ReFocus: The Films of Preston Sturges

ReFocus: the American Directors Series

Series Editors: Robert Singer and Gary Rhodes

Editorial Board: Kelly Basilio, Donna Campbell, Claire Perkins, Christopher Sharrett, and Yannis Tzioumakis

ReFocus is a series of contemporary methodological and theoretical approaches to the interdisciplinary analyses and interpretations of neglected American directors, from the once-famous to the ignored, in direct relationship to American culture—its myths, values, and historical precepts. The series ignores no director who created a historical space—either in or out of the studio system—beginning from the origins of American cinema and up to the present. These directors produced film titles that appear in university film history and genre courses across international boundaries, and their work is often seen on television or available to download or purchase, but each suffers from a form of "canon envy"; directors such as these, among other important figures in the general history of American cinema, are underrepresented in the critical dialogue, yet each has created American narratives, works of film art, that warrant attention. ReFocus brings these American film directors to a new audience of scholars and general readers of both American and Film Studies.

Titles in the series include:

ReFocus: The Films of Preston Sturges
Edited by Jeff Jaeckle and Sarah Kozloff

ReFocus: The Films of Delmer Daves
Edited by Matthew Carter and Andrew Nelson

ReFocus: The Films of Amy Heckerling
Edited by Frances Smith and Timothy Shary

www.euppublishing.com/series/refoc

ReFocus:
The Films of Preston Sturges

Edited by Jeff Jaeckle and Sarah Kozloff

EDINBURGH
University Press

Edinburgh University Press Ltd
The Tun—Holyrood Road
12 (2f) Jackson's Entry
Edinburgh EH8 8PJ
www.euppublishing.com

Typeset in 11/13 Monotype Ehrhardt by
Servis Filmsetting Ltd, Stockport, Cheshire,
printed and bound in Great Britain by
CPI Group (UK) Ltd, Croydon CR0 4YY

A CIP record for this book is available from the British Library

ISBN 978 1 4744 0655 0 (hardback)
ISBN 978 1 4744 0656 7 (webready PDF)
ISBN 978 1 4744 0657 4 (epub)

ACKNOWLEDGEMENTS

The editors wish to thank the following people for their invaluable assistance:
Robert Singer, Gary Rhodes, Barbara Lucas, Caitlan Moore, and Alice Royer.
Financial support came from Vassar Ford Scholars Program, Vassar College's
Research Committee, the William R. Kenan, Jr. Foundation, and the Betty and
Richard Duvall Foundation.

Contents

Figures

Notes on Contributors

Christopher Beach teaches film in the English Department of Williams College. He has published a number of books on literature and film, including *Class, Language, and American Film Comedy* (2002) and *The Films of Hal Ashby* (2009). His current project, *A Hidden History of Film Style: Cinematographers, Directors, and the Collaborative Process*, will be published in 2015.

Matthew H. Bernstein, Professor of Film and Media Studies at Emory University, is the author of *Walter Wanger: Hollywood Independent* (1994/2000) and *Screening a Lynching: Leo Frank on Film and Television* (2009). He has also edited or co-edited four anthologies, including *Controlling Hollywood: Censorship and Regulation in the Studio Era* (1999). In 2014, he provided commentary for the Criterion Collection's DVD edition of Don Siegel's classic prison film, *Riot in Cell Block 11*. He is currently completing a history of segregated movie culture in Atlanta, Georgia.

Diane Carson, Professor Emerita at St Louis Community College and former UFVA president (2008–10), is the co-author of *Appetites and Anxieties: Food, Film, and the Politics of Representation* (2014). She is also the co-editor of *Sayles Talk: New Perspectives on Independent Filmmaker John Sayles* (2006) and *More Than a Method: Trends and Traditions in Contemporary Film Performance* (2004).

Krin Gabbard is Professor Emeritus of Comparative Literature and Cultural Studies at Stony Brook University. Since 1971, he has taught courses in cinema studies, the cultures of jazz, and the history of literature. Since 2010, he has been Editor-in-Chief of Cinema and Media Studies for the online database Oxford Bibliographies. He is the author of *Hotter than That: The Trumpet, Jazz, and American Culture* (2009), *Black Magic: White Hollywood* *and African American Culture* (2004), *Jammin' at the Margins: Jazz and the American Cinema* (1996), and *Psychiatry and the Cinema* (2nd ed., 1999). His interpretive biography of Charles Mingus is forthcoming.

Leger Grindon is the Walter J. Cerf Distinguished Professor of Film Studies at Middlebury College in Vermont. He is the author of *Hollywood Romantic Comedy: Conventions, History, Controversies* (2011), *Knockout: The Boxer and Boxing in American Cinema* (2011), and *Shadows on the Past: Studies in the Historical Fiction Film* (1994). He is currently he working on an authorship study of the documentary filmmaker Errol Morris.

Jeff Jaeckle is the editor of *Film Dialogue* (2013). His scholarship on language in cinema, aesthetics, and Hollywood film has also appeared in *Film Quarterly*, *New Review of Film and Television Studies*, *Quarterly Review of Film and Video*, and the *Oxford Handbook of American Literary Naturalism*. He holds a doctorate from the University of Texas-Austin and teaches at Portland Community College.

Kristine Brunovska Karnick is Associate Professor of Communication Studies at Indiana University-Purdue University Indianapolis. She is co-editor of *Classical Hollywood Comedy* (1994) as well as articles on film and television history, gender, and film comedy.

Sarah Kozloff is Professor of Film on the William R. Kenan, Jr. Chair at Vassar College. She is the author of *Invisible Storytellers: Voice-over Narration in American Fiction Film, Overhearing Film Dialogue* (2000), *The Best Years of our Lives* (2011), and *The Life of the Author* (2014), and the co-author of *Introduction to Film Genres* (2014).

Martin Marks, Senior Lecturer in Music and Theater Arts, Massachusetts Institute of Technology, is a music historian whose principal research area is film music. He frequently performs live piano accompaniments for silent films, and he served as Music Curator for the series *Treasures from American Film Archives* from 2000 to 2011. He is the author of *Music and the Silent Film: Contexts and Case Studies, 1895–1924* (1997) and a contributor to *Music and Cinema* (2000), *Camille Saint-Saëns and His World* (2012), and *Michigan Quarterly Review*. His article "Screwball Fantasia: Classical Music in *Unfaithfully Yours*" appeared in *Nineteenth-Century Music*.

Joe McElhaney is Professor of Film Studies at Hunter College/City University of New York. His books include *The Death of Classical Cinema: Hitchcock, Lang, Minnelli* (2006), *Vincente Minnelli: The Art of Entertainment*

(2009), *Albert Maysles* (2009), and *A Companion to Fritz Lang* (2013). He has published dozens of essays on American, European and Asian cinema.

G. Tom Poe, an Associate Professor of Film and Media Arts at the University of Missouri-Kansas City, has published numerous journal articles and book chapters, including in *The Journal of Dramatic Theory & Criticism*, *The Journal of American History*, *Film History*, *American Journalism*, and the chapter on historical spectatorship for the anthology *Hollywood and Its Spectators* (1999).

Christian Viviani is Professor at Université de Caen-Basse Normandie and coordinator and co-editor of *Positif*. His books include *Le Western* (1982), *Les Séducteurs du cinéma américain* (1984), *Ernst Lubitsch* (with N. T. Binh, 1992), *Al Pacino, Robert De Niro, regards croisés* (with Michel Cieutat, 2000, updated 2005), and *Audrey Hepburn, La Grâce et la compassion* (with Michel Cieutat, 2009). He edited *Larousse du Cinéma* (2011) and has recently translated James Naremore's *Acting in the Cinema* (*Acteurs, le jeu de l'acteur au cinema*, 2014).

Virginia Wright Wexman is Professor Emerita of English and Art History at the University of Illinois at Chicago. She also served as President of the Society for Cinema and Media Studies from 1993 to 1995. Her books include *Creating the Couple: Love, Marriage, and Hollywood Performance* (1993), *A History of Film* (7th ed., 2010), and the anthology *Film and Authorship* (2002). She is currently working on a book entitled "Compromised Positions: The Directors Guild of America and the Cultural Construction of the Artist."

Introduction:
An Agile Mind—The Many
Stands of Preston Sturges

Jeff Jaeckle

Preston Sturges has long been a study in contrast, inspiring highly divergent characterizations such as genius and fluke, artist and entertainer,
auteur and sellout. These extremes seem warranted when considering his
startlingly eclectic life. A groundbreaking writer-director, Sturges was also a
songwriter, inventor, restaurateur, and engineer. He created some of the most
witty, acerbic, and hilarious comedies of the 1940s, yet his forays into dramatic
genres resulted in several dull and saccharine on-screen moments. He was considered the most "American" of Hollywood filmmakers, yet he lived in Europe
between the ages of eight and fifteen, and spent the final years of his life in
France. He was devoted to his globetrotting socialite mother, Mary Desti, yet
he had an abiding love and respect for his pragmatic, stockbroker stepfather,
Solomon Sturges. He was one of the highest-paid people in the USA in the
mid-1940s, yet he was consumed by debt and failure upon his death in 1959.

Antinomies like "auteur" and "sellout" are therefore useful for making
sense of Sturges; however, they also cast him as an ambivalent character in his
own story. This in turn has a narrowing effect, as all of the events and details
of his life are reduced to two extremes. Perhaps most famous are James Agee's
movie reviews for *The Nation*, in which he plays up Sturges's ambivalent
personality and finds, not surprisingly, that he suffers from a neurosis. Agee
contrasts Sturges's "retching, permanently incurable loathing for everything
that stank of 'culture,' of 'art'" with his "desperate respect and hunger for
success"; he argues that these twin drives resulted in films that are "paradoxical marvels of self-perpetuation and self-destruction."[1] Although these
characterizations smack of pseudo-psychoanalysis, Agee was not alone in spin-
ning such narratives. Andrew Sarris would rehearse (and tacitly endorse) this
view in 1968 when referring to Sturges's ambivalence, which derived from
"the incongruity of continental sophistication being challenged by American
pragmatism."[2] Richard Corliss would rehash a similar argument in *Talking*

Pictures when referring to the "schizophrenic showdown between two sides of the writer-director."[3]

These critical constructs, as G. Tom Poe's chapter reminds us, often tell us as much about the critics as they do about the object of study. The habit of seeing Sturges in terms of binary opposites was very much in tune with the pop-Freudianism of the mid-century, and it received additional fuel from structuralism, one of the most fashionable modes of film studies in the 1960s and 1970s. Foundational texts such as Peter Wollen's *Signs and Meanings in the Cinema* (1969) modeled the use of antinomies, often referred to as "structuring oppositions," as a way to "comprehend the system of differences and opposi-tions" in cinema, especially in the works of auteurs such as John Ford and Howard Hawks.[4] Sturges's ambivalent personality, as promulgated by Agee and others, was therefore ready-made for this form of interpretation. Yet not everyone endorsed this orthodoxy.

Brian Henderson lamented the lasting influence of this critical approach in his introduction to a 1985 collection of Sturges's screenplays, a seminal con-tribution to scholarship on the filmmaker both then and now. Finding Agee's reviews to be the most pernicious, Henderson observed: "no mere statement of facts or counter-argument is likely to prevail against it. It has become that most insidious of critical phenomena—an interpretation that is later taken as fact."[5] He concluded by expressing a hope that access to the screenplays, as well as future biographical and critical scholarship, might unsettle this perspective and "break the exclusivity of a reining single explanation."[6]

Indeed, the last thirty years have done much to enlarge and deepen our understanding of Sturges. Unlike Agee, who readily admitted to relying on a scant amount of evidence, current scholars and enthusiasts have a wealth of information at their disposal. The publication of three biographies, several critical studies, fourteen screenplays, a seven-DVD box set, and Sturges's own memoirs have afforded numerous insights into Sturges's films, career, and personal life. Much of this work has been made possible through access to the Preston Sturges Papers, an archive of production materials, inter-office memos, letters, and miscellany at the UCLA Charles E. Young library. These documents have enabled us to verify, correct, or complicate the dominant narratives about Sturges with a degree of scrutiny unavailable to early critics.

And yet, despite these advancements in scholarship on Sturges, the Agee model retains some allure, partly because it is so convenient but also because, like many clichés, it does contain some elements of truth—mother vs. father, USA vs. Europe, art vs. commerce, etc. We still see this binary model in passing remarks about Sturges in newspapers, magazines, and online forums, and we've witnessed it in our classrooms from students eager for a conceptual model to explain the man and his work. Following Henderson's lead, we aim to break the tidy, reining explanations, and so we propose new descriptive clusters or patterns that cut across every aspect of Sturges's life: *creator; businessman; wordsmith; skeptic; optimist.* We believe these terms provide a good sense of the personality, vitality, and talents that made Sturges such a compelling figure and such an excellent subject for the *ReFocus* series. The first three speak to Sturges's aptitudes and endeavors, while the latter two attempt to characterize his attitudes and worldview. Rather than set these terms in opposition, we put them in conversation to illustrate the complexities of Sturges's remarkable life.

Moreover, we do not see these terms as the *only* lenses through which to understand and appreciate Sturges; rather, they are entry points for the essays that follow, each of which combines primary documents from the UCLA archive, detailed analyses of the screenplays and films, deep engagement with previous scholarship, and thorough historical and cultural contexts. If we've done our jobs well, these terms and essays will shed light on why Sturges was, and continues to be, such a pivotal figure in Hollywood cinema and American culture.

STURGES THE CREATOR:
A VOLCANO OF INTERESTS AND PROJECTS

In the introduction to his collection of Sturges's early screenplays, Andrew Horton attempts to capture the sheer breadth of Sturges's creative talents:

> Before turning to Sturges the storyteller and screenwriter, we should consider the volcano of interests and projects that he indulged in beyond those related to writing and the silver screen. We are not speaking of a single-minded focused writer who gave all to his craft . . . There is also Sturges the inventor who delighted in devising new gizmos of all kinds. Listed in his archives at UCLA are patents registered for new planes, cars, a helicopter, a laugh meter (1934), and exercise machines, among more than thirty inventions.[7]

Sturges's aptitude for invention would begin early in life, when he found himself assisting his mother in launching her cosmetics company, Maison Desti, which he would go on to manage (first in Deauville and, later, New York), starting at age fifteen.

It was here, as biographer Diane Jacobs explains, that the young Preston began to tap into his creative potential: "Here he discovered how good he was with his hands and how, particularly when it came to solving practical conundrums, his mind was so much more agile than most people's."[8] In addition to designing boxes and posters, he improved the products themselves, most notably by inventing a kiss-proof lipstick, Desti's Red Red Rouge. After his mother resumed full control of the company in 1924, essentially forcing him out of the business, Sturges would shift his focus to mechanical inventions, including a photo-etching process, the "sturgephone" hearing aid, and a vertical-takeoff plane.

One of his central creative outlets was the Sturges Engineering Company, founded in 1937 to design diesel engines and yachting components; another was The Players, a supper club on Sunset Boulevard that also allowed him to try his hand at inventing, including tables mounted on tracks, revolving bandstands, and booths that mechanically ejected obnoxious customers. Although few of these inventions would bear fruit, Sturges would persist in his efforts. As Jacobs notes, "he wrote letter after letter to the patent office, and would continue to do so—and to conceive of instruments to make life easier and more interesting—all his life."[9]

Given his limited success in these areas, we might be tempted to view Sturges the inventor as distinct from Sturges the writer-director, yet these creative impulses spewed forth from the same volcano of ideas. An obvious connection between inventor and filmmaker is the appearance of mechanical devices in the films themselves, often in the form of tongue-in-cheek demonstrations of impractical technologies. For instance, the opening scene of *Christmas in July* (1940) is a conversation between Jimmy (Dick Powell) and Betty (Ellen Drew) about an apartment with revolving floors and walls (reminiscent of the tables and stages at The Players). Betty explains, "Then the sideboard turns around and turns into the bathroom . . . then another time it turns into a kitchenette, another time into a fireplace . . . it makes one room into four rooms." The next day, when the characters go on a shopping spree, they purchase the "Davenola," a couch that with the touch of a button springs open into a bed, complete with radio, reading lamp, telephone, and ashtray. In *The Palm Beach Story* (1942), Tom Jeffers (Joel McCrea) tries repeatedly to sell his invention for a suspended airport, an impractically large square of mesh stretched over a cityscape like a tennis racket; meanwhile, the film's fairy godfather, the Wienie King, explains to Gerry (Claudette Colbert) that he made his millions by inventing the addictive "Texas wienie." Much later in Sturges's filmmaking career, in *Unfaithfully Yours* (1948), he would subject his protagonist Sir Alfred de Carter (Rex Harrison) to a series of technological humiliations. Eager to frame his assistant for the murder of his wife, Sir Alfred attempts to impersonate her screams using the "Simplicitas" home recording machine, only to find his efforts thwarted by a devilish invention with the deceptive slogan, "so simple it operates itself!"[10]

Of course, Sturges's most famous inventions are the films themselves, especially his creation of unconventional, genre-breaking stories and fast-paced, highly articulate dialogue. Just as he wrote patent letter after patent letter,

Sturges also churned out story after story. In all, he wrote, adapted, or collaborated on 45 plays and screenplays between 1929 and 1957; yet even this is a fraction of his output, as many fascinating plays and scripts remain unproduced (see the chapters by Wexman, Karnick, and Jaeckle for examples). Part of Sturges's success derived from his sheer physical capacity—sometimes after weeks or months of procrastination—to dictate stories at length while acting out every part and performing every line of dialogue. His pace of creation was breathtaking; he was able to draft a full play or script in a matter of days or weeks. For instance, he completed his second produced play and breakout hit *Strictly Dishonorable* (1929) in six days.

Sturges was especially skilled at generating dialogue. As he famously boasted to Fox producer Darryl Zanuck, he could "spritz dialogue like Seltzer water. My trouble has never been in inventing it but rather throwing three-quarters of it away."[11] This talent brought him fame early in his screenwriting career, on *The Power and the Glory* (1933), when he invented "narratage," a dialogue device that combines flashbacks and voiceover in which the narrator speaks for the characters while also relaying the story. Success would come again in 1941, when Sturges won the first Academy Award for Best Original Screenplay for *The Great McGinty*; in 1945 he would be nominated *twice* for his screenplays for *Hail the Conquering Hero* and *The Miracle of Morgan's Creek*. Sturges often attributed these successes to what he called his "hook system," a writing style in which a word or concept in one character's speech is picked up, or hooked onto, by the next character, resulting in an elegant (and potentially endless) daisy chain of language. We hear this technique at work in *Sullivan's Travels* during Sully's rapid-fire three-way exchange with the studio heads about making *O Brother, Where Art Thou?*, and again in *The Sin of Harold Diddlebock* as the teetotaler Harold and a drunk named Wormy engage in a verbal fencing match using only aphorisms. In these and other memorable exchanges, the dialogue twists and turns, often breathlessly. "The problem," as Alva Johnston noted in a 1941 profile for the *Saturday Review*, "becomes that of making the dialogue end instead of keeping it going."[12]

This aptitude for brisk and voluminous composition directly impacted Sturges's approach to screenwriting, particularly when he was collaborating on or adapting existing stories. Rather than conserve the original plot, setting, or characterizations, he tended to toss out most of the material, saving only tidbits upon which to quickly and elegantly invent a new story. On his first assignment for Paramount, Sturges was to adapt the Vera Caspary story "Easy Living," about a working-class woman so eager to appear wealthy that she steals a fur coat, only to be caught and ostracized. Other than using the fur coat, which remains a central prop, Sturges radically reconceived the story, transforming the thief into an honest and affable woman, and abandoning the story's social message for a farcical and romantic romp. (See Kozloff's chapter

"To Write and Not Direct" for a thorough account of the adaptation and col-laboration processes behind this film.)

When adapting the Monckton Hoffe story "Two Bad Hats" into what would become *The Lady Eve* (1941), Sturges once again entirely reworked the plot, most notably by shifting the balance of power from the male to the female protagonist.[13] Even toward the end of his career, after he had suffered tremendously in terms of finances and reputation, Sturges's predilection for invention (and reinvention) remained undaunted, perhaps stubbornly so. In a famous anecdote about his collaboration on Ben Hecht's script of *Roman Holiday* (1953) for William Wyler, who wanted to send some work his friend's way, Sturges sneered, "There's one good line in it." Jacobs recounts the rest of the story this way:

> Sturges came back with a script substantively the same as Hecht's, but with every single line rewritten and elongated.
>
> After reading Preston's revisions, Wyler inquired: "Preston, remem-ber you said there was *one* good line. Where is it?"
>
> "I decided not to use it," Preston replied.[14]

Not surprisingly, Wyler went with Hecht's script and Sturges received no screenwriting credit.

As with his engineering company and restaurant innovations, Sturges's boundless capacity for story invention did not always serve him well. The vitality and energy coursing through his scriptwriting process could, at times, be excessive or uncontrollable, as was the case with *Roman Holiday*, result-ing in lots of stalled and unrealized projects. The same could be said of his tendencies as a businessman: never at a loss for a new venture idea, Sturges occasionally lacked the pragmatic skills of moderation and implementation to see it through or sustain it.

STURGES THE BUSINESSMAN:
THE ITCH TO MAKE GOOD AND MAKE MONEY

Sturges donned a number of professional hats during his lifetime, includ-ing head of Maison Desti, founder of Sturges Engineering Company, and restaurateur at The Players. We could add to this list the Sturges Music Publishing Company, Synder's restaurant, and the import/export venture Sturges & Company. The fact that all of these businesses ended in insolvency suggests that Sturges was ultimately a better creator—an "ideas man"—than he was a businessman. Nevertheless, he fought hard to develop and maintain this portion of his identity, once insisting in an interview: "I wanted to be a good businessman—like my father."[15] This insistence would find its way into his filmmaking career, both on- and off-screen, as Sturges's stories evince a fascination with business, while his observations on moviemaking and correspondence with studio executives speak to his desire to be taken seriously as a financially savvy filmmaker.

Sturges was especially concerned with audience enjoyment as an indicator of a film's potential success. Not content to rely on comment cards during pre-release previews, he often used a laugh meter to quantify a film's hilarity in terms of decibels, with four decibels denoting a winning moment. Sturges also quantified his scriptwriting process by drafting his eleven rules for box-office appeal. These rules build upon each other, each offering a better option to ensure audience enjoyment, such as "3. A bedroom is better than a living room" and "6. A chase is better than a chat," culminating in rule 11: "A pratfall is better than anything."[16] These audience-focused practices were meant to boost a film's grosses and, by extension, showcase Sturges's talent for producing winning investments.

This pragmatic approach to filmmaking comes through as well in Sturges's correspondence with studio executives, to whom he stresses his dual capacities as writer and businessman. In an undated letter to Fox producer Jesse Lasky (likely from early 1933), Sturges provides an impassioned cost–benefit analysis of script doctoring:

> I cannot re-dialogue a picture for two thousand dollars. It seems to me that the essence of good business is to put the deal through so this is my effort: I will re-dialogue the whole picture, however long it may take me, for 1% of the gross up to 500,000.00 and 2% on anything over that. As against this percentage you will give me an advance of $2000.00.[17]

Notable here is his emphasis on the mechanics and economics of his craft, not on his artistry. In signing off, he offers a series of maxims to reinforce these sentiments, including: "Whatever the story, a talking picture is only as good as it's [sic] dialogue. I believe good dialogue is the cheapest insurance a producer can buy: it makes good material magnificent and average material at least presentable. It is like good tailoring."[18]

This no-nonsense approach with Jesse Lasky arguably helped Sturges secure an unprecedented contract for the purchase of his script for *The Power and the Glory* (1933): a $17,500 advance as well as a percentage of the grosses;[19] this deal included a provision for Sturges to be present on the set to oversee any script changes, an unheard-of arrangement at the time. Henderson point outs, "Indeed, several performers averred they had never seen a writer before."[20] Sturges would once again break precedent and assert his business savvy when insisting that he direct *The Vagrant*, a 1933 script that would become *The*

Great McGinty (1940). As early as 1935, he pitched this writing-directing arrangement, once again taking a pragmatic approach. In a letter to Universal's general manager Fred Meyer of August 14, 1935, Sturges stresses that he is determined to make "Class A pictures for a great deal less than is expended upon them now."[21] When Paramount's William LeBaron finally gave him the opportunity to direct in 1939, remarkable for granting him the novel screen credit "Written and Directed By," Sturges maintained a businesslike approach to his craft, completing production three days ahead of schedule and $1,000 under budget, despite his contracting pneumonia in the middle of shooting.

Sturges maintained this workmanlike approach with his next few movies, *Christmas in July*, *The Lady Eve* (1941), *Sullivan's Travels* (1941), and *The Palm Beach Story*, bringing them in at or close to budget and within a few days of schedule. This feat is especially impressive considering that these four films were written, revised, shot, edited, and released in just over two years, between November 1940 and December 1942. He achieved this pace, in part, by balancing long bouts of stalling with intense periods of creation. This schedule, unsurprisingly, could make him irascible and intolerant of criticism, such as when he snidely replied to Darryl Zanuck, "I normally work seventeen hours a day but will try to do more in the future," when the producer questioned his shooting schedule for *Unfaithfully Yours*.[22]

Perhaps the greatest exception to this rule was *The Sin of Harold Diddlebock* (1947), which came in months late and $600,000 over budget. (See McElhaney's chapter for an extended account of the production woes.) The ample budget and unprecedented autonomy at California Pictures proved a detriment to Sturges, overwhelming his business sense with a hubris that sprang from unquestioned freedom and control. As Jacobs tells it, "He may have seen Cal Pix as an extension of The Players, a sort of fiefdom where he could play lord of the manor, lover, friend, sometime father, and filmmaker at once."[23] Yet no account of the troubles on set suggest that Sturges was anything other than the creative dynamo he had been on previous projects, or would be with any business venture he undertook until the end of his life.

Given the zeal with which Sturges pursued these ventures and cultivated his identity as an entrepreneur, it should come as no surprise that businessmen would figure prominently in his scripts and films. As Geoff Brown notes, "His characters had the Horatio Alger itch to make good and make money."[24] (See Beach's chapter for a fuller treatment of money and class; see McElhaney's chapter for a discussion of failure in business.) Indeed, businessmen characters are the rule, not the exception, in his stories, most notably Tom Garner (*The Power and the Glory*), J. B. Ball (*Easy Living*), The Boss (*The Great McGinty*), John D. Hackensacker (*The Palm Beach Story*), and Harold Diddlebock (*The Sin of Harold Diddlebock*). Even characters not explicitly in the role of "businessman" find themselves caught up in matters of finance. The director John

L. Sullivan (Joel McCrea) in *Sullivan's Travels* is proud of making profitable films, balking "Not from me, you haven't!" when the studio heads fret about losing money on his next venture. Sturges also binds business to sex and marriage, perhaps most explicitly in *The Lady Eve* when Eve (Barbara Stanwyck) comments to a smitten Charles (Henry Fonda): "They say a moonlit deck is a woman's business office." Moreover, for as much as Sturges ridicules businessmen in his films—whether by pelting them with tomatoes in *Christmas in July* or making them tongue-tied in *Hail the Conquering Hero* (1944)—he does not vilify business itself, especially the drive for success and financial gain. Audiences root for Dan (Brian Donlevy) to ascend the political ladder in *The Great McGinty* just as they hope Jimmy will win the slogan contest in *Christmas in July*.

This enthusiasm spurred Sturges's own business ventures, be they engineering contracts, real estate investments, or partnerships with Howard Hughes. Ultimately, however, Sturges was better at *generating* business ideas than he was at realizing and growing the profits made from them. Yet even if he had managed to retain the fortunes he made and lost throughout the years, his entrepreneurial spirit would likely not have waned but, like his predilection for creation, would have continued apace.

STURGES THE WORDSMITH: A CACOPHONY OF VERNACULARISMS AND UTTERANCES

Sturges's restless, boundless energy no doubt fueled his unparalleled achievements as a writer. Indeed, no account of his life would be complete without an acknowledgment of his genius for crafting language. He has, of course, been likened to other great screenwriters—Ben Hecht, Billy Wilder, Orson Welles—but his facility with words is so impressive as to invite comparisons with some of the greatest writers in history, among them Voltaire, Racine, Swift, and Twain.

Having left school at age fifteen to run Maison Desti, Sturges did not perfect these writing skills inside the classroom; rather, as an autodidact, he proved a quick study and a keen observer. He learned the basics of playwriting, for instance, by consulting Brander Matthews's *A Study of the Drama* (1910), which he read in 1928 during a six-week convalescence from peritonitis; while in the hospital, he wrote the operetta *Speaking of Operations*, which he ultimately discarded for being unfunny.[25] However, by 1930, he had completed and produced numerous plays, including *The Guinea Pig* (1929) and the highly successful *Strictly Dishonorable* (1929). When he wanted to write music and lyrics, he started by teaching himself composition. Dan Pinck explains that he purchased a course from the back pages of *Popular Mechanics* and "learned about passing chords, rolling bass, waltz bass, and ragtime bass—all in the key of G."[26] After founding his music publishing company, he eventually completed around sixty songs, often writing several per day. His nimble lyricism ranged from sentimental to sardonic, including the heartwarming "Home to the Arms of Mother" used in *Hail the Conquering Hero*, and the tongue-in-cheek "For You Alone" from the unproduced 1935 script *Song of Joy*, which includes the lyrics: "This is not a love song in the popular vein/Cause it's meant for you alone/I don't give a hang." (See Karnick's chapter for a detailed discussion of "Home to the Arms of Mother"; see Jaeckle's chapter for an in-depth analysis of *Song of Joy*; see Marks's chapter for a broader discussion of Sturges's uses of film scores.)[27]

Sturges's career move from playwright to screenwriter also proved quite easy, in part because he saw cinema as an extension of the theater, claiming that "the motion picture was theater in its modern form, being handy and cheap and necessary and used constantly by hundreds of millions of people worldwide."[28] If he seemed unperturbed by leaving behind the theater scene in New York for Hollywood in 1932, it's likely because he didn't perceive this move as a separation so much as a continuation. Biographer James Curtis recounts this exchange: "Asked when he was going to write another play for the theater, he replied, 'I have never stopped writing plays. This *is* the theater.'"[29] This connection between stage and screen no doubt influenced Sturges's approach to film dialogue, which is noteworthy for being highly literate, lengthy, and articulate.

Eschewing the dictum, common both then and now, that cinema is a visual medium, Sturges crammed his scripts and films with words, imbuing the language with a striking and unconventional density more akin to stage productions. As Geoffrey O'Brien explains, "The magnificence of his dialogue resides in what makes it difficult to excerpt. There are few one-liners or punchlines: the words careen off each other with manic expansiveness."[30] However, Sturges's dialogue is by no means "theatrical" in the sense of being stuffy or stagey. His characters may speak at length, but their speech is an energetic hodgepodge of erudition and slang, verses and vulgarities. *The Lady Eve*, for instance, shows an impressive range of verbal registers, from archaic ("meet me in yonder window embrasure") to aphoristic ("let us be crooked but never common") to goofy ("cock-eyed cookie puss"). *The Palm Beach Story* has its own sophisticated blend of poetry, speechifying, and outright gibberish, including Toto's (Sig Arno) three-word vocabulary of "yitz," "nitz," and "grittniks." Andrew Dickos captures this eclecticism well, claiming that it "establishes the standard of eloquence of poetry, a cacophony of Euro-American vernacularisms and utterances, peculiarly—and appropriately—spoken with scandalous indifference."[31]

Sturges added to this eclecticism by placing eloquent utterances in the mouths of both major and minor characters, so that a barman or butler is as likely to deliver a memorable speech as a banker or baron. As Manny Farber and W. S. Poster observe, "All of this liberated talk turns a picture into a kind of open forum where everyone down to the cross-eyed bit player gets a chance to try out his oratorical ability."[32] In *The Palm Beach Story*, for instance, the doddering Wienie King (Robert Dudley) delivers an eloquent speech on aging that begins, "Cold are the hands of time that keep along relentlessly, destroying slowly, but without pity, that which yesterday was young." In *Sullivan's Travels*, Sully's butler Burroughs (Robert Greig) corrects his employer's misguided views on poverty: "You see, sir, rich people and theorists—who are usually rich people—think of poverty in the negative, as the lack of riches—as disease might be called the lack of health. But it isn't, sir. Poverty is not the lack of anything, but a positive plague, virulent in itself, contagious as cholera, with filth, criminality, vice and despair as only a few of its symptoms." Minor players also get in good one-liners, often in the form of catchphrases that resonate throughout the films, such as the valet Muggsy's (William Demarest) insistence that Eve and the Lady Sidwich are "the same dame," or the studio executive LeBrand's (Robert Warwick) request in *Sullivan's Travels* that Sully make his social drama *O Brother, Where Art Thou?* "with a little sex in it."

These witty rejoinders can give the dialogue a feeling of spontaneity, as if tossed off in the moment, yet close analyses have repeatedly pointed up its thoughtful and painstaking construction. Timothy Paul Garrand's thorough study of screenplay design reveals Sturges's strategic reliance on a number of literary devices, among them epigrams, non-sequiturs, understatement, irony, and wordplay,[33] while Sarah Kozloff has analyzed elements of delivery and pacing, including the employment of repetition and overlapping speech.[34] My own research has uncovered Sturges's calculated use of misspeaking, especially malapropisms, mispronunciation, and exaggerated accents.[35] These verbal and vocal patterns illustrate that Sturges's genius came by the sweat of his brow. As Henderson notes, "the best-known features of Sturges's films—brilliant dialogue, break-neck pace, vivid characters—were in fact the result of tireless revision at every stage of production."[36]

Because Sturges often acted as both writer and director (and sometimes producer), he was able to extend and deepen this revision process up to the time of a picture's release. Henderson explains that he "had the opportunity to alter his dialogue, even to omit scenes or to change the order of scenes if he chose to, during shooting or in the editing."[37] On the set, Sturges was explicit about how a line should sound in terms of volume, pacing, and pitch. Sandy Sturges recounts this practice, saying that he "would tell the actors exactly and precisely how to say the line, how to deliver it . . . and every gesture to go with it."[38] (See Carson's chapter on Sturges's collaborations with actors.) However, this level of creative control brought with it a responsibility, since Sturges was thrust into the spotlight as the person to praise or to blame for what appeared on-screen.

The same goes for critical responses to his films. Since his characters deliver well-crafted and moving speeches on controversial topics ranging from gender inequality to patriotism to corporate greed, we look to Sturges the wordsmith to explain his films' themes or messages, be they progressive, regressive, or contradictory. (See Karnick's chapter on his treatments of gender, especially mothers; see Gabbard's chapter on his representations of people of color.) Yet Sturges's personal views have proven difficult to pin down, in part because he remained a slippery and self-contradictory commentator on his own work, establishing his reputation as an ideological agnostic.

STURGES THE SKEPTIC:
AN UNCOMMITTED OBSERVER

In recounting the familiar story of Mary Desti dragging the young Preston back and forth from Paris to Chicago and New York, critic Richard Schickel contends that these experiences engendered in Sturges a "partial alienation [that] shaped his sensibility."[39] This alienation, he argues, is why Sturges was such a talented wordsmith, especially when it came to appreciating American colloquialisms. It also developed in him a sense of skepticism: the ability to observe without judging, to mock without criticizing. While reviewers such as Agee cited this quality as evidence of Sturges's lack of moral seriousness, Schickel considers it a rare talent: "He was not, and never meant to be, a critic of society. Rather, he was an uncommitted observer, bemused and compassionate, but without any cures in mind for the conditions he observed."[40]

Sturges's observer status pervaded his personal and professional relationships. While his mother dabbled in various faiths and his first wife Estelle was a committed Catholic, Sturges remained steadfastly uncommitted to organized religion. In an undated letter to Estelle, presumably near the start of their marriage in 1923, Sturges explains, "Though I believe in God I don't believe in religion for everybody . . . I think a powerful conscience is worth all the religions put together."[41] This same detachment is evident in Sturges's stance on patriotism, particularly in the context of war. Although he scrambled to enlist for the Air Service during World War I, Sturges adopted a relatively neutral stance toward US involvement in World War II. In a 1943 letter to a friend, he admits, "The peculiar thing is that I have absolutely no *desire* to get in. Either this war has not been as well advertised as the last one or else there is a great difference between eighteen and forty-four, or else you don't fall for the same guff twice or something."[42] Jacobs hypothesizes that this detachment stemmed in part from Sturges's belief that all political movements, as with all religions, commit more evil than good, and are therefore best avoided altogether. (See Kozloff's chapter "To Write and Not Direct" for examples of how this stance differed from those of his contemporaries; see Wexman's chapter on this resistance as it pertains to the Directors Guild.)

This unwillingness to join a group or subscribe to a cause cropped up repeatedly during Sturges's time in Hollywood. He famously refused to join the Directors Guild, being the only recognized director not to do so. He also refused to aid the unionizing efforts of the Screen Writers Guild and the Screen Playwrights Guild. "Preston joined nothing and sided with no one," Jacob remarks about this period.[43] However, he *was* openly critical when others pursued causes he considered faddish. When filmmakers, for instance, advocated for political change, especially on screen, Sturges chastised them in print. In a 1942 *New York Times* article on *Sullivan's Travels*, he criticizes them for "wasting their talents in comstockery, demagogy, and plain dull preachment" and then proclaims his own democratic take on cinema and art in general: "I don't believe that now is the time for comedies or tragedies or spy pictures or pictures without spies or historical dramas or musicals or pictures without music. I believe that now is the time for all forms of art and that now is always with us."[44]

This avoidance of popular trends and movements often meant that Sturges adopted a relatively independent stance, both on- and off-screen. He consistently pursued any storyline or genre he thought best, even if that meant being unpopular or risking professional failure; indeed, this habit often came at the expense of his cultivated reputation for being business savvy. For instance, after the success of *Strictly Dishonorable* in 1929, Sturges was advised to take his time and then pursue another comedy. "Presenting two plays in a year was unwise," his friends cautioned, and "following a comedy with a drama was foolhardy."[45] And yet he did exactly that by producing *Recapture* (1930), a critical and commercial flop about a divorced couple's tragically failed attempt to rekindle their relationship. Much the same occurred twelve years later when, after the success of his early written-directed comedies, Sturges set out to make the drama *Triumph Over Pain* (also known as *Great Without Glory*) about the inventor of ether-based anesthesia, W. T. G. Morton. Rather than abandon the unpopular project early on, he persisted, Henderson explains, "even though it cost him the enmity of his studio and finally undid him, simply because he believed in the project."[46] Ultimately, Sturges lost control of the film, which languished for two years until Paramount's Buddy DeSylva had it recut and retitled *The Great Moment*. Released in 1944, it became one of Sturges's most dismal failures, both critically and commercially. (See Poe's and Viviani's chapters for broader discussions of Sturges's reception in the USA and France respectively.) Sturges would endure a similar disappointment years later during his vexed partnership with Howard Hughes, who recut, retitled, and even reshot portions of *The Sin of Harold Diddlebock*, releasing it as *Mad Wednesday* in 1950. (See Wexman's chapter on Sturges's fascinating yet vexed experiences with the studio system; see Bernstein's chapter on his equally vexed relationships with the Production Code Administration.)

Sturges's films embody his skeptical attitude in that they explore numerous and contradictory positions on a given subject, ultimately embracing a multiplicity of opinions over and above a single perspective or solution. For instance, the majority of *The Palm Beach Story*—originally titled "Is Marriage Necessary?"—seems to ridicule marriage and monogamy, as audiences see that Gerry, showered with financial and material support from a host of suitors, can get by just fine without Tom; meanwhile Maude's (Mary Astor) five marriages, all ending in divorce or annulment, suggest that marriage is outdated and love largely an afterthought. Yet the characters all find that marriage is, if not necessary, then at least preferable, as the film ends with two weddings and the "remarriage" of Tom and Gerry, who reluctantly admits, "You realize this is costing us millions," before embracing her estranged husband. Rather than answer the question about the necessity of marriage, Sturges takes audiences on an adventure that considers several hypothetical (and hilarious) scenarios.

Sturges's most famous satire, *Sullivan's Travels*, appears to skewer the shallowness and pomposity of Hollywood, with studio heads driven by profit motives and directors ruled by misguided notions of themselves as saviors. Yet the film also validates Hollywood on at least two fronts: Sturges renders scenes of poverty in ways that effectively illustrate the dramatic power of socially conscious cinema; he also underscores the value of film comedy, not because it is fashionable or politically popular, but because people sincerely benefit from it. Ultimately, then, he refrains from making any damning criticism of Hollywood. This decision stemmed, I would argue, not from a lack of conviction or fear of reprisal, but arguably from a desire to project (and protect) his reputation as an individualist and iconoclast who embodied what Penelope Houston calls "the notion of the film-maker as a universal man (if only on a Hollywood scale)";[47] however, this decision seems also to have come from an awareness of, and respect for, the sheer complexities of the Hollywood system, which render it both uniquely difficult and praiseworthy.

Sturges takes a similar stance when assessing the intertwined worlds of theater and cinema in a 1943 letter to author and journalist Emily Kimbrough:

> Hollywood is a medium, an invention, open to all. Anyone who can hold the attention of the selfish, vulgar, fearful, brave, learned and generous individuals who make up the theater-going public is welcome in the selfish, vulgar, fearful, brave, learned, generous and very much alive town of Hollywood.[48]

Once again, Sturges exposes the virtues as well as vices of an institution, and ultimately renders not a judgment so much as a sophisticated observation.

This capacity to perceive and appreciate the unresolved complexities of institutions (as well as people and events) was key to Sturges staving off the tides of cynicism that surrounded him, especially toward the end of his life; rather than give in to these pressures and transform himself into a defeatist or crank, he remained a cautious optimist.

STURGES THE OPTIMIST: TRIUMPH OVER PAIN

Sturges was anything but a wide-eyed romantic. He worked hard, knew the huge risks involved in his ventures, and experienced enough loss and failure for two lifetimes. And yet, his films and commentaries exude a resilient hope. For all of his skepticisms about ideologies and institutions, Sturges was nevertheless an optimist, though of a peculiar bent, as he readily admits in his memoirs:

> I am, always was, and always will be violently optimistic. I knew at twenty I was going to be a millionaire. I know it today. In between times, I have been.[49]

Striking here is the adverb "violently," a jarring descriptor that tempers the unalloyed connotations of "optimist." Agee's focus on ambivalence is apt here, as Sturges's optimism is itself pessimistic in that it accepts the necessity of pain for achieving triumph.

This violent optimism played out time and again in Sturges's life, up to and including his final months in 1959. At the time he started writing his memoirs, in February of that year, he had not made a film in Hollywood for a decade; Twentieth Century-Fox's *The Beautiful Blonde from Bashful Bend* (1949) was a box-office and critical flop; his cinematic forays in France had resulted in the mildly successful *Les Carnets du Major Thompson* (1955), which would turn out be his final film as a director; and his attempt to reenter Broadway, through directing a production of *The Golden Fleecing*, proved disastrous. Now living in the Algonquin hotel in New York, with much of his property in Los Angeles sold or repossessed, he was far behind on his mortgages and taxes. He was estranged from Sandy and his children and his health had also started to decline. He was, as Jacobs describes, "physically, as well as financially and emotionally, debilitated."[50] And yet we see in his memoirs here a glimmer of hope—"I know it today"—the absolute confidence that he would regain his position and fortune. He expressed a similar hope that April in a letter to his ex-wife Louise, insisting, "*luck does turn*, and the dice *will* come up the right way sooner or later. *That* you can be certain of."[51]

This sense of certainty reverberates throughout Sturges's films, typically during the final minutes, when the abused and downtrodden characters glimpse some hope that their luck is about to turn. This habit led Schickel to quip about Sturges, "How determined he was to permit his American Dreamers to preserve their dreams unvexed."[52] Indeed, in *The Great McGinty*, Dan loses his family and position as governor but is saved from jail and allowed to tell his fascinating story. Jimmy endures shame and ignominy in *Christmas in July*, but the last seconds of the film reveal that he has in fact won the slogan contest and will soon be back on top. In *Hail the Conquering Hero*, Woodrow Truesmith (Eddie Bracken) is tormented by his lies about being a Marine veteran, yet the town embraces him after he confesses to the masquerade. Charles and Eve psychologically abuse each other throughout *The Lady Eve*, only to survive and find each other again. Sully endures poverty, prison, and torture in *Sullivan's Travels*, but manages to learn a lesson about filmmaking, divorce his loathsome wife, and win the heart of The Girl (Veronica Lake). Norval (Eddie Bracken) is manipulated and mocked throughout *The Miracle of Morgan's Creek* (1944) yet ultimately receives everything he wants: a marriage with Trudy (Betty Grable) and the respect of the town. Even in Sturges's darkest film, *Unfaithfully Yours*, audiences are spared a tragic ending. After the jealous and crazed Sir Alfred schemes to murder his wife, or commit suicide, he discovers her to be faithful and proclaims, "A thousand poets dreamed a thousand years, and you were born, my love."

Since these endings blatantly employ a *deus ex machina*, they tend to be both unexpected and unsettling, leading Penelope Houston to liken them to the suspicious grin of the Cheshire cat.[53] Ray Cywinski goes further, suggesting that these endings, "far from being the standard commercial cop-outs as some critics aver, may actually testify to the opposite—a part of Sturges that believes *ultimate success is impossible*."[54] However, given all we know about Sturges's violent optimism as a creator, businessman, and wordsmith, Cywinski's argument about Sturges's cynicism doesn't hold up.

This is perhaps the most difficult aspect of Sturges's filmmaking career to grapple with: despite his predilections for satire, irony, and cynical *bon mots*, Sturges was a guarded optimist. Able to puncture the pieties of America's most beloved institutions, he was unwilling to destroy them, preferring to maim with style rather than kill with vengeance. Audiences could therefore entertain the complexities of his observations while leaving theaters with a smile. Apropos here is Sully's closing speech in *Sullivan's Travels*: "There's a lot to be said for making people laugh. Did you know that's all some people have? It isn't much, but it's better than nothing in this cockeyed caravan. Boy!" Corny as this line may sound—and it certainly does—it nonetheless characterizes Sturges's boundless store of optimism, which he would draw from his entire life. Despite finding that his creative triumphs were countered by financial flops, and despite seeing his verbal genius tarnished by entrepreneurial errors, Sturges pressed on ahead with confidence until his death.

Over half a century later, in sifting through scripts, films, letters, and other documents, what endures are numerous and conflicting portraits of a complicated man—the fascinating products of an agile mind. In the chapters that follow, contributors to this volume have analyzed selected aspects of Sturges's films, and the collection as a whole places these analyses in conversation with one another. As scholars well aware that we are embedded in our own cultural milieu, we adopt an approach that follows Robert Stam's advice that it be dialogic and marked by pluralization.[55] We have therefore interwoven primary research with textual analysis, sensitivity to many of the codes of filmmaking, and a detached historical understanding of the workings of Hollywood amid the social influences of the mid-twentieth century. More tolerant of ambiguity, and less moved to force Sturges into tidy binaries, we refocus attention on Sturges's complicated and enduring legacies.

Part 1, "Contexts: Genre, Studio, Authorship," locates and assesses Sturges's place in the Hollywood studio system, specifically his evolution from fledging screenwriter in the 1930s to top-grossing writer-director in the 1940s, pausing along the way to consider questions of collaboration, censorship, and contribution.

In "Preston Sturges and Screwball Comedy," Leger Grindon summarizes the key traits of the screwball comedy cycle and assesses Sturges's contributions to its late developments. Through careful examinations of *The Lady Eve* and *The Palm Beach Story*, Grindon considers how these films participate in the established traits of the cycle and how they develop fresh aspects of screwball.

Virginia Wright Wexman's "Preston Sturges, *Sullivan's Travels*, and Film Authorship in Hollywood, 1941" draws on archival materials housed at UCLA to examine the ways in which the film's production context sheds light on the discourses about Hollywood during this pivotal and transformational year. She reads the film as a critique not just of Hollywood moviemaking at this time, but also as an elevation of the status of the director at the expense of studios, producers, or stars.

In "To Write and Not Direct," Sarah Kozloff analyzes three of the scripts Sturges wrote and handed off to other Hollywood directors: *The Good Fairy* (Wyler, 1935), *Easy Living* (Leisen, 1937), and *Remember the Night* (Leisen, 1940). Although Sturges famously complained that others ruined his work, these sparkling comedies demonstrate the themes of the films that Sturges directed himself in the 1940s, and point to what others added to his vision.

Finally, Matthew Bernstein poses one of the most fascinating questions about Sturges's career in his chapter, "'The Edge of Unacceptability': Preston Sturges and the PCA." How did Sturges manage to insert so much sexual innuendo in his comedies of the 1940s, given the notorious vigilance of Joseph Breen and other members of the Production Code Administration? Through close examinations of script drafts and correspondence with the PCA, Bernstein explores how Sturges deftly negotiated with the censors to satisfy their demands while ensuring that his satires of war and sexuality made their way to the screen.

In Part 2, "Cultural Commentary: History and Identity," the contributors consider the current status of Sturges's films, including how they fare with respect to their complicated and somewhat fraught representations of gender, social class, race, and aging and decline.

Kristine Karnick begins her chapter, "Sturges's Many Mothers," by pointing out the relative rarity of mothers in Hollywood films, populated instead by aunts and grandmothers, whereas mothers abound in Sturges's films. Karnick's analyses of these representations reveal that his constructions of motherhood evolved during his career, progressing from cold and manipulative mothers in his early screenplays (which nod to Philip Wylie's notorious theories) and films to benevolent and sentimental characters that embody the outmoded Victorian ideal of "mother love."

Christopher Beach, in "'These Are Troublous Times': Social Class in the Comedies of Preston Sturges," argues that Sturges's romantic comedies of the early 1940s go much further in their treatments of class than the 1930s screwball comedies of Frank Capra, Gregory La Cava, and Mitchell Leisen. Sturges's films are more self-conscious about social conventions and more willing to comment on materialism, greed, and the desire for social status. Yet, like his views on motherhood, these representations evolved during his career, from straightforward class-based satires to parodic social fantasies.

In "'They Always Get the Best of You Somehow': Preston Sturges in Black and White," Krin Gabbard takes on Sturges's troubling reliance on racist stereotypes and finds that his black characters are both indicative of this historical period and often quite nuanced, expressing a wry suspicion of white characters through their scene-stealing dialogue. Gabbard also demonstrates the ways in which African American actors functioned as respected professionals in Sturges's repertory company, using their skills to transform one-dimensional bit parts on the page into memorable and compelling characters on-screen.

In "Falling Hard: *The Sin of Harold Diddlebock*," Joe McElhaney conducts an extended reading of this maligned and neglected film to understand its representations of aging and decline. McElhaney argues that Sturges's dramatizing of the ravages of time in the person of the film's star, Harold Lloyd, connects with the ossification of language and a thorough critique of the predations of capitalism and the American Dream of advancement.

In Part 3, "Technique: Scripting, Performance, Music," the contributors turn to questions of style and form, paying close attention to patterns of screenwriting, acting, and scoring that give Sturges's films their signature look and sound.

In "The Unheard *Song of Joy*," Jeff Jaeckle provides an in-depth account of the little-known script for *Song of Joy*, a backstage Hollywood musical that Sturges conceived, revised, and unsuccessfully pitched to four major studios between 1935 and 1941. In tracing the script's composition and controversies, he shows how its achievements in plotting, dialogue, and meta-cinema are actually more daring than those of Sturges's well-known films.

Diane Carson, in "The Eye of the Storm: Preston Sturges and Performance," demonstrates that Sturges's actors frequently present diverse facades and dramatically alter personality traits as they navigate elaborate and highly contrived plots. While these varied roles and shifting guises honor the acting conventions of the 1940s studio system, Caron finds that Sturges urged his actors to push the boundaries of performance in order to enliven the films' whip-smart dialogue and showcase acting itself.

In "*Presto(n) con Spirito*: Comedies with Music, Sturges-Style," Martin Marks begins by noting that audiences often forget about musical contributions in classical Hollywood films, since studios favored a relatively anonymous house style. Not so with Preston Sturges, who turned the studio's system to his advantage and developed a controlling musical consciousness of his own: planning films with musical enhancements in mind, so that they make strong contributions to the narrative form of his films.

The final Part, "Impact: Reception/Reputation," considers Sturges's legacy and influence as a filmmaker in the USA and France, both then and now, including his reception by critics and impact on contemporary filmmakers.

G. Tom Poe, in "Thrust with a Rapier and Run: The Critics and Preston Sturges," contends that Sturges's public persona as a "madcap" character in the history of the Hollywood studio system created a master narrative centering on his personal biography that influenced the critical reception of his films, serving as an early precursor to what would later be deemed "auteur criticism." Poe also finds that the theme of public spectacle in Sturges's life and films incited debates with regard not only to his place in American film history, but also to the purposes of film comedy.

In "Hail the Conquering Auteur: Preston Sturges in *La Revue du cinéma* (1946–1949)," Christian Viviani argues that Sturges was highly appreciated among French film critics, especially those writing for the short-lived but influential journal *La Revue du cinéma* (1946–9). Through detailed examinations of the journal's articles and reviews on Sturges, Viviani traces the filmmaker's critical reception in France while demonstrating how these debates served as an incubator for the major theoretical and critical angles that would come to characterize the highly influential publications *Cahiers du cinéma* and *Positif.*

Sarah Kozloff closes the volume with "O Preston, Where Art Thou?," which considers Sturges's ongoing influence in Hollywood and abroad. She suggests that while Sturges has not enjoyed the constant attention and adulation of

Hitchcock, Hawks, or Ford among film scholars, his themes, tone, and style lurk everywhere in contemporary films, especially in the works of Joel and Ethan Coen, Wes Anderson, Aaron Sorkin, and Pascal Caumeil. One reason we must bring him back into focus, she argues, is that so many modern film-makers can be counted as his offspring.

Indeed, Sturges is still very much with us, which is why this entry in the *ReFocus* series is so timely and relevant, but also why we hope it may prove an enjoyable and engaging read for scholars, students, and the Sturges fan in all of us.

NOTES

1   James Agee, *Agee on Film* (New York, NY: McDowell, Obolensky, 1958), 116–17.
2   Andrew Sarris, *The American Cinema* (New York, NY: Dutton, 1968), 114.
3   Richard Corliss, *Talking Pictures: Screenwriters in the American Cinema* (New York, NY: Penguin, 1974), 26.
4   Peter Wollen, *Signs and Meanings in the Cinema* (London: Secker & Warburg, 1972), 93.
5   Brian Henderson, *Five Screenplays by Preston Sturges* (Berkeley, CA: University of California Press, 1985), 24.
6   Henderson, 29.
7   Andrew Horton, ed., *Three More Screenplays by Preston Sturges* (Berkeley, CA: University of California Press, 1998), 5.
8   Diane Jacobs, *Christmas in July: The Life and Art of Preston Sturges* (Berkeley, CA: University of California Press, 1992), 27.
9   Jacobs, 56.
10 Sturges's *The Great Moment* (1944) is distinct in its reverent attitude toward inventions: W. T. G. Morton's use of ether as an anesthetic in 1846. For an extensive discussion of the role of inventions in this and other Sturges films see Geoff Brown, "Preston Sturges: Inventor," *Sight and Sound*, 55:4 (Autumn 1986): 272–7.
11 Jacobs, 143.
12 Quoted in Andrew Dickos's *Intrepid Laugher: Preston Sturges and the Movies* (Lexington, KY: University Press of Kentucky, 2013), 61. Paperback ed.
13 Henderson says of this revision, an adaptation of an adaptation by Jeanne Bartlett, "As had often been his practice as a screenwriter in the thirties whenever he 'rewrote' the work of others, Sturges in effect threw out the Hoffe and Bartlett stories and began again from scratch." Henderson, *Five Screenplays*, 329.
14 Jacobs, 408.
15 Quoted in James Harvey's *Romantic Comedy in Hollywood: From Lubitsch to Sturges* (New York, NY: Da Capo, 1998), 516.
16 Alessandro Pirolini, *The Cinema of Preston Sturges: A Critical Study* (Jefferson, NC: McFarland, 2010), 40.
17 Preston Sturges Papers (Collection 1114). Department of Special Collections, University Research Library, University of California, Los Angeles, Box 74, Folder 22.
18 Preston Sturges Papers, Box 72, Folder 22.
19 See Jacobs, 126, for a full breakdown of the contract terms.
20 Henderson, 13.

21 Preston Sturges Papers, Box 37, Folder 16.

22 Quoted in Jacobs, 258.

23 Jacobs, 344.

24 Brown, 276.

25 Henderson, 9.

26 Dan Pinck, "Preston Sturges: The Wizard of Hollywood," *The American Scholar*, 61:3 (Summer 1992): 406.

27 See Donald Spoto's biography of Sturges for a full list of songs. *Madcap: The Life of Preston Sturges* (Boston, MA: Little, Brown, 1990), 279–81.

28 Pirolini, 8.

29 James Curtis, *Between Flops: A Biography of Preston Sturges* (Lincoln, NE: iUniverse.com, 2000), 106.

30 Geoffrey O'Brien, "The Sturges Style," *The New York Review*, 20 December 1990, 6.

31 Dickos, 56.

32 Manny Farber, *Negative Space: Manny Farber on the Movies* (New York, NY: Da Capo, 1998), 97. Expanded ed.

33 Timothy Paul Garrand, "The Comedy Screenwriting of Preston Sturges: An Analysis of Seven Paramount Auteurist Screenplays," dissertation, University of Southern California, 1984.

34 Sarah Kozloff, *Overhearing Film Dialogue* (Berkeley, CA: University of California Press, 2000), 170–200.

35 Jeff Jaeckle, "Misspeaking in the Films of Preston Sturges," in *Film Dialogue*, ed. Jeff Jaeckle (London: Wallflower Press, 2013), 140–53.

36 Brian Henderson, "Sturges at Work," *Film Quarterly*, 39: 2 (Winter 1985–6): 16.

37 Henderson, 6.

38 Pirolini, 127.

39 Richard Schickel, "Preston Sturges: Alien Dreamer," *Film Comment*, 21:6 (November–December 1985): 33.

40 Schickel, 33.

41 Jacobs, 51–2.

42 Jacobs, 264.

43 Jacobs, 183.

44 Preston Sturges, "An Author in Spite of Himself," *The New York Times*, 1 February 1942, X5.

45 Jacobs, 88.

46 Henderson, 23.

47 Penelope Houston, "Preston Sturges," *Cinema: A Critical Dictionary: Volume Two*, ed. Richard Roud (New York, NY: Viking Press, 1980), 987.

48 Preston Sturges Papers, Box 73, Folder 39.

49 Preston Sturges, *Preston Sturges by Preston Sturges: His Life in His Words*, ed. Sandy Sturges (New York, NY: Simon & Schuster, 1990), 193.

50 Jacobs, 443.

51 Jacobs, 448.

52 Schickel, 34.

53 Houston, 990.

54 Ray Cywinski, *Preston Sturges: A Guide to References and Resources* (Boston, MA: G. K. Hall, 1984), 27.

55 Robert Stam, *Film Theory: An Introduction* (Malden, MA: Blackwell, 2000), 330.

Contexts:
Genre, Studio, Authorship

CHAPTER 1

Preston Sturges and Screwball Comedy

Leger Grindon

Romantic comedy remains among the most popular and vital of Hollywood genres. *The Proposal* (2009), *Silver Linings Playbook* (2012), and *Her* (2013) testify to its continuing success. While romantic comedy strives to incorporate new developments in courtship and culture in order to speak to its audience about contemporary experience, at the same time, the experience of the past exercises its influence. The screwball films produced in Hollywood between 1934 and 1942 are among the most celebrated cycles in the history of romantic comedy movies. These films continue to evoke fond memories, solicit repeated viewings, and inspire new work. Contemporary comedy incorporates the outrageous and the grotesque, striving to push the boundaries of humor into surprising territory. The spirit of Preston Sturges, so open to shifts in tone, so ready to press against the proper, and so thrilled to find laughter in the unexpected, is an inspiration for the romantic comedy of today.

Sturges wrote and directed two screwball comedies, *The Lady Eve* (1941) and *The Palm Beach Story* (1942), late in the screwball cycle. The 1941 release date of *The Lady Eve* falls within screwball's temporal parameters, while *The Palm Beach Story* was released months after the US entry into World War II. Closer inspection, however, reveals that Sturges was already working on *The Palm Beach Story* in the weeks before the Pearl Harbor attack, with the final screenplay draft completed in early November 1941. Shooting began on November 24. Thus, though the production was not finished until January 1942, and the US release was delayed until December 11, 1942, *The Palm Beach Story* was conceived and largely executed before Hollywood production felt the impact of the war. *The Lady Eve* is an acknowledged screwball classic; *The Palm Beach Story* is a crazy outlier, a mannered instance of an expiring legacy. The two films offer a rich counterpoint of sophisticated harmony and off-balance lunacy.

THE SCREWBALL MODEL

A review of key elements of screwball comedy establishes the perspective we need to evaluate Sturges's contribution. Nineteen thirty-four was a turning point in the history of Hollywood romantic comedy. *It Happened One Night* was released to popular acclaim and went on to win Academy Awards for Best Picture, Best Director, Best Screenplay, Best Actor, and Best Actress. The Frank Capra movie became the prototype for the most famous cycle in the romantic comedy genre, the screwball comedy. The tale of a runaway heiress, Ellie Andrews (Claudette Colbert), discovered and befriended by an unemployed, conniving reporter, Peter Warne (Clark Gable), as they travel by bus from Miami to New York remains one of the most influential films of the decade. This Columbia Pictures production sparked a cycle of award-winning comedies. The benchmark hits in the group include *My Man Godfrey* (1936), *The Awful Truth* (1937), *You Can't Take It With You* (1938), *The Philadelphia Story* (1940), and *His Girl Friday* (1940).

This fresh crop of romantic comedies expressed an optimism associated with Franklin Roosevelt's energetic New Deal. In 1933 the President assumed office, and he rallied the nation behind a series of federal programs trying to revive the national economy. The screwball comedies were set in Depression America and portrayed the economic distress marking the 1930s; they featured characters like Peter Warne, who had just been fired. But these familiar challenges were portrayed in a spirit of comic fun and with a belief that the crisis would be mastered. The screwball couple, such as Alice Sycamore (Jean Arthur) and Tony Kirby (James Stewart) in *You Can't Take It With You*, frequently matched the commoner with the wealthy, and the contrast in social standing sparked hostility. Though the commoner held our sympathy and the wealthy excited our suspicion, the screwball comedy engineered the reconciliation of class tension through the romance.

The term "screwball" first arose in response to *My Man Godfrey* to describe its heroine, Irene Bullock (Carole Lombard). The screwball leading lady was daffy, playful, and quick—in short, unconventional, assertive, self-reliant, and articulate; the screwball woman was ready for the battle of the sexes and often provoked it. Heroines like Lucy Warriner (Irene Dunne) in *The Awful Truth*, Tracy Lord (Katharine Hepburn) in *The Philadelphia Story*, and Hildy Johnson (Rosalind Russell) in *His Girl Friday* inverted the norms of male-dominated courtship by acting on their sexual desire. These fast-talking dames were frequently working women; together they embodied the social changes that were transforming gender roles in the years following World War I.

The screwball couple expresses attraction through aggression. Bickering and insults often lead to physical battles and schemes to get even. As Tamar Jeffers McDonald explains, "The emphasis on far-flung insults and violence, either threatened or carried out, as a main trope in screwball seems the most vital difference between the sub-genre and the wider romcom genre."[1]

Frequently screwball would have a free spirit like Susan Vance (Katharine Hepburn) in *Bringing Up Baby* (1938) pursue and harass a conventional stiff like David Huxley (Cary Grant), who would eventually be liberated by contact with this more free-spirited beloved. Together the couple indulged their eccentric battles and discovered a sense of fun that set them off from others and confirmed their unity in defiance of polite society. The quarrels sparked an attraction that eventually reeducated both the man and the woman. The relationship that blossomed between them established an equality that broke down the social roles dividing the sexes and allowed the couple to forge an elevating companionship. Their prospective marriage promised a union honoring each as autonomous individuals and finding its joy in their special partnership; child rearing and family values were beside the point. As a result, these lovers themselves often behaved like children. In many respects, Nick (William Powell) and Nora Charles (Myrna Loy) of *The Thin Man* (1934) embodied this new sense of marriage as a continuing adventure rather than a passage into the routine of family life.

Screwball plots included both courtship and infidelity variations. However, the infidelity films, like *The Awful Truth*, invariably reunited the married couple at the close, so Stanley Cavell dubbed them "comedies of remarriage."[2] Key to these films was the disruption of normal life. The world turned topsy-turvy, and daily experience became a crazy adventure. In *It Happened One Night*, Ellie Andrews escapes from her father's yacht without any of the safeguards that had sheltered her. David Huxley wants to raise funds for his scientific research, but soon finds himself chasing leopards in Connecticut. The disruption fosters spontaneity, masquerades, and drunken abandon. Having fun together unites the couple and leads to a liberating reeducation of the man and the woman. As Kathrina Glitre writes, "Above all else, perhaps, it is this sense of instability and inversion—a world turned upside down—that epitomizes screwball comedy."[3] The adventure changes the traditional relations between a man and a woman and leads to a fresh renegotiation of the common ground uniting the sexes.

Nineteen thirty-four also marked a much more stringent enforcement of censorship as the Hollywood film industry strengthened the Production Code Authority in response to complaints from various protectors of public virtue. The critique of marriage, so conspicuous in the romantic comedies of the early 1930s, gave way to a renewed respect in which courtship led to the altar and infidelity ended with the reconciliation of husband and wife. As Glitre explains, "under the moral guardianship of the Production Code . . . [t]he awful truth for screwball comedy is that there is no alternative to marriage."[4] Kissing and passionate embraces were restricted and ushered off screen; even the mention of sex was camouflaged in ambiguity. However, the censorship fostered the artful implication that allowed the innocent to suspect nothing but provoked the imagination of the experienced. The evasion required the combined talents of screenwriters, directors, and performers to suggest passion in artifice and persuasively stage a courtship while concealing its most fundamental motivation.

The simultaneous intensification of dialogue and censorship leads to the distinctive polyvalent language of screwball comedy. The conversation cultivates an ambiguity that both disavows and suggests the erotic. The twenty-first-century audience often is mystified by the elusive exchanges that characterize the screwball conversation, such as Walter Burns discussing his "dimple" with Hildy Johnson in *His Girl Friday*. Elliot Rubenstein explains, "the very style of screwball, the complexity and inventiveness and wit of its detours . . . cannot be explained without the recognition of the censors. Screwball comedy is censored comedy."[5] But censorship also has its rewards. The sensitive viewers congratulate themselves for finding the forbidden just beneath the surface of the ambiguous. The style of screwball comedy was emphatically verbal. Rapid-fire witticisms, overlapping delivery, and densely written insults establish wordplay as the chief vehicle for flirtation. At the same time, these carefully constructed conversations are delivered in a spontaneous and natural manner. These couples initiate their relationship with verbal duels that contribute to the unsentimental tone. Only later does each lover realize that the bond arising out of these exchanges identifies the beloved as the person with whom he or she experiences a special understanding. The wordplay sparks a current of erotic energy.

The screwball cycle moves beyond the sophisticated comedy of the early 1930s by integrating physical humor with the verbal fireworks. Johnny's somersaults in *Holiday* (1938) and the torn formal wear in *Bringing Up Baby* are among the many instances of knockabout gags integrated with the verbal jousting. The high comedy of manners is joined with the low comedy of pratfalls and the romantic couple is at the center of both the verbal and the physical humor. These wacky antics are generally childlike in their playfulness, but they also suggest the sexuality confined beneath the surface.

The screwball couple fought and made up, allied against outside threats, and acted like children playing out their feelings in disregard for polite society. Declarations of love, embraces, and kissing were replaced by piggyback rides and masquerades. The couple acted more like pals than lovers. As Tina Olsin Lent argues, the post-World War I concept of marriage based on a love companionship found expression in the cycle.[6] The screwball romances recognized the equality of men and women in love rather than relegating them to separate spheres. The weaker sex moved beyond the restrictions of the domestic, and the man strode into the world with a woman at his side. Female independence, and the couple's mutual interests and shared activities, welded the partnership into an emotional union that diminished restrictive gender roles. Both the man and the woman recognized in their beloved a screwball liberation that together, and only as a couple, they could realize.

America's entry into the World War brought an end to the screwball cycle. The feelings engendered by romantic comedy ran contrary to war. Rather than soliciting laughter from the union of the couple, the war separated couples by drafting young men and shipping them abroad in a life-threatening endeavor. After a few stragglers in 1942, Hollywood revised romantic comedies in light of the war effort, and the screwball model faded, though its influence continues to be felt today.

The Lady Eve and *The Palm Beach Story* are clearly grounded in the screwball cycle. They both feature unconventional heroines in Jean/Eve (Barbara Stanwyck) and Gerry (Claudette Colbert) who are assertive, self-reliant, and intelligent. They are fast-talking dames who invert the norms of male-dominated courtship by acting on their desire. Their attraction to Charles (Henry Fonda) and Tom (Joel McCrea) is expressed through aggression, both physical and verbal. Jean trips Charles to get his attention and her wit speeds at least two strides ahead of the naive, sheltered Mr. Pike. Gerry takes her husband Tom to dinner and to bed before fleeing their marriage and financial woes the next day. Both women take their men on crazy adventures.

Verbal wordplay and innuendo are central to the erotic heat of these comedies; many marvel that Sturges managed to get his sexy implications past the Hays Office. For example, in *The Lady Eve*, shortly after meeting, Jean replies to Charles's invitation to dance by cooing, "Don't you think we ought to go to bed?" Or in *The Palm Beach Story* John D. Hackensacker (Rudy Vallee) objects to his frequently divorced sister (Mary Astor), "You don't marry someone you met the day before . . ." and she replies: "But that's the only way, dear. If you get to know too much about them you would never marry them." Furthermore, the wisecracks are integrated with physical humor that remains a hallmark of the screwball cycle. Charles's repeated falls in his awkward pursuit of Jean or the antics of the Ale and Quail Club on the train to Florida are vivid examples. Finally the unsentimental tone diminishes the restrictive gender roles of traditional courtship and engineers a screwball liberation for the couple. As John D. notes, "Chivalry is not only dead, it's decomposed."

Film reviewers responding to *The Lady Eve* and *The Palm Beach Story* testified to the innovative and unusual quality of these films. *Time* called *The Lady Eve* "highly original,"[7] while *Variety* noted that "Sturges injects several new touches."[8] Bosley Crowther of *The New York Times* went head over heels for *The Lady Eve*, writing "Sturges is definitely and distinctly the most refreshing new force to hit American motion pictures in five years . . . suddenly the art of comedy-making is rediscovered . . . Mr. Sturges has taken one of the stock stories . . . and given it . . . such a variety of comic invention that it sparkles."[9]

The rousing reviews and commercial success of *The Lady Eve* were followed by the mixed response to *The Palm Beach Story*. But here, too, reviewers pointed to Sturges's "healthy rebellion against a mass of cinematic conventions" even while expressing disappointment.[10] Manny Farber writing in *The New Republic* expressed reservations about *The Palm Beach Story* but applauded Sturges for being "the most progressively experimental worker in Hollywood."[11] Sturges was recognized by the contemporary press as an innovator even as he worked within conventional Hollywood formulas.

So what are the distinctive qualities that made these works remarkable just as the onset of World War II upended the screwball sensibility? Two qualities distinguish the Sturges screwball comedies from the mainstream model: a dark undercurrent and cartoon sexuality. Later critics evaluating the achievement of Sturges have noted this darkness flowing through the romantic comedies. Jared Rapfogel writes of "a sharp perceptiveness and an acknowledgment of life's trials and tribulations that is generally treated with humor and bemusement but which always threatens to darken into something more painful."[12] Manny Farber and W. S. Poster were among the first to note that in Sturges's screwball comedies luck and coincidence, rather than virtue and determination, decided whether someone would be an abject failure or a celebrated achiever; so too with romance.[13] Typically, in screwball comedies, such as *It Happened One Night* or *His Girl Friday*, the central couple affirm their special partnership by working together in overcoming some obstacle or adversary. However, in the Sturges screwballs the couple fail to cooperate. Successful partnership with the beloved becomes wildly circumstantial and often undeserved. For example, the final reconciliation of Jean and Charles in *The Lady Eve* arises from an attempt on their part to forget nearly all their subsequent experience rather than from a genuine recognition of their intimate partnership and common destiny. In *The Palm Beach Story* the Wienie King's rescue of Gerry and Tom and Hackensacker's later support arise from unlikely, almost magical, intervention rather than as a result of devotion, development, or an epiphany. Worse, the cruelty the women inflict on their men exceeds aggressive flirtation and cultivates a sadistic pleasure in a partner's suffering. For example, James Harvey writes of the "energetic cruelty" inflicted on Charles by Jean in *The Lady Eve* that exceeds the typical humiliation of men widespread in screwball comedy.[14] As a result, the sexual inferences take on perverse implications. No wonder critics like Ray Cywinski argue that the happy endings Sturges fabricates are a mockery of Hollywood convention rather than an optimistic culmination to the romance.[15]

Manny Farber and W. S. Poster write of Sturges's tendency "to jumble slapstick and genuine humor, the original and the derivative together, and express oneself through the audacity and skill by which they are combined."[16] One distinctive aspect of these combinations is the incongruity of the cartoonish and the erotic, the childish and the sexual. The animated snake in the credit sequence of *The Lady Eve* is a vivid example. But character names also evoke the studio cartoons of the era. Hopsie, the nickname Jean calls Charles, refers to his brewery but reminds one of Bugs Bunny. Even though the doddering sausage maker hardly looks the part, the "Wienie King" sounds like the braggart with the biggest penis or a philandering playboy. But the incongruity of innocence and the worldly evokes the humor simmering just beneath the surface. For Sturges the juxtaposition of extremes makes the screwball ethos sharper in its bite and more disconcerting in its implications. Maybe the Hays Office was blinded by the extreme nature of these allusions and overlooked their perverse implications in the intersection of childish play and predatory sexuality.

Sturges's intentions help us approach the films. *The Lady Eve* announces itself as a revision of the Adam and Eve story from Genesis, particularly their fall and subsequent exile from the Garden of Eden. The Sturges comedy ignores the moral clarity demanded in the Production Code of Ethics ("the sympathy of the audience should never be thrown to the side of crime, wrongdoing, evil or sin") and cautions us about judgments and the presumptions of knowledge. Both Jean and Charles suffer for punishing their beloved's failures, and they can only unite when they dispense with their knowledge of each other's faults and embrace the impulse toward union. The general theme is benign and generous, but the bulk of the story portrays the lessons the lovers learn from their harsh judgments and cruel behavior, giving *The Lady Eve* its dark undercurrent.

Sturges outlines the idea for *The Palm Beach Story* in notes to his screenplay, highlighting two aspects: "1. Premise: That a pretty woman can do anything she wants and go anywhere she likes without money. 2. That a pretty woman can use her appeal for the advancement of her husband."[17] The sexual power of a beautiful woman allows her freedom and license. However, the humorous premise is fraught with moral questions as the men under the woman's influence may pursue sexual favors in exchange for their help or become hostile when such favors are denied. Moreover, the pretty woman's reputation may suffer from her exploiting her charms. As a result, this "comic" premise exhibits a sinister aura. In *The Palm Beach Story* Sturges cultivates a cartoon sexuality to deflect the compromising implications of a pretty woman seeking favors.

In another context, I have identified ten plot moves typical of Hollywood romantic comedy.[18] My analysis here will focus on these, namely: "unfulfilled desire," "the meeting," "fun together," "obstacles arise," "the journey," "new conflicts," "the choice," "crisis," "epiphany," and "resolution." Since *The Lady Eve* presents a typical courtship plot it follows the typical pattern closely. *The Palm Beach Story* has a more irregular infidelity plot, but adapts a variation on the typical pattern to structure its story. In particular, my analysis will draw attention to the dark currents in Sturges's screwball films as well as the integration of the childlike and the erotic producing a cartoon sexuality.

THE DARK CURRENT IN *THE LADY EVE*

Romantic comedies typically begin with plot move one: "unfulfilled desire." *The Lady Eve* poses the unfulfilled desire of Charles portrayed as the repression of his sexuality through his study of snakes. His apparent innocence is actually ignorance of an aspect of himself. Jean's predatory intentions pose her desire for money as a substitute, which will awaken her latent desire for a lover. Cartoon sexuality initiates the flow of a dark current through the film.

The credit sequence uses cartoon sexuality to elaborate on Genesis. An animated snake with a top hat, a big smile, and a maraca held to his tail plants three large apples on screen containing the title, *The Lady Eve*. As the credits scroll upward the snake coils down the tree on the left side of the image until the last title, "Written and Directed by Preston Sturges." Here the phallic snake wiggles through the "O" in "Preston," catching the letter around the middle of its body. The image of coitus finds the smiling snake with head bobbing to the music and the maraca in motion at the tail. Then the apple "Eve" falls from above, crushing his top hat over his head; the snake recomposes himself before exiting off screen. The humorous snake announces the comedy as a biblical revision readily displaying its erotic imagery as a cartoon.

The image changes to a waterway at the edge of a jungle (suggesting the Garden of Eden). A group of men in jungle attire bid Charles Pike goodbye, as the leader of the scientific expedition hands Charles a cage holding a snake, newly identified by these explorers. Charles tells his friends that he would like to spend all his time "in the pursuit of knowledge." As Charles expresses his noble aspiration, the image cuts to Muggsy (William Demarest) bidding farewell to a native woman, alluding to an absence in Charles's life. Muggsy, an older experienced man, serves as guardian to the heir of the Pike Ale fortune; he also functions as Charles's alter ego, sexually worldly, cynical and suspicious in contrast to his companion's innocence and idealism. Men from the expedition warn the departing Charles to watch out for the traffic and the dames. Charles replies, "You know me, Mac, nothing but reptiles." Charles's scientific knowledge of snakes contrasts with his ignorance of his own sexuality.

The Pike fortune pays a for a luxury cruiser to meet the launch carrying the heir back to New York, prompting a crowd of passengers to look at the young man climb aboard, speculating on his wealth. Among them are Colonel Harry Harrington (Charles Coburn) and his daughter, Jean, con artists eager to fleece a mark who is "dripping with dough." Jean expresses her affiliation with Eve by dropping her half-eaten apple onto the pith helmet of Charles as he climbs. Charles and Muggsy find their counterpart in Jean and Harry, prey and predators. In contrast to the naive Charles, Jean has plenty of experience "doing the dirty work," such as dancing with marks in the moonlight. She thinks money can satisfy her unfulfilled desire.

The Colonel is a counterpart for Muggsy. They are both charged with caring for their young companions and, like the conventional parent in romantic comedy, they become obstacles in the path of romance. In Genesis, God acts like an all-powerful parent creating, commanding and providing for his children, Adam and Eve. The snake entices Eve and Eve tempts Adam to satisfy his desire. From desire comes the experience of sexuality, which separates children from parents and poses choice. As a result, Adam and Eve enter the harsh world where they must toil, struggle and suffer. In *The Lady Eve*, Colonel Harrington and Muggsy fulfill parental roles that alert us to their godlike position in relation to their innocent charges. Jean and Charles must struggle and suffer.

Romantic comedies progress from unfulfilled desire to the second plot move, meeting of the couple. In *The Lady Eve* Charles sits in the dining room of the luxury liner trying to read *Are Snakes Necessary?* (an apparent reference to E. B. White and James Thurber's *Is Sex Necessary?* [1929]), but distracted by the overtures from the surrounding women. Charles starts to leave the room and Jean trips him. Sturges initiates the "fall" motif alluding to Charles falling in love as well as the fall of Adam and Eve. Jean insists that the young man take her to her suite for another pair of slippers. "See anything you like?" Jean inquires as she opens her trunk of shoes and displays herself.

In *The Lady Eve* Jean excites Charles's passion in order to fleece him, and the subversion of love for money provides a dark current. However, sexual attraction upsets the desire for money with an incongruity that fuels the screwball humor. The third plot move shows the new couple having fun together and a strong bond emerges to link the pair. The fun initially arises from card play and features money. The Colonel and his daughter manipulate Charles by allowing him to win $600 as a setup for their scheme. In response Charles invites the beautiful woman into his room to meet Emma, the object of his devotion. After Jean discovers that Emma, a slithering snake, has escaped from her cage, she runs screaming. The panic shatters Jean's aura of command and excites her. Now she makes Charles her protector, if only in fun. They exchange visions of their ideal mates. Jean explains that she always wanted to be "taken by surprise." And so she is. The next morning she awakes screaming and tells Harry, "That slimy snake, I've been dreaming about him all night." Later that evening she announces to Harry that she loves Charles. Charles takes Jean away from the parents to be alone at the bow of the ship. Entranced by the wind and the sea he proposes marriage, telling Jean that he has always loved her. They go way, way back, maybe as far as Adam and Eve.

Obstacles quickly arise to intensify the conflicts, marking the fourth plot move. In *The Lady Eve*, Muggsy pressures the authorities on the ship into revealing the cardsharps on board and Charles sees the incriminating photographs of Jean the morning after his marriage proposal. As Kathleen Rowe has noted, Charles "is guilty of the most ancient tendency to idealize women or vilify them, and, when in doubt, to judge them . . . with arrogance and self-righteousness."[19] In a moving scene whose superb pathos is a hallmark of the film's achievement, Jean finds Charles in a stony rage and warns, "You don't know very much about girls. The best ones aren't as good as you probably think they are, and the bad ones aren't as bad . . . not nearly as bad." Charles listens expressionless, while Jean, in a demonstration of Stanwyck's virtuosity, moves from the glow of fresh love to a breakdown in tearful sorrow.

Here the dark current shaping *The Lady Eve* invests the episode with its grim intensity. The discovery of a lover's flaws, an experience of every couple, is given a poignant expression and the plot pivots toward vengeance. Now the con as an analogue for courtship evolves into a bitter scheme to get even for a broken heart.

In romantic comedy's fifth common plot move, a journey takes characters outside their routine surroundings and sets the stage for transformation from independent individuals into a couple. Charles and Jean meet on an ocean cruiser; however, at midpoint a fresh scheme calls for a journey to a new setting. At a race track, Jean gains the inspiration for her vengeance scheme, that takes a dark turn as her party at the track bets on a loser. There she meets Sir Alfred McGlennan-Keith (Eric Blore), another con artist familiar to Harry and Jean as Pearlie. Jean wants to visit Sir Alfred at his home in Bridgefield, Connecticut, near the Pike estate, posing as his English niece because she has

Figure 1.1   *The Lady Eve*: Jean, in a demonstration of Stanwyck's virtuosity, moves from the glow of fresh love to a breakdown of tearful sorrow. Here the dark current shaping *The Lady Eve* displays its grim intensity.

some unfinished business with "that guy" Charles. This journey calls for a masquerade and the con as courtship deals another hand of cards as Harry is exchanged for Sir Alfred and Jean becomes the Lady Eve.

In romantic comedies the masquerade often reveals a search for identity, an exploration of a desirable aspect of the self that has been suppressed. What does Jean's masquerade as Eve reveal about her? Jean's ever-changing identity as a con artist speaks of an unstable, ill-defined self. Her desire for Charles arises from a need to construct a firm identity. Furthermore, she sees a kindred spirit in Charles because he also flees the destiny constructed by his parents (to be a brewer), and instead treasures his intellectual passion. Jean needs to leave her father and strike out on her own, and in a new direction. Jean is also humiliated by Charles's discovery of her illicit background. Her sense of inferiority rebounds and she imagines herself as a superior aristocrat, admired by all. So even as Jean executes her vengeance scheme, she also works to construct herself through her masquerade.

The new setting at the Pike mansion prepares for new conflicts, the sixth plot move. The Pikes throw a party to receive the visiting Lady Eve Sidwich, where Eve amuses the guests with her British mannerisms and laughs at American idiosyncrasies. Charles manages to fall not once, as on the boat, but four times before the close of the evening, puzzled and dazzled by the similarity between the con artist Jean and the aristocrat Eve. Eve captures Charles's heart in her masquerade as readily as she did aboard ship even as Muggsy protests that she is "the same dame." The next day Eve explains to Sir Alfred that she intends to charm the heir into proposing marriage and notes that Charles failed to recognize her "because we don't love each other anymore." Eve promises to realize her revenge for a broken heart. She enjoys the attention of Charles in Connecticut even as she torments him. However, a conflict develops between Jean and her alter ego, Eve; between the woman who fell in love with Charles and the one striving to get even.

The seventh plot move arises from a crucial choice posed by the new conflicts. In *The Lady Eve* the choice arises from Charles's marriage proposal and Jean's acceptance. Here the dark current reaches its high point. Stanley Cavell calls it "the most difficult moment of this comedy" carried "to virtuosic heights."[20] Harry takes Jean at her word that she hates Charles and asks, "Why did she do it?" The marriage proposal presents reverberations that are complex and conflicting in their resonance, delicate and painful in their humor. Jean begins the transition to the scene describing her plan in voiceover as the film visualizes the details. Her self-conscious ploy marks her as the "director" of the scene even as Charles's sincerity is compromised by the similarity between his first proposal and his second. The couple ride horseback, stopping to observe a forest sunset. (The horses evoke the racetrack where Eve hatched her scheme.) They are alone in a natural setting that excites their desire. Eve

Figure 1.2 *The Lady Eve*: Jean/Eve's gestures present a calculation mocking Charles's earnest declaration. Whereas in the earlier denouncement of her scheme aboard ship her vulnerability was on display, now she is in command.

exploits her memory of the earlier proposal and the Lady mocks the similarity of the suitor's words, all the while looking at the camera (and at the audience) and the sunset while Charles looks away or at her. Stanwyck's gestures of eyes, lips, head, voice, present a calculation mocking Fonda's earnest declaration.

Whereas in the earlier denouncement of her scheme aboard ship, Jean's vulnerability was on display, now she is in command. However, beneath the surface Eve hears again the words she has cherished: the desire that has provoked her tears. Her distance from them also measures her longing to make them come true. The romantic cliché of lovers destined for union since way, way back is rehearsed by these lovers in an ironical mix of mockery and sincerity. Of course, these two do go way back: back to the bow of the ship, back to their first passionate infatuation, back to Adam and Eve. Even as Charles's words seem like a well-rehearsed line that questions their spontaneity, the sincerity of the first proposal is confirmed by the similarity to the second, and the second reinforced by its repetition—because in spite of the masquerade these are the same two lovers, and in spite of their human flaws, a passionate destiny has brought them back to their deep yen for each other. In spite of Charles's pompous and manifestly untrue claim to careful deliberation, the force of those initial impulses has taken over. Now the conflict in Jean, the conflict between embracing the love or destroying it, will play itself out.

The eighth plot move brings on the crisis, a move toward marriage doomed by masquerade, in which the fate of the couple teeters on the edge of disaster. In the marriage montage Sturges elegantly contrasts Pearlie's financial concern with the Pikes' elaborate preparations. A beautiful wedding joins the couple as Eve harbors her scheme. The honeymoon train marks yet another journey of transformation, a journey through darkness. Charles's expectation of a virginal marriage bed evaporates as Eve springs her trap, revealing her elopement with "Angus" at age sixteen. Charles's initial impulse to "sweet forgiveness" fades with the ongoing litany of lovers (Herman, Vernon, John, Herbert . . .). The new Mrs. Pike is a promiscuous woman with a legion of indiscretions. The honeymoon montage, cutting feverishly between the speeding locomotive and the identification of yet another lover, counters the serene wedding montage. Jean repeats the debasement she experienced earlier when her illicit history was revealed to Charles on the cruiser. Now she is triumphant in shocking Charles with his misguided feelings for the idealized Eve. Eventually he carries his luggage off the train only to fall, once again, in the mud. Eve has her revenge. Behind in the sleeping car she lowers the shade and nods her head in a gesture of reflection and regret. Sturges challenges the propriety of the Production Code by having a marriage collapse under the dark cloud of a woman's licentious behavior, a pronounced reversal of the happy marriage convention of the romantic comedy.

The ninth plot move is an epiphany. In *The Lady Eve* lawyers crowd Horace Pike (Eugene Pallette), Charles's father, warning that the divorce negotiations are "entirely irregular." Charles sits silent and brooding. Jean wants nothing to do with lawyers, nor does she heed Harry's claim "that for once we have a chance to make some honest money." Money cannot distract Jean from love. Her only request is to meet with Charles "because there is something I want to say to him." Vengeance achieved and vengeance regretted. Just as Charles has suffered, so now Jean suffers in the knowledge of the love she has lost. With Jean's suffering, *The Lady Eve* achieves an emotional depth that arises from its darkness. The epiphany is Jean's realization of the terrible breach she has committed and the rising desire to make up for her foolish quest. After her original hurt, she could only imagine striking back. And indeed her strike returned Charles to her, his devotion even greater. But as she pushed him into the mud, she fell herself and now needs to save them both. Jean's epiphany transforms her. Only now does she recognize the depth and meaning of her love for Charles.

For its final plot move, the resolution, *The Lady Eve* returns to the ocean cruiser. Charles has decided on a trip to forget his romantic fiasco. He walks down the aisle to dinner carrying his book to guard against distractions. A camera movement glides in front of him as he strolls confidently into the dining room only to suddenly fall once more. "Hopsie," Jean cries. Without hesitation, Charles rises to kiss her and asks, "Can we go to your cabin?," swooping her away. As they enter her room Jean embraces him. "I've waited for you all my life," she declares, echoing his multiple proposals. Charles asks for forgiveness and adds, "I don't want to understand . . . I don't want to know . . . I adore you." But he continues, "I'm married." "So am I, darling, so am I," replies Jean, closing her door behind them. Muggsy steals from the room, telling the camera, "Positively the same dame." Now we know he is wrong. Jean is a woman transformed by love and suffering, and ready for marriage. As Rowe has noted, sexuality in Genesis leads to death and exile, but here desire redeems the couple who find salvation in their mutual love.[21] After the image fades the animated snake from the credits reappears, resting with eyes closed in a post-coital smile of satisfaction as the two apples he curls around read "The End." The gratifying conclusion reminds us of earlier episodes: the condensation of feeling and wit reminds us of the dark current navigated by these lovers on their journey to union. Though Charles declares that he doesn't want to know, the audience embraces a sweet understanding from the satisfying resolution. Though shaped with sophisticated artifice this ending strikes home without allowing any lingering questions, because the feeling of satisfied desire leaves us laughing with a sigh.

CARTOON SEXUALITY IN *THE PALM BEACH STORY*

While *The Lady Eve* is a courtship comedy, by contrast, *The Palm Beach Story* is an infidelity comedy that begins with the marriage of Tom and Gerry. The typical plot moves of romantic comedy generally arise from the dominant courtship model, whereas the infidelity plot offers a variation that veers from the dominant pattern.

The movie begins with a confusing credit sequence joining the couple at the altar after a frenzied dash to the church. The cartoon artifice has similarities to the animated credit sequence in *The Lady Eve*. However, here the cartoon tone pervades the entire film. The first two and a half minutes unfold with the credits displayed over the images; the William Tell overture plays as Gerry and Tom separately rush in their wedding finery, each desperately late. Most perplexing, a lookalike for Gerry, bound, gagged and locked in a closet, struggles to free herself. A maid faints repeatedly, in an exaggerated comic gesture at the surprising developments. There is no dialogue, only music, which makes the events more confounding. The accelerated chase to the altar is embellished with a few still images to display the credits and accent the comic distortion. The wedding ends with the title "And they lived happily ever after . . . or did they?" questioning the convention of romantic comedies. At the initiation of the project Sturges called his script "Is Marriage Necessary?," a question to the Hays Code found objectionable, but whose intention underpins the story.

Sturges begins his film where most romantic comedies end. Instead of flashing back to the initiation of a courtship, years propel us forward from 1937 to 1942 to see how the marriage is doing. As Farber and Poster have noted, Sturges adopts a key principle of the modern, "beginning a work of art at the climax and continuing from there."[22] However, these baffling events, particularly Gerry's imprisoned twin, pose plot questions that are apparently dismissed. But the cartoon exaggeration sets the tone. Desire appears satisfied, so only by eliminating satisfaction can our first plot move be initiated.

In the next scene, Gerry finds herself about to be evicted when an aging rich man supplies a rescue, raising questions about her fidelity. Plot move one, unfulfilled desire, organizes the episode around Gerry's unfulfilled desire—not for love—but for money. The half-deaf Wienie King acts like a fairy godfather to Gerry. Gerry's apartment is available because she and Tom are behind on the rent. The Wienie King tours the premises and Gerry in a negligée hides in the shower only to surprise the old man when he discovers the beautiful woman and quips, "I don't suppose you go with the flat." Nevertheless, when he learns of her hardship he doles out a wad of cash to the embarrassed but grateful woman. The Wienie King is the first of a series of sexless, cartoon suitors who will aid Gerry at every turn. The problem arises with her husband's reaction to Gerry's windfall.

In infidelity comedies a reversal of the initial meeting, plot move two, occurs in the estrangement of the couple. Tom returns from work to discover that Gerry has paid the rent and the bills, bought a new dress, and is ready to go to a restaurant. Over dinner, which she pays for, Gerry confesses to failing as a wife and being tired of living in debt. She wants a new life and thinks that Tom would be better off without her. Gerry declares, "We don't love each other anymore. We're just habits, bad habits." But when Gerry asks for help unhooking the back of her dress, she finds herself on Tom's lap. The husband gathers his wife in his arms and carries her up the stairs as she murmurs, "just a bad habit." Sexual attraction upsets the conflict between love and money with an incongruity that fuels the screwball humor.

The third plot move has the couple having fun together, but in *The Palm Beach Story* Gerry flees from Tom, having fun with other men. Gerry has decided that the marriage is over and departs with nothing but the clothes she is wearing. At Pennsylvania Station she entices the "Ale and Quail Club"—lunatic, aging millionaires on a hunting expedition—to take her to Palm Beach in their private rail car. The drunken revelers dance with Gerry and serenade her in bed before redirecting their sexual desire by shooting up the train. The Club is another example of cartoon sexuality, like dwarves in a child's fable rather than credible characters in a romantic comedy.

As with the Wienie King, the aging gentlemen offer Gerry extravagant favors without expectation, and like the Wienie King, they quickly disappear from the fiction.

In the fourth move an obstacle to the union of the couple arises. The obstacle appears as the rival, John D. Hackensacker III, a man of fabulous wealth in contrast to the penniless Tom. Gerry loses even the clothes of the previous day in the uncoupling of the Club's car. Then she steps onto John D. on her climb

Figure 1.3 *The Palm Beach Story*: the Ale and Quail Club, an example of cartoon sexuality, serenade Gerry before redirecting their desire by shooting up the train.

into the empty sleeping berth, twice breaking his glasses. ("I rather enjoyed it," John D. later confesses, suggesting sexual cruelty, another dark current often simmering beneath the Sturges screwball.) In the morning John rescues Gerry with breakfast and a shopping expedition, which allows Gerry to buy everything she wants and more. Yet another sexless, childlike man (though in this case an eligible bachelor) with intentions surpassing those of an upright Boy Scout provides for the beautiful woman. So when John D. offers a yacht trip to Palm Beach, Gerry appears to be a kept woman on the road to divorce, however much the film ignores the implication. Whatever the motive, the lack of feeling between Gerry and her string of male sponsors drains *The Palm Beach Story* of romantic charge. Rather than offering a challenge to Tom for Gerry's affection, John D. is simply a cartoon exaggeration of what Tom lacks: unlimited wealth.

Elaborating on the "journey" move, Gerry finds herself aboard Hackensacker's yacht where she hatches a scheme, a modest variation on the masquerade in which she assumes a new identity, somewhat like *The Lady Eve*. Once she realizes John D.'s unlimited wealth Gerry puts a price on her freedom. To secure a divorce, she needs $99,000 for her estranged spouse, angling for the capital Tom needs to fund his crazy project, an airport invention he introduced to a reluctant investor at the beginning of the film. The chivalrous Hackensacker assumes that Gerry has been abused. Was her husband a drunk? Had she been beaten? The brute . . . hound . . . reptile . . . The scene develops John's naiveté and Gerry's underlying affection for Tom. Once again Sturges portrays what "a long-legged gal can do without doing anything."

In *The Palm Beach Story* Tom arrives at Palm Beach to reclaim Gerry, but new conflicts arise between the husband and various embodiments of cartoon sexuality when Tom meets John D., John's sister, Princess Maude Centimilla (Mary Astor), and Toto (Sig Arno). Toto, the Princess's kept man, provides the most extreme case of cartoon sexuality. He strains to be humorous, speaking in indecipherable gibberish, and parades in ridiculous costumes while assuming foolish poses between occasional pratfalls. Maude even dismisses Toto with "This is not for children." Childish eroticism involves no exchange. As parents give to children without expectation of reciprocal return, Gerry's alliance with a series of men characterized by cartoon sexuality implies no mutual giving and receiving. Sturges defuses the prospect of male rivals by undermining the sexuality of Gerry's suitors. The elaboration of this childish eroticism invests *The Palm Beach Story* with weightless frivolity and marks Sturges's bizarre variation on screwball.

Gerry introduces Tom as her brother Captain McGlue, another cartoon name, and the Princess immediately latches onto the handsome American and invites the sister and brother to stay in her mansion. Tom squirms behind his masquerade and jealously watches John court his wife, while fending off the advances of the Princess. He is a humorless moralist who believes in balance: something received implies something exchanged. Tom's objections to Gerry's maneuvers leave him a straight man without development. As Sarah Kozloff has noted, "Tom Jeffers is a thankless role; he speaks in a sullen monotone and is deprived of wit."[23]

Gerry must solve the conflict between money and love by seducing a wealthy patron while quieting Tom's jealousy and circumventing his manly pride. There seems little chance that Gerry will surrender herself simply to money or that she intends to live without it. None of the cartoon rivals offers a credible challenge to her marriage, so Gerry's feelings flitter during her adventure but never express passion. The emotional tone of *The Palm Beach Story* glides along the surface of the plot and, in spite of Claudette Colbert's charm, the conflict between money and love functions like a dramatic device rather than expressing an abiding human concern. Sturges's concept of a beautiful woman's power never builds into a crisis of character.

Gerry must choose between John D. and Tom: the men embody the conflict between money and love that propels the film. The conflict reaches its climax at the ball where the Princess pursues Captain McGlue and John D. presses Gerry for an engagement. Gerry secures the $100,000 for Tom's airport twice, both for her brother and for her ex-husband. Tom tries to resist his good fortune by blowing the masquerade, but Gerry's pleas and Hackensacker's generosity sabotage Tom's frankness. The cartoon sexuality of the Hackensackers knocks into Tom's stolidity as the conflict rises to a head.

For Gerry the crisis intensifies after the ball. At her door John promises a surprise, "if you just leave your window open under the balcony." But Gerry has little to fear from the childlike Hackensacker. When Tom declares his love for his wife, Gerry retreats, repeating, "It's all over." Nevertheless, Tom asks for a goodnight kiss. As their lips meet the music is heard from the garden. Instead of climbing through her window for clandestine lovemaking, John serenades Gerry with a full orchestra and a song, "Good Night Sweetheart." Ironically the song excites the feelings of wife and husband for each other. Gerry can't unclasp her dress without help and ends embracing Tom. "I hope you realize this is costing us millions," she declares between kisses.

The morning after his serenade John D. arrives at Gerry's room with an engagement ring. However, Tom and Gerry are back together and packing. Love appears to have triumphed over money until Hackensacker decides to affirm his support for the airport project. So the conflict dissolves without an epiphany and dissolves again when Tom and Gerry reveal they both have identical twins! So neither John D. nor the Princess will be deprived. Thus, Sturges defuses the conflict without allowing Gerry or Tom to experience any significant transformation.

Many have criticized Sturges for his abrupt and unconvincing resolutions. As noted above, some find in the awkward closing a critique of the happy ending convention in romantic comedy. Certainly the ending to *The Palm Beach Story* represents one of the most exaggerated in the Sturges canon.

The Palm Beach Story returns abruptly to the altar where Tom and Gerry were wed, reminding us of the cartoon tone of the opening. Now the mysterious twin of Gerry's, once bound and gagged in the closet, reappears to marry John D. Tom also produces an identical twin to satisfy the Princess. No further explanations arise, even as Toto remains standing behind Maude.

The marriage conveys a sense of the arbitrary and irrational nature of romance elaborating on Charles Pike's remark, "I don't want to know."

Figure 1.4 *The Palm Beach Story*: the return to the altar where Tom and Gerry were wed presents the double marriage of John D. and the Princess with the identical twins of Tom and Gerry. Toto impatiently observes the ceremony.

Rather, the earlier qualified cliché "and they lived happily ever after . . . or did they?" returns with a crash on the soundtrack. Are these blank alter egos merely a shallow reflection of how little Tom and Gerry have developed in the course of the fiction? The repetition implies that a genuine reconciliation is doomed. As Kozloff has pointed out, "*The Palm Beach Story* is perhaps the least romantic of screwballs . . . the very arbitrariness of the device of the twins deliberately satirizes movie conventions of love and courtship."[24] The exaggeration and repetition question more than convention—they question the elevating nature of union itself, returning us to Sturges's original title "Is Marriage Necessary?" Matched with the lack of epiphany, this resolution suggests that lovers never learn, that prospects for development are ephemeral. Maybe Sturges's own multiple marriages, not to mention his then-current adulterous affair with his secretary Jeannie La Vell, made the filmmaker cynical about any prospect of a harmonious and lasting union. In questioning the prospect of a happy marriage, the dark undercurrent of *The Lady Eve* re-emerges from behind the cartoon sexuality of *The Palm Beach Story*.

Attention to the common plot moves of Hollywood romantic comedy reveals the classical shape of both *The Lady Eve* and *The Palm Beach Story*. Although the infidelity comedy offers some variation on the dominant court-ship model, especially in the early episodes, the plotting generally conforms to the typical structure. However, an examination of the plotting highlights other distinguishing qualities, for example, the absent epiphany in *The Palm Beach Story*, which sets up the crazy conclusion. It also makes the distinctive elements Sturges brought to screwball more evident.

Preston Sturges contributed to screwball both a cartoon sexuality and a dark current of suffering that run contrary to the ethos of romantic comedy. The childish eroticism of *The Palm Beach Story* carries a jarring, off-balance humor that finally robs the comedy of passion even as it mocks the sexuality filtered, and often buried, by Hollywood's facile censorship. Suffering gives *The Lady Eve* a depth of feeling and complexity of wit, allowing the viewer to ascend with the lovers in the closing embrace.

I believe these characteristics distinguish Sturges's approach to screwball. One might ask if the cartoon figures are simply inadequate rivals who high-light the attractive qualities of the right partner, for example, Bruce Baldwin (Ralph Bellamy) in *His Girl Friday* or George Kittredge (John Howard) in *The Philadelphia Story* (1940). But Baldwin and Kittredge are handsome and youthful, normal—if intellectually limited—suitors. By contrast, the cartoon figures of Sturges (the Wienie King, the Ale and Quail Club, the Hackensackers and Toto) are eccentric, extremes of aging or naivety and exaggerated in their behavior; their names immediately mark them as humorous caricatures. One might also point to dark currents in other screwball comedies, such as the urban corruption or the Earl Williams case in *His Girl Friday* or

the philandering father in *The Philadelphia Story*. But these disturbing qualities are foils for the central couple to combat together. In *The Lady Eve*, Jean's
vengeance quest is directed against *the beloved*, and the harsh behavior of both
Charles and Jean toward each other is disquieting.

So what can contemporary romantic comedy learn from Sturges's contributions to screwball? Cartoon sexuality is often grotesque and can undermine the
passion driving the romantic pursuit. *There's Something About Mary* (1998)
offers a vivid and influential example of cartoon sexuality in contemporary
romantic comedy. The loser Ted (Ben Stiller) and his various rivals for Mary
(Cameron Diaz) are repellent, exaggerated caricatures of male types. Even Mary
appears to be a silly confection of male desire (beautiful, wealthy, loves sports,
genial, nurturing) rather than a credible woman. The improbable courtship of
opposites pokes fun at the unlikely prospect of love. Suffering, on the other
hand, elaborates on the intensity of passion and the dangers of romance, and
prepares the audience for a powerful ascent into the happy union of a couple.
Though Jules's (Julia Roberts) quest to sabotage Michael's wedding in *My
Best Friend's Wedding* (1997) evokes Jean's vengeance quest in *The Lady Eve*,
perhaps a better example of a powerful dark current in contemporary romantic
comedy is *Eternal Sunshine of the Spotless Mind* (2004). Only after portraying
the agony of separation do the memories of Joel (Jim Carrey) and Clementine
(Kate Winslet) resurrect their love and prompt a reconciliation. The suffering
of the couple, as well as the flaws of both lovers, intensify the passion of the
romance. The convoluted flashbacks draw upon the European art cinema, but
the emotional trajectory of *Eternal Sunshine* might well have found a source in
The Lady Eve. The Sturges contribution to screwball still percolates through
contemporary romantic comedy, and audiences are richer as a result.

NOTES

1   Tamar Jeffers McDonald, *Romantic Comedy: Boy Meets Girl Meets Genre* (London:
    Wallflower Press, 2007), 20.
2   Stanley Cavell, *Pursuits of Happiness: The Hollywood Comedy of Remarriage* (Cambridge,
    MA: Harvard University Press, 1981).
3   Kathrina Glitre, *Hollywood Romantic Comedy: States of the Union, 1934–65* (Manchester:
    Manchester University Press, 2006), 25.
4   Glitre, 44.
5   Elliot Rubenstein, "The End of Screwball Comedy: *The Lady Eve* and *The Palm Beach
    Story*," *Post Script* 1:3 (Spring–Summer 1982): 45.
6   Tina Olsin Lent, "Romantic Love and Friendship: The Redefinition of Gender Relations
    in Screwball Comedy," in *Classical Hollywood Comedy*, ed. Kristine Brunovska Karnick
    and Henry Jenkins (New York, NY: Routledge, 1995), 314–31.
7   *Time*, "The New Pictures: *The Lady Eve*," 10 March 1941, 86.

8 Walt, "*The Lady Eve*," *Variety*, 26 February 1941, 16.

9 Bosley Crowther, "*The Lady Eve* . . .," *The New York Times*, 26 February 1941, 17.

10 *London Times*, "*The Palm Beach Story*," 26 August 1942, 6.

11 Manny Farber, "Preston Sturges: Satirist," *New Republic*, 21 December 1942, 827.

12 Jared Rapfogel, "The Screwball Social Studies of Preston Sturges: Laugh It Up," *Cineaste*, 31:3 (Summer 2006), 10.

13 Manny Farber with W. S. Poster, "Preston Sturges: Success in the Movies," *Negative Space: Manny Farber on the Movies* (New York, NY: Praeger, 1971), 98–9. Originally written in 1954.

14 James Harvey, *Romantic Comedy in Hollywood from Lubitsch to Sturges* (New York, NY: Knopf, 1987), 570.

15 Ray Cywinski, *Preston Sturges: A Guide to References and Resources* (Boston, MA: G. K. Hall, 1984), 27.

16 Farber and Poster, 91.

17 Brian Henderson, *Four More Screenplays by Preston Sturges* (Berkeley, CA: University of California Press, 1995), 32.

18 Leger Grindon, *The Hollywood Romantic Comedy: Conventions, History, Controversies* (Malden, MA: Wiley-Blackwell, 2011), 9–11.

19 Kathleen Rowe, *The Unruly Woman: Gender and Genres of Laughter* (Austin, TX: University of Texas Press, 1995), 164.

20 Cavell, 60–1.

21 Rowe, 162.

22 Farber and Poster, 97.

23 Sarah Kozloff, *Overhearing Film Dialogue* (Berkeley, CA: University of California Press, 2000), 195–6.

24 Kozloff, 198.

CHAPTER 2

Preston Sturges, *Sullivan's Travels,* and Film Authorship in Hollywood, 1941

*Virginia Wright Wexman**

Thanks to the growing influence of the auteur theory, many people today think of directors, even Hollywood directors, as the authors of their films. In the 1930s and 1940s, however, few directors were well known and most were struggling. Audiences of the time commonly viewed movies not in relation to their directors but as products of the studios where they were made or as vehicles for the stars who appeared in them. Even within the studios claims to authorship were challenged as directors vied with screenwriters and others for authority. Preston Sturges's 1941 production *Sullivan's Travels,* which focuses on a Hollywood director, necessarily confronts this issue and addresses a series of questions. How could a moviemaker working in the American film industry at that time be seen as an author whose art emerged from a passion for aesthetic expression? If a studio movie is made by a group rather than a single individual, how could people understand it as the expression of the inner life of a unique creative genius? And how was it that such a genius became identified with the role of director?

The idea of artists who work together in groups to create art for commercial gain has been a problematic concept at least since the nineteenth century. M. H. Abrams's classic study *The Mirror and the Lamp* argues that the modern focus on the solitary artist as the source of meaning in an artwork grows out of the idea of the originary genius developed during the Romantic period, when the notion of art as an imitation of nature gave way to an idea of art as the expression of the imaginative vision of its author.[1] Since that time, Western societies have increasingly looked upon works of art as artifacts representing the complex inner lives of unique individuals. Economic gain was supposedly not part of the equation. In addition, the honor traditionally accorded to skill and craftsmanship was largely supplanted by a reverence for inspiration and personal passion. Hollywood movies pose a problem for such an understanding of art. They are made for profit, not from passion. And, rather than representing unique personal visions, they are manifestly produced by groups, not individuals. Furthermore, studio-made movies do not typically flaunt their uniqueness; rather, they adhere to formulas associated with both the tropes of popular genres and the strict formal grammar of the classical Hollywood style.

Sturges's own views about film authorship were pieced together from two very different worlds: his early life in Europe and his professional experiences in Hollywood. Having lived in Paris during his youth, he had been exposed to a European tradition of art cinema in which auteurs were far more prominent than in Hollywood. The ciné-clubs and film journals that took root in Paris during the teens and twenties celebrated auteurs. And the avant-garde movements that flourished on the continent during these years included short, abstract films intended to be seen as the expression of unique creative individuals.[2] Given such a background, it is not surprising that many of Sturges's statements about cinema indicate a belief that good movies express the vision of a single person. In his autobiography Sturges stated, "The results of collaboration have never equaled the results of a single effort."[3] As a screenwriter, Sturges, unlike most of his colleagues, usually worked alone. Once he became a director, his own practice bore out his conviction that movies should be made by a single person, for he took charge of every phase of his productions. As his friend William Wyler once put it, "He wrote everything, directed everything, played everything out for the actors."[4] Few other Hollywood filmmakers of the day exercised a comparable level of control.

For someone like Sturges, who saw his films as expressions of his own distinctive sensibility, participants in the studio filmmaking process such as executives, producers and actors were useful tools, but he did not view them as true collaborators. In *Sullivan's Travels* he pays homage to two celebrated Hollywood colleagues, Orson Welles and Charlie Chaplin, who personified an ideal of singular authorship within the Hollywood system, functioning as one-man bands wielding authority over every aspect of their films. Sullivan's first adventure as a hobo takes him on a wild ride with a young boy driving a hot-rod, a reference to 1914's *Kid Auto Races at Venice*, Chaplin's first appearance as the little tramp. And the striking shot in the screening room as the lights come up at the conclusion of the opening film-within-the-film references a similar image in *Citizen Kane*, a production that was being shot on the Paramount lot as Sturges was writing his own movie.[5]

Such figures as Chaplin and Welles were rarities, however, for the studio system was predicated on the supposition that many people shared credit for the movies made under its auspices. In *Sullivan's Travels*, a story about a Hollywood author, Sturges presented his hero as a kindred spirit to Chaplin and Welles by characterizing him as someone set apart from the studio and its many creative artisans, including executives, producers, actors and writers as well as directors. He also designed the film itself in a way that minimized the

Figure 2.1 The screening room with its projector light.

contributions of collaborators in order to put a spotlight on his own image as a singular author.

EXECUTIVES AND PRODUCERS

The most obvious challenge for anyone who attempted in 1941 to create an artist hero was how to situate such a person in a world where capital is King. "We must never forget that cinema is an art," Sturges once said. "But it is an art which is so much more costly than the others . . . that the artist must tie himself to the businessman."[6] His early experiences in the movie industry gave him a privileged perspective on this issue, for he was treated almost as a solitary genius while still a screenwriter. His association with Paramount Studios and its executives furthered his image as a unique creative artist, and he responded to the star treatment he received there by creating a warm view of top studio personnel in *Sullivan's Travels*.

From its earliest days, Paramount had cultivated an aura of prestige by promoting eminent stars from the realms of high culture; as such it was well-situated to foster the notion of singular artists in the high art tradition. The studio and its founders Adolph Zukor and Jesse Lasky initially constructed a cinema of quality by tying its productions to the names of revered celebrities of the day. Zukor initially named his business The Famous Players Film Company. For his first project in 1912 he acted as the American distributor for the French film *Queen Elizabeth*, which starred legendary stage actress Sarah Bernhardt. In 1916, Zukor joined forces with Jesse Lasky's Feature Play Company, a studio built on a similar principle. Lasky had begun his career in the film industry in 1914 by teaming up with the DeMille brothers, William and Cecil, scions of a well-known theatrical family. In 1915 Lasky enhanced the new company's cachet by luring renowned opera diva Geraldine Farrar to star in a film version of the popular opera *Carmen* under Cecil DeMille's direction.

As the company evolved into Paramount Pictures it began to promote its own filmmakers as artists as well as appropriating celebrities from more established art forms. The first such figure was Cecil B. DeMille. "I think it a very good business move for us to build up [Cecil's] name," wrote Lasky in 1915. "[T]he public go to see a Griffith production, not because it may have a star in the cast, but because Griffith's name stands for so much. [L]et Cecil stage the plays that have no stars[,] and his name in large type on the paper, advertising, etc. would undoubtedly, in time, take the place of a star's."[7] During the 1930s, despite some bouts of financial distress, Paramount continued to be a home for artists. Unlike rivals like MGM, whose productions were all expected to display the bland, glossy look the studio promoted as its brand image, Paramount supported auteurs who created distinctive stylistic signatures. Besides DeMille, the studio's directorial stable included Joseph von Sternberg, Rouben Mamoulian, and Alfred Hitchcock. Between 1935 and 1936 the famed German émigré director Ernst Lubitsch served as head of production. He was replaced by William LeBaron, himself a former playwright. By 1941, the year in which *Sullivan's Travels* was made, Paramount's artist-centered strategy had paid off—*Barron's* rated the studio as the most profitable in Hollywood.[8]

Sturges's claim to authorship benefited from such author-oriented policies. His first big Hollywood success came about through Lasky. Though Lasky had by then left Paramount and was working as a producer at Twentieth Century-Fox, he continued to follow the strategies he had been instrumental in developing at his former studio. After reading Sturges's radically structured screenplay for *The Power and the Glory* in 1933 Lasky agreed to film it as written, pronouncing it "the most perfect script I have ever read."[9] Sturges was permitted to be on the set every day and to participate in the editing. And his contract gave him a percentage of the profits. No other writer of the day had ever received such perks. When the film opened, Lasky insisted that Sturges's photograph, along with a copy of his script, to be prominently displayed in the lobby of New York's Gaiety Theater.[10]

As a writer in Hollywood during the early 1930s, Sturges had bounced between various projects and studios with little sense of job security, but his career stabilized when William LeBaron offered him a long-term contract at Paramount in 1936. In 1939 LeBaron gave Sturges a chance to direct one of his own screenplays, thereby giving him unprecedented control over his work. Sturges was the first writer in Hollywood permitted to make the leap into directing. LeBaron's gamble was richly rewarded, for the resulting film, *The Great McGinty*, was both a critical and a commercial hit. Sturges's credit on the front roll of *McGinty* read "Written and Directed by Preston Sturges," another Hollywood first. As subsequent Sturges films were released, Paramount aggressively promoted the name and image of its star filmmaker. Publicity stills of the director were labeled "Genius at Work."[11] One of the studio's ads for the 1940 hit *Christmas in July* featured Sturges rather than the film's star Dick Powell. For the movie's opening at the Rivoli Theatre in New York City, ads showed a picture of Sturges alongside those of Ford and Hitchcock. The ads read, "Great directors make great pictures. Alfred Hitchcock for suspense, John Ford for drama. And now, just for fun, Preston Sturges."[12] A story in *Vogue* at around the same time claimed, "Lubitsch and Hitchcock, each with the stamp of a great personality on his work, are names not half as familiar to the public [as Preston Sturges]."[13]

The support Sturges enjoyed at Paramount during this period had given him a warm view of the studio system. "I loved Paramount and did not wish to leave," he later wrote.[14] In this spirit he created two studio executives in *Sullivan's Travels*, LeBrand (Robert Warwick) and Hadrian (Porter Hall), who are seen as sympathetic and supportive in their relations with their star filmmaker, John L. Sullivan (Joel McCrea). By contrast, Sturges's 1935 screenplay for *Song of Joy*, written while he was still a freelance writer for Universal, features an obtuse, inefficient and self-protective mogul, Mr. Apex, who is outraged to discover that his screenwriter Jasper Balcom has included a scene in which a producer trips over a pig. Apex comments, "I wouldn't put a dime in a Hollywood story . . . What are you trying to do? Give the industry a black eye?"[15] Sturges's industry colleagues at the time concurred with this judgment about movies made about Hollywood. Universal's Carl Laemmle, Jr., remained wary of *Song of Joy*; and even Edward Sutherland, who had directed *Diamond Jim* from Sturges's script and whom Sturges considered a friend, demurred, "I am sure that making fun of producers, writers, etc. is not entertainment," he wrote to Laemmle.[16] By contrast, the studio executives in *Sullivan's Travels*, LeBrand (whose name brings to mind that of Paramount chieftain William LeBaron) and Hadrian, are both caring and reasonable. They may argue with their star moviemaker but they stand ready to indulge him in his desire to make a non-commercial film.[17] Even when it seems that Sullivan has died, they make good on a pledge to take care of The Girl (Veronica Lake), whom Sullivan has befriended.

Such a benign portrait of two studio heads complicated Sturges's ability to distance his artistically ambitious filmmaker hero from the commercial side of Hollywood. *Sullivan's Travels* addresses this difficulty on a stylistic level during its opening and closing sequences. The opening features Sully discussing his next project with LeBrand and Hadrian. After they view the concluding scene of a recently released film in which two men fight to the death on the top of a train, they adjourn to Hadrian's adjoining office for a conference. An exchange follows in which the three circle about each other as Sully attempts to justify his desire to make a picture like the one they have just seen. LeBrand and Hadrian counter this proposal by stressing the importance of creating a commercial property that will bring in revenue to the studio. Their conversation is captured by a bravura four-minute tracking shot executed by Sturges's cinematographer John F. Seitz. In this much-lauded shot the camera stalks the three men as Sully attempts to extricate himself from the profit-oriented point of view of his bosses. Only when he determines to strike out on his own does he escape from the camera's relentless embrace. By contrast, the camera remains stable in the film's concluding scene, which again features the two

Figure 2.2 Sullivan surrounded by studio supporters.

studio executives in conversation with Sullivan. He is now in agreement with his bosses, but his motive for making the movie they want has changed. In the course of his travels, Sully has discovered the importance of laughter to lighten people's lives.[18] His new perspective enables him to exist within the business-oriented environment of Hollywood without being tainted by it. Now the camera's steady gaze centers itself firmly on Sully, who sits amid an admiring group of studio personnel. LeBrand and Hadrian are positioned somewhat below him, one on either side. Sturges thus securely situates his hero in the heart of the movie business while he simultaneously manages to rise above it.[19]

In Hollywood, commerce is represented not just by studio moguls but also by the representatives of such powers on the sets of movies themselves: producers. Without ever depicting a producer, *Sullivan's Travels* alludes to the movie's actual producer, Paul Jones, in ways that make him appear trivial and even ridiculous. Jones gives his surname to the bloviating publicist played by one of Sturges's favorite character actors, William Demarest. An image of Paul Jones also appears in the film, because the producer posed for the photograph we see of Joseph, the deceased husband of the sexually predatory farm widow, Miz Zeffie (Esther Howard). As Sully attempts to escape from his room at the farm after Miz Zeffie has locked him in, the portrait's eyes shift in a furtive manner to track his movements. But the picture is ultimately impotent, merely an image plastered on the wall that can only observe, not act. These sly references demean the producer of *Sullivan's Travels* and, together with the portrait Sturges paints of the accommodating studio executives LeBrand and Hadrian, have the effect of lifting the movie's filmmaker-hero above the commercial realm that surrounds him.

ACTORS

Stars formed the backbone of most Hollywood movies in 1941, bringing in the crowds and frequently shaping the vehicles they headlined. As a skilled Hollywood professional Sturges crafted effective showpieces for some of the industry's biggest names, including Betty Hutton in *The Miracle of Morgan's Creek* (1944) and Harold Lloyd in *The Sin of Harold Diddlebock* (1947). He also cultivated a number of highly accomplished character actors like William Demarest, Esther Howard, Eric Blore, and Jimmy Conlin, who became known as the Sturges stock company. He made good use of the expertise such performers brought with them, sometimes incorporating bits of business they suggested into his productions.

At bottom, however, Sturges viewed all performers as less than full creative partners. His actors were encouraged to follow his screenplays to the letter. When he became a director he customarily demonstrated how to play each scene by acting out all the parts for the cast members. "All my actors wear tailor-made parts down to the woman who sells flowers in the street," he once said, "What you see is the work of one man; what you hear is his voice."[20] In *Sullivan's Travels*, a story about a Hollywood auteur, he discounts the role of actors by marginalizing the issue within the diegesis. Save for a brief glimpse of a movie set on which The Girl works, we never see the messy process by which studio films are staged. Instead, his film focuses on the Romantic notion of the artist's moment of inspiration, not the actual working out of his idea.

Though *Sullivan's Travels* never overtly addresses the nature of actors' creative input, Sturges's casting of Veronica Lake as The Girl implicitly raises this issue, for he used her in a way that minimized her creative contributions. Sturges wanted Lake for the role, and he kept her on even after discovering that she was six months pregnant at the start of filming. Why? One can readily imagine that his reasons had much to do with the image she presented on screen. Lake was at the time an emerging star known for her "peek-a-boo" coiffeur, which featured a wave falling over the left side of her face. The style became a sensation after her breakout performance as Sally Vaughn in Paramount's 1940 production *I Wanted Wings*, and women all over the country copied it. The press response to *I Wanted Wings* (no doubt prompted by an energetic Paramount publicity department) frequently focused on Lake's coiffeur. "Veronica Lake is a newcomer, an exotic young blonde with a fantastic hairdo and makeup," Eileen Creelman gushed in the *New York Sun*. Howard Barnes of the *New York Herald-Tribune* was similarly enthusiastic. "She has a startling hairdo, with overlong blonde tresses that she occasionally strings out as though she were about to use her head as a violin," he wrote.[21] One of the posters for *Sullivan's Travels* features a sketchy caricature of the star consisting largely of a rendering of her famous wave. The studio was exploiting an established asset, and Sturges was a partner in this effort.[22]

Lake's signature hairstyle was not a feature she naturally possessed. Like the movie itself, her coiffeur was artificially created. The behind-the-scenes labor and skill involved in fashioning Lake's distinctive look was sometimes brought to the fore in the publicity surrounding her. Such publicity tied the Hollywood industry to the marketing of a changing array of beauty products. An article published by *Life* magazine in 1942, for example, detailed the work that went into maintaining the star's hairstyle. "Her hair was washed each morning before appearing in front of the cameras, once in Nulava shampoo and once in Maro oil," the article claimed, "and then it was rinsed in vinegar."[23] The work as well as the expense implied in this description is obliquely referenced in *I Wanted Wings* during Lake's final scene. While Sally is on the run from the

Figure 2.3 Poster for *Sullivan's Travels*.

police her hair appears disheveled and frizzy, signaling that the character has lost the time as well as the financial wherewithal to care for it.

The publicity surrounding Lake's hair was part of a larger trend in which female stars were made into models for women to look up to and follow. The rise of mass-market magazines, modern advertising techniques, and low-priced chain stores in the 1920s enabled beauty rituals to be readily exploited by corporate interests, and Hollywood quickly became a willing partner in this enterprise.[24] Having managed his mother's cosmetics business while still in high school, Sturges was well-aware of all the facets of this new phenomenon, from the array of products it encompassed to the nature of the care and upkeep required to apply them.[25] And his studio, Paramount, was at the forefront in promoting an ideal of feminine loveliness. During this period the studio was home to a number of the most famous beauty queens of the day, including Gloria Swanson, Marlene Dietrich, Carole Lombard, and Claudette Colbert, all of whom represented ideals women could try to emulate. Of particular relevance in relation to *Sullivan's Travels* is the example set by another Paramount star, Louise Brooks, whose flapper bob set the style for many American women in the 1920s. In 1928's *Beggars of Life* Brooks plays a beautiful waif whose iconic coiffeur is concealed in scenes where she, like Lake in *Sullivan's Travels*, dons a cap in order to disguise herself as a boy as she rides the rails with co-star Richard Arlen.[26]

Though it provided fodder for glossy magazines and the advertising that supported them, the work of beautification routinely engaged in by Hollywood actresses is rarely evident in the movies themselves. As Virginia Postrel observed in her 2013 book *The Power of Glamour*, part of the appeal of the ideal of glamorous beauty Hollywood purveys in the images of female stars like Veronica Lake depends on conveying an impression of effortlessness.[27] Phrases used to described such stars, such as "the camera loves them" and "she has star quality," operate to obscure the work of the army of support personnel such as cinematographers, cosmeticians, hair stylists and costume designers, whose efforts, along with those of the performers themselves, play a major role in crafting actresses' on-screen personas. The Hollywood mystique of glamour, with its hidden level of labor and expertise masked by an aura of effortlessness, also downplays the contributions of such female stars and, by extension, advances the claim of directors to be thought of as authors in the high art tradition. For if actresses are thought of as mere images, directors are the ones who manipulate them.

By treating Veronica Lake as an image whose creative contributions could be discounted, Sturges was following long-established Hollywood tradition. But he was capable of acknowledging the effort that went into constructing her image in subtle ways. Such an acknowledgment is evidenced in two brief scenes in *Sullivan's Travels* in which women converse about beauty work.[28] Both scenes are staged as two-shots that emphasize the common bonds between the women and the intimacy they encourage. The first scene takes place when Miz Zeffie confides to her sister Ursula (Almira Sessions) that she needs a permanent wave and comments, "Some are blind to beauty . . . while others . . . are not." The second exchange occurs between The Girl and the studio secretary (Margaret Hayes) when the secretary offers The Girl her makeup. "Thanks," replies The Girl; "I can use it." To which the secretary responds, "You sure can!"

Sturges also took pleasure in poking fun at the mystique of female beauty that Hollywood promulgated. Several of his films feature male characters so completely enthralled by a woman's fetching appearance that they are blind to any of her other qualities. For such men, the woman's image is all. Sturges pairs these males up with women who look identical but who are not in other ways similar. Thus, in both *Diamond Jim* and *The Palm Beach Story* two beautiful women who look alike are presented as interchangeable romantic partners—and in both cases the women are even played by the same actresses: Jean Arthur in *Diamond Jim* and Claudette Colbert in *The Palm Beach Story*.[29] *The Lady Eve* features a variation on this motif. Jean (Barbara Stanwyck) pretends to be another woman, Lady Eve Sidwich, and Charles (Henry Fonda), the man who loves her, falls in love with Lady Eve as well. "It would never have happened if she didn't look so exactly like you," Charles confesses to Jean at the story's conclusion. Such self-conscious jibes at Hollywood's beauty culture do not appear in *Sullivan's Travels*; instead, the glamorous image of Veronica Lake simply becomes part of the movie's décor.

WRITERS AND DIRECTORS

Sturges discounted the creative contributions of a female star like Veronica Lake with some ease, but he faced a more complicated issue in relation to the competing claims of writers and directors to be considered as authors of Hollywood films. Tellingly, *Sullivan's Travels* never makes the job of its hero explicit. Is he a writer-director or just a director? Sturges had good reason to maintain this ambiguity, for in the Hollywood culture of the day the question of Sully's job description was problematic. Long before Sturges arrived in Hollywood, writers and directors had been vying for authorial supremacy within the American film industry.

At the beginning of his career, Sturges himself believed not only that films should have single authors but also that those with the best claim to be authors were screenwriters. "[T]the writers alone can bring motion pictures to the high level they are destined to occupy," he once wrote.[30] During his years at Paramount he worked alongside some of the best, including Joseph L. Mankiewicz, Billy Wilder, and Samson Rafelson.[31] Wilder, who became a writer-director hyphenate soon after Sturges did, voiced an opinion similar to that of Sturges about the pre-eminence of the writer when he claimed "I have always thought of myself primarily as a writer."[32] Another of Sturges's contemporaries, Orson Welles, concurred. "In my opinion, the writer should have the first and last word in filmmaking," he once said, "the only better alternative being the writer-director, with the stress on the first word."[33]

The right of screenwriters to claim authorship of Hollywood movies was not uncontested: directors had long made a similar claim. The struggle between the two groups had been going on since the beginning of the twentieth century. In the early days of cinema it appeared that writers might come out on top. In contrast to directors, whose craft has little in the way of an official history, screenwriters can evaluate their work in the context of a distinguished tradition of high literary art. In addition, writers create material that can be readily identified as original: plots and dialogue. In their struggle for control over their work, screenwriters looked to the traditions of theater. The Dramatists Guild represents playwrights, and the group's first contract in 1919 gave them copyright protection for their work. Producers could license a play, but they were required to consult the author about directors, casting and script changes.

Yet the realities of moviemaking prevented screenwriters from achieving a similar level of control over their work. Screenplays are broken down and reorganized to maximize efficient filming by production executives; locations are often far-flung; and technical considerations involving camera angles, film stock, lighting and editing further compromise the integrity of a script. The erosion of the writers' authority occasioned by all of these circumstances encouraged studios to adopt the practice of assigning several writers or teams of writers to work on scripts in tandem or serially. At Warner Bros., screenwriter Julius Epstein, one of the many writers who worked on *Casablanca*, described the practice:

> You were assigned a script, and when you were through with it, the studio would give it to another writer. And someone else would polish it, and, if you were good at a particular thing, you would do that kind of scene on one picture and another and another.[34]

When screenwriters began to organize in the early 1930s into what eventually became the Writers Guild of America, elevating their status as authors was at the top of their agenda; but they had by then lost so much ground on issues like piecework, on-set revisions, and multiple credits that they could make little headway in this area. In addition, many writers were strongly committed to left-wing causes, and, as a result, both political pressure from without and rifts within their own ranks weakened the organization throughout its early years.[35]

Directors, for their part, struggled as well, competing for control with cameramen and producers as well as with writers. In the earliest days of moviemaking cameramen who exercised a purely mechanical function, were in charge. Between 1901 and 1904 cameramen began to be paired with directors, whose main responsibility was to supervise actors and staging. Only gradually did directors assume superiority. Magisterial figures like D. W. Griffith were crucial in advancing the fortunes of directors. Recalling his career at Biograph studios, Billy Bitzer stated, "Before [Griffith's] arrival, I, as cameraman, was responsible for everything except the immediate hiring and handling of the actor. Soon it was his say whether the light was bright enough, or if the make-up was right."[36] Film historian Tom Gunning attributes this shift in power not merely to Griffith's charisma and public relations efforts but to the growing ascendency of narrative. "With the director's new involvement in the visualization of the film," he writes, "the equivalent of the theatrical director appeared in a film: a role that integrated elements of a production around a unifying center . . . The dramatic purpose within a scene determined its visual presentation as well, creating a filmic discourse which expressed dramatic situations."[37] Recognizing this power, American critics and journalists advocated for the idea of directors as authors as early as 1915, when one writer opined, "The director is the man. The movie director has command of everything."[38]

By the 1920s, top directors wielded considerable clout, though studios often resisted them. A 1927 article in *The New York Times* reported on the growing tendency of directors to go over budget and over schedule, a propensity which the industry typically viewed as the result of their commitment to making artistic films.[39] New bank oversight of the studios in the 1930s curtailed this trend, and directors were not as free as before to impose their own styles on the productions they helmed. During this period strong producers like Irving Thalberg and Darryl Zanuck had the most right to claim responsibility for a film's artistic coherence.[40] In 1936 John Ford complained:

> They've got to turn the picture making over to the hands that know it . . . As it is now, the director arrives at nine in the morning. He has not only never been consulted about the script to see whether he liked it or feels fit to handle it, but he may not even know what the full story is about. They hand him two pages of straight dialogue or finely calculated action. Within an hour or less he is expected to go to work and complete the assignment the same day, all the participants and equipment being prepared for him without any say or choice on his part. When he leaves at night he has literally no idea what the next day's work will be.[41]

Even worse, an assembly-line production model was taking hold in some studios, a practice which saw different directors assigned to helm selected scenes in a given production. Yet even as they saw their authority eroding, directors continued to hold sway on the set, and studio heads respected them.

Sturges campaigned long and hard to become a director not because he saw directors as the creative heart of moviemaking but because he saw them as the aristocracy of the industry. "When I went to Hollywood I saw that directors were treated as Princes of the Blood, whereas writers worked in teams of six like piano movers," he wrote to his stepfather in 1957. "In the beginning I tried to prove that writers were at least as important as directors, then one day I realized it would be easier to become a Prince of the Blood myself than to change the whole social order. This did not change the relative merits of directors and writers (who are actually vastly more important), but it changed my salary and the way people treated me."[42] Though Sturges remained committed to the cause of writers, once he became a director himself his experience on the set made him ready to give directors a certain amount of credit. "If anyone knows how a scene should be played it is the fellow who wrote it," he once stated. "Or so I once thought. I agreed with very few directors when I was merely writing. They argued tremendously, and sometimes they lost out. I look upon them now as brave fellows who went down with their colors flying. I don't as a director, film a scene exactly as the writer—who was myself—wrote it."[43] By the time he became a member of the Academy of Motion Picture Arts and Sciences in 1941, he had come to attach great value to the prestige directors enjoyed, objecting when the Academy categorized him as a writer. "As it took me eight years to become a director," he wrote to the Academy, "you might as well give me credit for it and list me with the directors."[44]

Though Sturges avoided explicitly pitting the cause of writers against that of directors in *Sullivan's Travels*, he addressed the issue in two other projects. *Song of Joy* contains a number of scenes in which a team made up of a screenwriter, director, and producer collaborates on a screenplay. Though all make contributions to the finished product, the screenwriter consistently shows up as the most creative, knowledgeable, and articulate participant.[45] *Unfaithfully Yours*, released in 1948, does not concern moviemaking, but the position of its main character, the orchestra conductor Sir Alfred de Carter (Rex Harrison), is similar to that of a Hollywood director, just as the composer is analogous to the screenwriter.[46] Lionized as a major celebrity, Sir Alfred nonetheless singles out composers as the ones who truly deserve credit. "I have made some small success by playing exactly what I saw before me in black and white," he says at one point, and at another moment he states that his goal is "to follow the wishes of the composer, clearly expressed by the composer."[47]

Despite his bias in favor of writers, Sturges understood that directors are the ones who receive most of the credit for a film's success. He himself spoke about *Sullivan's Travels* as a movie about directors, not writers. "After I saw a couple of pictures put out by some of my fellow comedy directors which seemed to me to have abandoned the fun in favor of the message," he stated, "I wrote *Sullivan's Travels* to satisfy an urge to tell them that they were getting a little too deep-dish; to leave the preaching to the preachers."[48] In his conversations with the two studio executives, Sully mentions Frank Capra as an inspiration for his newfound desire to make a socially conscious film, suggesting that Capra was one of the filmmakers Sturges had in mind who had abandoned fun in favor of the message. Two years before *Sullivan's Travels* Capra had made *Mr. Smith Goes to Washington*, more a politically progressive melodrama than a comedy, and the film had been attacked as Communist-influenced by right-wing members of the press. Yet it was the *writer* of *Mr. Smith*, Sidney

Buchman, who was a communist; Capra himself was a conservative.[49] Sturges ignored this inconsistency, for despite his belief in the validity of the writer's claim to creative authorship, he recognized that directors were the ones who possessed the fame and authority to make such a claim credible. And for him personally the distinction was moot, for he was both a writer and a director.

At the very moment Sturges was making *Sullivan's Travels*, when his power and reputation had peaked, forces were at work in the American movie business which would ultimately undermine his ability to think of himself as a solitary artist within an industry marked by many competing interests. During the years when he rose to fame in Hollywood most of his fellow directors had concluded that they could not rely simply on their own talent to shape their future careers; they would need institutional support. Driven by this conviction, they banded together to form the Screen Directors Guild.[50] The level of autonomy Sturges enjoyed in the industry at that moment led him to cast a cold eye on their project. He was the only recognized director in the industry who rebuffed the nascent organization, just as he had earlier turned down an invitation to join the Writers Guild. In his reply to the SDG's invitation to become a member, he wrote:

> It is only because of my very deep conviction that guilds are principally useful to the lawyers whom they enrich that I must take a rain check on the invitation . . . I failed to make myself clear to my friends Mr. Frank Capra, Mr. Frank Lloyd or Mr. Wyler. Certainly also I failed to make myself clear to my friends of the screen writers guild during the years I was overpowered by my desire not to join their organization.[51]

His decision was a mistake, for unlike the Writers Guild, which Sturges had shunned years before, the Directors Guild was not a left-leaning union roiled by political strife. Instead, the underlying idea driving the SDG's creative agenda was one that Sturges would have found congenial: that a director should be the sole author of a Hollywood film.[52] Frank Capra had formulated this version of the directorial persona as early as the 1920s when, together with his publicist Scoop Conlon, he devised the slogan "One man, one film." Capra's autobiography returns again and again to the principle of the artist as a solitary figure. "The 'one man, one film' idea took hold slowly," Capra wrote, "against opposition from entrenched executives—and today many directors have a box office value as big, or bigger than the stars."[53] When he became president of the SDG in 1936, Capra made this sentiment into the mantra of the Guild. The idea behind his slogan, that a single director should stand as the creative center of every Hollywood movie, has led the SDG to impose ever-stricter rules governing the conditions under which a director may be replaced on any given production. The Guild has also sponsored policies that have increasingly marginalized the contributions of other creative personnel who work with directors.

For example, standard DGA contracts now bar screenwriters from film sets; and the right to a director's cut, negotiated by the Guild in the 1980s, places editors under directors' control. All of these policies strengthened the position and image of directors, largely at the expense of writers.

CONCLUSION

Sturges's conviction that he could assert his own claim to authorship within a Hollywood industry that was becoming ever more complex and corporate without some kind of institutional support such as that offered by the SDG was ill-founded. Friends and peers like Billy Wilder, Joseph Mankiewicz, and John Huston, who, like Sturges, had begun their careers as writers, nonetheless understood the value of the SDG's mission and worked to advance it. In the years ahead their careers flourished. Partly as a result of their efforts and those of other members of the SDG, directors have become, for many people, the unquestioned authors of Hollywood films.

In 1941, however, executives, producers, stars and writers could credibly cast themselves as creative partners in the moviemaking enterprise. In *Sullivan's Travels*, Sturges made light of the pretentions of the first two groups and avoided dealing with the third. But the ambivalences and hesitancies that mark the film have little meaning for critics today. A commentary by playwright Christopher Guest on the 2002 Criterion DVD release of *Sullivan's Travels* reflects the modern view, for Guest hails John L. Sullivan as a lone author and does not even consider that he might be a writer as well as a director, let alone that executives, producers, and actors could be significant collaborators in successful Hollywood moviemaking. Sullivan "must struggle alone to reveal the truth, as artists do," Guest states. "This is a film about the sovereignty of the director over the studio system . . . It's about how directing is a noble profession."

NOTES

* I would like to thank the research staffs at the UCLA Special Collections Department and the Margaret Herrick Library for their assistance in locating materials for this essay. Special thanks are due to Jenny Romero at the Herrick. I am also grateful to the editors of this collection, Jeff Jaeckle and Sarah Kozloff, for helpful information and guidance.
1 M. H. Abrams's *The Mirror and the Lamp: Romantic Theory and the Critical Tradition* (New York, NY: Oxford University Press, 1971). Clifford Siskin's *The Historicity of Romantic Discourse* (New York, NY: Oxford University Press, 1988) offers a more materially oriented version of the romantic idea of art.
2 For a history of French film culture during this period see Richard Abel, *French Film*

Theory and Criticism: A History / Anthology, 1907–1939. Volume 1: 1907–1929 (Princeton, NJ: Princeton University Press, 1993).

3   Preston Sturges, *Preston Sturges by Preston Sturges*, ed. Sandy Sturges (New York, NY: Simon & Schuster, 1990), 75. Sturges subsequently reiterated these sentiments in a letter to Alva Johnston written on February 10, 1941.

4   Quoted in Axel Madsen, *William Wyler* (New York, NY: Thomas Y. Crowell, 1973), 104.

5   It was widely believed at the time that the script for *Kane* had been influenced by Sturges's 1933 script for *The Power and the Glory*, and Welles confessed to having screened Sturges's earlier *succès d'estime* several times as he worked on *Kane* with screenwriter Herman Mankiewicz.

Sturges himself characterized *Sullivan's Travels* as a whole as an exercise in parody in which a range of films were burlesqued. "*Sullivan's Travels* started with a discussion about movie-making," he stated, "and during its unwinding, tried a little of every form that was discussed" (quoted in Jacobs, 184). Elliot Rubenstein ("Hollywood's Travels: Sturges and Sullivan," *Sight and Sound* 47 [Winter 1977–8]: 50–2) discusses the many references to other movies and works of art the film contains, as do Alessandro Pirolini (*Preston Sturges: A Critical Study* [Jefferson, NC: McFarland, 2010]) and Kathleen Moran and Michael Rogin ("'What's the Matter with Capra?' *Sullivan's Travels* and the Popular Front," *Representations* 71 [Summer 2000]: 106–34) I note additional references to other films in *Sullivan's Travels* below where relevant to my argument.

6   Quoted in Diane Jacobs, *Christmas in July: The Life and Art of Preston Sturges* (Berkeley, CA: University of California Press, 1992), 419.

7   Quoted in Sumiko Higashi, *Cecil B. DeMille and American Culture: The Silent Era* (Berkeley, CA: University of California Press, 1994), 19–20.

8   Douglas Gomery, *The Hollywood Studio System: A History* (London: British Film Institute, 2008), 91.

9   Quoted in James Curtis, *Between Flops: A Biography of Preston Sturges* (New York, NY: Harcourt Brace Jovanovich, 1982), 82.

10   Jacobs, 130.

11   Curtis, 142. Sturges himself backed away from the "genius" label the press pinned on him. "If I have any success," he told a journalist in 1940, "it's an act of God." Molly Hollywood, "Sturges Spurns Genius Tag," *Los Angeles Examiner*, 25 August 1940.

12   Curtis (illustrations), 116ff.

13   Quoted in Pirolini, 1.

14   *Preston Sturges*, 299.

15   Screenplays for *Song of Joy* are on file at the Special Collections, Margaret Herrick Library (Academy of Motion Picture Arts and Sciences), Beverly Hills, CA, Paul Kohner Agency Records, Box 136, Folders 1363, 1364; and Preston Sturges Papers (Collection 1114). Department of Special Collections, University Research Library, University of California, Los Angeles, Box 27.

16   Quoted in Jacobs, 168. See Jeff Jaeckle's chapter on *Song of Joy* for a detailed account of the script and its controversies

17   The name of the movie's hero, John L. Sullivan, casts him as an individual of formidable prowess in Hollywood, since it refers to a famous prizefighter of the day. Sturges was an avid boxing fan and included a minor character called John L. Sullivan, who is a nightclub bouncer with "a fine pair of dukes" in *Diamond Jim*.

18   Sturges's emphasis on the significance of comedy in *Sullivan's Travels* leads him to brush aside issues of social injustice, softening them by means of a film's lighthearted style. He repeatedly turns aside from the political implications of its depictions of poverty through

self-reflexive intrusions, comic interludes, and musical accompaniments that emphasize whimsy and pathos over political outrage. James Harvey offers an insightful discussion of *Sullivan's Travels'* strengths and weaknesses as a comedy in his book *Romantic Comedy in Hollywood: From Lubitsch to Sturges* (New York, NY: Knopf, 1987). Moran and Rogin offer an extended critique of the way in which Sturges's emphasis on comedy leads to a somewhat cavalier treatment of the political issues the film raises.

19 Sturges later claimed that Sullivan was not intended to represent him. "The less [Sullivan] had of other things, the more important became laughter. So as a purveyor of laughter he regained the dignity of his profession and returned to Hollywood to make laughter . . . That was Sullivan's conclusion, not mine. I don't believe that now is the time for comedies or tragedies or spy pictures without music. I believe that now is the time for all forms of art and that art is always with us" (quoted in Curtis, 157).

20 Quoted in Curtis, 204.

21 Quoted in James Robert Parrish, *The Paramount Pretties* (New Rochelle, NY: Arlington House, 1972), 413. In her autobiography, Lake complains that the style was a consequence of her fine, hard-to-manage blonde hair. According to Lake, Busby Berkeley first marked her distinctive style as part of her appeal on the set of *40 Little Mothers*. "Let it fall," she quotes Berkeley as saying. "It distinguishes her from the rest." Lake also claimed that Arthur Hornblow, Jr., the producer of *I Wanted Wings*, cast her in the film because of her coiffeur. See Veronica Lake with Donald Bain, *Veronica* (London: W. H. Allen, 1969), 16.

22 Sturges betrays some embarrassment about using Lake in this way, for he simply refers to her as "The Girl." He also has Sully acknowledge that all Hollywood movies must have "a little sex" in them. Sully also responds to a question put to him by a policeman by asserting, "There's always a girl in the picture; don't you ever go to the movies?"

23 Parrish, 413. The article also went into minute detail in describing Lake's hair. "Veronica had about 150,000 hairs," the article stated, "each measuring about 0.0024 inches in cross section, with the locks 17 inches in front, 24 inches in back, and falling about 8 inches below her shoulders."

24 Feminist critics have long decried the way in which this regime of beautification virtually forced women (or the beauticians they could afford to hire) to take on considerable work and expense. See e.g. Rosalind Coward, *Female Desires: How They Are Sought, Bought and Packaged* (New York, NY: Grove Press, 1983); Sandra Lee Bartky, *Femininity and Domination* (New York, NY: Routledge, 1990); and Naomi Wolf, *The Beauty Myth* (New York, NY: Morrow, 1991).

25 Sturges's association with the beauty culture continued into adulthood, when he had a long affair with Frances Ramsden, a model famed for her role in marketing fashion and cosmetics.

27 It is impossible to determine whether Sturges saw *Beggars of Life* while he was working as a playwright in New York. Other films of the period, including *Wild Boys of the Road* (1933) and *Sylvia Scarlet* (1935), also feature actresses who cover their tresses to appear as boys, but the publicity surrounding Louise Brooks's paradigm-shattering hairstyle during a time just after Sturges had left his mother's beauty business makes *Beggars of Life* the most intriguing precursor.

27 Virginia Postrel, *The Power of Glamour* (New York, NY: Simon & Schuster, 2013). For other explorations of the phenomenon of glamour, see Stephen Gundle, *Glamour: A History* (New York, NY: Oxford University Press, 2008); and Carol Dyhouse, *Glamour: Women, History, Feminism* (New York, NY: Zed Books, 2010). Dyhouse reports that the 1930s became known as the Golden Age of Glamour (29).

28 In her book *Hope in a Jar: The Making of America's Beauty Culture* (New York, NY:
    Henry Holt and Company, 1999), Kathy Peiss has examined the ways in which strictures
    surrounding beauty regimens have fostered female empowerment and relations among
    women.

29 Sturges claimed he was inspired to make *The Palm Beach Story* (which he plunged into
    directly after *Sullivan's Travels*) to examine what he called "the aristocracy of beauty."
    Preston Sturges, 296.

30 Quoted in Harvey, 519.

31 Many members of Paramount's illustrious stable of writers were recruited by Joseph
    Mankiewicz's brother Herman, who had been named head of the scenario department in
    1927.

32 Quoted in Burt Prelusky, "An Interview with Billy Wilder," in *Billy Wilder: Interviews*,
    ed. Robert Horton (Jackson, MS: University of Mississippi Press, 2001), 184.

33 Quoted in Richard Corliss, *Talking Pictures: Screenwriters in the American Cinema* (New
    York, NY: Penguin, 1975), xxii.

34 Quoted in Aljean Harmetz, *"Round Up the Usual Suspects": The Making of Casablanca*
    (New York, NY: Hyperion Books, 1993), 56. For histories of Hollywood screenwriters see
    Richard Fine, *West of Eden: Writers in Hollywood, 1928–40* (Washington, DC:
    Smithsonian Institution Press, 1979); Tom Stempel, *Framework: A History of
    Screenwriting in the American Film* (New York, NY: Continuum, 1991); Jorja Prover,
    No-one Knows Their Name: Screenwriters in Hollywood (Bowling Green, OH: Bowling
    Green University Press, 1994); Sean Mitchell, "Hereinafter Referred to as the Author,"
    [written by] *The Magazine of the Writers Guild of America* (June 2000): 40–9; and Steven
    Price, *The Screenplay: Authorship, Theory and Criticism* (New York, NY: Palgrave, 2010).

35 The Writers' Union was originally called the Screen Writers Guild. For a history of the
    group focusing on their political woes see Nancy Lynn Schwartz and Sheila Schwartz, *The
    Hollywood Writers Wars* (New York, NY: Knopf, 1982).

36 Billy Bitzer, *His Story: The Autobiography of D. W. Griffith's Master Cameraman* (New
    York, NY: Farrar, Straus & Giroux, 1973), 69.

37 Tom Gunning, *D. W. Griffith and the Origins of Narrative Film: The Early Years at
    Biograph* (Champaign, IL: University of Illinois Press, 1991), 47.

38   Quoted in Richard Koszarski, Introduction. *Film History* 7:4 (1995) (Special Issue:
    Auteurism Revisited): 355.

39 James O. Spearing, "Directors Are Human!," *The New York Times*, 31 July 1927; repr. in
    The New York Times Encyclopedia of Film, ed. Gene Brown (New York, NY: New York
    Times Books, 1984).

40 Thomas Schatz has explored the power of producers in the old-style studios in *The Genius
    of the System: Hollywood Filmmaking in the Studio Era* (New York, NY: Pantheon, 1988).

41 Quoted in Dan Ford, *Pappy: The Life of John Ford* (Englewood Cliffs, NJ: Prentice-Hall,
    1979), 97.

42 Quoted in Jacobs, 130, 461, n. 39.

43 Quoted in Curtis, 183.

44 Letter to Donald Gledhill, 26 August 1941, UCLA, Box 92, Folder 2.

45 The name of the screenwriter, Jasper, probably alludes to John Jasper, who was then at the
    center of a labor dispute at the Writer's Club, of which Sturges was a board member. The
    character of Vladimir, the director, may refer to Rouben Mamoulian, a Russian émigré
    director with whom Sturges had worked on *We Live Again* in 1934 just before he wrote
    Song of Joy. Sturges was later to put down Mamoulian, saying, "My friend Mamoulian
    told me he could make the audience interested in whatever *he* showed them, and I told

him that he was mistaken. It is true that he can bend my head down and force me to look at a doorknob when my reflex wants to see the face of the girl saying goodbye, but it is also true that it stops my comprehension of the scene, destroys my interest and gives me a pain in the neck" (quoted in Jacobs, 153).

46 Sturges himself later confessed, "It was the opinion of almost everyone who knew me that I not only wrote, directed and produced [*Unfaithfully Yours*], but that I also played the lead" (*Preston Sturges*, 308). Sturges began the script for *Unfaithfully Yours* in 1932–3, though it was not completed until 1948. The inspiration for the story came from an experience he had while he was writing the script for *The Power and the Glory* in 1931 and noticed that his rewrites of a certain scene were influenced by the different pieces of music he heard playing on a radio in the next room. This anecdote suggests that Sturges's aim in *Unfaithfully Yours* was as much to highlight issues related to the creative process as it was to examine Sir Alfred's jealousy. Such an understanding of the genesis of the film is supported by its original title, "Unfinished Symphony," which emphasizes Sir Alfred's vocation rather than his love life. (The title was eventually changed because producer Darryl Zanuck decided that audiences would stay away from any movie with the word "Symphony" in its name. [See Memo from Darryl F. Zanuck to Preston Sturges, 11 October 1947, UCLA Box 24, folder 3.]) For more information about the film's production history, see Brian Henderson, *Four More Screenplays by Preston Sturges* (Berkeley, CA: University of California Press, 1995), 755–822. For a superb analysis of *Unfaithfully Yours* as a study in jealousy, see Henry Jenkins, "'The Laughingstock of the City': Performance Anxiety, Male Dread and *Unfaithfully Yours*," in *Classical Hollywood Comedy*, ed. Kristine Brunovska Karnick and Henry Jenkins (New York: Routledge, 1994), 238–64.

47 For a discussion of comparisons between classical music performance and film authorship, see Sarah Kozloff, *The Life of the Author* (Montreal: Caboose Books, 2014), 46.

48 *Preston Sturges*, 295.

49 In her commentary on the Criterion DVD of *Sullivan's Travels*, Sturges's widow Sandy Sturges identifies Leo McCarey as another of the "deep dish" directors Sturges was thinking of when making his film. McCarey had been let go from Paramount in 1937 after he had departed from his practice of directing lighthearted comedies to helm *Make Way for Tomorrow*, a poorly received study of the effects of the Depression on an elderly middle-class couple. Max and Dave Fleischer were also undoubtedly among those Sturges was critiquing when he made *Sullivan's Travels*, for Sturges's film parodies the Fleisher Brothers' 1939 *Gulliver's Travels*, a feature-length animation which flopped at the box office and led Paramount to sever its relationship with the Fleischer Studios.

50 The organization is today known as the Directors Guild of America.

51 Letter from Preston Sturges to J. P. McGowan, 30 August 1940. UCLA Box 100, Folder 34.

52 Brief histories of the Directors Guild can be found in: "Screen Directors Guild History," *The Hollywood Reporter*, 16 June 1955, n.p.; Frank Capra, "Introduction," *Directors in Action Selections from the Official Magazine of the Directors Guild*, ed. Bob Thomas (Indianapolis, IN: Bobbs-Merrill, 1973), vii–ix.; David Robb, "Directors Guild Born out of Fear 50 Years Ago," *Daily Variety*, 29 October 1985, 21–50ff.; Jerry Roberts, Ted Elrick and Tom Carroll, "Sixty Years of Action: A History of the Directors Guild of America," *DGA Magazine* (November–December 1996, January–February 1997), 58–82; Virginia Wright Wexman, "The Directors Guild of America," *The Encyclopedia of Labor and Working Class History*, ed. Eric Arnesen (New York, NY: Routledge, 2006), 366–8; and Directors Guild of America, *Fifty Years of Action* (Documentary Film, 1986).

53 Frank Capra, *The Name Above the Title* (New York, NY: Macmillan, 1971), 207.

CHAPTER 3

To Write and Not Direct

Sarah Kozloff

When Mother Theresa passed away, God meets her at the Pearly Gates.
"Theresa! How wonderful to see you! You have been a favorite of mine, so
kind, so selfless, so close to god, I mean, to me . . . So tell me, now you are
here and the kingdom of heaven is yours, what would you like to do first?"

To which she replies . . .

"Well, what I really want to do is Direct."

Sturges was no Mother Theresa, but, like everyone else in the film business,
he aspired to the director's chair for years.[1] Some of this yearning had to do
with ambition: he wanted to be at the top of the food chain. "When I first went
to Hollywood," he wrote in a 1957 letter to his stepfather, "I discovered that
the directors were treated as Princes of the Blood . . . In the beginning I tried to
prove that writers were easily as important as directors, then one day I realized
that it was easier to become a Prince of the Blood myself than to change the
whole social order."[2] Another factor lay in his inherent sociability; he disliked
working alone so much that he hired secretaries/assistants to take down his
scripts to provide a receptive audience as he dictated and acted the parts out
loud, into the small hours of the night. Being the director meant that he could
turn the set into hospitality venues, where he could welcome visitors and press,
distribute gifts, and preside over a congenial caravan much as he presided over
long nights at the Players, the Los Angeles dinner club into which he poured
his energies and disastrously sank his fortune.[3] Of course, Sturges also had
artistic and professional reasons for wanting to direct. From the time he started
as a playwright in the late 1920s, he hated compromising over casting and
hated producers and others changing his texts. As his biographer Diane Jacobs
noted, "If Sturges had his way, he'd do everything himself."[4]

Sturges was unusual among Hollywood screenwriters in that he typically
worked on original material (or if it was an adaptation, he changed it radically),

and he generally wrote solo, not in the assembly line or partnered fashion then so common. Actually, in his early years, when producers hired him as a script-doctor of other writers' work, he often completely rewrote the screenplay.

Sturges's unhappiness with passing off his scripts to others has led to the misconception that other directors didn't do as good a job with his gems as Sturges himself would have done. Yet when, for instance, one studies *The Sin of Harold Diddlebock*, on which Sturges had complete control (he wrote, cast, directed, budgeted and produced the film—in fact he served as chief production head of Howard Hughes's company, California Pictures), one starts to see the benefits of checks and balances, and the ways in which collaboration can lead to better films. For *Diddlebock*, Sturges cast his then-current lover, Frances Ramsden (who had never acted before), as the romantic interest. Her inexperience forced him to keep her screen time so minimal that the love story aspect of the plot is only vestigial. Moreover, Sturges wanted Harold Lloyd so badly that he allowed him a contract that gave Lloyd a great deal of say. Lloyd had a terrible time with Sturges's dialogue and he was uncomfortable with the physical demands of the role and proximity to the lion. Star and director clashed repeatedly, and finally, they shot many scenes in two versions. According to Kevin Hagopian:

> They screened the two versions together, and picked whichever seemed the best approach for that scene. What resulted is one of the most manic enterprises ever put on the American screen, a non-stop marathon of bits, shtick, and gags woven into a narrative so fast-paced it sometimes seems like an amphetamine jag . . . Lloyd believed that a film had to build sympathy for the leading character, so that when he was put in jeopardy in the comic moments, the audience would feel a melodramatic involvement with him. Sturges, on the other hand, as Lloyd's astute biographer Tom Dardis put it, believed in treating his comic protagonist "as a half-mad dolt, caught up in a whirlwind of chance events."[5]

This is not a situation any experienced studio producer would have allowed to occur. The film went wildly over-budget and got only lukewarm reviews.

Although the auteur theory venerates the writer-director above all other professional categories because the theory sees this combination as most responsible for conveying a singular artist's unique vision, at least in this case, giving the artist free rein did not necessarily do his vision any favors. Although no one held Sturges back, at the same time no one compensated for his weaknesses or facilitated his strengths.

To investigate the tension between screenwriting and directing, I have chosen three of Sturges's screenplays, *The Good Fairy*, *Easy Living*, and *Remember the Night*, which were made into successful films by William Wyler and Mitchell Leisen. By comparing the finished films with Sturges's scripts, I hope to demonstrate that the directors and studios brought Sturges the screenwriter's imagination to fruition and the changes that they made improved upon Sturges's original plans. Actually, I believe that Wyler and Leisen did more than advance the initial vision: they helped to draw out from the scripts what was unique about them, and they modeled for Sturges how to become the full-blown writer-director we see in later films. Obviously, not being a fly on the wall during the shoot and editing sessions, I cannot know whether these changes were solely the personal decisions of the directors, whether producers had a hand, whether the actors offered suggestions, or even whether Sturges himself—visiting the set—contributed. What we can determine from the finished films is that the collaborative enterprise helped Sturges create the style we will see in later films.

But at the same time, I wish to pursue a contradictory aim: I want to give Sturges the screenwriter his fair due. Although *The Good Fairy* script includes no visual details, in the later screenplays Sturges *visualized* the scenes as he wrote. His scripts are full of details about what the camera should be doing, how the lighting should look, instructions about physical business, and how the lines should be read. He was not merely a wordsmith (writing clever *bon mots*), nor a daring constructor of plots (stretching and breaking Hollywood conventions). His scripts are not blueprints, but rather imagined movies, flickering in his midnight visions.[6]

THE GOOD FAIRY (WILLIAM WYLER, 1935), UNIVERSAL

Carl Laemmle, Jr., the head of production at his father's studio, had bought *The Good Fairy* for Margaret Sullavan, then a rising star under contract.[7]

Ferenc Molnár's play *The Good Fairy* had had a successful run on Broadway in the early 1930s starring Helen Hayes. The original play takes place in Budapest; it follows Lu, a coquettish but poor movie usher, who increases a rich businessman's attraction to her by claiming that she is married (and thus not a woman of easy virtue). However, as she explains to the Waiter, she loves to do good deeds. She decides to do someone a favor by claiming him as her husband: she chooses the elderly lawyer, Max Sporum, out of the telephone book. By promising to sleep with the businessman if he makes her faux-husband wealthy, Lu finagles him into hiring Max at a fantastic sum. Sporum, informed of the deception, at first reluctantly agrees to it and then feels great relief when the Waiter saves Lu from going through with the bargain. The lawyer marries his long-devoted secretary, while Lu gets engaged to the Waiter and helps him start a restaurant named The Good Fairy. An epilogue, however, informs us that subsequently Lu broke off this engagement and married a rich diplomat, Dr. Metz.

William Wyler was already a director of stature when he directed *The Good Fairy*. After winning acclaim for *Counsellor-At-Law* (1933), he had one foot out of the door of Universal, the studio where he had worked for fifteen years, on his way to bigger budgets directing *Dead End* (1937), *Jezebel* (1938), *Wuthering Heights* (1939), *Mrs. Miniver* (1942), and *Best Years of Our Lives* (1946). Throughout his career, Wyler leaned toward prestige adaptations, social dramas, and romantic melodramas; his comedy tends to be slower than Sturges's and much more bittersweet. Studying *The Gay Deception*, a screwball comedy he made at Fox in 1935, the comic scenes of *The Westerner* (1940), or *Roman Holiday* (1953), reveals that the comedy arises mostly from the gestures and faces of the performers, such as a small flash of unease that shows they are lying or telling tall tales. Wyler rarely resorts to slapstick or chaos.

Neither Alan Hale, Reginald Owen, Frank Morgan (the Wizard of Oz) nor Eric Blore were under contract with Universal. Universal hired them all for this project, creating an early version of a Sturges stock company of older men with odd speaking styles: Hale's bluff American forcefulness, Owen's lower-class British accent, Morgan's stutter and dithering, and Blore's pomposity. This foursome serves to contrast with Herbert Marshall; Marshall's melodious upper-class British baritone give Sporum continental charm and sex appeal.

Sturges changed the story of *The Good Fairy* radically. Now Luisa is an orphan, the Waiter (renamed Detlaff) her protector, and Sporum her love interest. New locations, including the orphanage, the movie theater, and the department store where Max and Luisa go shopping, "open up" a play that originally transpired solely in a private dining room and the lawyer's office. These new settings create opportunities for comic business, such as Luisa's swinging from a light fixture or inept ushering.

Along with Molnár and Sturges, we should consider another "author" of the film: the Breen Office.[8] Why Universal ever thought that this play about lechery, infidelity, ruses, and greed could be transplanted to the screen after July 1934, when the Breen Office started strictly enforcing the Production Code, is something of a mystery. Sturges made many changes to Molnár's original, principally in trying to make Luisa Ginglebusher virginal and innocent of the facts of life. In the film, Luisa doesn't even understand what Konrad wants:

Detlaff: I won't have it! Don't you understand something terrible is going to happen to you if you go up there?
Luisa: What?
Detlaff: An A-number-one calamity! A catastrophe! Something so terrible I can't bring myself to mention it! A regular cataclysm!

Note the typical Sturges alliteration.

Still, the script Sturges completed on August 11, 1934 was so risqué that alarm bells started ringing throughout the PCA office. On September 14, 1934, Breen wrote to Will Hays that *The Good Fairy* was the film on their docket presenting the most serious difficulties.[9]

Because of contract commitments, shooting started without a completed or accepted script. From late September to early October, Universal kept submitting new scenes to the PCA, which turned these emendations around very swiftly, if often with renewed demands. Every method by which Sturges attempted to illustrate Luisa's ignorance about sexuality made the issue prominent, so the Breen Office kept watering these scenes down. Other problems stemmed from Sturges's deliberately taunting the censors. For instance, Sturges wrote about Max Sporum's desire to keep his beard:

> Dr. Sporum: Secondly, it keeps me warm in winter and cool in summer *besides giving me something to play with when I'm nervous.*
> Lu: *You could find something better than that.*[10]

The emphasis comes from the Breen Office, which insisted those lines be cut out. Thus Sturges remained on the set, writing and rewriting with Wyler, who always took an active hand in the scripts he directed, under Joseph Breen's vigilance, throughout the film's production.

Because the script was literally being rewritten in chunks, no complete version is available with Sturges's papers in the archive. However, comparison of the August draft shows several major ways in which Wyler both honored Sturges's story and characterizations and changed the script in major ways.

Aspects of the August script that made it into the final film include most of the funny bits, such as the crazy names, including "Luisa Ginglebusher," the absurd overblown melodrama projected in the movie theater with the endlessly repeated command "Go!," and the physical comedy, such as Konrad's tripping over a lamp when he tries to answer the door, Detlaff's second wild rescue of Luisa, and Konrad's chase through the hotel. However, several secondary characters were pared away. Sturges had written in lines for the movie theater doorman, projectionist, projectionist's assistant, and telephone bill collector. All vanished.

Moreover, some of the dialogue of the major characters was trimmed. Theater owner Maurice Schlapkohl (Alan Hale) plays a smaller role. Detlaff (Reginald Owen) looses his poetic flights of fancy: for instance, "I have always such beautiful thoughts in my head. Now when you look at a roast beef, you just see a roast beef, but me . . . I see a sweating team of oxen yoked to a noble plow. Cheerfully they struggle on."[11] Moreover, Detlaff no longer spills food all over Konrad during the dinner in the private dining room.

Thirdly, most of the characters become nobler in the final version. In the August script, Konrad is married, yet in the film he improbably confesses he actually isn't a Lothario intent on illicit affairs. He ends up proposing to Luisa. "I'm really not a butterfly, I just look like one," says Konrad (though no one ever looked less like a butterfly than Frank Morgan).

In the film, Max Sporum is poor because he is one of the rare, ethical lawyers. As he tells Luisa, he is overjoyed to have been hired by the meatpacking firm, because

> it vindicates what I've always contended: that right is right and that integrity is a shortcut to success . . . For years I've starved in this very spot where you now see me surrounded by expensive luxuries. For years, my dear child, for years, understand, I've dreaded every pull on that doorbell knowing that it meant always a summons for the rent or a man to shut off the water or some individual bent on the removal of my gas meter. And why, I ask you, why? I'll tell you why . . . Because I uphold the standard of ethics and such a lawyer is useless to people interested only in gouging their fellow man.

Max's delight that Konrad has sought him out because of his reputation for integrity is touchingly naive, and it motivates a major plot point: Luisa can't tell him that she sent Konrad to hire him because this would shatter his illusion.

Of all the characters, Luisa changes most radically from screenplay to film. In the script she tells Sporum about the deception early on, but is willing to sleep with Konrad so that Sporum can still enjoy his newfound riches. In the film, she is still willing to keep her appointment with Konrad, but she sacrifices herself not for Sporum's lifestyle, but rather for his noble dreams, and so that she can carry through on her own goal of doing something for someone else, a pleasure denied her all her life because she is an orphan, without family to sacrifice for. Speaking to Max on the phone before her appointment, knowing full well he will reject her if she is not chaste, she says, "After I hang up, think of me for a little while. Think of me kindly, almost as if I loved you."[12]

Sullavan's line reading here is poignant. Wyler coaxed a moving performance out of Sullavan (falling in love and eloping with her in the process). The film contains many close-ups of Sullavan, often wearing simple, round, Madeline-style hats and school girlish clothes, to emphasize her youth and innocence.

Wyler's camera movements and compositions enhance the film. Stupefied, Max ponders his newfound riches, talking aloud to himself, uneasily occupying the side of the screen, while his dusty, antiquated furnishings take center stage. A sidewalk café breakfast sparkles with reflections in a glass partition, while a gay awning flutters overhead. Max and Luisa visit a department store to spend his newfound riches: she sees herself in a "genuine foxine" wrap in

Figure 3.1 Max's point of view, as Luisa tries to sneak away. Shooting through hallways and doorways in deep focus is Wyler's habitual method of emphasizing unforgettable moments. Sure enough, Max races to the vestibule and avows his love.

an infinite string of mirrors and mimics the movie melodrama she watched earlier. Moments later Max and Luisa sit in a swinging seat before a diorama of a house with a porcelain dog at their feet: this is the stable (middle-class) home that neither of them has had.

Wyler's touch is most apparent at the end. All the confusions have been cleared up, but Luisa is crying:

> Max (with sad resignation): There's nothing to cry about. It's been very funny. Mr. Konrad has lost a little money of which he has plenty. I've lost a little hope. That's about all. You haven't lost anything. Why are you crying?

The viewer knows that Luisa's tears stem from her belief that Max doesn't care for her anymore. She is stealthily leaving the apartment when Max notices.

Working together, Wyler, Sturges, and Universal took a frothy, semi-naughty Broadway play and turned it into a fairy tale about longing for love, accepting reality, and granting forgiveness.

EASY LIVING (LEISEN, 1937), PARAMOUNT

Easy Living began life in 1935 as an unpublished screen story by Vera Caspary in Paramount's story collection about a manicurist who steals a mink coat, falls in love, and is eventually found out.[13] According to Andrew Horton, Sturges threw away everything from this rather bitter tale but the title and the coat.

Mitchell Leisen was Paramount's ace director of the late 1930s, so successful that not one of his films lost money. Leisen had started in the film business designing costumes for Cecil B. DeMille; after he gained experience in amateur theatricals he began designing sets for William De Mille; he then returned to the younger brother's films as a production designer.[14] In addition to the two films written by Sturges, Leisen's memorable movies include *Hands Across the Table* (1935), *Swing High, Swing Low* (1937), *Midnight* (1939), *Hold Back the Dawn* (1941), *To Each His Own* (1946), and *No Man of Her Own* (1950). *Midnight*, starring Colbert and written by Billy Wilder, justly belongs in the canon of great screwball comedies, while *Hold Back the Dawn* and *To Each His Own* are classic 1940s melodramas starring Olivia de Havilland.

Sturges's biographers present contradictory information about his relationship with Leisen. James Curtis claims that Sturges "saw him as a bloated phony" and made fun of his homosexuality.[15] Diane Jacobs recounts that Sturges thought of him merely as an interior decorator.[16] Andrew Horton, however, reports that Sturges went around Paramount brass to ask Leisen to direct *Easy Living*.[17] For his part, Leisen seems to have been genuinely appreciative of Sturges.[18]

Jean Arthur had been under contract to Paramount, and had worked previously on the Sturges script *Diamond Jim* (1935) and with Leisen on *Swing High, Swing Low*. But the studio had let her go, and then had to borrow her back from Columbia.[19]

Ray Milland, a handsome Paramount contract player, plays her love interest, Johnny Ball. Edward Arnold plays his father, J. B. Ball, "The Bull of Broad Street," a barrel-chested tycoon in the mold of Ellie Andrews' father (Walter Connolly) in *It Happened One Night* (1934), or Alexander Bullock (Eugene Pallette) in *My Man Godfrey* or, for that matter, Horace Pike (Eugene Pallette) in *The Lady Eve*. (During the Depression, physically big actors embodied the rich.)

Both script and film begin with J. B. Ball's fury over his wife's purchase of yet another sable coat. He throws it off the rooftop, and it lands on Mary's head, crushing her hat feather. Sturges's script precisely describes the coat's fall, Mary's startled reaction, and the turbaned fellow passenger who enigmatically pronounces, "Kismet." Ball gives Mary the coat on a whim and decides to buy her a new hat to replace the damaged one. From here the script and film stress the runaway power of misleading appearances and gossip, because the milliner, Van Buren (Franklin Pangborn) assumes that Mary is J. B.'s mistress, and spreads this rumor, causing the hotelier Louis Louis and others to pamper her in hopes of thus currying J. B.'s favor. Meanwhile, Mary's superiors fire her from her job at the magazine *The Boy's Constant Companion* because they also suspect her virtue. Almost starving, she goes to an automat, where she meets Johnny, who is working there to prove his independence from his father. Mary and Johnny fall in love, but by unguarded words to one of J. B. Ball's competitors they inadvertently almost make his financial firm go bankrupt. At the end, the firm is saved; everyone understands that J. B. and Mary are not having an affair; Ball hires Johnny to work for him; and Johnny and Mary reconcile.

Easy Living did not prompt Breen to set the dogs on Paramount. However, again, the premise caused problems:

> In order to avoid the possibility of a basically objectionable flavor, care should be taken to remove from the story all material, which may be said to be a suggested comedy treatment of morality. This has to do with the situations based on the mistaken idea that Mary is Ball, Sr.'s mistress. As you know, any comedy treatment of sex situations is unacceptable from the point of view of the Production Code.[20]

Since "comic treatment of sex situations" was the whole point of the script, Paramount ignored this general warning. But the April 1937 screenplay did make the changes specified on small matters such as making Louis Louis' (the hotel owner) nationality ambiguous. And it cut out all mention of real people or companies, including Mrs. Astor, Rockefeller, Cartier's, Macy's, Rolls Royce and various real banks, thus softening Sturges's social satire.[21] (For more on Sturges's calculated negotiations with the PCA, see Matthew Bernstein's chapter.)

Leisen's basic approach to Sturges's script was to prune the beginnings of scenes, most of the exposition, and some of the dialogue in order to add in *more* comic business. In the opening, when J. B. is trying to get the fur coat from his wife, Jenny, Leisen inserts J. B. getting caught up in the folding doors of the closet and landing under the breakfast tray in the bedroom. While Sturges specified that in the earshot of the servants the angry couple would speak "with false sweetness," Leisen has Jenny speak lovingly while throwing a pail and bucket down the attic stairs to trip up her pursuing husband. While Leisen follows Sturges's precise instructions when Mary is breaking open her piggy bank, only in the film does softhearted Mary cover up the little piggy's eyes before executing him. Leisen also extends the scene in the automat, creating even more mayhem with more stunts after Johnny accidentally presses open the doors to all the food plates. Sturges specifies that when Mary believes she has come into riches her first desire is to buy a sheepdog—in the film she buys *two*. And only in the film does Mary mush the dogs in order to break into Ball's

Figure 3.2　Mary holds her two new dogs close as she escapes from the Ball family and the scandal it has drawn her into.

office. Leisen goes for maximum chaos, a quality that, of course, will be salient in later Sturges films.

Much of the dialogue in the film appears just as Sturges wrote it. Louis Louis mangles English idioms over and over, for example "Too far is enough" and "You are a sight for eyesore!" Ball keeps trying to think of ways to teach Mary about compound interest, including writing her a letter from his office about Willie Jones and his marbles. But the funniest line in the movie, Mary's riposte to J. B., "You know, you don't have to get mad just because you're so stupid!," is not in the August script. Since Sturges was periodically on the set, perhaps he thought it up Johnny-on-the-spots.

Leisen's experience with art direction shows throughout the film. Mary's hotel suite offers a fantasy of art deco design, receding into deep space on the largest stage in Paramount. And the wonderful shot of Johnny and Mary falling asleep while lying in opposite directions on the overlong couch so that only their faces line up manages to be both chaste enough for the Production Code and dreamily romantic.

Moreover, Leisen/Paramount changed the script's ending. Sturges had resolved the market crash and cleared up the misunderstandings. The film goes one step further: Johnny proposes to Mary, and J. B. again throws the coat into the air. It lands on another unsuspecting young woman and breaks her hat-feather. As Diane Jacobs remarks:

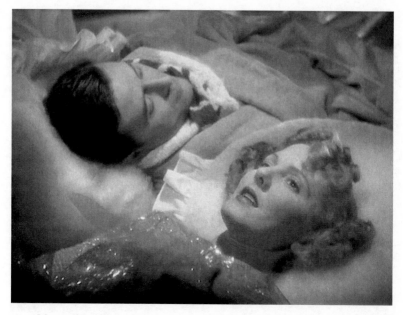

Figure 3.3 Mary offers Johnny a place to sleep after he has lost his job. She is dressed in a glittery number given to her by Van Buren; he wears a bathrobe because they both accidentally got soaked in an art deco bathtub. Leisen vignettes their faces to create mystery and romance. This is not the type of shot one will see in the films Sturges directs.

Easy Living is the first script where Sturges, imposing a farcical plot on screwball protagonists, discovers a structure to mirror his uneasiness about luck and virtue. The film's ending, where another fur coat lands on the hat of yet another working girl, underscores the very arbitrariness of Mary and Johnny's story, the capriciousness of their happy union now. But they're happy nonetheless, for this is, after all, comedy, rejoicing in order restored and the miracle of success.[22]

The ending was not Sturges's, but Leisen and Paramount precisely convey Sturges's characteristic uneasiness about luck and virtue.

Easy Living is as daring in its physical comedy as anything Sturges later attempted. Moreover, it showed that one could stir together verbal inventiveness, wild slapstick, and social satire. Add a touch of glamour, flambé the sexual attraction of the two leads, and voila: kismet.

REMEMBER THE NIGHT (LEISEN, 1940), PARAMOUNT

With *Remember the Night*, Sturges didn't even have a short story to throw away. The script is completely original.

Every commentator has remarked on *Remember the Night*'s unusual tone, in that this film is less comic and more romantic than was Sturges's wont. Some relate this to Sturges's happiness with his new marriage to Louise, his third wife, and point to the film's original titles. The first title, "Beyond These Tears," comes from an anonymous, traditional Scottish love poem.[23] When Paramount rejected this suggestion, Sturges used "The Amazing Marriage" as a working title, even though no one gets married in the script.

Other critics, such as Jack Shadoian, attribute the film's depth of feeling to the director. As Shadoian writes, "Part of the rap against Leisen is that his marshmallow nature interfered with the courageously caustic wit of a bona-fide writer and wild nut like Sturges, and that he willfully dulled the edges of his (and Billy Wilder's) scripts."[24] Victoria Wilson, author of a recent study of Barbara Stanwyck, concurs with Shadoian: "Sturges wrote comedy with flashes of feeling and warmth; Leisen directed pictures that were warm with bursts of comedy."[25]

Although Sturges had written the script believing that Lombard would star,[26] Leisen, serving as his own producer, wisely chose Barbara Stanwyck and Fred McMurray as the leads: Lee Leander, a jewel thief who has been caught, and John Sargent, an ambitious assistant attorney who finagles a continuance of Lee's trial because he knows juries are reluctant to convict women at Christmastime. Then, feeling guilty that Lee will have to spend the holidays in jail, Sargent arranges for her bail. The bail bondsman, Fat Mike, assumes that Sargent wants to have an affair with Lee (shades of *Easy Living*) and delivers her to his apartment. Since they are both from Indiana, Sargent offers to drive her home for the holidays, but when Lee's mother rejects her, he takes her on to his home instead. Lee, so hardboiled and cynical, is touched by Sargent's loving, old-fashioned home life, especially the warmth of his mother (Beulah Bondi) and Aunt Emma (Elizabeth Patterson)—actresses who (coincidentally?) both appeared in *The Good Fairy* as orphanage employees. On the drive back to New York City, Sargent offers to allow Lee to escape in Canada, but she refuses, and when he tries to throw the case, she confesses on the stand. Their love will have to wait until after she has served her prison term.

One of the main ways Leisen changed the script was by tailoring it to his leading players. According to Wilson, Fred MacMurray was rather shy and uncomfortable before the camera. Leisen trimmed Sturges's longer speeches for him, and cut out much of the exaggerated miming Sturges had written. David Chierichetti, the author of the only book on Leisen, argues, "Cutting MacMurray's lines down to the minimum, Leisen played up the feeling of gentle strength MacMurray could project so well. It was a far cry from Sturges's highly articulate hero."[27]

In *Remember the Night*, under Leisen's direction, Stanwyck invents the prototype of a role she will reprise in *Ball of Fire* (Hawks, 1940) and *The Lady Eve*. Lee is a woman wise to the ways of the world, amoral, sparkling and

Figure 3.4 Returning to New York City, John and Lee detour through Canada. In front of Niagara Falls, John urges Lee to flee. She refuses, and remarks that they don't have to delay their honeymoon, because they are already here. Though nothing is shown, the inference is that they consummate their love. Leisen films their silhouettes in front of a glass shot of fake falls, an effect he and Paramount worked hard to create. This scene captures a depth of sexual passion foreign to Sturges's works.

funny until she falls in love with a sap. Then her eyes fill with tears of hurt and dismay as she regrets the life she has lived. Leisen's Stanwyck takes obvious glee in her pre-redemption naughtiness and yet makes her tears heartbreaking. When Sturges saw Stanwyck's performance here, he decided to write her a comedy—the script that became *The Lady Eve*.

Leisen's other changes improve the film as well. The script was too long: at 130 pages it was over Paramount's usual maximum running time of 100 minutes.[28] Sturges the writer has a tendency to be too explicit: the script included numerous shots of a clock to stress the passage of time on the day before Christmas (gone), a scene of Lee being touched by a minister's sermon (gone). In the final courtroom scene, Sturges wrote in aural flashbacks of Lee recalling Sargent's comment that juries will turn against a prosecutor who is rough to a female defendant—Leisen cuts the flashbacks completely.

Although script and film contain some vaguely humorous moments of Lee and John lost during a road detour—including an encounter with a cow that prefigures the sublime scene with the horse in *The Lady Eve*—what comedy the film offers lies mostly in Lee's amazement at the suckers of the world. Leisen cut out a silly scene of John and Lee bobbing for apples, and he also (thankfully) cut out Sturges's instructions for Willie (Sterling Holloway), the handyman, to have a stutter.[29] Leisen also radically cuts the scenes and dialogue of John's servant, Rufus, which were even more racist than the scenes as played. (Here is a lesson that Sturges the director failed to learn.)

Other scenes transpire almost exactly as Sturges wrote them. When John and Lee come to Lee's house and Lee's mother grudgingly invites the couple in, Sturges even specifies the lighting effect:

THE PARLOR
We see the light in the hall through the cracks in the door. Now the door opens and Lee's mother comes in carrying the lamp. Lee and Sargent follow her. She puts the lamp on the table then turns with HER BACK TO US.[30]

The camera is situated *in* the dark parlor, so the crack of light spilling in from the hallway shows how little warmth fills Lee's maternal home. The room's décor of stiff, formal furniture and out-of-date Victorian do-dads (little ornaments), however, comes from Leisen and Paramount's art directors.

The film as a whole has a quality of directness about it. Sargent tells his mother about Lee's past the first night he introduces them. When the mother exclaims that such a sweet person couldn't possibly be guilty, Sargent disabuses her. The line that Sturges subsequently gives Sargent, "But that doesn't mean that she wasn't unhappy and lonely and a human being like the rest of us," is possibly the most humanistic line he ever wrote. It prefigures Jean's line about naughty girls not being nearly as bad as Hopsie thinks they are.

Although Lee does "corrupt" John to the extent that at the end of the film he is willing to bend the law for her, as Jay Rozgonyi comments, the film's "primary theme" is

the power of love, its ability to create a strong person, and its unlimited potential to redeem those who have been deprived of it. Along with this redemption comes a clearer knowledge of right and wrong, or a moral imperative that goes beyond mere written law.[31]

Leisen, working from Sturges's blueprint, was able to make a film that captures the power of love.

CONCLUSION: THE *WRITER AS AUTEUR*

Some twenty years after the French proposed the auteur theory, Richard Corliss countered with his book, *Talking Pictures: Screenwriters as Auteurs*.[32] Corliss argues that too much credit has been given to directors, and not enough to the professionals who dreamed up the stories and wrote the dialogue. In a recent study, Steven Maras usefully shifts the battleground away from "credit and control" to "conception and execution."[33] Because Sturges as screen-writer worked solo, radically changed source material, and eventually became a writer-director (a Prince of the Blood), in these scripts we have a rare chance to study the screenwriter's conception. A number of themes tie together these three examples, and/or link these early scripts with Sturges's later work:

Theme 1. In Sturges's worldview money is not earned or deserved, but capriciously falls from the sky like the Kolinsky coat or a name picked out of a phone book by eenie meenie minie mo. No rhyme or reason explains why someone is rich or poor, or rich one day and poor the next (see *Christmas in July*, *Palm Beach Story*, *Diddlebock*). Material objects, such as a foxine stole, the sable coat and hat or the diamond bracelet, call out to characters/viewers with a bewitching appeal. Poverty is neither noble nor fun: Sturges stresses that it means hunger, deprivation of all beautiful things, and a numbing of the soul (see *Sullivan's Travels*).

Theme 2. Appearances are usually deceiving; you can't/shouldn't judge people too quickly. People have an amazing ability for self-deception, such as Sporum believing that his virtue has been rewarded. Moreover, society as a whole is easily duped, and people will easily sink to thinking the worst about others. Luisa is not married to Max Sporum, nor is she using Konrad as a way to get luxuries for herself. *Easy Living* highlights how the whole town is eager to believe that J. B. has a mistress and tries to capitalize on this fact. What makes Mrs. Sargent and Aunt Emma special is that they see the best in Lee, while Fat Mike and the Judge assume the worst of the prosecutor and the criminal. See also *The Lady Eve*, *Hail the Conquering Hero*, *Unfaithfully Yours*.

Theme 3. Self-sacrifice is a special way to prove one's love. Luisa is willing to sacrifice her virtue for Max; Johnny loses his job out of sympathy for Mary; Sargent and Lee are equally willing to suffer for the other's benefit. See also: *The Palm Beach Story*, and especially *The Miracle of Morgan's Creek*, in which Norville's willingness to marry a woman pregnant by another man marks *him* as a Prince of the Blood.

Characters. Women leads are unruly in the sense that Kathleen Rowe speci-fies: breaking traditional rules of decorum, sweetness, and patience.[34] They break these conventions unintentionally and out of good motives (Luisa); out of strength of character (Mary angrily knocks her boss over the head with a picture and slaps Louis Louis in *Easy Living*); or out of a strain of larceny and impatience with society's strictures (Lee). Leading men are tall, baffled by their women, and more than a touch naive (Sporum, Johnny, Sargent). According to Sturges, old men, foreigners, hicks, homosexuals, and black servants are ripe for comic treatment. We will see all these characters again and again in later Sturges-directed films.

Style. One sees too all the elements that will recur throughout Sturges's films. Mayhem—especially many people talking at once (preferably with many telephones ringing and perhaps dogs barking)—is funny. Falling down is funny in *The Good Fairy* and *Easy Living* (and throughout Sturges's later films). Wild names are funny, almost as funny as mangled idioms, alliteration, and general wordplay.

Did Sturges learn anything from Leisen's or Wyler's execution about how to place the camera or light a scene? Sturges did not work with Leisen's director of photography, Ted Tetzlaff (who would go on to film *Notorious* [1946]), preferring to work instead with Victor Milner or John Seitz on the majority of films he directed. And, as James Harvey asserts, he generally avoided close-ups, or at least the diffused, glamour close-ups we see in these three films.[35] It is more likely that Sturges absorbed from Wyler and/or Leisen some of their skill with casting or coaxing performances out of actors. (See Diane Carson's contribution to this volume.)

These early films do not show the strain of caustic satire against American mores that pervades Sturges's works of the 1940s. In *Remember the Night*, Sturges wrote into the initial trial scene swipes at the Judge's inattentiveness and the jury's foolish gullibility. Leisen cut out all of this. I posit that Wyler and Leisen's warmer sensibilities acted as a break on Sturges's tendencies. *The Power and the Glory* and *Diamond Jim* show more of Sturges's dark side.

Let us conclude by paraphrasing Charles Foster Kane, who once said to a correspondent, "You provide the prose poems; I'll provide the war." Sturges provided the comedy; Wyler and Leisen provided the romance. There was certainly "genius at work" on these three films, but much of it stemmed, as film historian Thomas Schatz reminds us, from the genius of the studio system.

NOTES

1 Diane Jacobs, *Christmas in July* (Berkeley, CA: University of California Press, 1992), 171.
2 Richard Corliss, "Still Talking," *Film Comment* 28:6 (November 1992), 11.
3 Donald Spoto, *Madcap: The Life of Preston Sturges* (Boston, MA: Little Brown, 1990), 146.
4 Jacobs, 150.
5 Kevin Hagopian, "*The Sin of Harold Diddlebock* Film notes." Available at <http://www.albany.edu/writersinst/webpages4/filmnotes/fnfo2n8.html.> (last accessed 17 April 2015).
6 The same of course is true for the later scripts he wrote. See Brian Henderson, *Five Screenplays by Preston Sturges* (Berkeley, CA: University of California Press, 1985).
7 Jan Herman, *A Talent for Trouble: The Life of Hollywood's Most Acclaimed Director, William Wyler* (New York, NY: Da Capo Press, 1997), 126.
8 Thomas Doherty, *Hollywood's Censor: Joseph I. Breen and the Production Code Administration* (New York, NY: Columbia University Press, 2007).
9 Breen to Will Hays, 14 September 1934. *History Of Cinema. Selected Files From the Motion Picture Association Of America Production Code Administration Collection. The Good Fairy.* Reel 11, p. 23.

10 Breen to Harry Zehner, 10 October 1934. *History of Cinema. Selected Files from the Motion Picture Association of America Production Code Administration Collection. The Good Fairy.* Reel 11.

11 Preston Sturges Papers (Collection 1114). Department of Special Collections, University Research Library, University of California, Los Angeles, Folder 3. Script A, 11 August 1934.

12 This scene implies that Luisa knows that she has essentially made a bargain with Konrad to sleep with him. But the film is just indirect enough that children might not understand, which was the goal of the Breen Office.

13 Andrew Horton, "Introduction to *Easy Living*," in Andrew Horton, ed., *Three More Screenplays by Preston Sturges* (Berkeley, CA: University of California Press, 1998), 148.

14 David Chierichetti, *Mitchell Leisen: Hollywood Director* (Los Angeles, CA: Photoventure Press, 1995), 5.

15 Curtis, 110–11.

16 Jacobs, 174.

17 Andrew Horton, ed., *Three More Screenplays by Preston Sturges* (Berkeley, CA: University of California Press, 1998), 141.

18 On January 10, 1940, Leisen wrote Sturges a lovely note about how the success of *Remember the Night* was due to the strengths of the screenplay. Preston Sturges Papers (Collection Number 1114). Department of Special Collections, University Research Library, University of California, Los Angeles, Box 21, Folder 1.

19 Tino Balio, *Grand Design* (New York, NY: Scribner, 1993), 276.

20 Letter from Breen to Hammell dated March 1, 1937, PCA File *Easy Living*, Special Collections, Margaret Herrick Library (Academy of Motion Picture Arts and Sciences), Beverly Hills, CA.

21 Letter from Breen to Hammell dated March 1, 1937, PCA File *Easy Living*, Margaret Herrick Library.

22 Jacobs, 173.

23 Curtis, 123.

24 Jack Shadoian, "I Take My Work Seriously and I Do It Well," *Film Comment* 34:7 (1998): 47.

25 Victoria Wilson, *A Life of Barbara Stanwyck: Steel-True 1907–1940* (New York, NY: Simon & Schuster, 2013), 805.

26 Harvey, 560.

27 Chierichetti, 128.

28 Chierichetti, 126–7.

29 The stutter was one of many issues with the script that Albert Lewin, a Paramount producer, pointed out as faulty in a four-page memo to William LeBaron, April 27, 1939. He also noted that the freezing cold weather of Indiana seemed to change haphazardly and objected to the detour through Canada. All of his points are sensible, but only a few were followed. Preston Sturges Collection. Box 21, Folder 1.

30 Horton, 413.

31 Jay Rozgonyi, *Preston Sturges's Vision of America: Critical Analyses of Fourteen Films* (Jefferson, NC: McFarland, 1993), 38.

32 Richard Corliss, *Talking Pictures: Screenwriters in American Cinema* (Woodstock, NY: Overlook Press, 1974).

33 Steven Maras, *Screenwriting: History, Theory and Practice* (London: Wallflower Press, 2009), 101–16.

34 Kathleen Rowe, *The Unruly Woman: Gender and the Genres of Laughter* (Austin, TX: University of Texas Press, 2011).

35 Harvey, 525.

CHAPTER 4

"The Edge of Unacceptability": Preston Sturges and the PCA

*Matthew H. Bernstein**

Particular Applications . . .
II. Sex
The sanctity of the institution of marriage and the home shall be upheld.
Pictures shall not infer that low forms of sex relationship are the accepted
or common thing . . .
2. Scenes of Passion
    a. They should not be introduced when not essential to the plot.
    b. Excessive and lustful kissing, lustful embraces, suggestive postures
    and gestures, are not to be shown . . .
3. Seduction or Rape
    a. They should never be more than suggested, and only when essential
    for the plot, and even then never shown by explicit method.
    b. They are never the proper subject for comedy.
                    —Motion Picture Production Code (1930)

How *did* Preston Sturges's major romantic comedies earn seals from the vigilant Joseph I. Breen and the Production Code Administration (PCA)? The films are full of "suggestive postures;" their central topic is often seduction, which is frequently "more than suggested" through staging and dialogue; hints of extramarital sex abound; and the films ridicule "the sanctity of the institution of marriage" into the ground. To quote Elliot Rubenstein, "If Sturges's scenarios don't quite invade the province of the flatly censorable, they surely assault the border outposts, and some of the lines escalate the assault into bombardment."[1]

Sturges's heroines drive these assaults on the censorable. They embody Kathleen Rowe's unruly women who "[create] disorder by dominating, or trying to dominate, men," and by being "unable or unwilling" to stay in a women's traditional place.[2] In *The Lady Eve* (1941), the con artist/cardsharp

Jean (Barbara Stanwyck)—having been rejected at the height of an unexpected, exhilarating romance on the high seas—achieves revenge by persuading ale heir Charles "Hopsie" Pike (Henry Fonda) to marry her in disguise and then teaching him a lesson in forgiveness and humility. In *The Palm Beach Story* (1942), the practical and hardheaded Gerry Jeffers (Claudette Colbert) abandons her poor, hapless inventor husband Tom (Joel McCrea) to pursue marriage with a rich millionaire (Rudy Vallee) who can finance Tom's ridiculous ideas. Trudy Kockenlocker (Betty Hutton) in *The Miracle of Morgan's Creek* (1944) gets married and pregnant during an all-night goodbye party for departing soldiers; unable to recall what transpired, and even her husband's name, Trudy desperately needs the infatuated Norval Jones (Eddie Bracken) to stand in as her husband and future father of her child(ren).[3]

In each case, the Sturges heroine's actions and her overwhelmed partner's reactions generate the potentially offensive material—especially the compromising sex scenes and ever-present innuendo—that the Production Code tried to proscribe. True, by each film's conclusion, the Sturges heroine agrees to get or stay married, fulfilling the genre's conventions and the PCA's stipulations, which worked hand in hand. Yet the manner in which marriage is achieved or affirmed, that is, the roller-coaster path to that conclusion, ridicules its basic meaning and deflates its "sanctity."

As Sturges put it in his autobiography, "it was actually the enormous risks I took with my pictures, skating right up to the edge of nonacceptance, that paid off so handsomely."[4] Here, Sturges was describing his insistence, against the views of his friends and colleagues, that Charles would fall four times during Eve's coming-out party in Connecticut. Yet this is an apt description of Sturges's overall approach to comedy. In the case of the romantic comedies, I would argue, the PCA skated up to that edge with him.

Received wisdom has it that the PCA (and the Studio Relations Committee before) were in the business of prohibiting the making of risqué films. Certainly the rhetoric of the Code's language, as quoted above, created that perception, as did the Motion Picture Producers and Distributors Association's publicity about the PCA: Joseph Breen and his staff would keep the movies clean, so as to avoid federal censorship, or, more fundamentally, to prevent for as long as possible the dismantling of the major studios' oligarchic dominance of the American film industry, a distinct possibility after the Department of Justice's anti-trust suit in 1938. Yet, in her pioneering study of the PCA's work, Lea Jacobs points out that "self regulation was an integrated part of film production under the studio system."[5] She argues that censorship was "a constructive force, in the sense that it helped to shape film form and narrative."[6] Breen's associate and successor Geoffrey Shurlock told an interviewer in the mid-1970s, "No, we never refused seals. We were in the business of granting seals. The whole purpose of our existence was to arrange pictures so that we could give seals. You had to give a seal."[7] "Arranging pictures" meant suggesting modifications to plot lines, scenes, and lines of dialogue so that a filmmaker's ideas remained intact and no official censors were offended.

The PCA (like the Studio Relations Committee before it) had been obsessed since the early 1930s with the regulation of female sexuality on screen. Its particular focus on "sex pictures," and melodramatic fallen woman films, resulted in its insistence that errant characters be condemned by a "voice of morality" and/or punished by death or redeemed by marriage.[8] Comedy, however, presented a problem where female sexuality was concerned, as was demonstrated by the early comedian comedies of Mae West, the original screen unruly woman—particularly her unabashed expression of female desire, her autonomy, and her inevitable seduction of and triumph over men. With West, and with many subsequent comedy heroines (including *The Lady Eve*'s Jean and *The Palm Beach Story*'s Gerry), the fallen woman became a comic gold digger, trading—or promising to trade—sexual favors for cash.

The creation of the PCA in 1934, with its close regulation of film content, was a major factor in the genesis of the screwball comedy. Elliot Rubenstein puts it well: "the very style of screwball, the complexity and inventiveness and wit of its detours around certain facts of certain lives, the force of its attack on the very pieties it is pledged to sustain, cannot be explained without recognition of the censors. Screwball comedy is censored comedy."[9] Of course, every Hollywood genre (gangster films, melodramas, musicals, westerns) was a censored genre after 1934; but none flaunted, even parodied, the strictures of the Production Code more than screwball comedy did, especially by the late 1930s. Sturges's own script for *Easy Living* (1937), with its heroine's unintended new identity as a millionaire's mistress, is a key example (see Sarah Kozloff's chapter). As Kozloff has commented:

> These comedies shy away from bald declarations or moral commentary; everything is conveyed through irony, through inference, through undercutting . . . Sex is never mentioned but always inferred. Romance is consistently mocked, but it is the motivation for everything that happens . . . These films insist that we are so sophisticated we don't need everything spelled out for us. Screwball comedies invite us to join the game.[10]

With *The Lady Eve*, Sturges took these tendencies beyond the limits of what had been previously acceptable. He was just getting warmed up.

Context is a crucial factor here. By the late 1930s, Hollywood romantic comedies were growing more risqué by the month. Shortly after the release of Sturges's second film *Christmas in July* (1940), MPPDA attorney Charles C. Pettijohn warned association chief Will Hays and Breen that a "*legislative censorship epidemic*" was underway, with anywhere from four to eleven

states considering bills to establish boards, and several others contemplat-
ing the barring of 10-, 12- or 14-year-olds from movie theaters. *The Great
McGinty* (1940) was among a varied group of films cited as offensive (not for
sexuality, but for its breezy and cynical depiction of graft and political corruption in general). The biggest offense, according to Pettijohn's sources in
theater management and statehouses, lay in a series of 1940 films—*My Little
Chickadee*, *The Philadelphia Story*, *The Road to Singapore*, *Too Many Husbands*,
The Primrose Path, *Strange Cargo*, and, especially, *This Thing Called Love* (a
marriage comedy about a husband trying to seduce his abstinence-obsessed
wife), all of which featured excessive drinking and extensive sexual innuendo.
Pettijohn summarized: "There is a definite feeling that the bars have been let
down [previously] in Hollywood, and that the present crop of pictures indicates there has been no improvement." One of his sources asked him directly,
"Doesn't Mr. Hays have any influence with the producers any more, and has
that fellow Breen out there killed himself or has he just been compelled to walk
the gangplank?"[11]

Why *did* Breen grow more permissive in his application of the Code? He
never explained this publicly, but several reasons appear. He was bombarded
with such material. Leonard J. Leff and Jerrold L. Simmons write, "As the
European war clouded the future of American pictures abroad and Hollywood
competed more aggressively for domestic box office dollars, producers weakened their Production Code commitment."[12] For Breen, negotiating on
paper and in person with Hollywood creative personnel for seven years had
exhausted him and wore down his resistance (he resigned temporarily in
spring 1941).[13] If business was behind this shift, so was the quasi-collaborative
nature of the PCA's work: one industry reporter explained in May 1941 that
"Breen, in an effort to cooperate with producers, permitted dialogue and situations to stand which, a year or two ago, would have been summarily deleted,"
leading to the rise of "the dreaded *double entendre*," among other problems.[14]
Breen biographer Thomas Doherty sees the PCA leader adjusting to changing
domestic mores:

> In the juggling act that was self-regulation, Breen was bobbling the
> ball—in part because the center of cultural gravity had shifted. As
> wartime mobilization heated up, the equipoise between the normal tem-
> perature of the popular audience and the boiling point of the bluenoses
> became harder to calibrate.[15]

When self-regulation was well-calibrated—a moment-to-moment, scene-
by-scene, film-by-film achievement—two interpretations of a sexual encounter
could be read by two different viewers. For example, in *The Lady Eve*, the fade
out from Charles's and Jean's passionate embrace in the bow of the ship at night

to the fade in of the ship's prow slicing through the ocean the next morning would suggest to the naive viewer that they kissed for a while and went to bed. After all, we see that Jean is getting dressed in her stateroom and talking with her father, while Charles is alone on the deck waiting to see her. The sophisticated viewer would understand that the fade out (with or without the ocean spray) indicated what Joseph Breen routinely called "a sex affair." Jean's subsequent statement to Hopsie after she is unmasked as a cardsharp sustains both readings: "I'm glad you got the picture this morning instead of last night, if that means anything to you . . . it should." The challenge to Sturges and the PCA was to maintain this duality of meaning. As Lea Jacobs notes, "the screwball comedies of the late thirties and early forties proved to be a constant source of irritation and complaint for the MPPDA precisely because they were so adept at exploiting the sorts of denial mechanisms typically favored by the Production Code Administration"—that is, that striving for interpretive ambiguity where scenes and dialogue involving sex were concerned.[16]

The PCA's dual mandate—to try to give filmmakers the maximum freedom to create risqué situations but to uphold the Code—was a tightrope walk; with Sturges and other filmmakers, Breen and his staff often lost their balance, either by not diminishing the overtly sexual material enough, or not even noticing elements that could give offense. Like any Hollywood director, Sturges was warned about giving offense to politicians, religious officials, doctors and the American soldier. However, for the romantic comedies, the PCA most closely examined language or staging that suggested illicit female desire, or sexuality or a "sex affair."

Sturges was clearly a persuasive negotiator, as the PCA correspondence on these films reveals; the agency rescinded countless directives it initially ordered. It is entirely likely that the Breen Office gave Sturges greater room to maneuver in admiration of his gifts for outrageous comedy. He certainly conceived of unprecedented challenges to the Code's strictures about the sanctity of marriage and "low forms of sex." As Sturges played the PCA game, his convoluted romance and marriage plots stuck to the letter of the Code, but could wreak havoc with its spirit—with the PCA's sanction. Did the PCA leaders and staff realize the extent to which Sturges's scenarios in effect came to mock their work relentlessly by the time of *The Miracle of Morgan's Creek*'s premiere? It is difficult to say, but I believe it is quite likely.

After negotiations, which grew more elaborate with each title, each Sturges romantic comedy received a seal; at this point, the PCA staffers believed they had done their job. The requested eliminations from state censor boards and outraged letters of protest from ordinary viewers, as well as the commentary of contemporary critics, suggest the agency often failed badly in predicting the reception of these films' moral tone. Part of it was in the PCA's quixotic mandate; part of it arose from the filmmaker's greater skill in exploiting the

Code; part of it also stemmed from changing, more expansive conceptions of what met the Code's requirements. These, in a nutshell, are the crucial reasons Sturges "got away with it"—in addition to his prolific comedic imagination, he was often aided by the very body that was alleged to be censoring him.[17]

THE CARDSHARP'S STATEROOM AND THE TELLING CIGARETTE

The PCA correspondence regarding *The Lady Eve* is surprisingly brief—Breen sent only two letters to Luigi Luraschi, Paramount's liaison on censorship matters, prior to the film's completion and the issuing of a seal. They illustrate how cooperative Breen could be, especially when it came to potentially offensive scenes regarding illicit sex.

When he read Sturges's October 7, 1940 first complete script, Breen had objections to many "questionable lines of dialogue."[18] Jean's rapid-fire description of Hopsie's many female admirers in the Main Dining Room of the SS Southern Queen originally contained comments about women who were "a little flat in the front" or "a little flat behind," which, unlike the "lady wrestler" gag, had to be cut because they were too physiologically specific. We hardly miss them, as Jean had plenty of remaining dialogue along these lines. However, Breen wrote the word "in" alongside certain demands he had made for eliminations in his October 9 letter, indicating that Sturges and Luraschi had persuaded him to relent. Take Breen's eventual acceptance of this exchange after Charles suggests they could go dancing:

> Jean: Don't you think we ought to go to bed?
> Charles [after a pause]: You're certainly a funny girl for anyone to meet who's just been up the Amazon for a year.
> Jean [after a pause]: Good thing you weren't up there two years.

Breen's next letter (October 21) on Sturges's revised script expressed satisfaction with all the changes made, noting that Jean's line about heading to bed "will be delivered without any suggestive inference, or reaction."[19] There is nothing arch about Stanwyck's almost parental delivery of the first line, delivered as she looks straight ahead and stubs out her cigarette before she turns to face Charles; likewise, her delivery of the second line is almost compassionate, not mocking. (See Diane Carson's chapter on acting for a discussion of Stanwyck and Fonda's work in the film.) Still, the connotation remains that Jean is suggesting they sleep together. In fact, the couple proceeds to Charles's cabin to meet his snake Emma and thence to Jean's cabin, wherein the celebrated chaise longue scene transpires.

Indeed, Breen's greatest concern with the script concerned sexual matters. These could be allusive, purely the product of dialogue, as with Sir Alfred's (Eric Blore) account to Charles at the Pike's party of what the former labels "Cecilia or the Coachman's daughter, a gaslight melodrama." Breen insisted that Sir Alfred deliver a line indicating that Jean's mother divorced her elderly earl before taking up with "Handsome Harry" and giving birth to Jean, so that Jean's birth would not seem illegitimate. Sturges obliged, yet somehow persuaded Breen to permit a later portion of the Alfred–Charles exchange, also alluding to an adulterous affair, to remain in:

Charles: They [Jean and Eve] look *exactly* alike!
Sir Alfred: We must close our minds to that fact . . . as it brings up the *dreadful* and thoroughly unfounded suspicion that we must carry to our tombs, you understand . . . as it is absolutely untenable . . . that the coachman, in both instances . . . need I say more?

Why did Breen let Sturges keep this in without modification? It is hard to say. Sir Alfred articulates a suspicion that Eve was also the product of an adulterous affair as had been the case for Jean in the first completed script. True, the offending line concerns a "suspicion" voiced by Sir Alfred, rather than a fact; but Charles immediately affirms its likelihood: "But *he did*, I mean, *he was*, I mean . . ." before being shushed for nth time by Sir Alfred. Here again, Breen consented to Sturges's use of questionable material.

Breen's greatest objection in his initial letter concerned pp. 70–4 of the first submitted script, which suggested "a sex affair": "Inasmuch as this is treated without the proper compensating moral values, it is in violation of the Production Code, and will have to be eliminated entirely from your finished picture." The offending pages outlined a scene between Charles and Jean set on the deck of Jean's cabin at the end of their first evening together. Just previously, Jean had caught him and her dad, the Colonel, playing double or nothing. Charles had been called away to receive the incriminating photo of Jean, the Colonel and Gerald. Charles then returned to the exchange with Jean about all women being adventuresses, before asking if they can go down to her cabin. There, Charles lights Jean's cigarette; he then "struggles to say something" but Jean tells him, "Kiss me," and he obeys ("he crushes her in his arms" as she "sinks back against the chaise longue"). The film would then cut to a shot of the rail of Jean's deck and of "the moonlit water beyond. A lighted cigarette arcs over the rail and down into the water. FADE OUT."

Brian Henderson notes that this early plot sequencing—in which Charles sleeps with Jean even though he already knows she is a cardsharp—would make Charles a reprehensible cad, far worse than the prig that he is in the finished film.[20] Sturges eventually solved this issue by having Charles learn of Jean's duplicity on the morning of their third day together at sea. But before

Sturges did, Breen's October 9 letter directed that Charles could not say the line about going down to her cabin, that the scene could not play out on Jean's private deck, and that "it would be better to have the embrace with the couple standing up." The shot of the cigarette thrown over the railing also "should be omitted, on account of its connotations." Sturges in effect watered down the offending scene of passion and relocated it to the bow of the ship, where Charles recites his "I've always loved you" speech and they embrace as the scene fades out, creating, as described earlier, ambiguity about what transpired next of the kind that the PCA and Sturges strove for. Here, Sturges's solution to a problem of plot and characterization went hand in hand with the strictures of the Production Code. I speculate that Sturges wrote the passionate deck scene knowing full well that Breen would demand its elimination/transposition; his immediate agreement to revise it was a kind of bargaining ploy to earn Breen's goodwill to bank against other potential deletion directives.[21] In any case, the MPPDA issued its seal on December 26, 1940. Released in mid-March 1941, *The Lady Eve* passed the censors in the city of Chicago, and the states of Massachusetts, New York and Virginia, without cuts.

With *The Lady Eve*, Breen's instincts were strong. He had advised against Sir Alfred's sketch of the Handsome Harry plot. He had eliminated the overt sex affair scene in Jean's cabin. Yet he missed many elements as well. Besides those cut by state and city censors, there were ostensibly innocent lines such as "See anything you like?" delivered as Jean leans back with a bare midriff against her shoe trunk, while Charles searches for a pair of new shoes. The constantly repeated phrase "been up the Amazon for a year" not only references Charles's extended sexual privation and naivety, and consequent susceptibility to Jean's wiles; it also evokes female anatomy itself. There's also Breen's neglect of the phallic imagery of the animated credit sequence (see Leger Grindon's chapter). Whether the neglect of these details was a function of Breen's increasing tolerance or the limits of his discernment, their sparkling effects cannot be denied.

THE GOLD DIGGER AND THE PROMISCUOUS PRINCESS

Sturges's next romantic comedy came under the scrutiny of Breen's associate Geoffrey M. Shurlock (Breen was a production executive at RKO between April 1941 and June 1942). Shurlock in the 1950s succeeded Breen and recognized the need to liberalize the Production Code; in 1941, however, he was generally unmovable when filmmakers tried to work around him.[22] Yet the fate of *The Palm Beach Story* at the PCA was similar to that of *The Lady Eve*: Shurlock, like Breen before him, chipped away at details without successfully challenging Sturges's narrative premises, extreme characterizations and free-flowing sexual allusions.

Shurlock's November 12, 1941, five-page, single-spaced response to Sturges's November 8 script for *Palm Beach* demonstrates how rigorous the PCA leader was. The first of *four* letters he would write through December 6, it listed many abiding concerns, such as the extensive drinking and violent carousing done by the Ale and Quail Club members on the train to Palm Beach. As with *The Lady Eve*, what made Sturges's first draft "unacceptable" were "the sex suggestive situations and the sex suggestive dialogue that runs throughout the script."[23] These were concentrated in two areas: the first three scenes between Tom and Gerry (at home, in the restaurant, and at home again) and all the scenes involving the much-married Princess Centimilla, a.k.a. Maude (Mary Astor).

In Tom and Gerry's first scene together, Tom suspects that the Wienie King's gift of $700 was the result of a sexual transaction and questions Gerry's desire to marry for money. Shurlock found their lines dialogue "overpointed in their reference" and wrote that they "must be rewritten in order to eliminate the sex suggestive offensiveness."[24] Offending examples included:

Tom: [asking about the cash from the Wienie King] Seven hundred Dollars . . . what for?
Gerry: [describing how she could help support Tom if they divorced] . . . you have no idea what a long-legged gal can do without doing anything . . .

In their restaurant scene, where their argument continues ripe with innuendo, Gerry suggests that Tom simply regards her as "something to keep you warm at night." Later, when they prepare to leave and return home, Tom sarcastically asks Gerry, "Or do you object to spending the night under the same roof with me?" Gerry answers, "I'm not worried about the roof."

Luraschi and Sturges persuaded Shurlock to keep all these lines in with subtle modifications: Tom's question about the $700, "what for?" became "why?" in the finished film; "something to keep you warm at night" became "something to snuggle up to and keep you warm at night like a blanket"; and "I'm not worried about the roof" became "I wasn't thinking about the roof." Shurlock's letter of November 17 confirmed that the "long-legged gal" line, which encapsulates a key idea informing the film, "should be acceptable if delivered straight."[25] Colbert does deliver the line without archness and very quickly as she moves on to make other points. On the other hand, Sturges was compelled to omit yet another exchange entirely: for example, Gerry comments, while listing the many failures of their marriage, "We didn't even increase the world population"; Tom replies, "Well, you can't say we didn't try."

Shurlock's copy of his November 12 letter indicated places where he relented or was willing to reconsider his decrees for these early scenes. He wrote, "This entire business where Tom kisses one of Gerry's vertebrae right through the fade out, is unacceptable." His notation alongside this reads "will be handled"—meaning Sturges had assured him he would stage it acceptably. In the finished film, this appears to be the case: Gerry insists that the kisses "mean nothing" to her. The playful mickey-mousing, descending string passages that accompany each kiss on the soundtrack, further downplay the erotic elements of their physical intimacy, along with Gerry's protests that she is ticklish. However, Gerry visibly melts at the first such kiss, even if she quickly recovers, and subsequent events undercut her assertions: she fully embraces Tom on the sofa, her ankles extend as they kiss, the music surges romantically, and Tom quiets her half-hearted protests with a kiss as he carries her up the stairs and the scene fades out.[26]

Prior to this charming exchange, Gerry speaks one of the most outrageous lines in the entire film: "When love's gone, there nothing left but admiration and respect." Elliot Rubenstein notes that this dialogue

> flies loose of its moorings of personage and situation and into the sky of audacity ... whither are fled the pieties of Hollywood marriages? Without "admiration" and "respect," what is the audience to take for love? Just what the rest of the movie demonstrates: it is McCrea's cowboy physique, not his dull soul, that Colbert can't resist.[27]

Figure 4.1 *The Palm Beach Story*: Gerry melts after Tom has kissed her back while undoing her dress at their apartment.

Tom and Jerry's sexual connection is the core of their marriage, as demonstrated definitively when they repeat this series of events and reunite in the Hackensacker mansion. There is no sparkling wit and witty repartee of the kind we see between, say, Hildy (Rosalind Russell) and Walter (Cary Grant) in 1940's *His Girl Friday*. Tom is too stolid, boring, befuddled and literal-minded (more like Ralph Bellamy's Bruce Baldwin) to participate, and Gerry talks in metaphorical circles around him.[28] At least Charles could wax poetic (if repetitively) about his love for Jean and Eve going back years and years. The PCA never commented on this characterization of Tom and Jerry's almost exclusively erotic connection, only on the most overt evidence of it.

By contrast, Maude, the Princess Centimilla, was Shurlock's biggest target: "This characterization of the Princess as having been married and divorced eight times is unacceptable, in accordance with the provisions of the Production Code re the sanctity of marriage."[29] Sturges did reduce the number of Maude's marriages from the original eight to five in the film when Gerry and John D. discuss her on the yacht; yet John D.'s count of three, by dismissing her two annulments, effectively mocked Shurlock's request. This and all the other changes that ensued were small victories; they did little to diminish Maude's characterization as a determined woman who keeps a gigolo on call and for whom marriage provides the Code-approved cover for fresh sexual conquests.[30]

As Shurlock recognized, most of Maude's dialogue reinforced this point; he targeted her lines nearly twice as often as Gerry's or Tom's, and while she is a fast talker, she appears only in the final thirty minutes of the film. Again, Sturges obliged, but only up to a point. He cut many of her lines: referring to her past marriages, she at one point tells her brother "It isn't how long it was . . . it's how nice it was," which Shurlock accurately judged in his November 25 letter as "unacceptably sex suggestive and susceptible of a very offensive double meaning." Still, many of Maude's "unacceptable" lines remained in with Shurlock's "OK," such as, in reply to Gerry's statement that she herself is not divorced yet, "I don't think I'm quite through with the Prince yet." Alternately, as with the number of Maude's marriages, Sturges's revisions were arguably worse than the original. When Maude's line "I'm thinking of trying an American for a change" became "I'm thinking of an American at the moment, it seems more patriotic," Sturges previews the sex-obsessed patriotism that gets Trudy into trouble in *The Miracle of Morgan's Creek*, while confirming Maude's very vague awareness of anything besides "Topic A."

While no baldly sexual scenes appear in *The Palm Beach Story* comparable to the one Sturges drafted in Jean's cabin deck, the many outrageous lines Maude utters in the first script draft might have served as a comparable bargaining chip. In any case, in his November 25 letter, Shurlock asked for some

final changes and thanked Sturges and Luraschi for their "splendid coopera-
tion in discussing and revising this script."[31] Suddenly, on December 6, and
twelve days into shooting, Shurlock sent Luraschi a new letter informing him
that the PCA staff "have re-read with great care" the script they had already
approved "and respectfully wish to call your attention to elements in this story
that cause us great concern." These items all related to multiple marriages and
dialogue allusions to sex, which were, in the case of Maude, the same thing.
Gerry's line "I wasn't thinking about the roof" was out. Maude's statements
about being nearly divorced and choosing an American husband next had to
go. Her revelation to Gerry and Tom of John D.'s plan for a mock marriage
with Gerry, and other dialogue, were now unacceptable. There had been no
problem previously with Gerry having the best of both worlds by the end of
the film—staying married to Tom and getting John D's support for Tom's
airport idea. Now, Shurlock wrote:

> We must insist that some line be inserted here to show that the wife was
> not successful in her morally questionable procedure of trying to get
> money to finance her husband's projects. This is a technical request but,
> under the circumstances, very important.[32]

Shurlock went so far as to describe dialogue to solve this problem, which
Sturges, thankfully, did not use. Finally, Shurlock wrote: "We must insist
that the characterization of the Princess as a *much-divorced* woman be dropped
entirely . . . Some less offensive characterization must be found."

Brian Henderson ponders the reasons for this late-inning turnabout,
wondering if "Shurlock had taken his time in reading the script, or if he had
awakened one night and realized what he had, in essence, approved by remaining silent." (He also speculates that the events of December 7, 1941 further
distracted the PCA from monitoring the production closely.) Shurlock *did*
awaken to the possible offense *The Palm Beach Story* would generate, chiefly
because of the storm that erupted after the November premiere of the Greta
Garbo vehicle *Two-Faced Woman*. In George Cukor's film, a straying Melvyn
Douglas neglects traditional wife Greta Garbo in the mountains to pursue
Garbo's impersonation of a non-existent, more sexually alluring sister in the
city. The film unfortunately inspired Garbo's retirement from the screen;
more importantly for Shurlock and Sturges, it provoked cries of condemnation from the Legion of Decency "for its immoral and un-Christian attitude
toward marriage and its obligations; impudently suggestive scenes, dialogue,
and situations; [and] suggestive costumes." Shurlock had given the film a seal,
a decision that nearly cost him his job.[33]

Shurlock, in other words, was in a panic as he reread the script for *The
Palm Beach Story*, and he scrambled to ensure that Sturges's film would not

be as catastrophic for him, the PCA and the industry in general as the Garbo feature had been. The December 5 letter contained Shurlock's multiple apologies that alluded to this situation, beginning with the very first paragraph, which described how "stories centering around the theme of a light treatment of marriage and divorce . . . has been a source of serious complaint."[34] Shurlock now "earnestly request[ed] that you give full consideration to our suggestions below, where it will be asked that you help minimize what might be called 'constant irritation' of a sensitive public." He concluded, "We know you will appreciate our concern from the standpoint of the best interests of the industry, and will cooperate fully." Sturges did not, in fact, "cooperate fully." Shurlock must have calmed down in subsequent days and Sturges, as he so capably had done throughout the negotiations, reassured the PCA head once again that these details would be handled in an acceptable manner.

Some of Shurlock's concerns proved prescient, however, in late 1942, when local censors screened *The Palm Beach Story*. Only New York and Kansas passed the film without eliminations. Elsewhere, many of the suggestive elements that Shurlock had criticized were cut.[35] Yet other elements of the film were accepted without comment by both Shurlock and local censors. For all the worries in early 1941 about excessive drinking in the movies, no one inside the industry or out seemed to notice or care that Gerry and Tom are certifiably smashed at dinner and upon their return home as they discuss splitting up—Tom has to catch Gerry to prevent her from falling on her face before she sits on his lap. More generally—the Ale and Quail Club aside—virtually all of *The Palm Beach Story* mocks the sanctity of marriage. There's the madcap opening credit sequence of Tom and Gerry's own wedding, which requires that Gerry tie up her twin sister to get to the altar first; there's Gerry's determination to be a gold digger to benefit Tom; and there's John D.'s desire for a mock marriage. Then there's the "happy ending," with its farcical notion that John D. and Maude accept Gerry and Tom's identical twins solely on the basis of their physical appearance (Tom and Gerry are grinning broadly for the first time in the film since their wedding ceremony, but their twins look bewildered at the altar). Sarah Kozloff calls *The Palm Beach Story* "perhaps the least romantic of screwballs," noting that "the very arbitrariness of the device of the twins deliberately satirizes movie conventions of love and courtship."[36] Elliot Rubenstein noted, "If the end of *Eve* stands for sex at long last emancipated from betrothals and marriages [because the marital status of Charles and Jean/Eve at the end of the film is uncertain to Charles and to us], the end of *Palm Beach* epitomizes the utter impertinence of all weddings."[37]

Even before the ending, the Princess alone (albeit with Toto [Sig Arno] in tow) would have been reason enough to reject the film. When we first see her, Gerry speculates that Toto might be a duke; John D. replies quickly "It might be her tailor too. She'll go out with anything." Their famous exchange about marriage says it all:

> John D.: You don't just marry somebody you just met the day before.
> Maude: But that's the only way, dear. If you get to know too much about them you'd never marry them. I'd marry Captain McGlue tomorrow, even with that name.
> John D.: And divorce him next month.
> The Princess: Nothing is permanent in this world except Roosevelt, dear.

For Maude, because of the Code, marriage and sex are identical. In this, she looks back to the Lady Eve and her multiple imaginary marriages and forward to Trudy who, because of the Code, must be married so she can be pregnant.

In short, *The Palm Beach Story*'s thorough demolishing of the sanctity of marriage demonstrates what Sturges and the PCA could achieve, especially when some of the most objectionable dialogue is delivered swiftly and most of the characters are caricatures with, according to Leger Grindon's chapter in this volume, cartoon sexuality. For this reason as well, *The Palm Beach Story* encountered fewer cuts from censors than *The Lady Eve*: many viewers saw no need to take the characters as seriously.[38] Shurlock, in spite of his reversals and panics, ultimately skated up to the edge of acceptability with Sturges—as Breen had before him.

THE MIRACLE OF THE PCA SEAL

The Miracle of Morgan's Creek constituted the apex of Sturges's absurdist approach to romantic comedy; not coincidentally, it was the apotheosis of his Production Code provocations. As biographer Diane Jacobs summarizes:

> The Breen office, which had found it hard to accept Maude's multiple marriages in *The Palm Beach Story*, was beside itself over Preston's latest project. It was not just the pregnant girl with no husband in sight, or the blasphemous miracle, or the mockery of a wedding that disturbed them, but that Sturges was actually making fun of the war effort. A soldier gets a girl pregnant and leaves the hard part of father to a draft reject. What an idea, at a time when Hollywood was desperately trying to solace the War Department.[39]

James Agee famously wrote in his review that "the Hays office has been either hypnotized . . . or raped in its sleep."[40] However, as Brian Henderson correctly observes, "they may have been raped, ultimately, but they were not sleeping. They were defeated less by Sturges perhaps than by their own certainty that meanings can be policed."[41] That certainty, of course, was the very foundation of the PCA's work.

The day after his October 20, 1942 meeting with Sturges and Luraschi to discuss Sturges's initial script draft, Breen (back in the saddle at the PCA) wrote Luraschi a seven-page, single-spaced letter announcing that "much of this material in the present script . . . appears to us to be unacceptable, not only from the standpoint of the Production Code, but, likewise, from the viewpoint of political [i.e. city and state] censorship."[42] In making his case, Breen singled out over 46 pages of the 116-page *incomplete* script that contained dialogue that could not stand. Beyond the strictures of the Code, *Miracle* involved enough objectionable material to offend, if not *everybody*, then a broad array of groups and institutions (the Legion of Decency, lawyers, police officers, ministers of the peace, the military, and stutterers).

Miracle takes a dramatically different approach to romantic comedy from *The Lady Eve* and *The Palm Beach Story*.[43] In Trudy, Sturges created (and Breen confronted) a different kind of comic heroine from Jean and Gerry. Trudy's unwavering determination to dance with the soldiers and kiss them goodbye makes her an unruly sister-in-arms with her predecessors. However, Jean and Gerry are experienced, sophisticated, witty, sexy, capable manipulators of men; moreover, they are well aware of their seductive charms (the entirety of *Palm Beach* supports Gerry's claims about "what a long-legged gal can do without doing anything"). Trudy, on the other hand, is an adolescent, impulsive, airheaded sexual naïf; all of these traits lead her to those dire straits the morning after the party. She is aware of her popularity, but seemingly unaware, or only vaguely aware, of how her sexuality affects men. In this way, even after getting married and sleeping with a soldier, she retains an overwhelming sense of innocence, a quality she shares with the utterly incompetent Norval. The latter's quest to win Trudy's heart is a central narrative concern, but there is no erotic heat—or heat of any kind, or *intentionally* witty byplay—arising from Trudy and Norval's interactions.[44]

Where Jean and Gerry relent upon achieving their goals at the conclusion of each of their films, the adolescent Trudy quickly regrets what she has done. Jean runs to the ship to meet Charles and start all over at the end of *The Lady Eve*. Gerry finally acknowledges her love for Tom. After consulting Dr. Meyer (Torben Meyer) to confirm the pregnancy and the lawyer Mr. Johnson (Al Bridge) to learn she has no legal recourse, Trudy gives up on finding her husband. Instead, she, Norval and her smart 14-year-old sister Emmy (Diana Lynn) struggle to figure out how they can save her from the catastrophe that will befall her if the town finds out. Trudy and Norval's efforts to get married under assumed names, and their attempts to deal with the consequences of their failure, occupy the final third of the film. As Brian Henderson notes, "one of the dark wonders of the film is the way that the two characters, by pooling their intelligence, create disaster after disaster—each greater and more calamitous than either could have created alone."[45]

A number of scholars have detailed the lengthy negotiations between the PCA and Luraschi and Sturges.[46] The PCA found most worrisome Trudy's night out, the failed marriage ceremony, and the dialogue involved in both.[47] Of course, how Trudy got pregnant was a subject of great concern to everyone. Sturges initially showed her getting drunk. Breen's October 21 letter ruled this out: "We understand from our discussion of yesterday that Trudy will, at no time, be shown to be drunk, nor will there be any reference to the fact that she was drunk. It is acceptable to indicate that she, along with the others, did drink some champagne, but she should not be shown drunk."

Thus, Trudy's partying behavior plays out equivocally in the film. While champagne is bought for everyone at the Country Club, Trudy is seen drinking only "Victory Lemonade" in the church basement. She and the soldier beside her wince as they partake, suggesting it's been spiked with alcohol. However, a sign next to the bowl explains, "save sugar for victory." The bump Trudy receives on her head from being lifted to the dance floor lamp is supposed to explain her impulsive, semi-conscious behavior for the rest of the

Figure 4.2 *The Miracle of Morgan's Creek.*

evening. In the morning-after scene, in which Trudy returns Norval's car, she hits the curb before she stops, and speaks slowly, lolling her head from side to side and struggling to pronounce the word "punctual."

She could be exhausted from being out all night and she denies drinking anything stronger than lemonade but, as Norval comments, "Well, you certainly don't get what you've got on lemonade." Sturges and the PCA fulfilled their obligations to the Code by providing the material for more than one interpretation of Trudy's behavior, but as Diane Jacobs put it, "For all the talk of lemonade and marriage licenses, Sturges's point—that Trudy got drunk and slept with a soldier—came across loud and clear."[48]

In Sturges's previous romantic comedies, kisses at any fade out suggested a sex affair. In *Miracle*, Trudy and Norval kiss only once and briefly at that, during their invalidated marriage ceremony. Instead, Sturges alluded to sex via dialogue and especially visuals. Leger Grindon notes that at each party site—the church basement, the country club where a wealthy man buys everyone champagne, and the roadhouse club—the action gets wilder:

> The increasing pace of the shots, the focus on moving legs, Trudy's ecstatic lift, and finally the moral implication of her fall evoke sex, and the immediate consequences inform us of Trudy's passion. The farewell party montage is a vivid example of how a classical Hollywood filmmaker could suggest everything and show nothing.[49]

Significantly, when Breen screened the finished film, he had no comment on this sequence.

Moreover, Trudy's consequent marriage and pregnancy constituted the key component of the film's outrageousness, taking the same logic that had informed Maude's multiple marriages (though the latter apparently used effective birth control). As Grindon describes it, "The Sturges dialogue plays upon the implied substitution of the forbidden for the respectable. The equation of sex with 'marriage' is a repeated gag that becomes a pivot for humor . . . The morning after the drunken farewell party Trudy can't remember whom she 'married.'"[50] Though the dialogue honors the restrictions of the censor, much of its humor arises from a codified system of double meanings.

Breen's correspondence with Sturges about *Miracle* focuses on the literal and the details; on paper, at least, Breen plays Tom to Sturges's Gerry. For example, beginning with his very first letter, Breen acknowledged, "It is agreeable—and necessary for plot purposes—to establish the fact that Trudy is pregnant. The unacceptability of much that follows is due to the fact that the point is hit several times, and thus gives out a flavor and an atmosphere which, in our judgment, is unacceptable." Sturges had so internalized the PCA's application of the Code that he solved in advance, albeit in the flimsiest possible way, the major offensive element of his *Miracle* scenario: Trudy got pregnant, but she got married first to a virtual non-entity. Interestingly enough, Sturges never referenced the Code in his notes as he worked out Trudy's quandary.[51] He didn't need to. He knew what Breen would say if Trudy were not married before she got pregnant.

Once Breen and his associates accepted the very premise of the story, negotiations focused on details such as reducing the number of times the word "pregnant" was uttered (it appeared on five pages of the initial script), much as Shurlock asked that "divorce" be rarely uttered in *The Palm Beach Story*. Sturges, having learned from his experience on *Palm Beach*, may well have sprinkled "pregnant" around the script as a bargaining chip, knowing that the PCA would object to its "in your face" effects. Sturges likewise may have seen the eliminations he made at Breen's request as providing more leverage: in the first draft, the Doctor (Torben Meyer) tried to console Trudy by noting, "These situations are frightening but not terribly unusual . . . unfortunately"; and "Just remember one thing . . . it's perfectly natural." Both were cut. Sturges revised many others: the lawyer's query as to whether the marriage was "consummated? They usually are" was revised to "celebrated" in the finished film.

More often, however, Sturges ignored Breen's directives. Breen made no notations on his letter to indicate he was giving in on any of these points, and yet he did. For example, Breen warned that the scene in which Trudy reveals her condition to Norval seemed "certain to give offense inasmuch as the reaction is certain to be one of comedy about pregnancy." There is comedy aplenty in Norval's repeated experience of "the spots" as Trudy first tells him she is married and then that she is pregnant.

Norval and Trudy's "prexy" marriage ceremony (as Trudy mangles the term) was another key point of concern for Breen (who wanted the "marriage by proxy" concept explicitly stated so audiences would not think Trudy was committing bigamy). Breen deemed it "imperative" that "once the marriage ceremony gets under way there be no interruptions whatever until it has been completed. It is permissible that any gagging necessary to carry the scene be played either before or after the marriage ceremony; but in no case may there be any interruptions or gagging while the ceremony is under way." Sturges obliged; the actual performance of the ceremony has no comic interruptions. Everything and everyone calms down for this 30-second rite, as Trudy and Norval solemnly listen to the minster's words and say, "I do." They kiss to a swell of orchestral music. However, the Justice absolutely mangles their impossible names:

Minister: Ignatz Razly Wazly, do you take this woman Gertrude Sockenbocker for your lawful wedded wife . . .?
Norval: I do.

Minister: Gertrude Krockendocker, do you take Ignatz Razby Wazby for your lawful wedded husband . . .?
Trudy: I do.

Thus, no audience member can take the performance of the ceremony seriously.

Moreover, the moments before and after the ceremony are among the funniest in the film. Porter Hall's Justice of the Peace (whose sign in the first submitted script was to read "Marriages performed at any hour" and who was to ask his wife "They want *a room* or a marriage?"—both deleted) attributes the young couple's nervousness to marriage jitters. His performance here—as a man jaded by performing many such "military" marriages and eager to get back to looking at his stereopticon photos—provides the perfect contrast to Trudy and Norval's paralyzing fear as they try to lie. Neither can pronounce their names easily (although Trudy has the edge, since she is giving her real name this time). Trudy, understandably panicked, struggles to answer the routine question, "Have you ever been married before?" Norval can't pronounce the named of his alleged Army base as his stuttering goes into overdrive.

The script then called for the Justice to say "That will be $2.00 please." Breen directed that "there is to be a distinct pause after the conclusion of the marriage ceremony" before the Justice speaks. After Norval and Trudy are pronounced man and wife, Sturges cuts to a waist-up two-shot of the pair as they beam at each other and kiss, while the witness (Esther Howard) looks adoringly at them and the music swells. This soaring moment, lasting all of five seconds, is quickly undercut when Sturges cuts back to the master shot in the scene as the Justice demands payment. Moreover, the Justice's nasal, rapid-fire delivery of the marriage vows and his quick quips about marital unhappiness—"Don't be nervous. People do it every day. The bad part comes later" and (to Norval, who says the ceremony made him nervous) "If you knew what it was like, it would make you still nervouser"—further undercut any sense of the ceremony's gravity. Here, staging, performance, shooting, editing and music combine to provide a hilariously ambivalent representation of a marriage ceremony, which is, after all, false.

A legitimate marriage is of course Trudy and Norval's goal. They achieve it only by fiat of the corrupt Governor (Brian Donlevy) and the Boss (Akim Tamiroff), who declare their previous marriage to be valid (a power the PCA repeatedly reminded Sturges no governor would have[52]). Between Trudy's forgotten marriage to a forgotten soldier, her attempt at a mock marriage to Norval, and the *deus ex machina* of the Governor, *The Miracle of Morgan's Creek*, like *The Palm Beach Story*, tossed the concept of marriage's sanctity around like a limp rag.

As might have been expected, *Miracle* passed New York without eliminations; inexplicably it was approved in Maryland, Massachusetts and Ohio. Yet

Miracle, even after conferences with the Legion of Decency and the armed forces, provoked plenty of outrage upon its initial release, including "indignant complaints . . . by ministers, civil groups and reformers in general," according to Columbia Pictures President and production chief Harry Cohn.[53] Sturges personally received numerous letters of complaint about the film, many of which linked the film to the growing problem of juvenile delinquency. Given the growing panic around this subject, Paramount's delay in distributing *Miracle*—it was completed in spring 1943 but released in January 1944— exacerbated its controversial reception.[54]

One fascinating assessment of *Miracle* came from Geoffrey Shurlock, now head of the PCA, eleven years after the film's initial release. Paramount wanted to remake the film (this became the 1958 Frank Tashlin– Jerry Lewis vehicle *Rock-a-Bye Baby*). Shurlock noted that the "basic sordidness" of the story was hidden by its setting "during the hysteria of war," and that Sturges's "frantic and slapstick manner" of direction "helped cover up this fundamental unpleasantness. Told in a more leisurely fashion, the camouflage would probably turn out very thin." Shurlock suggested to Luraschi that the remake pay "more attention . . . to a proper appreciation of marriage": the script could indicate that the marriage to the soldier was invalid "because it occurred when the girl was not in full possession of her faculties." The Trudy character could make a speech "indicating her remorse for having made such a shambles of marriage, which up to that time she had considered a sacred obligation." Shurlock concluded by noting that the Legion of Decency might use such a production "to prove their complaint that the industry was seeking out the most questionable material they could find for re-make."[55] Even over a decade later, then, *Miracle* had the potential to create trouble.

In terms of PCA process, Breen had many reasons to issue a seal to *The Miracle of Morgan's Creek*. Diane Jacobs rightly reports that the Breen Office and even the Legion of Decency "both abhorred *Miracle* and found it 'very funny . . . from a strictly entertainment standpoint.' That despite (or because of?) its audacity, they found it funny and timely and true."[56] In continuing to ease his demands for adherence to the Code, Breen tolerated Sturges's increasingly elaborate Code-stretching schemes, which in turn helped Sturges and Paramount create a continuing string of hit comedies. Sturges handled the elaborate process of PCA review masterfully, alternately accepting and ignoring the agency's directives.

In terms of the completed film, one could argue that the highly allusive nature of *Miracle*'s plot and dialogue made it incomprehensible to innocent viewers and certainly children; that so far as sophisticated viewers are concerned, Trudy is not truly married to the soldier, but because she thought she was, their sex was legitimate; and that because she is not truly married, she is not committing bigamy with Norval.[57] One can further argue that the cartoonish qualities that Brian Henderson and Leger Grindon identify in *The Palm Beach Story* permeate *Miracle* more thoroughly, making its offenses more tolerable. All of these considerations helped shape the film's happy fate at the PCA.

CONCLUSION

In his three romantic comedies, Sturges presented the PCA staff with narrative situations, scenes and dialogue that increasingly "skated to the edge of non-acceptability." Yet, they were acceptable in their overall narrative framework, given Sturges's loose adherence to the conventions of romantic comedy. The formation (or reformation) of the couple required each of Sturges's heroines to ultimately relent in her unruliness. Outrageous as narrative developments might be, some viewers could feel that the desirability and elevated state—if not the sanctity—of marriage were ultimately upheld.

In the negotiating process, the PCA was not Sturges's "enemy." Instead, the agency worked *with* Sturges to represent questionable material to the fullest extent they judged the Production Code to allow. They did so in fulfillment of the PCA's paradoxical mission of both awarding seals to films and avoiding or downplaying overtly offensive sexual material, wherever they turned up—in details of plot, scene, and/or dialogue. The process ideally made possible ambiguous interpretations of suggestive material. The PCA's work was to regulate the representation of sex, not to eliminate or repress it. The agency's success in doing so varied film by film, often scene by scene, and also according to the historical context in which each title appeared. One element remained constant: the potentially offensive material, large and small, came so thick and fast that the agency could not possibly catch everything. Many suggestive situations and lines of dialogue and scenes were first noticed by local censors and ordinary viewers.

Even when the PCA noticed problematic elements, Sturges responded by accepting eliminations, by cooperating through rewriting material (sometimes to greater potential offense than his original formulation), by ignoring the problems, or by assuring the agency he could handle the material to minimize infractions and gain its blessing. The entire process left Sturges a great deal of room to maneuver; in fact it paradoxically enabled Sturges's satire to soar far beyond Code restrictions. As with the best screwball and romantic comedies of the 1930s and 1940s, his achievement is his, but it is also inseparable from the work of the PCA.

NOTES

* I thank Jeff Jaeckle and Sarah Kozloff for their editorial acumen, and Jenny Romero and, especially, Kristine Krueger of the Margaret Herrick Library of the Academy of Motion Picture Arts and Sciences for their invaluable assistance.

1 Elliot Rubenstein, "The End of Screwball Comedy: *The Lady Eve* and *The Palm Beach Story*," *Post Script* 1:3 (Spring–Summer 1982): 35. A number of books have recounted certain aspects of Sturges's negotiations with the PCA. See e.g. James Curtis, *Between Flops: A Biography of Preston Sturges* (New York, NY: Limelight, 1982); Diane Jacobs, *Christmas in July: The Life and Art of Preston Sturges* (Berkeley, CA: University of California Press, 1994); Brian Henderson, *Five Screenplays by Preston Sturges* (Berkeley, CA: University of California Press, 1985); Brian Henderson, *Four More Screenplays by Preston Sturges* (Berkeley, CA: University of California Press, 1995); and Andrew Horton, ed., *Three More Screenplays by Preston Sturges* (Berkeley, CA: University of California Press, 1998).

2 Kathleen Rowe, *The Unruly Woman: Gender and the Genres of Laughter* (Austin, TX: University of Texas Press, 1995), 31. Rowe discusses *The Lady Eve* specifically on pp. 161–8.

3 Marriage is rarely straightforward in *any* of Sturges's films (a fact very likely related to his personal biography as the son of Mary Desti and a multiply-married man). Only three of Sturges's great films of the 1940s portray marriage in a conventional way, i.e. as the culmination of a traditional courtship—1940's *Christmas in July*, 1944's *Hail the Conquering Hero* and *The Great Moment*. In his other films, characters get married for political gain (1940's *The Great McGinty*) or for tax advantages (1941's *Sullivan's Travels*).

4 Preston Sturges, *Sturges by Sturges*, adapted and edited by Sandy Sturges (New York, NY: Simon and Schuster, 1990), 294.

5 Lea Jacobs, *The Wages of Sin* (Berkeley, CA: University of California Press, 1997), 21.

6 Jacobs, 23.

7 Jacobs, 20. Jacobs quotes here from Geoffrey Shurlock in James M. Wall's unpublished manuscript "Oral History with Geoffrey Shurlock," 1975, Louis B. Mayer Library, American Film Institute, Los Angeles, CA.

8 See Lea Jacobs, Ch. 1 and 2.

9 Rubenstein, 43.

10 Sarah Kozloff, *Overhearing Film Dialogue* (Berkeley, CA: University of California Press, 2000), 200. Contra Kozloff, sex *is* mentioned explicitly by Gerry when arguing with Tom about the Weenie King's gift of $700, but this is an exception which proves the rule.

11 "C.C.P." [Charles C. Pettijohn], Memo to Mr. Hays and Mr. Breen, 17 February 1941, in *The Great McGinty* File (AMPAS).

12 Leonard J. Leff and Jerrold L. Simmons, *The Dame in the Kimono: Hollywood, Censorship, and the Production Code*, rev. ed. (Lexington, KY: University Press of Kentucky, 2001), 83.

13 Leff and Simmons quote from Breen's resignation letter, 114.

14 Ivan Spear, "Spearheads," *Box Office*, 3 May 1941, quoted in Thomas Doherty, *Hollywood's Censor: Joseph I. Breen and the Production Code Administration* (New York, NY: Columbia University Press, 2007), 139–40.

15 Doherty, 139.

16 Lea Jacobs, 113.

17 One could write a monograph on Sturges's PCA negotiations. Here, for reasons of space, I focus only on the representation of female sexuality and marriage.

18 Joseph I. Breen, Letter to Luigi Luraschi, 9 October 1940, in *The Lady Eve* File, in *History of American Cinema: Hollywood and the Production Code*, Microfilm edition, Reel 18 (hereafter "*The Lady Eve* File").

19 Joseph I. Breen, Letter to Luigi Luraschi, 21 October 1940, *The Lady Eve* File.

20 Brian Henderson, "*The Lady Eve*," in *Five Screenplays by Preston Sturges* (Berkeley, CA: University of California Press, 1985), 332–3, 342–5. See also Brian Henderson, "Sturges at Work," *Film Quarterly* 39:2 (1985/6), 18–20.

21 Breen, in his October 9 letter, objected to Jean and Charles's final exchange about who can forgive who before the cabin door is shut, "by reason of its reference to the aforementioned sex affair." Breen's reading here—and it's worth remembering that it's an interpretation forged before Sturges relocated the clinch scene from Jean's private deck to the bow of the ship—is that the exchange refers only to the sex affair, rather than to everything that transpired between them on the S.S. Southern Queen, including Charles's narrowmindedness and Jean's duplicity. Given the key importance of forgiveness to the entire meaning of the film, it is fortunate that Sturges was able to keep this exchange.

22 See Doherty, "Intermission at RKO," in *Hollywood's Censor: Joseph I. Breen & the Production Code Administration*, 132–51, for a discussion of the PCA just before and during Breen's brief tenure at the studio. On pp. 136–9, Doherty discusses directors' and producers' ploys to get around PCA directives; he discusses Shurlock's firmness on p. 145.

23 Geoffrey Shurlock, Letter to Luigi Luraschi, 12 November 1941, in *The Palm Beach Story* File, in *History of American Cinema: Hollywood and the Production Code*, Microfilm edition, Reel 19 (hereafter "*The Palm Beach Story* File").

24 Geoffrey Shurlock, Letter to Luigi Luraschi, 17 November 1941, *The Palm Beach Story* File.

25 Geoffrey Shurlock, Letter to Luigi Luraschi, 17 November 1941, *The Palm Beach Story* File.

26 This is a tender, mutual and far more demonstrative staging of Rhett Butler (Clark Gable) carrying Scarlett O'Hara (Vivien Leigh) up the staircase in 1939's *Gone with the Wind* for what is spousal rape. Here it is Tom, not Scarlett, whom we find smiling in bed the morning after.

27 Rubenstein, 35–6.

28 Kozloff, 195–6. See also Leger Grindon's chapter in this volume for his discussion of Tom and his sex-less rivals for Gerry's affections.

29 Geoffrey Shurlock, Letter to Luigi Luraschi, 17 November 1941, *The Palm Beach Story* File.

30 At one point, Maude cannot even remember the name of her third ex-husband ("the tall one with the scar, what *was* his name?," she asks her brother). Significantly, Sturges retained the character of Toto in the film in spite of Shurlock's insistence that eliminating his gigolo characterization was "imperative." Clearly, Toto's status—a running gag based on his absolute impotence and irrelevance to the Princess Centimilla—eased Shurlock's concerns.

31 Geoffrey Shurlock, Letters to Luigi Luraschi, 17 and 25 November 1941, *The Palm Beach Story* File.

32 Geoffrey Shurlock, Letter to Luigi Luraschi, 6 December 1941, *The Palm Beach Story* File.

33 Doherty, 143; the Legion of Decency quotation appears on 144; Doherty quotes Shurlock's interview with James M. Wall about nearly losing his job on p. 143.

34 Geoffrey Shurlock, Letter to Luigi Luraschi, 5 December 1941, *The Palm Beach Story* File.

35 See the censorship reports in *The Palm Beach Story* File.

36 Kozloff, 198.

37 Rubenstein, 38.

38 Brian Henderson broaches the cartoon elements of Sturges work in "Cartoon and Narrative in the Films of Frank Tashlin and Preston Sturges," in Andrew Horton, ed., *Film/Cinema/Theory* (Berkeley, CA: University of California Press, 1991), 153–73; he focuses primarily on the romantic comedies from pp. 165 onwards.

39 Jacobs, 297–8, and Leger Grindon, *The Hollywood Romantic Comedy: Conventions, History, Controversies* (Malden, MA: Wiley Blackwell, 2011), 106–16.

40 James Agee, *Agree on Film: Reviews and Comments* (Boston, MA: Beacon Press, 1966), 74.

41 Henderson, 25.

42 Joseph Breen, Letter to Luigi Luraschi, 21 October 1942, in *The Miracle of Morgan's Creek File*, in *History of American Cinema: Hollywood and the Production Code*, Microfilm edition, Reel 21 (hereafter, *The Miracle of Morgan's Creek* File).

43 Diane Jacobs sees *Miracle* as more about families than romance (297–8); Leger Grindon places it as a wartime romantic comedy (106–16); Kristine Karnick sees it as a late screwball comedy (see her chapter in this volume).

44 Jacobs, 298, argues that Trudy would never have married Norval except for her calamity and speculates that Trudy would forswear sex with him after what she has been through.

45 Henderson, 536.

46 See e.g. Curtis, 179–81 and 184 and Jacobs, 298–301, 305. See also Henderson, 550 and 560–1. Henderson also discusses the extensive retakes demanded by the War Board, 589–91.

47 The comparison of Trudy's birthing of sextuplets with the birth of Christ was another major focus of PCA worries.

48 Jacobs, 301.

49 Grindon, 111.

50 Grindon, 108.

51 See Henderson's account in *Four More Screenplays*, 527–44. David B. Pratt suggested to me, in an email of September 28, 2014, the notion of Sturges's internalization of PCA maneuvers in drafting *Miracle*'s narrative.

52 See e.g. Joseph I. Breen, Letter to Luigi Luraschi, 3 December 1942, *The Miracle of Morgan's Creek* File.

53 Harry Cohn, Letter to Joseph Breen, 22 August 1945, *The Miracle of Morgan's Creek* File.

54 At the same time, the film had many fans, including military officials and ordinary soldiers. Commander A. J. Bolton, serving as the US Navy's Motion Picture and Radio Liaison Office, wrote to Sturges on March 1, 1944 that he and his wife had brought some friends to see it: "I have never had a better time . . . It was truly a howling success in my opinion just the sort of screen fare we can use a lot of in these trying times." A. J. Bolton, Letter to Preston Sturges, 1 March 1944, *The Miracle of Morgan's Creek* Correspondence, 1944, Box 40, Folder 29, Preston Sturges Collection, Special Collections, Charles Young Research Library, UCLA, Los Angeles, CA. Bolton's praise is especially striking given the extensive rewrites and the day of retakes that Sturges shot to earn the military's approval of the film.

55 "G.P.S." (Geoffrey P. Shurlock), "Memo for the files," 1 December 1955, in *The Miracle of Morgan's Creek* File.

56 Jacobs, 298–9. Jacobs here quotes from Russell Holman, *CONFIDENTIAL* letter to Luigi Luraschi, 5 October 1943, explaining the Legion of Decency's many objections to the film and its acknowledgment of its humor.

57 These ideas were formulated to me by Thomas Doherty, email to author, 23 July 2014.

PART 2

Cultural Commentary: History and Identity

CHAPTER 5

Sturges's Many Mothers

Kristine Brunovska Karnick

Perhaps the first notable feature of the mothers in Preston Sturges's films is that they exist at all. After all, Hollywood comedies, and specifically screwball comedies, are full of aunts, sisters, dowagers, and guardians—but very few mothers. Especially scarce are the mothers of female leads. As Stanley Cavell has noted, "in the fiction of our films the woman's mother is conspicuously and problematically absent."[1] Indeed, mothers are scarce in screwball comedies, not just in the remarriage comedies that Cavell describes, but also in most romantic comedies of the period. Whereas mother–daughter relationships are a staple of Hollywood melodramas, comedies tend to avoid those potentially problematic relationships. When Hildy tells Walter that "mother" will accompany her and Bruce on their honeymoon in *His Girl Friday*, Walter assumes she is referring to her own mother and responds incredulously: "Mother? Why, your mother kicked the bucket!"

Mothers of male leads in classical Hollywood comedies don't get much more attention. One clue to Dan Leeson's unsuitability to be Lucy Warriner's new husband in *The Awful Truth* is his possession of and relationship to a mother, an impression he confirms as their relationship is ending: "Well, I guess a man's best friend is his mother." Whereas fathers are well-represented in Hollywood comedies, most often as *senex* figures who constitute obstacles the male lead must overcome to win the young woman of his choice, the diegetic world of comedies has little room for mothers—except in the works of Preston Sturges.

In films either written or written and directed by Sturges, mothers are not only present but also, in fact, integral to the development of the narrative; they exhibit a powerful influence over their worlds in both his dramas and his comedies. Because Sturges has often been lauded for his progressive, proto-feminist approach to gender construction, we should consider his take on motherhood, a topic he addressed repeatedly in his films.

Sturges's construction of motherhood is both complex and nuanced. As his career in Hollywood progressed, his conception of motherhood, as seen in his films, changed. Perhaps as a working out of his complex relationship with his own mother,[2] the mothers in Sturges's early films are cold and manipulative (*The Power and the Glory*, Lee's mother in *Remember the Night*). This image is consistent with a popular critique of motherhood at the time. However, in the later part of his career, that image give way to a far more benevolent and at the same time outdated, sentimental image of ideal Victorian "mother love" (*The Miracle of Morgan's Creek, Hail the Conquering Hero*).

RETHINKING MOTHERHOOD IN MODERN AMERICA

In foregrounding the impact of motherhood, Sturges weighed in on a critical reformulation of the concept during the first half of the twentieth century. This period brought a shift away from the century-old set of values surrounding the concept of moral motherhood. Emerging to replace it was a new maternal ideal based on scientific principles and a reformulation of the political and economic order in which women were increasingly demanding a role not as wives and mothers but as individuals.

Until the early twentieth century, prevailing notions of motherhood emphasized "mother love," an emotion so powerful, enduring, and selfless "as to border on the divine."[3] This near-divine status was based partly on the hazardous, potentially life-threatening nature of childbirth. Consequently, motherhood was accorded the same honor as military service: "Just as the soldier risked life and limb for his country, so the childbearing woman bravely descended into 'the valley of the shadow of death' to bring forth the nation's future citizens."[4] In a similar vein, when the governor of Washington proclaimed Mother's Day a state holiday in 1910, he urged every citizen to wear a white flower "in acknowledgement and honor of the one who went down into the valley of the shadow of death for us."[5] The set of ideas surrounding this construction assumed a special role for mothers in their children's moral development. It sentimentalized motherhood while effectively restricting a mother's scope of influence to the home and to social issues involving domestic and child-related matters. Motherhood, argues historian Linda Kerber, "was discussed almost as if it were a fourth branch of government, a device that ensured social control in the gentlest possible way."[6]

Religious and moral concerns were seen as the goals of childrearing. Mother love, traditionalists believed, "had the capacity to transform and redeem: it could turn a shallow and vapid woman into a noble character; it could recall a wayward son or daughter to the path of virtue; it could mold a poor and scrawny boy into a great and powerful leader."[7]

In the early twentieth century, notions of moral motherhood were beginning to give way. Modernists saw motherhood as just one stage in the life of women, who would be helped through an organized set of scientific principles and cultural ideals reflecting the shift in their political and social status. As methods of improving maternal and infant health and mortality developed, mothers were flooded with opinions by "experts" on childrearing. Motherly instinct, a hallmark of the previous order, went out of fashion, as a growing cadre of experts "fostered new psychological expectations for motherhood and encouraged women to measure their mothering against ever-changing notions of what was 'normal' for themselves and their children."[8]

A consequence of the new emphasis on science was a move away from religious and moral concerns. Whereas, earlier, moral mothers had focused on children's spiritual and religious development, the modern mother worried about children's potentially harmful habits, such as thumb-sucking and masturbation. Children's behavioral problems and psychological inadequacies came to be seen as the result of improper guidance.

As the clash of discourses surrounding motherhood became more pronounced, writers and scientists placed increasing blame on women who seemed to cling to the old order. Mother love came to be replaced by mother hate and blame. Although often associated with Philip Wylie's 1942 screed, *Generation of Vipers*, ideas about the damage caused by improper (Victorian) mothering appeared more than a decade before that book's publication. Geoffrey Gorer traces the development of the "mom" figure to the publication of Sidney Howard's play *The Silver Cord* in 1927.[9] In a speech given in 1937, Smith College president William Allan Neilson remarked, "Mother love used to be regarded as one of the most beautiful things in the world. I do not believe in mother love. I think in nine times out of ten, mother love is self-love."[10] Journalist Dorothy Dix ridiculed the concept as well, referring to mother love "as an old tradition that when a woman bears a child she is automatically metamorphosed into an angel and filled with altruistic devotion to her offspring."[11]

The scientific community encouraged the increasing skepticism toward mother love. Psychologist Dr. John Watson wrote of "the dangers of too much mother love," claimed that it "is a dangerous instrument," and stated that most parents "should be indicted for psychological murder."[12] Historian Jodi Vandenberg-Daves writes, "Watson castigated mothers who cuddled and kissed their children . . . he lambasted maternal sentimentality and even argued that kissing a baby was 'at bottom a sex-seeking response.'"[13]

The publication of Wylie's *Generation of Vipers*, and its bestseller status, significantly amped up the volume on the debate over motherhood.[14] Wylie (1902–71) was a prolific writer whose output included hundreds of short stories along with numerous screenplays, novels, radio programs, newspaper columns, and social criticism. His early science fiction works, including

Gladiator (1930), *The Savage Gentleman* (1932), and *When Worlds Collide* (1933), were influential in the development of twentieth-century science fiction.[15] In fact, he worked with Sturges on the screenplay for James Whale's *The Invisible Man* (1933), though neither ultimately received screen credit. Wylie had already entered into the debate over mothers and motherhood in 1931, in a short story published first in *Redbook* and later developed into the novel *Footprint of Cinderella*. Wylie endowed the spinster character "Chloe" with attributes that he and others would eventually ascribe to "moms": snobbery; selfishness; an obsession with preserving outward appearances; a drive and willfulness to achieve her desires at the expense of others; spiteful-ness; and above all, hypocrisy and self-righteousness. Wylie's description of Chloe would be reworked over the next decade in numerous other publica-tions and eventually incorporated into his denunciation of moms. Although *Generation of Vipers* attacked numerous institutions Americans held in high regard—businessmen, statesmen, professors, the political establishment, and the military—some of its most searing criticism was reserved for women, and especially for "mom."

Wylie originated the term "Momism" in *Generation of Vipers*, and it quickly made its way into the popular lexicon.[16] Momism refers to the woman "who clings to the notion that she deserves worship, money, and power" and who "displays her self-serving, voracity and incredible stupidity by interfering in politics, law, religion, education, art, and science, consistently defeating all attempts at reform or enlightenment."[17] The term gained immense popularity throughout the 1940s as *Generation of Vipers* became a bestseller. Published with a modest initial run of 4000 copies, consistent with Wylie's earlier writ-ings, the book sold out within a week. By 1954, it had sold more than 180,000 copies.[18]

The mother hatred of Momism soon found its way into Hollywood films. In describing Wylie's impact on Hollywood, Mike Chopra-Gant has exam-ined the representation of domineering motherhood in Alfred Hitchcock's *Notorious* (1946). However, I believe that Wylie's influence was evident long before *Generation of Vipers*. The screenplays written by Sturges in the 1930s, most notably *The Power and the Glory* (1933) and *Remember the Night* (1940), directly address the impact of traditional, domineering mothers with characteristics similar to those in Wylie's works.

The moms that Wylie describes not only dominate their husbands but also spoil their male children to such a degree that they have "produced generation after generation of infantilized men, incapable of breaking free from the 'apron strings' and the 'silver cord' the 'mom' used to bind her children to her."[19] *The Power and the Glory* (1933), for which Sturges wrote the screenplay, pre-sents Sally Garner (Colleen Moore) as manipulative and domineering. Her actions toward her husband, Tom Sr. (Spencer Tracy), and her son, Tom

Jr. (Phillip Trent), are explicitly portrayed as destructive. Tom Jr. is in fact a compelling case study of the disastrous impact of "antiquated notions" of mother love. When Tom Jr. returns home after being expelled from college, Tom Sr. (Spencer Tracy) expresses his frustration to Sally: "You've spoiled him, and you ought to have sense enough to see it. You treated him like a baby his whole life. Look at him—irresponsible, useless, kicked out of college for a nasty mess. I'd like to be proud of him, Sally. I'm ashamed of him."[20] When Tom Sr. says that he is leaving to stay at the club, Sally replies, "Stay as long as you please, for all I care." Once Tom leaves, mother and son embrace, as they commiserate over their difficulties:

> Tom Jr.: That's telling him, mother. Thanks.
> Sally: You don't know what I have to put up with.
> Tom Jr.: There, there.

The monstrous aspect of the relationship between this mother and son becomes evident after Sally's death, as Tom's new wife, Eve, not only has an affair with Tom Jr. but also becomes pregnant with his child.[21]

The power and influence of mothers is even more pointed in *Remember the Night* (1940), where we see a clear and compelling contrast between two very different conceptions of motherhood. Lee Leander's (Barbara Stanwyck) hateful and hypocritical mother mouths Christianity but raises a thief, whereas loving Mrs. Sargent (Beulah Bondi) has brought up an upstanding and charitable district attorney. In trying to finalize a title for the film, studio correspondence aptly summed up Sturges's ideas on the narrative: "On Remember the Night we would like to get title which suggests some of the story theme, namely: that environment of love and affection in home contrasted with environment of hate makes for two different personalities in two main characters in later life."[22]

Sturges's next film, *The Great McGinty* (1940), moves the focus of motherhood away from negative portrayals such as the characters of Sally Garner and Lee Leander's mother. What emerges instead, however, is not progressive, 1940s-style modernity, but rather a return to Victorian ideals of motherhood. Dan McGinty's (Brian Donlevy) marriage to his secretary, Catherine (Muriel Angelus), is presented as a matter of political expediency, and it provides him with not just a wife but also two children. As Dan grows increasingly fond of the children and devoted to Catherine, she uses her role as a mother to shape his social conscience, a process which begins when she tells Dan that her son fought with a boy who called McGinty a "grafter." McGinty is contrite, and he begins to listen to her opinions on social issues as he experiences "the temptation of goodness." Catherine pleads, "Doesn't it mean anything to you to stop little children from being exploited in dark, airless factories when they ought to be out playing in the sunshine?" Her pleadings originate from her position as a mother, and the concerns she raises are consistent with traditional conceptions of acceptable political involvement for women, namely causes involving children.

Throughout his career, Sturges continued to adjust his portrayal of motherhood. Three works in particular have at their core the construction of and appreciation for the ideal mother. These include an unproduced screenplay, titled *Matrix*, and two films, *The Miracle of Morgan's Creek* and *Hail the Conquering Hero*. Each emphasizes a distinct and different period in a woman's life. *Matrix* posits motherhood as a woman's primary instinct even before marriage, which can cause dysfunction in her other relationships. *The Miracle of Morgan's Creek* takes up the onset of motherhood. Finally, *Hail the Conquering Hero* presents the mature, older mother. Through these works Sturges constructs the ideal mother in traditional, Victorian terms, as passive, serene, wise. Importantly, however, Sturges ascribes to this role an immense power. Sturges's mothers, when "properly" constituted, provide the moral core for their worlds.

THE DEARLY LOVED BUT UNPRODUCED MATRIX

> It is one of the two stories I have carried around in my head since landing in Hollywood, one of the two stories I tried for many years to persuade someone to let me direct.
>
> —Preston Sturges on *Matrix* (1947)[23]

Sturges began pitching the idea for *Matrix* in 1933. Over the next twenty-five years, he would continue to revise the screenplay for a number of different studios. His efforts resulted in the sale of the script several times, most notably to Twentieth Century-Fox in both 1936 and 1946.[24] Darryl Zanuck, however, had little interest in the project: "I frankly was not very enthusiastic and neither was Julian [Johnson] . . . I sincerely do not believe it has the freshness or originality associated with your previous accomplishments."[25] Sturges's response to Zanuck acknowledged frustration that "no one has ever seen eye to eye with me on it." He then continued to revise a script he was deeply invested in.

Indeed, *Matrix* is a curious project. Although no mother appears in the screenplay, its principal theme is motherhood. In a foreword to the script written in 1950, he explains the point of the story: "You have often heard it said, 'What can she possibly see in that bum? Why does she stick to him?' This is an attempt at an explanation."[26] In a different draft of the story, Sturges explains, "This is the story of a woman whose love impulses were somewhat mixed up and whose life, as a consequence of this condition, became complicated."[27]

The *Matrix* story involves three characters, a young woman named Madeleine, a somewhat handsome, poor, ne'er-do-well named Tommy, and a rich, handsome, and tall executive named Gerald Craig.[28] The orphaned Madeleine lives with her spinster aunt. To make ends meet, Aunt Emmy takes in a boarder, Tommy, whom Sturges describes as follows:

Tommy had honey-colored hair and black eyebrows and deep blue eyes but that should not have blinded a person to the fact that he was a tramp, at least not a person as intelligent as she [Madeleine]. When I say tramp, I exaggerate, but you will know what I mean. His mouth was the giveaway. It was a little too loose and a little too small and the lips curled pettishly when he was crossed. He had been spoiled since infancy, of course . . . You will have noticed that there is an aristocracy of beauty, the members of which do not obey the ordinary laws of social intercourse . . . Tommy belonged to this aristocracy, women adored him, and even sane men.[29]

The third member of the triangle, Gerald Craig, is described by Sturges as follows: "easily as good looking, although not beautiful, two inches taller, and one year younger [than Tommy]. His mouth was firm and his expression pleasant."[30] Sturges then lays out the shape of this triangle: "Gerald could have any woman in the world and adored Madeleine. Madeleine could have Gerald and the Craig millions and adored Tommy. Tommy tolerated her . . . and everybody else. It was very irritating."[31]

While living with Madeleine and Aunt Emmy, Tommy falls in love with Madeleine, who works at a company run by Gerald Craig. At a company party, Gerald meets and immediately falls in love with Madeleine as well. Tommy senses Gerald's feelings and, while drunk, picks a fight with him. Tommy loses the fight, and Madeleine, feeling sorry for him, rushes to comfort him while admonishing Gerald for picking on someone weaker than he. Tommy capitalizes on that pity, and soon he and Madeleine elope. Eventually, Madeleine realizes her mistake in marrying Tommy:

The scales fell from her eyes, and she saw what she had married: not a conquering hero, not a brain to conjure with, not an embryo tycoon, not even a good bond salesman. Just a dub. A little too handsome, a little too weak, a little too dumb to get along, much too conceited, but pleasant if you rubbed him the right way.[32]

As Madeleine contemplates her mistake, she comes to realize that she cannot leave Tommy, because she is "tied to him by the strongest bond there is." Sturges describes this bond:

It isn't pity exactly nor could one call it a bond of weakness, but it is that thing which turns mother rabbits into tigresses when their young are imperiled, that thing which causes congenital weaklings to be cherished instead of strangled, that thing which makes the runt the favorite of the litter. His failures, his hopes, his stupid conceit become as the faltering steps, the vacant expression and the idiotic utterances of a first-born to its mother.[33]

Madeleine, in other words, loves Tommy as a mother rather than as a wife. She has confused mother love with romantic love. Sturges makes that explicit in describing her differing attitudes toward the two male central characters, as he describes Madeleine's feelings for both men:

She loved Tommy as one loved the puling child, tenderly, angrily, pityingly, hoping to one's private self that it will grow up some day perhaps and go away. She loved Gerald as one loves a man. She loved his strength, his mind, and, must I say it, his physical self. She owned Tommy. She wishes to belong to Gerald.[34]

Madeleine stays with Tommy, finds a job for him, and puts up with and excuses his excessive drinking because of a perceived need to protect him. She realizes that she will not be able to leave him until he is able to stand on his own: "Not until he did not need her any more. Thus spoke her mother love. Thus spoke her conscience."[35]

Sturges struggled to come up with an appropriate ending for *Matrix*. Of course, Madeleine and Gerald are joined in the end. Perhaps the most significant difference between many versions of the script lies in *how* the plot resolves. In one version, Tommy commits suicide. In another, he is publicly humiliated when it is discovered that he has known about his wife's affair with Gerald for years and put up with it because it provided him with a good job with Gerald's company. However, Sturges's last version, written in 1958, conveys his clearest thinking on motherhood. Sturges explains:

One day she [Madeleine] feels ill but the illness turns out to be a very normal one. She is going to have a child . . . her mother love, finally will be centered upon that for which it was intended. Everything must be done to protect the child, to put it in the safest place, to give [it] every chance in life! Her husband comes home whining, another deal has flopped, he has been drinking a little, he wants sympathy. The girl looks at him through entirely new eyes. She tells him to go to hell, to drink himself to death, to do what he likes. She is leaving. Happily she puts on her hat. Happily she picks up her gloves and snaps her bag shut. Happily she throws open the door. Sunlight floods in upon her with a burst of music. The music swells as she trips gaily down the stairs, faster and faster. We know exactly where she is going.[36]

In all versions of the *Matrix* script, Madeleine is presented as a sympathetic character who simply lacks the proper object for her love. The ending of the script is similar to the conclusion of *The Miracle of Morgan's Creek*. As we shall see, in both, motherhood or impending motherhood turns women who have been faced with serious difficulties into mature, properly focused mothers. Though *Matrix* was never produced, it provides a fascinating commentary on Sturges's conception of women and motherhood. Women are born to be mothers. Motherhood is their primary instinct. Sturges makes this point repeatedly in all versions of the script. His association with it for so many years points to his tremendous interest in the topic of motherhood and its place in women's lives. Even late in his life, Sturges continued to pitch *Matrix*, as in a letter to the writer Leonard Lewis Levinson:

Matrix has to do with the two different kinds of love that all women have . . . and that sometimes conflict: the passionate and the maternal. It's an awfully nice story and every woman in the world will recognize herself in the heroine.[37]

Later that same year, Sturges changed the title to the more universal *A Woman's Story*, hoping that the new title would help Hollywood studios recognize the market potential of his efforts. However, some of the sharpest criticism of this project came from women, as in a letter from Paramount's Margaret Webster, in which she writes, "the only danger seems to me to be that one dislikes Tommy so heartily all the way through that Madeleine seems like a kind of dope by being bothered with him!"[38]

MOTHERHOOD AS MIRACLE

He [Sturges] has spoofed that most sacred institution, that most unapproachable mystery—motherhood.
          —Bosley Crowther on *The Miracle of Morgan's Creek*[39]

Especially illustrative of the emphasis placed by Sturges on mothers and motherhood are two comedies released in the same year (1944), which take up the issue from two ends of the maternal spectrum. Whereas *The Miracle of Morgan's Creek* casts a jaundiced eye at society's rules about the onset of motherhood, *Hail the Conquering Hero* looks at the power of an aging mother whose very existence influences the actions of those around her. *The Miracle of Morgan's Creek* and *Hail the Conquering Hero* also represent the box-office high points of Sturges's career.[40]

Pre-Sturges screwball comedies tend to share a common set of characteristics, including upper-class settings and characters, an urban milieu, stylish apartments, glamorous costumes, integration of slapstick physical comedy, no children, and a nearly complete absence of mothers. As Sarah Kozloff has indicated, these films also "share common narrative/thematic threads, in that they generally celebrate play, spontaneity and romance, and revolt against dullness, propriety, and stuffy conventionality."[41] Although the female characters in these films have been celebrated for their unruliness,[42] other assessments argue that the genre focuses on the taming of an all-too-threatening female.[43]

By the time Preston Sturges began filming *The Miracle of Morgan's Creek*, the elements of screwball comedy were firmly in place and recognizable to both producers and audiences as salient generic features. In fact, some critics argue that this period, and U.S. involvement in World War II, signaled the end of screwball comedy (see Leger Grindon's chapter in this volume for a fuller treatment of this genre). The war reshaped social attitudes in numerous ways, and it led Sturges to modify and reshape many of the genre's conventions. First, at the level of iconography, upper-class settings and characters ensconced in stylish urban apartments are gone, replaced by working-class characters living in small-town America. The pace of the big city, so often integral to screwball settings, features childless couples. As David Shumway notes, "the suburban and small town environments of Updike and Lurie are the expected settings for married couples, just as cities are where we expect to find singles and childless couples . . . Couples in cities have children too, though you would barely know it from seeing the relationship films."[44] Sturges's setting, which features both singles and children, is a "family-oriented" small town. In fact, the fear and shame felt by Trudy Kockenlocker (Betty Hutton) upon finding out about her pregnancy leads her to use the "resources" of the town itself to plot her own demise as she contemplates jumping from a bridge into Morgan's Creek. The irony inherent in Sturges's critique of the small town and its residents is direct and unambiguous, as it satirizes the gossiping, judgmental, holier-than-thou neighbors who lead Trudy to contemplate suicide and eventually drive the Kockenlockers out of town. The inherent hardship of Trudy's predicament, and her own role in creating her difficulties, are treated far more sympathetically by Sturges.

The construction of the central couple, as well as their road to marriage, is decidedly different in *Miracle* than in earlier screwball comedies. Part of what makes the ideal couple in screwball comedies easily identifiable is their ability to communicate effortlessly. They speak the same language. As Kozloff has noted, "in screwball, the lovers learn that the other is the only one he/she can converse with."[45] Trudy Kockenlocker and Norval Jones (Eddie Bracken) can hardly talk to one another. The lilt and assuredness of Trudy's speech, particularly in the first half of the film, contrast with Norval's halting stutter. Conversely, Trudy communicates effortlessly with the young soldiers who visit her at work and with whom she spends time at the dance, perhaps suggesting that the soldier she initially "marries"—Ignatz Ratzkiwatski—might have been her ideal partner. The strong, handsome soldiers presented first at Mr. Rafferty's store talking to Trudy and later at the dance provide a striking contrast to the bumbling, 4-F-designated Norval, who is much more reminiscent of screwball comedies' "unsuitable suitors"—such as Dan Leeson, Bruce Baldwin, Miss Swallow, and Julia Seton (*Holiday*). Joe McElhaney has summarized this aspect of Sturges's films: "When a couple is formed in a Sturges film, there is almost always something lopsided and implausible about the pairing. Rarely is there a sense of the meeting of equals central to much romantic comedy of the 1930s."[46] Sturges reverses the order of the traditional romantic love triangle so that the mismatched couple wind up together in the end. Under the category of "be careful what you wish for," Norval Jones, Trudy's repeatedly spurned suitor, eventually gets what he has desired since childhood.

Not only do the setting and characters in *The Miracle of Morgan's Creek* depart from conventional screwball comedy standards, the film's plot really begins where other screwball comedies end. Traditional screwball comedies end with marriage, remarriage, or the promise of marriage. Here only *after* Trudy has become a mother is the way paved for her family to be properly constituted. In a scathing review, James Agee saw in this premise evidence of a basic disdain for the characters: "It seems to me clear that Sturges holds his characters, and the people they comically represent, and their predicament, and his audience, and the best potentialities of his own work, essentially in contempt."[47] Certainly, for Sturges a key theme in the film is suffering. Sturges wanted both characters to suffer mightily before the *deus ex machina* miracle saves them. In a fairly early treatment, Sturges itemized his thoughts on "what happens to the girl":

She loses her job
She is expulsed from the church
She is thrown out by her family
She steals money from her father and is nearly put in jail
She discovers that she is pregnant
She gets put off a train without ticket and loses her baggage

She is nearly attacked by a motorist and is then arrested when she beats
him up
She is threatened with prosecution by the doctor to whom she goes
She is nearly sent to reform school
She actually commits bigamy and is in danger of going to the peniten-
tiary when . . .
She triumphs over all.[48]

Although some of these actions did not make it onto the screen, the list provides a clear indication of the trials Trudy would have to undergo. It also
indicates Sturges's perspective on her condition: giving birth to sextuplets
and marrying Norval is her "triumph over all." As Sturges describes her,
"Trudy Kockenlocker is quite a girl but being innocent, she is also the elect of
God and accordingly protected . . . her greatest trouble brings her fame and
fortune."[49]

Our introduction to Trudy is marked by her comic unruliness, and that
unruliness, expressed partly through her laughter, leads to her troubles. She
laughs as she finishes singing a comic rendition of "The Bell in the Bay" for
soldiers in the record shop. Trudy is initially surrounded by signs of sexual
unruliness as well, from her suggestive last name, Kockenlocker, to the poster
for "The Nutcracker Suite" that is positioned directly behind her as she turns
down Norval at his request for a date.[50] Trudy makes a spectacle of herself,
and she takes pleasure in that ability. The rest of the film, however, examines
the consequences of that act and its motives. Her laughter is brief, lasting
only until the end of the party. From the next morning on, she rarely laughs.
Furthermore, almost every subsequent scene ends with Trudy in tears—until
the last scene. Her last dialogue line is "I'm so happy."

Virtually all screwball comedies use the deferral of sexual fulfillment as a
plot device to prolong narrative suspense. In *The Miracle of Morgan's Creek*,
the entire process of courtship, engagement, marriage, and pregnancy occurs
within the diegetic space of one night, and a little under four minutes of
screen time in the first quarter of the film. When Papa Kockenlocker (William
Demarest) refuses to allow Trudy to go to the dance that will prove her
undoing, his decision is met with derision by "wise" 14-year-old sister Emmy
(Diana Lynn): "People aren't as evil-minded as they used to be when you
were a soldier, Papa," and later, "If you don't mind my mentioning it, Father,
I think you have a mind like a swamp." Papa is right, however, and Emmy's
decidedly more modern approach to relationships proves to be naive at best.

Although both critics and audiences generally acclaimed *The Miracle
of Morgan's Creek*, it came under pointed attack for its comic treatment of
wartime marriages and promiscuity. It led James Agee to surmise, "The Hays
office must have been raped in its sleep."[51] When confronted repeatedly for

promoting immorality, Sturges gave an explanation that sounds suspiciously like Papa Kockenlocker's admonition to Trudy:

It so happens that I intended *The Miracle of Morgan's Creek* as anything but evil, meretricious and destructive of moral standards. I wanted to show what happens to young girls who disregard their parents' advice and who confuse patriotism with promiscuity. As I do not work in a church I tried to adorn my sermon with laughter, so that people would go to see it instead of staying away from it . . . For failing to make you laugh then, I apologize, but I refuse to plead guilty to "contributing to the delinquency of minors."[52]

The film itself suggests that he was indeed stating his true attitude here. Whereas the litany of proposed hardships experienced by Trudy listed above is presented as a consequence of her indiscretion, the consequences proposed for Norval come as the result of his overreaching desire for Trudy. In the same treatment, Sturges outlines his plan for "what happens to the boy":

He nearly gets pneumonia waiting for her
He is threatened with a shotgun by her father
He is punched in the eye by her brother
He tears his best suit, helping her into the house
He is arrested as a prowler while coming to see her, after having a pot dropped on his head by her sister
He borrows a friend's car but forgets to leave word
He signs his draft registration falsely
He is threatened with Mann Act prosecution for taking her across the state line
He is locked out somewhere without his clothes
He loses his job
He is held up and robbed of all his savings
He smashes up his boss' car
He is fired at by her father
He commits bigamy two or three times in two or three places and
He becomes a national hero, with a commission and a medal.[53]

Furthermore, Sturges proposed that the following crimes be charged to Norval:

1. Impairing the morals of a minor
2. Perjury
3. Impersonating a member of the armed forces

4. Rape
5. Being a spy—agent of a foreign government
6. Vagrancy
7. Abduction
8. Seduction

In the film's final scene, all charges are dropped, and Norval receives his commission and medals. Without either proposing or saying "I do," Norval finds himself the married father of six. Emmy succinctly describes Norval's potential as a patsy—and a father (though decidedly not as a lover): "He was made for it . . . like the ox was made to eat . . . and the grape was made to drink." The romantic conception of marriage imagines a couple whose love is "radically separate" from any relationship to children. As Shumway argues, "children are to be expected, but they have nothing to do with the parents' relationship with each other."[54] Trudy and Norval's relationship, by contrast, begins with the specter of children—many children. Family, instead of romance, is at the core of their relationship. The inference is that Trudy's entire existence from now on will be tied to her role as mother. Her relationship with Norval promises to be anything but "radically separate" from children. Trudy's increasingly tender feelings toward Norval are presented as motherly affection rather than passion.

Most screwball comedies posit outside forces as impediments to the eventual constitution of the romantic couple, whose union is preordained, fated, and written in the stars. Those forces, be they professional imperatives, parental objections, or other societal pressures, must be overcome in order for the pair to be united and/or reunited. Norval and Trudy's union, by contrast, is actually orchestrated by those outside forces. Their marriage is brought about in the same way as most of their earlier difficulties, by sociopolitical forces outside of their control. The sexual activity that leads to Trudy's pregnancy is not nearly as objectionable as her failure in managing the circumstances. "She ought to be ashamed of herself," lawyer Johnson observes of Trudy's situation, "I mean because of her carelessness." Until the birth of the sextuplets, the Kockenlockers are relegated to a rundown farmhouse far outside of town, where Papa struggles to keep livestock out of the house. The only reason Trudy and Norval are praised and commended at the end of the film is because there is something in it for the town and the state—fame, celebrity, and the likely influx of money. When it looks like the town might profit from Trudy's predicament, a would-be tragedy becomes cause for celebration. The reaction of the town and the state to the birth of sextuplets is reminiscent of (and would have been recognizable to wartime audiences as) the celebrity surrounding a real-life set of quintuplets in Canada. *The Miracle of Morgan's Creek* was released less than ten years after the much-celebrated birth of the

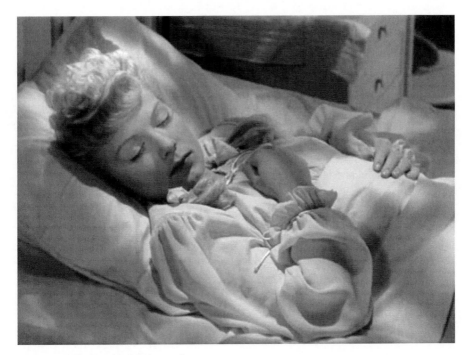

Figure 5.1 The beatific Madonna shot.

Dionne quintuplets, and during their much-publicized childhood. Audiences of the time would have been well-aware of the incredible lengths to which the Canadian authorities, politicians, and medical establishment went in drawing attention to and making money from that family.[55]

Though Trudy and Norval find themselves married at the end of the story, the film doesn't include a wedding scene. Their wedding is "spoken" for them, as the state government declares them to be legally wed—no "I do's" needed.

The final shots of the film make clear Sturges's perspective on Trudy, Norval, and their relationship. Through the miracle of childbirth, Trudy is transformed from a wild, free-spirited youth into a serene and mature mother. This is the endpoint in a transformation that began nine months earlier, the morning after the party. The fullness of her transformation is encapsulated in a single, soft-focus, low-key medium-close-up of Trudy after the birth of the sextuplets.

Rarely does a single shot express so much. Trudy's fast speech and over-excited demeanor (she commented earlier in the film: "You know me. I never get tired") have been replaced by the serene look of an angel. As Kathleen Rowe argues, "Ideology holds that the 'well-adjusted' woman has what Hélène Cixous has described as 'divine composure.' She is silent, static, invisible—composed and divinely apart from the hurly-burly of life, process, and social power."[56] That seems at first glance an apt description of new mother Trudy. The film's final image of her is also visually reminiscent of the ideals inscribed in Victorian, moral motherhood. The agitation at the hospital during childbirth, with scurrying doctors and nurses, suggests a complex and possibly dangerous situation. This is followed by Trudy's supremely heroic accomplishment, and the serene composure that attends it does appear divinely inspired. To underscore this particular irony, the birth takes place at Christmas to a mother who has no memory of getting pregnant. However, while serene in the hospital, Trudy is not without social power. Her power to influence the decisions and actions of all those around her has just begun.

Sturges's conception of motherhood in *The Miracle of Morgan's Creek* is decidedly traditional. Trudy's brief moment of laughter and spectacle-making not only affects her speech and actions but in fact creates in her an increasingly "grotesque" physical body, one which must be hidden from society and the audience. Only a miracle can save her from social banishment. Had Trudy delivered only one child, the consequences for her entire family would have been dire. Instead, the final image of mother Trudy endows her with characteristics of Victorian motherhood: love that exists somewhere between the sentimental and the divine.

HAIL THE VICTORIAN MOTHER

> He [Sturges] is laughing his head off at what someone has called our "cult of Mom" and is making some rather saucy sport with the good old "mother" refrain.
>
> —Bosley Crowther on *Hail the Conquering Hero*[57]

In writing the screenplay for *Hail the Conquering Hero*, Sturges composed "Home to the Arms of Mother," a song that would play a prominent role in the film:

> Home to the arms of mother
> Far away though I may roam, dear
> Hard as the days may appear
> Still every night I go home, dear
> Home to the arms I hold dear.
> *Chorus:*
> Home to the arms of mother
> Safe from this world's alarms
> That's where I spend each night . . . in my dreams
> Far from all daily harms . . . and it seems

I can see you once more
By the old cottage door
As you wait in the gloaming
To welcome me home
Home to the arms of mother . . .
Never again to roam.

Although the song was initially treated as "something to laugh about," Famous Music's Sidney Kornheiser, in a letter to Decca Records, envisioned its commercial potential, hoping it could be a vehicle for Bing Crosby: "I think that if you have the same feeling on this that I have, it can turn out to be a tremendous thing. The subject matter and type of song and everything else is real groovy right now."[58] The song was written during World War II, and Sturges and Paramount hoped that postwar euphoria accompanying the return of soldiers would create a market for it.

"Home to the Arms of Mother" is shamelessly sentimental in its reflection on traditional conceptions of motherhood. The values implicit in the song's lyrics—sacrifice, mother love, comfort—would clearly have resonated with wartime audiences. As Vandenberg-Daves has noted, "mothers were expected to sacrifice on the home front, and Americans sentimentally honored the sacrifice of mothers' sons to the larger cause."[59] However, *Hail the Conquering Hero* was released at a time when Wylie's *Generation of Vipers* was also enjoying both popularity and notoriety. Wylie's preface to the book comments directly on the war, ascribing blame to virtually everyone for the "the peace that failed."[60] Wylie refers to war as the failure of reason and "the infantilism of man,"[61] arguing that the soldier's job is to rationalize that infantilism and to reduce it to "an adult level of efficient co-operation and intelligent action which will bring about . . . the restoration of peace."[62] However, he further argues, soldiers are not equipped to do this. Why?: *MOM*: "It is difficult to put young men in the mood for war when they come to arms fresh from reviling arms, and in the panty-waist, besides, which their moms had put upon them."[63]

Although *Hail the Conquering Hero* does target soldiers and their relationship to moms for humor and irony, Sturges's approach is far less castigating than Wylie's. One reviewer stated, "There is in Sturges' work a kind of obsessive nihilism which drives him to violent and ribald satire of America's most hallowed institutions, motherhood and hero-worship."[64] Yet unlike Wylie's bitter attacks on these institutions, *Hail the Conquering Hero*, like Sturges's earlier *The Miracle of Morgan's Creek*, ultimately refrains from such condemnation, as that same review later points out: "At the end he [Sturges] seems to be saying that he is privileged to satirize such sentiments because he also shares them."[65]

Mrs. Truesmith (Georgia Caine, ironically also the cold-hearted mother who originally set everything in motion in *Remember the Night*) is the center of the film, around whom everything revolves. She is the reason Woodrow (Eddie Bracken) has been hiding out of town, afraid and ashamed to reveal his 4-F status. He cannot bear to disappoint his mother. After all, she is heroic, having sacrificed her husband to the cause. Her living room is a shrine to her late husband, whom she calls "my sergeant."

The six soldiers Woodrow meets at the bar at the beginning of the film are responsible for bringing Woodrow back home. They are also responsible for constructing the increasingly elaborate set of lies that hide Woodrow's true military status, though they are only trying to help. The six soldiers, with Woodrow as number seven, take as their mission and calling the protection of Woodrow's mother, much as the seven dwarfs saw their role as protecting the equally pure and angelic Snow White (Disney's version appeared in 1937). Like Snow White's dwarfs, each soldier has his own unique and easily identifiable personality, and as such they constitute a constellation of comic characters revolving around and committed to the protection of Woodrow's mother. From gruff Sergeant Heppelfinger (William Demarest) to the film's breakout star, Bugsy (Freddie Steele), these Guadalcanal soldiers have just that one ostensible goal. As such, they constitute what Brian Henderson refers to as "flat," cartoonlike characters, a feature he finds in other Sturges films.[66] The wellbeing of Woodrow's mother gives them purpose, much as the Snow White dwarfs are committed to her protection. Each plays his small role, consistent with his abilities, in trying to bring happiness to Mrs. Truesmith. Bugsy is the first to try to remedy the situation, phoning Woodrow's mother from the bar in the opening scene. Later, he doesn't sleep, instead standing guard over the group throughout the night. Heppelfinger does the scheming that he feels is necessary to bring her peace of mind. The rest of the soldiers help construct the fiction that ultimately unravels.

Hail the Conquering Hero most clearly echoes the ideas espoused by Wylie and other Momism critics in its depiction of military life. Wylie described war as final proof of man's "failure to achieve adulthood." Similarly, psychiatrist, prolific author, and consultant to the U.S. Army E. A. Strecker argued that the army was structured such that it could become a surrogate mother, and "the stage would seem to be set for 'child-soldier,' 'mom-officer' relationships, dangerously promoting immaturity."[67] Sturges's soldiers descend on Oakridge much as orphans looking for a surrogate mom, and Mrs. Truesmith becomes exactly that. She takes them all in, cooks for them, cares for them, and loves them. She refers to them as her heroes. In return, the soldiers all do what they can to make her happy.

The character who received perhaps the most attention from both audiences and the industry was Bugsy, played by Freddie Steele. Steele had appeared briefly in *The Miracle of Morgan's Creek*, where Sturges, impressed with his performance, promised to write for him a bigger role in a subsequent film.[68] His strength and size made him an ideal "Bugsy," an orphaned soldier whose condition the sergeant describes by saying, "He got a little shot up, that's all." Bugsy speaks slowly, with the drawl of someone who has suffered a brain injury. He keeps repeating the line, "You shouldn't do that to your mother." James Harvey describes him as a monomaniac, whose "quiet, lowering, steadily watching way" is singularly focused on Woodrow's mother.[69] Woodrow ascribes to him a "mother complex."

The lies concocted by Woodrow and the rest of the soldiers eventually unravel. However, the means by which the truth emerges provide the key to Woodrow's maturation to adulthood. Risking disappointment in his mother's eyes, Woodrow reveals the truth to the entire town in a speech at the end of the film. In other words, he risks the loss of his mother's love on top of having no military "mother substitute" to fall back on. Such is the price of entry into adulthood. For this honesty and maturity (perhaps as a substitute for military bravery), Woodrow, in another "miracle" ending, is rewarded by retaining not only the mother's love he treasured most, but also the "love" of the entire town.

Whereas *The Power and the Glory* paints an entirely negative portrait of traditional motherhood, *Hail the Conquering Hero* contains what may be Sturges's most optimistic treatment of it. First, motherhood here, as in *Miracle of Morgan's Creek*, is a powerful yet passive force. Woodrow's mother does nothing directly to advance the narrative. However, all the narrative actions revolve around her. Her position as a mother makes those around her go to great lengths to protect her. This is a perspective consistent with traditional conceptions of motherhood and mother love. The film depicts an exceedingly sentimental societal view of motherhood. When the townspeople band together in welcoming Woodrow home, they burn the mortgage on his mother's house in a ceremony at the church, and the Reverend Dr. Upperman explains their sentiments:

Homecoming ... what a beautiful word. Home to the arms of his mother, the widow of yet another hero cut down in the bloom of young manhood. The arms of a mother who struggled through poverty and privation to raise her boy rightly and courageously, that he might follow in the honorable footsteps of his father. The years were hard, not always was there work and the winds of reality blew coldly against this frail woman protecting her infant son.

Yet here, as in *The Miracle of Morgan's Creek*, the small town's actions are far more suspect than are those of Woodrow and the soldiers, who simply want peace and happiness for Woodrow's mother. The townspeople have more complex motives. They didn't burn the mortgage when Mrs. Truesmith lost her husband; they left her alone to struggle through those times. When Woodrow returns as a "hero," when they can bask in a bit of his glory and can benefit from his fame and celebrity, then the mortgage is forgiven.

In *The Miracle of Morgan's Creek* and *Hail the Conquering Hero*, the difficulties the protagonists must overcome are largely the result of towns-people's meddling. Social forces in both films act as foils against which the passive goodness of Trudy and Mrs. Truesmith shines more brightly. Sturges refers to such characters in his scripts as "busybodies" and "gossip-ing old maids." In the towns that crowd Sturges's characters, individuals see themselves as representing constituencies, and as such they see their role not as individuals making moral judgments but instead as selfless agents of larger forces—the bank, the law, the government, the military, the town—doing what is required to exert and maintain social control. Set against this unruly and garrulous backdrop, the restoration of order in both films involves the reaffirmation of mother's proper place as the moral core of the reconstituted society.

Wylie's writings and Sturges's films address and at times attack the "problem" of motherhood. Yet the two writers place the blame for such problems on distinctly different sources. For Wylie, the Victorian mother is at fault for the problems plaguing American society; she acquires power by instilling guilt and shame and then uses her immense power to emasculate and destroy those around her. Sturges played with that concept early in his career, as is especially evident in *The Power and the Glory*. His later comedies, however, fully refashion the source of the problem. Sturges does indeed mock "Momism," but, as both *The Miracle of Morgan's Creek* and *Hail the Conquering Hero* demonstrate, the power of mothers must struggle against an almost equally powerful social force: a hypocritical, greedy, self-serving society.

Motherhood, for Sturges, is a powerful and admirable force. It is far from Kathleen Rowe's conception of the powerful, unruly woman. It is equally distinct from Wylie's construction of motherhood as a plague upon civilization. The properly constituted society at the end of Sturges's films is matriarchal. Mrs. Truesmith's moral authority is one of the rare, consist-ently commendable impulses in *Hail the Conquering Hero*. Similarly, Trudy Kockenlocker/Jones provides the town of Morgan's Creek with its most prominent and noteworthy achievement. Although they cannot overcome the selfish impulses and idiotic decisions of the surrounding society, such mothers accomplish great things. Sturges, whose own "unruly" mother wanted to live life to the fullest,[70] turns out to be the comic screenwriter-director who values Victorian motherhood—properly separated from roman-tic love—the most. In this, as in so many other matters, Sturges's vision worked against the grain.

NOTES

1 Stanley Cavell, *Pursuits of Happiness: The Hollywood Comedy of Remarriage* (Cambridge, MA: Harvard University Press, 1981), 18.

2 Sturges's relationship to his mother, Mary Desti, has been well documented. Married and divorced numerous times, Desti moved with Preston to Europe when he was very young. The two lived a rather bohemian lifestyle, where they travelled with her good friend Isadora Duncan, and associated with an assortment of well-known figures including Aleister Crowley, Paris Singer, Theda Bara, and Marcel Duchamp. Sturges famously said that although he loved his mother, he didn't seek her approval. He did, on the other hand, crave approval from his bourgeois businessman stepfather, Solomon Sturges. Writing about Preston's early relationship with his mother, Geoffrey O'Brien states: "[Mary] had little interest in tending to the emotional needs of her son . . . It would be poor form for [Sturges] to show his hurt any more bitterly, but he gets his revenge through satiric demolition of everything she took seriously. His accounts of her husbands and lovers leave an aftertaste of sullen jealousy." Geoffrey O'Brien, *Castaways of the Image Planet* (Washington, DC: Counterpoint, 2002), 62. Along similar lines, Diane Jacobs comments on the psychological implications of Preston's childhood on his films: "[portrayals of motherhood] can be read . . . as wish fulfillment alternatives to the self-interested and volatile Mary Desti." Diane Jacobs, *Christmas in July* (Berkeley, CA: University of California Press, 1992), 162.

3 Rebecca Jo Plant, *Mom: The Transformation of Motherhood in Modern America* (Chicago, IL: University of Chicago Press, 2010), 2.

4 Plant, 119.

5 Quotation from Eugene Pharo, "This Mother's Day Business," *American Mercury* 41 (May 1937), 62.

6 Linda Kerber, *Women of the Republic: Intellect and Ideology in Revolutionary America* (Chapel Hill, NC: University of North Carolina Press, 1980), 200.

7 Plant, 5. Such transformation is certainly a fitting description of the characters played by Eddie Bracken in Sturges films.

8 Jodi Vandenberg-Daves, *Modern Motherhood: An American History* (New Brunswick, NJ: Rutgers University Press, 2014), 6.

9 Geoffrey Gorer, *The Americans: A Study in National Character* (London: Cresset Press, 1948), 45.

10 Transcript of the Twentieth Anniversary Dinner in honor of President William A. Neilson, p. 59, 16 November 1937, Smith College Club of New York City records, quoted in Plant, 1.

11 Dorothy Dix, "Life Lines: 'Mother Love' That Shuts Door of Opportunity Is the Worst Type of Self Love," quoted in Plant, 4.

12 Vandenberg-Daves, 97.

13 Vandenberg-Daves, 97–8.

14 Truman Frederick Keefer, *Philip Wylie* (Boston, MA: Twayne, 1977), 102.

15 *Gladiator* helped inspire the character of Superman and *When Worlds Collide* inspired the comic strip *Flash Gordon*. Keefer, *Philip Wylie*, 48.

16 Wylie, *Generation of Vipers* (New York: Farrar & Rinehart, 1942), 185.

17 Keefer, 100. On the origins of "Momism," see *Oxford English Dictionary* [online resource]. Available at <http://www.oed.com.proxy2.ulib.iupui.edu/view/Entry/121023?> (last accessed 22 August 2014).

18 Wylie himself insisted that he was not a misogynist. His supporters have argued him to be a proto-feminist, whose goal was to free women from the ideas and ideals inherent in moral motherhood – ideals which were intended to keep women tied to the domestic.

19 Chopra-Gant, "Hollywood's 'Moms' and Postwar America," 127.

20 Sturges's screenplay for *Easy Living* (1937) also addresses the dysfunctional family relationship between successful husband, extravagant spendthrift wife and lazy, spoiled son, but from the perspective of comedy.

21 The writing of *The Power and the Glory*, coming so soon after Sturges's work on *The Invisible Man*, may well have been influenced by the destructive conceptions of motherhood espoused by Wylie. Certainly, Sally (who bears the same name as Wylie's ex-wife) exhibits characteristics consistent with Wylie's attack on motherhood.

22 "Night letter to New York," dated 8 November 1939. Preston Sturges Papers (Collection 1114). Department of Special Collections, University Research Library, University of California, Los Angeles.

23 Letter from Sturges to Darryl Zanuck, 24 February 1947. Preston Sturges Papers.

24 Contract between Preston Sturges and Twentieth Century-Fox Film Corporation, 16 December 1946. Preston Sturges Papers.

25 Letter from Darryl Zanuck to Sturges, 20 February 1947. Preston Sturges Papers.

26 Matrix screenplay, 1950. Preston Sturges Papers.

27 Matrix screen story, 1933. Preston Sturges Papers.

28 In subsequent drafts of the screenplay the names are changed. The woman's name changes from Madeleine to the more girlish Candy and then to Cissy. The rich, handsome suitor is later named Stephen Craig. However, the ne'er-do-well is always known by the childish nickname "Tommy." It is interesting that by 1957, when Sturges is again attempting to sell the story in an extended treatment, all three of these characters remain nameless, known only as "the orphaned girl," "the boarder," and "the rich and powerful man."

29 Matrix screen story, undated. Preston Sturges Papers.

30 Matrix screen story, undated. Preston Sturges Papers.

31 Matrix screen story, undated. Preston Sturges Papers.

32 Matrix screen story, undated. Preston Sturges Papers.

33 Matrix screen story, undated. Preston Sturges Papers.

34 Matrix screen story, undated. Preston Sturges Papers.

35 Matrix screen story, undated. Preston Sturges Papers.

36 Synopsis for Matrix, 21 March 1957. Preston Sturges Papers.

37 Letter to Leonard Louis Levinson, Esq. from Sturges, 18 July 1958. Preston Sturges Papers.

38 Letter from Margaret Webster to Sturges, 6 August 1940. Preston Sturges Papers.

39 Bosley Crowther, "The Screen," *The New York Times*, clipping in Preston Sturges Papers.

40 At the box office *The Miracle of Morgan's Creek* outperformed all of Sturges's earlier films. On a budget of $775,000, *Miracle* registered domestic returns of nearly $9 million in 1944, making it (according to biographer Curtis) the biggest hit of the year. James Curtis, *Between Flops: A Biography of Preston Sturges* (New York, NY: Limelight Editions, 1984), 190.

41 Sarah Kozloff, *Overhearing Film Dialogue* (Berkeley, CA: University of California Press, 2000), 171.

42 Kathleen Rowe, *The Unruly Woman* (Austin, TX: University of Texas Press, 1995), 125–36.

43 Diane Carson, "To Be Seen But Not Heard: *The Awful Truth*," in *Multiple Voices in Feminist Film Criticism*, ed. Diane Carson, Linda Dittmar, and Janice Welsch (Minneapolis, MN: University of Minnesota Press, 1994), 213–25.

44 David Shumway, *Modern Love: Romance, Intimacy, and the Marriage Crisis* (New York, NY: New York University Press, 2003), 201.

45 Kozloff, 173–4.

46 Joe McElhaney, "Fast Talk: Preston Sturges and the Speed of Language," in *Cinema and Modernity*, ed. Murray Pomerance (New Brunswick, NJ: Rutgers University Press, 2006), 287.

47 James Agee, "Films; *The Miracle of Morgan's Creek*," *The Nation*, 5 February 1944, clipping in Preston Sturges Papers.

48 "Miracle Story," 27 July 1942. Preston Sturges Papers.

49 "Design for the story," 22 July 1942. Preston Sturges Papers.

50 It is interesting to note that these two jokes suggest confinement and emasculation of the man, and further the notion of matriarchy in the film.

51 Agee, "Films: *The Miracle of Morgan's Creek*."

52 Letter from Sturges to Mrs. George F. Kaufman, 4 April 1944. Preston Sturges Papers.

53 Letter from Sturges to Mrs. George F. Kaufman, 4 April 1944. Preston Sturges Papers.

54 Shumway, *Modern Love*, 201.

55 The Dionne quintuplets were born on May 28, 1934 in Ontario, Canada. All five were girls. They were the first known set of quintuplets to survive infancy. Just months after their birth, the quintuplets' parents were found to be unfit, and custody of the children was given over to the government of Ontario. Under the Dionne Quintuplets Guardianship Act of 1935, the sisters were made Wards of the King. The DaFoe Hospital and Nursery was built near the girls' birthplace, and Dr. Allan Roy DaFoe became legal guardian. The hospital's outdoor playground included an observation area where tourists could view the girls from behind one-way screens at regular times each day. The quintuplets became a popular tourist attraction in Ontario, where it is estimated that 6000 tourists per day, and 3 million overall visited what became known as "Quintland." The attraction brought in to the Ontario government approximately $51 million. See esp. Pierre Berton, *The Dionne Years: A Thirties Melodrama* (New York, NY: Norton, 1978).

56 Rowe, 31.

57 Bosley Crowther, "The Screen," *The New York Times*, 10 August 1944, clipping in Preston Sturges Papers.

58 Letter to Dave Kapp, Decca Records, from Sidney Kornheiser, 27 October 1943. Preston Sturges Papers.

59 Vandenberg-Daves, 173.

60 Wylie, iii.

51 Wylie, 256.

62 Wylie, 260.

63 Wylie, 260.

64 "Hollywood: 1944 style: A review of last year's best performances," *New Leader*, 6 January 1945, clipping in Preston Sturges Papers.

65 "Hollywood: 1944 Style: A Review of Last Year's Best Performances," *New Leader*, 6 January 1945, clipping in Preston Sturges Papers.

66 Henderson comments on this aspect of Sturges's work in relation to *Sullivan's Travels* with his description of "the eight stooges" who follow Sullivan on his journey. Brian Henderson, "Cartoon and Narrative in the Films of Frank Tashlin and Preston Sturges,"

in *Comedy/Cinema/Theory*, ed. Andrew Horton (Berkeley, CA: University of California Press, 1991), 168–70.

67   E. A. Strecker, *Their Mother's Sons: The Psychiatrist Examines an American Problem* (Philadelphia, PA: J. B. Lippincott, 1946), 119.

68   Letter from Sturges to Cpl. Norman Geld, 14 July 1944. Preston Sturges Papers.

69   James Harvey, *Romantic Comedy in Hollywood, from Lubitsch to Sturges* (New York, NY: Knopf, 1987), 641.

70   In one of her last conversations with Preston, Mary Desti explained the reasons for the rather unorthodox, bohemian lifestyle she imposed on both herself and Preston: "I know that you don't approve of very much in my life. But believe me, I was only trying to find happiness."

CHAPTER 6

"These Are Troublous Times": Social Class in the Comedies of Preston Sturges

Christopher Beach

In the first act of Preston Sturges's screenplay for the 1937 screwball comedy *Easy Living*, the film's female protagonist Mary Smith (Jean Arthur) is riding on the upper level of an open-roofed double-decker bus when a very expensive sable coat falls out of the sky onto her head. As it turns out, the coat has been thrown from the balcony of a Park Avenue residence by J. B. Ball (Edward Arnold), a wealthy Wall Street banker. This incident initiates a series of events that hinge on class differences, their endless comic possibilities, and their ultimate resolution at the end of the film. Though *Easy Living* was directed by Mitchell Leisen, Sturges's imprint on the film can be felt most strongly, both in the class-based theme and in the zany comic tone. The scene in which the coat falls on Mary's head is not only one of the most memorable moments in any 1930s screwball comedy; it is also emblematic, I would argue, of Sturges's characteristic treatment of social class.

Sturges adapted the screenplay of *Easy Living* from a "screen story" by Vera Caspary, in which a working-class girl steals a mink coat from a wealthy woman. Sturges takes the detail of the coat from Caspary, but he turns the narrative completely around: instead of the coat being stolen by an angry young woman who feels slighted by her employer, it falls on the head of an innocent young woman who has no idea either of the value of the coat or of the identity of its owner. The falling sable and its aftermath—in which Mary is mistaken for Ball's mistress and given a suite at a luxury hotel before meeting and falling in love with his son—is a variation both on the good-fairy narrative and on the rags-to-riches narrative. Yet at the same time, the film is a devastating satire of class relations during the Depression years. It is, in fact, Mary's level-headed intelligence that ultimately saves Ball from bankruptcy and facilitates both the preservation of his fortune and his reconciliation with his son. As I will demonstrate in this essay, Sturges used variants of these same class-based themes in a number of his films, sometimes moving more toward a conventional form of social satire and sometimes gravitating toward a form of parody in which the levels of irony are so densely woven as to make a clear satirical message unreadable.

The fact that the films written and directed by Sturges frequently deal with issues of social class should hardly come as a surprise, given that the period during which he established his career—first as a playwright, then as a screenwriter, and finally as a director—coincided with the years of the Great Depression. As Andrew Horton notes, Sturges appears to have had a fascination with both rags-to-riches and inter-class narratives, and a number of his plays, screenplays, and films contain "sudden transitions in socioeconomic status."[1] Sturges explores class difference and various forms of social mobility in so many of his works that class can be said to constitute the single most important motif of his oeuvre. His 1932 play *Child of Manhattan*, subsequently made into a movie by Columbia Pictures (Edward Buzzell, 1933), involves the relationship of the son of the immensely wealthy Paul Vanderkill with a dime-a-dance girl. In Sturges's script for *The Power and the Glory* (William K. Howard, 1933), the protagonist Tom Garner (Spencer Tracy) rises from an uneducated railway "trackwalker" to become a powerful railroad tycoon. In *Remember the Night* (Mitchell Leisen, 1940), a young attorney from a respectable middle-class family (Fred MacMurray) develops a romantic relationship with the working-class shoplifter (Barbara Stanwyck) whose case he is assigned to prosecute. In *The Great McGinty* (1940), the protagonist rises from a homeless "bum" to become mayor of a large city and then governor of the state. Among Sturges's most memorable female characters are Jean Harrington (Barbara Stanwyck) in *The Lady Eve* (1941) and Gerry Jeffers (Claudette Colbert) in *The Palm Beach Story* (1942), both of whom are able to use their intelligence, cunning, and physical appearance to manipulate the class system, exploiting the stupidity and gullibility of the upper classes in order to improve their own position.[2]

In this essay, I focus on three comedies written and directed by Sturges in the early 1940s: *Christmas in July*, *Sullivan's Travels*, and *The Palm Beach Story*. While each of these films comments on such issues as social class, social ambition, and social status, each takes a very different approach to these issues. *Christmas in July* contains a relatively straightforward form of class-based satire, involving a working man's attempt to improve his economic and social status by means of winning first prize in a slogan contest for a coffee company. *Sullivan's Travels* involves the almost diametrically opposed (and largely failed) attempt of a wealthy and commercially successful director of film comedies to experience the life of the common man. Finally, in *The Palm Beach Story*, Sturges creates a social fantasy located somewhere between a cartoon and a fairy tale. Here, I will argue, he shifts from a mode of satire to one of parody in his treatment of a social world in which class relations are so fluid as to be practically meaningless.

The distinction between satire and parody is important for an accurate understanding of the treatment of social class within American film comedy. Though it is similar to satire in establishing a critical distance from its target through the use of irony, parody differs in its more self-reflexive or inter-textual reference to established conventions, genres, or historical figures. As a mode of what Dan Harries has called "heightened heteroglossia," parody "proudly displays its multi-voicedness by appropriating from a variety of preformed sources," including individual films, film genres or cycles, and performers within those films.[3] Since parody is a mode that always involves a doubleness—referring to previous source-texts as well as to a real world of social particulars—it is also less univocal in its articulation and critique of class distinctions and their impact on individuals or groups.

As Jeff Jaeckle notes in the introduction to this volume, Sturges's own class background was itself the product of a complex set of ancestral, social, and economic factors. His mother, born Mary Dempsey, was the daughter of poor Irish-Catholic parents in Chicago. Wishing to escape the dreary circum-stances of her family background, Mary did everything she could to raise her social rank as well as that of her son. After a brief early marriage during which she gave birth to Preston, Mary began a liaison with the wealthy stockbroker Solomon Sturges, who raised Preston and gave him his name. The young Preston considered Solomon Sturges his father, and he did not find out the truth about his relation to the Sturges family until the age of twelve, when his mother asked for a divorce. Yet while Solomon's marriage to Mary conferred on the young Preston an identity as a member of the solid upper-middle class, it also brought with it an awareness that Preston's class status was based on a fortunate turn of events, that vicissitudes of good and bad fortune were arbitrary, and that changes in social and economic position could occur at any time. This idea would inform the situations of many of his characters, as when Mary Smith is elevated to the upper class through the accidental fall of a fur coat onto her head, when Jimmy MacDonald is suddenly elevated to a higher socioeconomic status by winning the $25,000 prize in a slogan contest, or, in the opposite way, when John Sullivan suffers a blow to his head that throws his life into a frightening downward spiral.

Another important early influence on the formation of Sturges's ideas about social class was Paris Singer, the lover of Isadora Duncan and a friend of both Sturges and his mother. Raised and educated in England, Singer was heir to a sizable portion of the estate of Isaac Singer, founder of the Singer Sewing Machine Company. With an income estimated at $15,000 a week (the equivalent of perhaps a million dollars a week in today's terms), Singer was a member of the idle, extravagantly wealthy upper class that Sturges would at times satirize in his comedies.[4] Preston's adolescent attitude toward Singer, however, appears to have been one of wide-eyed admiration. Sturges would later tell his wife Louise that Singer "had vastly more to do with shaping my character than Mother had," and that as a boy he had "wanted to be like him."[5] Like the characters of Hopsie Pike in *The Lady Eve* and John D. Hackensacker III in *The Palm Beach Story*, Paris never had to work for a living and remained "the dilettante par excellence," with interests in antiques, airplanes, yachts, cars, technological gadgetry, and beautiful women.[6] Also like Hackensacker, Singer had a sister who had become a princess by marriage into the European aristocracy.

Sturges's thinking about the intricacies of social status had been formed by the time he met his second wife, the upper-class heiress Eleanor Hutton, but his interactions with Eleanor and her family further clarified his class attitudes. The granddaughter of cereal magnate C. W. Post and stepdaughter of Wall Street financier Edward F. Hutton, Eleanor grew up surrounded by wealth and privilege, with an estate in Long Island and a mansion and 350-foot yacht in Palm Beach. Preston and Eleanor's courtship and marriage by elopement transpired like a cross-class romantic comedy: in fact, aspects of Frank Capra's *It Happened One Night*, in which an heiress escapes from her father to share a road adventure with a socially questionable newspaper reporter, may have been drawn in part from Sturges's relationship with Eleanor.[7] The Huttons, socially ambitious and wary of fortune hunters, strongly opposed their daughter's liaison with Sturges, at one point even sending private detectives to follow him in New York City. When Sturges married Eleanor in the spring of 1930, he was 31 and she only 20. Their marriage lasted only two years before it was annulled, but during that time Sturges heard a number of stories from Eleanor about her parents and her grandfather, whose rise from poverty to found an economic empire was the model for the protagonist of Sturges's screenplay *The Power and the Glory*. As Diane Jacobs suggests, Eleanor and her family were a source of fascination and ultimately of artistic inspiration for Sturges: "real American dynasty builders," they were "ruthless in a way, crude certainly, but inventive, philanthropic, fantastically energetic, and among the most powerful people in America."[8] Sturges would never be entirely comfortable with the socioeconomic status of Eleanor and the Huttons, and his affection for Eleanor would not be enough to overcome the differences in culture, wealth, and class affiliation that separated them.

CLASS SATIRE IN *CHRISTMAS IN JULY*

It was during his marriage to Eleanor that Sturges wrote the play *A Cup of Coffee*, which would serve as the basis for *Christmas in July* nearly a decade later. Jacobs calls the play Sturges's "first attempt to grapple with success in America," and we could equally well say that it is his first attempt to deal in a meaningful way with issues of social class.[9] The protagonist, a young coffee salesman named Jimmy MacDonald, works for a company called Baxter's Best Coffee, but enters and wins a slogan contest sponsored by the rival company, Maxford House. Given the fact that the actual Maxwell House Company belonged to Sturges's in-laws, we can safely assume that the play is at least partly informed by Sturges's own experience, especially with respect to its treatment of class.

Sturges did not write the screenplay for the film until the spring of 1940, and the differences between the theatrical and film versions highlight both Sturges's considerable development as a writer and the manifold changes in the social and economic situation of the country, which was emerging from a decade-long economic depression. Though the unemployment rate remained high—an average of 14.6 percent for 1940—it had already fallen considerably from 25 percent in the early 1930s and 19 percent as recently as 1938, and it would continue to decline throughout the first half of the 1940s.[10] The film's protagonist—like that of the play—is a young clerk in a coffee company, whose only hope for socioeconomic advancement appears to be winning a contest that will allow him the financial security to marry the woman (Betty) he loves. When Jimmy enters the Maxford House Coffee slogan contest, three of his co-workers decide to play a practical joke on him, sending a fake telegram announcing that he has won the $25,000 grand prize. In fact, the jury making the decision is still locked in debate, with no winner declared. Since the owner of the company, Dr. Maxford, is unaware of this fact and assumes the telegram to be legitimate, he gives Jimmy a check for $25,000, on the basis of which Jimmy is able to gain a promotion, buy expensive presents for his friends and family, and propose to his fiancée. When events reveal that Jimmy has not won the contest after all, Dr. Maxford confronts him, tears up the check he had given him, and accuses him of dishonesty. The film ends with a final plot twist: the jury decides that Jimmy's entry is the winning slogan after all. Though Jimmy has not yet received the telegram and does not know that he has in fact won, the audience can reasonably assume that another rise in his fortunes will soon take place. Nevertheless, in what would become a trademark of Sturges's films, the "happy ending" remains a somewhat ambivalent one. As Brian Henderson notes, the film's ending leaves Jimmy "stranded on his island of self-doubt, indeed so much so that the twist that he's won the contest after all seems only the film's final gag, necessary to tie up some plot ends but not a resolution of its themes."[11]

The central character of the film is, as Henderson suggests, a more coherent figure than the one we find in the play.[12] The Jimmy of the play starts out as a kind of "1920s wise guy," a less than completely likable character who boasts of being able to con his customers. The play's politics are also more strongly articulated than they are in the film. In his first speech of the play, Jimmy espouses a vaguely socialist ideology, telling his fiancée (named Tulip in the play) that "with things going the way they are now, pretty soon there'll be a sort of general bankruptcy, and then the working man will come into his own." When Tulip asks him if he means to suggest that there will be a revolution, Jimmy replies, "No, just a sort of readjustment," adding that he hasn't "got it all figured out yet." At the same time that Sturges presents him as an exponent of leftist rhetoric, Jimmy is also a more cynical character in the play than he is in the film, claiming that such slogan contests as the one he is entering are "all fixed anyway." In Act II, Jimmy enacts a cynical parody of a celebration of robber-baron capitalism, telling his boss Mr. Baxter that he has no patience for the "namby-pamby methods" of "fair" competition, preferring the practices of men like "Johnny Rockefeller, the elder Morgan, Hill, Fisk, Vanderbilt, Astor, and the rest of them."

By the time Sturges came to write the screenplay in early 1940, it would have seemed an anachronism to cast his protagonist in such overtly ideological terms. In the film, MacDonald's leftist political leanings and boldly cynical attitude have been replaced by an unflappable optimism in the face of constant failure, accompanied by a motivating desire for material success. Though he is more ambitious than most, and perhaps more talented as a writer of slogans, he is essentially the anonymous everyman of corporate America. This change surely reflects Sturges's growing assurance as a writer of comedy: in *Christmas in July*, we witness Sturges's ability—unique among Hollywood writers and directors of the era—to combine a prodigiously brilliant comic sensibility with an ironic viewpoint that is always threatening to puncture the comic veneer.

Already in the film's opening scene, Sturges sets up the class dynamic. Jimmy's girlfriend Betty (Ellen Drew) is describing to him a new kind of efficiency apartment she has just read about, in which a device can turn one room into any of four different rooms, "so that young people without much money can have a lovely four-room apartment for the price of a one-room apartment." The four-rooms-in-one apartment is not only highly impractical for rather obvious reasons which Jimmy quickly points out, but it is also a commodity marketed to potential consumers who desire a more upscale lifestyle but cannot in reality afford it. Like the slogan contest itself, it holds out the illusory promise of quickly attained riches and all the perks that accompany them. When Jimmy points out the flaws in the idea, Betty complains, "Nothing's good enough for you except a palace on Fifth Avenue." Betty's assessment is not far from the truth: Jimmy, as his mother tells him, is "a dreamer," more comfortable in the world of ideas and slogans than in the everyday grind of his job as an office clerk.[13] Jimmy tells Betty that every time he enters a contest and fails to win, it doubles his chances of winning the next one: "It's what you call the law of averages," he confidently proclaims. Jimmy even insists on a new "scientific theory" proving that coffee, rather than keeping people awake at night, actually helps them to sleep. This counter-intuitive belief leads to his slogan, "If you can't sleep at night, it isn't the coffee, it's the bunk."

The social circumstances of the play's other characters have changed as well in terms of their class positioning. Where the Baxter Company of the play is a family business founded by the patriarchal Ephraim Baxter and to be inherited by his sons, the Mr. Baxter of the film is of the second generation and has already inherited his father's money. Anticipating the characters of Hopsie Pike in *The Lady Eve* and John D. Hackensacker in *The Palm Beach Story*, J. B. Baxter (Ernest Truex) is a cautious man who has done nothing to build on his inherited business, and who is unable to act on his own. As he tells Jimmy, "I'm no genius. I didn't hang on to my father's money by backing my own judgment, you know." Baxter's lack of "judgment" allows him to promote Jimmy to a higher-paid position with his own office when he believes him to be the winner of the contest, even though, as Jimmy points out, his ideas are no better after his winning of the contest than they were before.

One of the film's sequences that foregrounds class issues most clearly is that in which Jimmy, believing he has won the $25,000, goes on a shopping spree and brings presents home to his mother and the other members of her working-class ethnic neighborhood. In contrast to the rather static *mise-en-scène* of the office scenes, the street scenes are shot in an almost documentary

Figure 6.1 Jimmy McDonald (Dick Powell) is confused by events in *Christmas in July*.

manner, capturing the communal spirit and proletarian ethos of the local populace. It is also the only part of the film in which Sturges indulges his fondness for slapstick. When the forces of capitalism arrive on the scene—Mr. Schindel (Alexander Carr) to take back his merchandise, and Dr. Maxford (Raymond Walburn) to take back his check—they are pelted with various objects, including a pie, a toy airplane, a rubber-tipped arrow, and, in the case of arch-capitalist Maxford, a large fish and some very ripe tomatoes. The street sequence would be the last time in any of his films that Sturges would depict class conflict in such unambiguous, though thoroughly comic, terms.

Though much of *Christmas in July* can be viewed as fairly broad comedy, the film also reveals a darker argument about social class. The American Dream of material success that Jimmy so wholeheartedly embraces is certainly a fallacy, and perhaps even a joke. (It is, quite literally, a practical joke on Jimmy that makes him think he has won the contest, setting the wheels of the film's plot in motion.) As if to underscore this social critique, Sturges repeats the words "success" and "succeed" in several different contexts. Mr. Waterbury, the office manager, tells Jimmy that although he never expects to have $25,000 of his own, "I'm a success, and so are you if you earn your own living and pay your bills and look the world in the eye." Later, in trying to convince Mr. Baxter to let Jimmy keep his office, Betty tells him that even though most of those who are given their own offices are never "going to succeed," they will still be better off "because they had their chance."

The slogan contest is a potent metaphor for the inherent contradiction between the promotion of a desire for material success and the vast odds against the possibility of ever achieving it. Despite its fairytale plot, the film's vision of America shows clear-eyed realism: for every Jimmy MacDonald who wins first prize in a contest, thousands of lowly clerks sit in long rows of desks with other anonymous clerks. As Mr. Waterbury puts it, "No system could be right where only one half of one percent were successes and all the rest were failures." And yet that is exactly the system that prevails in the world of *Christmas in July*: Jimmy's "success"—itself made possible only by the miraculous intercession of a stubborn employee named Bildocker (William Demarest)—will not change the underlying class system, and it will not help his co-workers to escape their dreary routinized lives or to buy the material goods they desire.[14]

CLASS TRANSVESTISM IN *SULLIVAN'S TRAVELS*

If the representation of class issues in *Christmas in July* is relatively straightforward, that of *Sullivan's Travels* is more difficult to evaluate. On its surface, the film's plot would seem to offer a recipe for a treatment of class relations in prewar America: John L. Sullivan (Joel McCrea), a director of commercially successful Hollywood comedies, decides that instead of making yet another crowd-pleasing comedy he will direct a serious film that will allow him to explore "the modern condition" of "suffering humanity." Donning the attire of a hobo, Sullivan takes to the road, where he hopes to acquire first-hand experience about the lives of the poor and downtrodden, and thus to gain a greater appreciation for their situation.

As written and directed by Sturges, *Sullivan's Travels* is not the politically-engaged satire of the kind one might expect from such a narrative; instead, it is a radically intertextual film that engages in a highly self-conscious discourse about the problem of social representation; as such it is not about class so much as about the representation of class. As Kathleen Moran and Michael Rogin suggest, while the director within the film (Sullivan) desires to "open up a Popular Front window on society," the director of the film (Sturges) "turns that window into a self-reflecting mirror."[15] Both the tone and the genre of *Sullivan's Travels* are highly unstable: just as the protagonist travels to a variety of locales, the film moves through a series of disparate genres, including the road movie (or parody of one), the slapstick comedy, the screwball romantic comedy, the social satire, the melodrama, and the chain-gang prison film. The film also participates in the literary genre of what Eric Schocket has called "class transvestism," in which a middle-class writer, journalist, or, in this case, film director, attempts to "pass" as a member of the working or destitute classes by means of clothing, language, or behavior.[16] Thus, in contrast to the straightforward message about systemic economic inequality in *Christmas in July*, *Sullivan's Travels* presents a more ambiguous narrative, one that highlights both the chasm that divides members of different social classes and the belief that it can be voluntarily bridged.

The differences between the character of Sullivan and the real-life Sturges are themselves telling. While Sullivan is determined to make a social protest film and is only dissuaded from doing so by an encounter with poverty that results in his serious injury, loss of memory, and incarceration, Sturges was infamously apolitical, rarely mentioning Roosevelt or the New Deal, refusing to join either the Screen Writers Guild or the Screen Directors Guild, and contributing virtually nothing to the war effort.[17] We must assume, then, that the entire premise on which the film is based—that a film director would need to go on the road disguised as a hobo in order to discover the truth about the lives of the poor and needy—is not intended to be taken at face value. In fact, as Brian Henderson points out, Sullivan is not a particularly admirable or likable character: "a smug, thick-skinned success, haunted by no fear of failure," Sullivan is "protected as it were by his very mediocrity."[18] Yet, if Sullivan himself represents the "fantasy figure of success" at the beginning of the story, the film's narrative supplies "a return of the Sturgean repressed,"

introducing into the ostensible comedy of Sullivan's voyages "the ghost haunt-
ing all success in Sturges's films—the ghost of failure and poverty."[19]

Moran and Rogin read *Sullivan's Travels* as a parody both of road films such
as William Wellman's *Wild Boys of the Road* (1933) and Capra's *It Happened
One Night* and of Depression-era films of class reconciliation such as *My
Man Godfrey* (1936) and *The Devil and Mrs. Jones* (1941). While the film does
participate in the road movie narrative and tropes intertextually on the road
genre (as do other Sturges films such as *Remember the Night* and *The Palm
Beach Story*), Sturges's use of the road movie does not amount to parody. As
Moran and Rogin note, the decade of the 1930s saw the road narrative used
as a container for everything from socially conscious melodrama (*Wild Boys
of the Road*), to screwball comedy (*It Happened One Night*), to musical fantasy
(*The Wizard of Oz*), to quasi-documentary social problem film (*The Grapes
of Wrath*). While Sturges's movie does not treat these genres in an overtly
parodic way, it does, I would argue, engage in a form of class satire.

Sturges clearly intends the opening sequences of the film as satire, focusing on the excesses and vapidity of the movie business, and in a larger sense
on class privilege and its tendency to isolate the rich and successful from any
accurate understanding of the world outside their protective walls. Sullivan's
speech to his two producers, Mr. LeBrand (Robert Warwick) and Mr. Hadrian
(Porter Hall), is little more than a patchwork of well-worn clichés: Sullivan
talks about holding up "a mirror to life," making a "commentary on modern
conditions," creating "a true canvas of the suffering of humanity," and realizing "the potentialities of film as the sociological and artistic medium that it
is." The speech of the producers—famously punctuated by their interjection
of the line "with a little sex in it" whenever Sullivan tries to describe his ideas
for a serious message film—is equally as vapid in their crass commercialism.

In order to convince Sullivan not to direct *O Brother, Where Art Thou?*, the
producers represent themselves as having worked their way up the socioeconomic ladder from the bottom. When Sullivan makes the argument that he
needs to direct *O Brother, Where Art Thou?* as a response to these "troublous
times," one of the producers asks him the pointed question, "What do you
know about trouble?":

Hadrian: You want to make an epic about misery. You want to show
hungry people sleeping in doorways.
LeBrand: With newspapers around them.
Hadrian: You want to grind out 10,000 feet about hard luck. And all I'm
asking you is, what do you know about hard luck?
Sullivan: What do you mean, what do I know about hard luck? Don't you
think I have. . .
Hadrian: You have not! I sold newspapers till I was twenty, and then

I worked in a shoe store and put my way through law school at night.
Where were you at twenty?
Sullivan: Well, I was in college.
LeBrand: When I was thirteen I supported three sisters and two brothers
and a widowed mother. Where were you at thirteen?
Sullivan: I was in boarding school. I'm sorry!

The producers go on to remind Sullivan of his rapid climb to the top ranks
of Hollywood directors. Alternating rapid-fire dialogue between the two of
them, they enact a parody of the American success story: Sullivan made $500
a week by the age of twenty-four, $750 at twenty-five, $1,000 at twenty-six,
and $2,000 at twenty-seven. This funny scene comprises the only moment
in the film in which Sullivan's class background is explicitly discussed: while
we do not learn the details of his social class, we learn enough to understand
the difficulty he will have in leaving the comfort of his class position, even on
a temporary basis.[20] Though it is Sullivan and not the more pragmatically-
minded Hollywood producers who are the primary object of Sturges's satire,
viewers note at the end of the scene that the stories of economic hardship told
by the producers turn out not to have been entirely authentic. In a film that is
so much about things not being quite what they seem, it turns out that Hadrian
never sold newspapers, and LeBrand, while he did operate a shooting gallery,
borrowed money from his uncle to open it.[21]

Sturges underscores the degree to which Sullivan is removed from any
real understanding of social conditions in the following sequence. When
Sullivan's butler Burrows (Robert Greig) first sees Sullivan wearing the
hobo costume, he turns the tables on his employer, remarking with evident
sarcasm: "Fancy dress, I take it." The butler goes on to tell Sully that he has
"never been sympathetic to the caricaturing of the poor and needy." When
Sullivan insists that he is not attempting to caricature the poor but instead
hopes to gain first-hand experience of their conditions in order to make a film
about them, Burrows admonishes him further. "If you'll permit me to say so,
sir, the subject is not an interesting one. The poor know all about poverty,
and only the morbid rich would find the topic glamorous." When Sullivan
remonstrates that he is "doing it for the poor," the butler replies skeptically,
"I doubt if they would appreciate it, sir. They rather resent the invasion of
their privacy." Sullivan, unwilling to heed the sound advice of his servant,
sets forth on the first of his "travels."

The master–servant dynamic in the film is an interesting one, as the
relationship of Sullivan with his butler and valet stands as a kind of socially-
contained proxy for the more violent expression of class dynamics in later
sequences. Though the butler and valet are clearly subservient to Sullivan
(and economically dependent on him), they do not exhibit any fear of speaking

their mind to him, and they participate actively in his affairs, sewing identity cards into the lining of his boots, bailing him out of jail when he is arrested for stealing his own car, and making arrangements for him to jump onto a freight train as a "tramp." In the prison sequences, the master–servant dynamic is reenacted in far more negative terms in the relationship of the prisoners to the warden, who is known simply as "The Mister." In one scene, we see The Mister floating on a lake on a boat while the chain gang works around him: the iconography is clearly that of the southern plantation master and his slaves, setting up a contrast with the seemingly well-off congregation of the all-black church where the prisoners go to see the picture show.

The longest section of the film—lasting from near the beginning until about the midway point of the narrative—depends on the class-based irony generated by the difficulty Sullivan has in escaping Hollywood, and by extension escaping the world of wealth and privilege to which he belongs. By my count, Sullivan undertakes a total of six "voyages" (not including the unintentional train voyage he takes while in a state of amnesia after being knocked unconscious by the tramp). The first voyage is orchestrated by the studio: Sullivan walks along the road, dressed in his hobo garb, followed closely—in one of the film's marvelous sight gags—by a large "land yacht" containing a retinue including his press agent, a chef, a secretary, a writer, a doctor, a cameraman, and a radio

Figure 6.2 John Sullivan (Joel McCrea) in search of life in *Sullivan's Travels*.

man. Sullivan ends this brief voyage by hopping into a "whippet tank" driven by a precocious thirteen-year-old boy, hoping to escape the land yacht but ending up in a field where the members of his entourage quickly find him.

In his second voyage, Sullivan is once again unable either to make contact with the poor, or to escape Hollywood for any length of time. After taking a job as a handyman for a middle-class widow with the ridiculous Sturgean name of Zeffie Kornheiser (Esther Howard), who dresses him up in her husband's old suit to take him to the movies, Sullivan has to make a quick escape from the house when he becomes the object of her affections. Hitching a ride with a truck driver (already a step down the class ladder from his previous modes of transport), Sullivan realizes on waking the next morning that the end of the driver's route was Hollywood. This sets up the next plot twist: the meeting of Sullivan and "The Girl" (Veronica Lake), a down-on-her-luck actress who has run out of both money and hope. Here, the real and imagined class positions of the two characters take a novel turn. Taking Sully for a real tramp, the girl insists on buying him a plate of ham and eggs. Sullivan, feeling sorry for the girl, offers to help her, prompting her to accuse him of acting "Ritzy." Temporarily abandoning his determination to live as a penniless hobo, he "borrows" his own car (an expensive convertible) and offers to drive the girl wherever she wants to go. This third journey ends quickly when Sullivan is arrested for the theft of the automobile, is bailed out by his butler and valet, and is subsequently returned to his Hollywood home. Here, the class implications are obvious: not only does Sullivan feel entitled to take his car (abandoning the entire objective of his social experiment), but, unlike a real tramp, he receives no punishment for doing so. This humorous episode foreshadows Sullivan's more serious run-in with the law later in the film, when he is arrested and imprisoned for striking the rail yard guard.

The fourth voyage is the first in which Sullivan actually experiences a hint of the life of the tramp. He and the girl ride on a freight train together, both now dressed as hobos. Even in this sequence, however, Sullivan fails to make any real contact with the poor and desperate whose lives he hopes to study. Despite their best efforts to engage a pair of tramps in conversation, Sully and the girl are dismissed as "amateurs" and left alone in a railway car that smells strongly of hog manure. When they get off the train, they are in Las Vegas, where they find the land yacht awaiting them. More pampered than the girl and thus less able to tolerate the life of a tramp, Sullivan has caught the flu during his ride on the freight train and needs several days of bed-rest before he can resume his travels.

The fifth trip is an extraordinary seven-minute montage sequence that takes place in the slums of an unidentified city at night. Sturges presents this sequence with a musical score but no dialogue, taking full advantage of the atmospheric visuals provided by John Seitz's cinematography. This sequence is the turning point in the film, both tonally and narratively. For the first time, we feel we are no longer in a comedy, as Sullivan and the girl finally experience at first hand the life of the desperately poor. They live on the streets, catch fleas and have to be disinfected, attend a Salvation Army sermon, and sleep in a homeless shelter, where Sullivan's boots are stolen by another tramp. Even here, however, the experience of poverty is not entirely authentic: at one point during the night, they take a romantic walk together by a lake in the moonlight, thus demonstrating their ability to leave this assumed life of poverty at any time. The voyage ends when they are forced to look in garbage cans for food: finding the experience too disgusting, they decide to end the adventure.

The sixth and final voyage is taken by Sullivan himself, who, as his publicity agent (William Demarest) tells the press, is "just going out for a quick tour" to hand out $1,000 in $5 bills to the tramps of Kansas City "in gratitude for all they've done for him." Here the irony is clear: not only have the tramps done nothing for Sullivan, but in their few interactions with him they have ridiculed him, refused to speak to him, and stolen his shoes. In a second silent montage, a tramp follows Sullivan into an abandoned train yard, knocks him out and steals his remaining money. When a train kills the tramp as he attempts to pick up loose bills dropped on the tracks, everyone assumes the body to be that of Sullivan, since he is wearing the boots he stole with Sullivan's identity sewn into them.[22] Sullivan wakes up with amnesia and hops on a train for his final, unintended voyage, one that takes him somewhere in the Deep South. When he gets off the train, still groggy from being knocked out, he strikes a railroad guard with a rock and is tried and sentenced to six years hard labor. At this point, because of his hobo clothing and amnesia, Sullivan has literally entered the class that he all along aspired to understand. Sullivan does not regain his memory of who he is until he is in prison, by which time it is too late, since the sadistic warden (Alan Bridge) refuses to listen to him and punishes him for his arrogant attitude.

In the prison, we see further evidence of Sullivan's inability to understand the experience of poverty. When the sympathetic prison trusty (Jimmy Conlin) suggests that Sullivan will have to serve out his time like all the other inmates, Sullivan, who does not seem to have learned anything about the real "suffering of humanity," replies, "They don't sentence picture directors to a place like this for a little disagreement with a yard bull." The trusty is skeptical of Sullivan's identity, since without a shave and a clean set of clothes he hardly looks the image of a film director. "Don't I look like a picture director?" Sullivan asks him. "I've never seen one," the trusty replies. "To me, you look more like a soda jerk, or a plasterer, maybe." Where Sullivan's earlier efforts to play the part of the downtrodden tramp were rejected as phony or amateurish, he is now identified—much to his displeasure—with the members of a working class to which he has never belonged and to whom he feels superior.

Here, more than anywhere else in the film, Sturges seems to be mocking the pretensions of the rich and "successful" who take their success and class privilege for granted. Sullivan does not identify in any way with his fellow prisoners, who are the true representatives of the very class he set out to comprehend.

Several commentators have discussed the sequence in the film in which the minister of an all-black church invites the prisoners to attend a picture show, but the treatment of social class in the scene rarely assumes prominence. In this scene, the issue of socioeconomic class with which the entire film has been concerned is further complicated by the introduction of race. The congregation of the church appears to be well-dressed (most of the men wear coats and ties) and "respectable" members of the black community: if not quite middle-class, they are at least well-removed from obvious signs of poverty. In a highly ironic moment, the minister instructs his parishioners not to act "high" toward the prisoners, since "we is all equal in the sight of God." As they watch the movie, a comic cartoon, all distinctions of both race and class seem to vanish, as all members of the audience laugh together. This moment of idealized social and racial solidarity is of course short-lived: the prisoners go back to their prison, Sullivan gains his release once his identity is revealed (with, apparently, no additional punishment for having hit the railroad guard), and he decides, much to the consternation of his producers and publicists, that he no longer wants to make *O Brother, Where Are Thou?*.

The film's ending leaves us with an ambivalent message. On the one hand, Sullivan's decision to continue to make comedies is motivated by an egalitarian notion that his greatest service to humanity is through providing films that will appeal to the poor and working classes as much as the highbrow audiences that would have seen his more serious film. On the other hand, Sullivan's failed attempt to experience the life of the poor in any meaningful way indicates that any escape from the social class to which he has been conditioned by birth, education, and career success is, in fact, impossible. Like *Christmas in July*, *Sullivan's Travels* presents a forceful message about the systemic inequality and intransigent class stratification of American society. The impact of that message, however, is substantially weakened by the final sequence of the film, in which upbeat sentiments about the salutary effects of comedy almost dispel the concerns about poverty and inequality that Sullivan had earlier seemed so eager to address.

CLASS PARODY IN *THE PALM BEACH STORY*

As Kathleen Rowe has observed, many romantic comedies of the 1930s map the "slippery" issue of social class onto "the more readily managed ones of gender and generation," thus "bridging the gap between social class[es]" by uniting the male and female protagonists, who often represent different social classes, at the end of the film.[23] We might be tempted to see *The Palm Beach Story* as just such a case of the displacement of social class onto issues of gender and marriage. As I will argue, however, Sturges's film parodies such an easy resolution of class conflict. Where *Christmas in July* offered a clear message about workers trapped in a system of inequality, and *Sullivan's Travels* is an extended commentary on the ways in which members of the upper class are trapped within their own system of social and economic privilege, *The Palm Beach Story* is more complex in that it refuses to provide a clear message concerning social class or to resolve class conflicts in easily identifiable ways.

Like *Sullivan's Travels*, *The Palm Beach Story* has a plot structure based on a cross-country voyage, though in this case the voyage ends halfway through the film, the remainder of which takes place in the eponymous Palm Beach, Florida. Like Sullivan, Gerry Jeffers (Claudette Colbert) sets out on a quest, encounters a variety of unusual characters, and experiences a dramatic reversal of fortune. The open structure of *The Palm Beach Story*—like that of *Sullivan's Travels* and very different from the more tightly controlled narrative structure of *Christmas in July*—allows Sturges to introduce a diverse cast of characters from a wide range of social classes, forcing the protagonist to navigate radically different social milieus.

On another level, however, the social trajectories of *Sullivan's Travels* and *The Palm Beach Story* move in opposite directions. Where Sullivan tries to engineer a temporary move downward on the social ladder, Gerry attempts to move upward on the ladder to escape a life of economic disappointment and instability. As Sturges's notes for the film make clear, Gerry is a gold digger: "A young woman works her way to Palm Beach to see what life holds for her: a husband or adventure . . . She chose Palm Beach because it contained more wealth in the shape of rich men per square mile than any other locale."[24] If Sturges's treatment of Gerry is gently mocking, his treatment of Hackensacker and the other wealthy characters in the film is a broad parody. In fact, as has been pointed out by various commentators, Hackensacker, his sister, and the other characters Gerry encounters on her trip to Palm Beach are so highly exaggerated as to appear to be cartoon-like caricatures.[25] John D. is fabulously wealthy—wealthier, in fact, than the upper-class characters in Sturges's previous comedies such as *The Lady Eve* and *Sullivan's Travels*—but at the same time he is further removed from the origins of his wealth. It was his grandfather (John D. Hackensacker I) and not his father (as in the case of Mr. Baxter in *Christmas in July* and Hopsie Pike in *The Lady Eve*) who made the original family fortune. John D. himself confesses to this fact in his conversation with Gerry: "I'm not my grandfather of course. . .he's dead anyway. I'm John D. the Third." So unoriginal is John D. that he uses his grandfather's yacht and follows his habit of writing his accounts in a notebook. In the case of his grandfather, this habit was presumably attached to some actual thriftiness, but in the case of the current John D. it is simply an affectation with no real significance. Hackensacker is continually writing down every penny he spends, while claiming that "tipping is un-American." At the same time, however, he never adds up his expenditures and thinks nothing of buying an expensive ruby bracelet and a new wardrobe for Gerry.

If John D. is a weak copy of his grandfather, he is also deficient in the ways that make him a dubious potential husband for Gerry. So ineffectual is John D. as a suitor that he never manages a proposal to Gerry, despite his obvious desire to marry her. His inadequacy as a potential mate is demonstrated most tellingly in the brilliant comic set piece toward the end of the film in which he serenades Gerry from below her bedroom window while Tom seduces her. In a wonderful comic image, Tom helps Gerry to undo her dress as we hear John D. (played, ironically, by the famous singer Rudy Vallee) singing outside.[26] Gerry delivers her punchline from Tom's lap—"I hope you realize this is costing us millions"—and the scene ends as John D. hits the high note while Tom and Gerry embrace. John D.'s sister Maude (Mary Astor), who from one of her marriages has picked up the title of Princess Centimilla (another reference to

Figure 6.3 Gerry Jeffers (Claudette Colbert) is stuck between eccentric millionaires J. D. Hackensacker III (Rudy Vallee) and Princess Centimilla (Mary Astor) in *The Palm Beach Story*.

the hundred-thousand-dollar figure), is an equally exaggerated portrait of the empty-headed high-society woman who has little to occupy her other than the question of what man she will marry next: "I'll marry anybody," she at one point admits to Tom. She has already been through three divorces and two annulments, and she keeps as her current "pet" a babbling foreigner of indeterminate nationality named Toto. Sturges had hinted at the idea of marriage as an essentially financial arrangement in *The Lady Eve*, but here it is made far more explicit. In the scene on Hackensacker's yacht, when Gerry first discovers the truth about his identity, she levels with him about her own designs, explaining that her husband, from whom she is now seeking a divorce, needs $99,000. Hackensacker, though initially appalled by the implication that Gerry's husband would offer to "sell" her, is forced to admit that Gerry is "probably worth twice that. . .three times," a comment that in its awkward attempt to compliment Gerry ends up commodifying her. Gerry, not put off so easily, is prepared to play along, adding that her husband would want the money "in cash."

The tropes of marriage and money are constantly at play in *The Palm Beach Story*, undermining our sense of the film as a conventional romantic comedy. Diane Jacobs calls the film "a sort of mannerist recreation" of a screwball comedy, "with atmosphere and narrative ploys intact, but no real suffering or affirmation."[27] If the frequent reference to the $99,000 figure is reminiscent of the $58,000 sable coat in *Easy Living*, here the absurdity of the amount (so close to and yet not an even $100,000) is taken even further. Gerry, not shy about asking John D. for money, has to ask for the amount twice: once as a "payoff" for her husband, and once to help her "brother" build his airport. In fact, money is treated more as an abstraction than as any real signifier throughout the film. Through Gerry's successive encounters with the Wienie King, the members of the Ale and Quail Club who buy her train ticket and adopt her as their mascot, and finally John D. himself, we have a vision of a world in which another millionaire can apparently be found around just about any corner.

Sturges's satire in the film—caustic as it may appear—is not in the service of any real social critique. Unlike *Christmas in July*, in which class divisions are rigidly maintained (though temporarily put on hold when Jimmy appears to have won the contest), and *Sullivan's Travels*, in which class divisions are readily apparent on the level of dress, behavior, and speech, no class distinctions arise on the level of language, manners, or education. The fact that both Tom and Gerry are physically attractive seems to count for more than their social or economic status: as a result, the issue of class remains a relatively superficial one. As Elizabeth Kendall observes, the differences that do exist are economic rather than social: Gerry "is allowed to understand, in the course of prolonged contact with the Hackensackers, that 'money' and 'class' don't necessarily go together."[28] Though economic disparities are clearly foregrounded, they are prevented from having any real social significance—or much impact on the lives of Gerry and Tom—by the procession of wealthy eccentrics, by the constant intervention of fairy-godfather benefactors, and by the existence of a pair of identical twins who can marry the Hackensackers in their stead.

The difference between social classes in *The Palm Beach Story* remains a rather arbitrary and superficial one. As if to ironize the resolutions of previous screwball comedies such as *It Happened One Night* and *Easy Living*, Sturges manufactures an extremely artificial and emotionally unsatisfying ending: Gerry and Tom do *not* marry their respective partners from the upper class at the end of the film: instead, in one of the most cartoon-like scenarios to be found in any Sturges comedy, John D. marries Gerry's twin sister as the Princess marries Tom's twin brother. The double sets of twins function as figures of non-difference—or even as the erasure of difference—within the social world of the film, further contributing to the sense of class position as an irrelevant factor. Further, in *The Palm Beach Story*, a combination of sex appeal and the hunt for financial reward has replaced the virtues of spunk, hard work, and principled independence that allowed characters to overcome class differences in 1930s screwball comedies. The mercenary attitude of Gerry Jeffers throughout most of the film anticipates that of Lorelei Lee (Marilyn Monroe) in Howard Hawks's *Gentlemen Prefer Blondes* (1953) more than it resembles that of Mary Smith in *Easy Living*.

The tensions in *The Palm Beach Story* have less to do with the film's plot than with its complex tone, which hovers between ebullient optimism, materialistic yearnings, and profound cynicism. If, as Sarah Kozloff notes, *The Palm Beach Story* is "the least romantic of screwballs," it is also the most cynical.[29] The film's portrayal of the upper class—who display even less in the way of redeeming qualities than the wealthy in screwball comedies of a few years earlier—suggests that Sturges's real message may have been darker than its falsely optimistic narrative suggests. As Duane Byrge and Robert Miller note, after having "kidded and pushed the screwball conventions to. . .a fantastic extreme" throughout the film, Sturges ends with the "and they lived happily ever after" title that was already questioned at the beginning of the film. This time, however, it is written on a sheet of glass that is shattered off-screen, suggesting "the shattering of the illusion implied by the 'happy endings' of all previous screwball comedies."[30]

If the shattering of the screwball happy endings in the final moments of the film confirms its status as parody, that status is already suggested by the film's title, which tropes on the title of George Cukor's classical screwball comedy of two years earlier, *The Philadelphia Story*. *The Palm Beach Story* is an outrageously irreverent parody of Cukor's film, which represents the romantic comedy in its most conventional manifestation. As Stanley Cavell rightly argues, *The Philadelphia Story* is very much about class: it stages a debate about the "nature and the relation of . . . classes" and about "whether the upper class, call it the aristocracy, is to survive and if so what role it may play in a constitution committed to liberty."[31] In the course of the film, class issues are introduced only to be deflected by a story that focuses on the growing emotional attachment and ultimate remarriage of the two upper-class characters, Tracy Lord (Katherine Hepburn) and C. K. Dexter Haven (Cary Grant).

Whereas the title of *The Philadelphia Story* contains a certain gravity— provided by associations with the city of Philadelphia and its part in our national history—*The Palm Beach Story* has none. Palm Beach, unlike Philadelphia, has no "story," no significant history other than the fact that it is home to a number of very rich people. The Palm Beach "aristocracy" is not the old-money social establishment represented by Tracy Lord, but a fabulously wealthy and completely tasteless society represented by the Hackensackers. Even the name "Hackensacker," while clearly an allusion to "Rockefeller," is a play on the lower-middle-class town of Hackensack, New Jersey, as well as a commentary on the way in which the family accumulated its wealth by ravaging and plundering the American people ("hack and sack"). The allusion to the Rockefellers is not the only one in the film, which, as Kozloff notes, is marked by its "thoroughgoing double-layeredness."[32] The film references earlier films such as *It Happened One Night*; it stars Claudette Colbert, whose role both repeats and inverts that of Capra's 1934 film; and it alludes to specific events in Sturges's life.

Released at the end of 1942, *The Palm Beach Story* was the last of Sturges's comedies in which social class would appear as a central theme. The themes of class mobility and inclusion in the new consumer society that were much in evidence in *Easy Living* and *Christmas in July* have become ripe for parody by the time of *The Palm Beach Story*. In Sturges's next two films—*The Miracle of Morgan's Creek* and *Hail the Conquering Hero*—he abandons those themes altogether. The movement away from issues of class in Sturges's later films may reflect his loss of interest in the topic, but it also coincides with a more general waning of a thematic concern with class variations in American film comedy. This decrease in the frequency of class-based plots in American comedies may itself be related to changes—observed by sociologists such as C. Wright Mills—in the class stratification of American society, as well as evolving attitudes about wealth and social class.[33] In keeping with changing attitudes about class, Hollywood retreated from its Depression-era preoccupation with class mobility, inter-class romantic relationships, and "success-up-the-class-ladder" plots. Comedies of the mid-to-late 1940s rarely engaged in the kind of satirical or parodic treatment of class issues that directors like Frank Capra, Mitchell Leisen, Gregory La Cava, and Sturges himself had perfected within the confines of the screwball comedy genre.[34]

NOTES

1   Andrew Horton, ed., *Three More Screenplays by Preston Sturges* (Berkeley, CA: University of California Press, 1998), 17.
2   See my discussion of the treatment of social class in these two films in *Class, Language, and American Film Comedy* (New York, NY: Cambridge University Press, 2002).
3   See Dan Harries, *Film Parody* (London: BFI, 2000), 24.
4   In terms of "economic status," a measure of how individual wealth relates to overall GDP, a 1910 dollar is equivalent to over one hundred dollars today. See the website measuringwealth.com. (last accessed 14 July 2014).
5   Diane Jacobs, *Christmas in July: The Life and Art of Preston Sturges* (Berkeley, CA: University of California Press, 1992), 22.
6   See Peter Kurth, *Isadora: A Sensational Life* (Boston, MA: Little, Brown, 2001), 250–1.
7   See Elizabeth Kendall, *The Runaway Bride: Hollywood Romantic Comedy of the 1930s* (New York, NY: Knopf, 1990), 241.
8   Jacobs, 95.
9   Jacobs, 105.
10 According to most estimates, the Depression-era unemployment rate in the U.S. peaked at 25 percent in 1933. However, unemployment figures prior to 1940, when unemployment statistics began to be kept by the Department of Labor Statistics, are not entirely reliable.
11 Henderson, 205.
12 See a discussion of the differences between the play, screenplay, and film in Brian Henderson, *Five Screenplays by Preston Sturges* (Berkeley, CA: University of California Press, 1985), 190–9.
13 In a scene later in the film when Jimmy is invited into Mr. Baxter's office to share some of his marketing ideas with the other executives, he comes up with the slogan "Baxter's Best, the blue-blood coffee: it's bred in the bean." If the reference to the quality of the company's coffee beans as a surrogate for social class is not sufficiently clear, Jimmy adds that the slogan suggests how every bean has its own "pedigree."
14 Henderson makes the interesting suggestion that the pranks played by Jimmy's office mates are their means of coping with "their faceless, automaton-like work, just as contests are for Jimmy" (199). This reading seems consistent with other elements of the film: for example, the office set is probably intended by Sturges as an allusion to King Vidor's *The Crowd* (1928), a decidedly non-comic study of urban mechanization and anonymity, while the names of the three co-workers—Tom, Dick, and Harry—are another sign of their anonymous status.
15 Kathleen Moran and Michael Rogin, "'What's the Matter with Capra?' *Sullivan's Travels* and the Popular Front," *Representations* 71 (Summer 2000), 107.
16 Eric Schocket, "Undercover Exploration of the 'Other Half': Or the Writer as Class Transvestite," *Representations* 64 (Fall 1998): 109–33.
17 For a discussion of Sturges's lack of political commitment, see Jacobs, 183–4.
18 Henderson, 522.
19 Henderson, 522.
20 Sullivan's class position is largely modeled on that of Sturges himself. Sturges attended private schools in France and Switzerland, and he boasted to Solomon Sturges in 1935 that he was the highest-paid writer in Hollywood, with a salary of $2500 a week.
21 As Henderson suggests, Sturges's portrayal of the producers is not an unflattering one. Despite their mild hypocrisy in claiming to have risen from the gutter, they clearly have

far more real-life experience than Sullivan, and they are actually giving him good advice. The producers—"reasonable men" and "nice guys" (521)—are presumably based on Hollywood producers who had helped Sturges over the years.

22 One wonders how The Girl could have failed to notice that Sullivan's boots were stolen in the shelter and replaced with another pair, thus rendering spurious the identification of the tramp's body as that of Sullivan.

23 Kathleen Rowe, *The Unruly Woman: Gender and the Genres of Laughter* (Austin, TX: University of Texas Press, 1995), 125.

24 Quoted in Brian Henderson, *Four More Screenplays by Preston Sturges* (Berkeley, CA: University of California Press, 1995), 46.

25 Whether the names "Tom" and "Gerry" are a reference to the *Tom and Jerry* cartoon is debatable: the first cartoons in the series were released in 1941, the same year *The Palm Beach Story* was written and filmed.

26 The scene receives another layer of irony from the fact that Vallee had in fact written and successfully recorded the same song, "Good Night Sweetheart." See Henderson, *Four More Screenplays*, 78–9.

27 Jacobs, 271. Also see Leger Grindon's chapter in this volume.

28 Kendall, 259. Kendall takes this reading of the film a bit further than I would. Her argument that Gerry finally understands "why she, and therefore America, must reject rich people" seems somewhat facile, suggesting a direct analogy between Gerry and the national psyche that I do not believe exists.

29 Sarah Kozloff, *Overhearing Film Dialogue* (Berkeley and Los Angeles, CA: University of California Press, 2000), 198.

30 Duane Byrge and Robert Miller, *The Screwball Comedy Films: A History and Bibliography, 1934–1942* (Jefferson, NC: McFarland, 1991), 132–3.

31 Stanley Cavell, *Pursuits of Happiness: The Hollywood Comedy of Remarriage* (Cambridge, MA: Harvard University Press, 1981), 153.

32 Kozloff, 199.

33 Over the period from the mid-1930s to the late 1940s, Mills identifies decreases in the gap between the earning power of white-collar workers and "urban wage-earners" such as skilled manual laborers, and he points to an accompanying decline in the prestige of white-collar workers. See *White Collar: The American Middle Classes* (New York, NY: Oxford University Press, 1951), 72–3. Changes in personal income tax rates also reflect changing attitudes toward the very rich. The top tax bracket in 1935, for individuals earning over $1 million a year, was 63 percent. By 1944, those earning only a fraction of that amount—$200,000 and above—were taxed at a far higher 94 percent rate.

34 Some examples of representative postwar comedies are *Without Reservations* (Mervyn LeRoy, 1946), *The Egg and I* (Chester Erskine, 1947), *The Bachelor and the Bobby Soxer* (Irving Reis, 1947), *Mr. Blandings Builds His Dream House* (H. C. Potter, 1948), *Adam's Rib* (George Cukor, 1949), and *I Was a Male War Bride* (Howard Hawks, 1949).

CHAPTER 7

"They Always Get the Best of You Somehow": Preston Sturges in Black and White

Krin Gabbard

I am often surprised when friends in the jazz studies world turn out to be as devoted to movies as they are to the music. One night about twenty years ago, a jazz writer and I were sitting in a club between sets when I discovered that we both had a passion for Preston Sturges. He soon asked, however, "Have you ever noticed how every Sturges film has a scene with a demeaning stereotype of a black person?" I immediately thought of what may be the single most memorable moment in the entire Sturges canon, the drunken rampage by the Ale and Quail Club in *The Palm Beach Story* that begins with two of the members blasting away with shotguns while a terrified black bartender throws soda crackers into the air. The English journalist John Pym lists the bartender first when he writes about "the coloured characters" in *The Palm Beach Story* who make up the one "discordant and profoundly unappealing note" in a film he otherwise finds to be nearly flawless.[1]

To make matters even more "unappealing," Fred Toones, the actor playing the bartender, is identified in the end credits only as "Snowflake." Although Paramount probably chose to identify Toones in this way, the actor came up with the nickname, just as Lincoln Perry called himself "Stepin Fetchit," and Willie Best often billed himself as "Sleep and Eat." Nick Stewart may have been a bit more self-aggrandizing when he called himself "Nicodemus." Nevertheless, the dehumanizing name Snowflake reinforces the image of the childlike, timorous, desperate-to-please servant in *The Palm Beach Story*. But is this scene really typical of Sturges? And even if this scene were an anomaly—which it is not—how do we adjust our evaluation and appreciation of Sturges as a filmmaker?

When I was asked to contribute an essay on Sturges and race to this collection, I again thought of the terrified black bartender ducking behind the bar and looking even more ridiculous when he emerges wearing an ice bucket on his head for protection. But I quickly learned that my jazz writer friend was wrong when he said that *all* of Sturges's films are insulting to black people. In a few of his films, there are no African Americans at all!

But what can I say about the several films in which blacks are in fact demeaned, as well as those films in which they are not actually humiliated like the bartender but nevertheless embody familiar stereotypes? Sturges was not a crusader for integrating the races or for granting African Americans their full weight as human beings. But then neither were the vast majority of Hollywood filmmakers of the late 1930s and early 1940s, who were as comfortable with the old racist stereotypes as were the vast majority of white Americans in those days. But since Sturges employs multiple functions for his African American characters, we need to consider a number of approaches to the issue of Sturges and race. A list of these approaches should start with an understanding that, *contra* the auteur theory, which assigns responsibility for every aspect of a text to the director's personal genius or unconscious inclinations, Sturges was no different from other filmmakers in accommodating the dominant racism of his day. Second, we need to look more closely at representations some would consider negative or simply neutral. Today we can condemn Sturges for making the bartender in *The Palm Beach Story* look ridiculous, but simply by presenting a black man as a bartender on a Pullman car, Sturges acknowledges—consciously or not—that few other occupations were available to African American workers at that time. Third, we may even be able to regard some portrayals as positive or at least more nuanced. I'm thinking of the witty, even scene-stealing dialogue that Sturges wrote for his black characters in *Christmas in July* and *The Palm Beach Story*, as well as the many scenes in *Sullivan's Travels* in which blacks and whites share in their humanity. At other moments in the Sturges canon blacks function as foils, placed in the narrative primarily to allow white characters to reveal something about themselves. And finally, we need to get past mere representation and consider African Americans actors as respected professionals, at least two of whom were part of Sturges's repertory company.

BALUCHISTAN AND CLOSER TO HOME

In one sense, the black characters in Sturges's films are not that much different from the many thickly-accented ethnics he also presents: the angry Jewish neighbor in *Christmas in July*, the temperamental Russian chef in *The Lady Eve*, the indignant Irish cop in *The Palm Beach Story*, and the *gemütlich* German bearing sausage in *Hail the Conquering Hero*. In these films the humor comes from accent and syntax, as when the Jewish neighbor complains about noise by saying, "You have up there a horse yet?" Sturges's ethnic humor reaches a tipping point with Toto (Sig Arno) in the *The Palm Beach Story*.[2]

The Princess (Mary Astor) is not sure, but she thinks that Toto may be from "Baluchistan." More commonly known as Balochistan, such a place truly exists on the Iranian plateau in what is now Pakistan. But since few members of Sturges's audience know anything at all about the natives of that region, he has full license to pile on multiple stereotypes, turning Toto into a vain, clueless, effeminate, argumentative, incomprehensible, free-loading drunkard.[3] Except for the actual residents of Balochistan (who were not watching Paramount films), no one can be genuinely offended by Toto. As for the rest of Sturges's stereotypical ethnics, most of us can laugh at them innocently—or as innocently as any joke ever allows—because the stereotypes are *not* based on centuries-long histories of slavery and oppression.

On the one hand, at least since the nineteenth century, ethnic stereotypes have driven a great deal of American humor. On the other hand, jokes at the expense of African Americans emerge from the "love and theft" of minstrelsy, which has a very different history.[4] As Michael Rogin observes, in the nineteenth century Irish and Jewish immigrants could put burnt cork on their faces and hide their ethnicity behind the minstrel mask.[5] At a certain stage in the history of minstrelsy, everyone was white when the masks came off. African American performers, even when they too became minstrels, would always be black. Thus Conchita (Olga San Juan), the Mexican companion of Freddie (Betty Grable) in *The Beautiful Blonde from Bashful Bend*, has something in common with African American characters—she *looks* different and is thus regarded as Native American and hence dim-witted. For Sturges, such negative stereotyping was simply another way to get a laugh.

In this sense, Sturges counts as just one more American director buying into well-established Hollywood traditions. We know very little about his actual views on race. Diane Jacobs never once mentions race in her biography of the director, and Sturges's passing references to non-white people in his autobiography tell us very little about his own attitudes. While the vicious racism of *Birth of a Nation* and a handful of other films from the 1910s and 1920s was soon proscribed, Hollywood films of the 1930s and early 1940s casually perpetuated an institutionalized racism that consigned blacks to a limited range of occupations, temperaments, and social roles. *Gone With the Wind* (1939), for many years the single most popular film in American history, is entirely typical of Hollywood in Sturges's day. White audiences were obviously not offended by Mammy and Prissy or by the film's romanticized view of slavery.

Even Orson Welles did not rock this particular boat. In *Citizen Kane* (1941), released only a year before *The Palm Beach Story*, the one scene with African Americans opens with a tight close-up of a round-faced black man who strongly resembles Fred "Snowflake" Toones. Alton Redd, the performer in the close-up, is singing a popular song of the era, "In a Mizz," while the leader of the band, drummer Cee Pee Johnson, is energetically beating out a rhythm in the background. Redd and Johnson are now forgotten figures in jazz history, and Welles may have deliberately chosen a mediocre band for a scene in which practically no one—least of all Kane—is paying attention to the entertainment. After directing a "Voodoo Macbeth" with an all-black cast on Broadway in 1936, a production that brought new levels of timelessness to Shakespeare and new levels of distinction to African American performers, Welles scores no points as a Hollywood liberal for making Cee Pee Johnson's band the only African American performers in his film.

In this context, I should also mention Frank Capra, a director who was only one year older than Sturges and to whom he was often compared, even by Sturges himself. (In *Sullivan's Travels*, the protagonist holds up Capra's films—perhaps ironically—as the kind of work he is hoping to direct.) On several occasions, Capra worked with a talented actor named Clarence Muse (1889–1979), at one point patronizingly calling him "my pet actor."[6] In addition to being a very busy performer with 157 credits on the Internet Movie Database, Muse was a renaissance talent who sang opera and founded the Harlem Lafayette Theatre. He also wrote the screenplay for one of the most thoughtful films in the cycle of all-black-cast or "race" films, *Broken Strings* (1940). Clarence Muse's best-known work as a songwriter is "When It's Sleepy Time Down South," which he co-wrote with the brothers Leon and Otis René.[7] Capra, however, cast Clarence Muse in typical secondary parts, including the black sidekick of the hero in *Broadway Bill* (1934), where he plays, in the words of Thomas Cripps, a "singing flunkie."[8] With my own obsession about jazz in film, my most vivid recollection of a black character in a Capra film is the pianist with a derby and a cigar playing boogie-woogie in a saloon, as if to add an additional note of decadence and corruption to Pottersville in the fantasy sequence of *It's a Wonderful Life* (1946).

Sturges never associated blacks with corruption, but neither did he make a film like *The Negro Soldier* (1944), a compromised celebration of the achievements of African Americans with progressive intent.

"YASSUH, YASSUH"

The scene in *The Palm Beach Story* when the bartender tries to stop the Ale and Quail Club from shooting up the place by pounding on the bar like an angry child will never be confused with a scene from *The Negro Soldier*. We can say the same about the scene with a black chef played by Charles Moore in *Sullivan's Travels*. When Sullivan (Joel McCrea) takes to the road in hobo drag, a "land yacht" follows him containing a crew dispatched for the occasion by the studio bosses LeBrand (Robert Warwick) and Hadrian (Porter Hall). The crew includes a press agent, a photographer, a doctor, a secretary, a short-wave operator, and a butler as well as the black chef. We first see the chef serving breakfast to the publicist Jones (William Demarest) and the doctor (Torben Meyer). Broadly smiling, he offers pancakes to Jones:

> Chef: Can I sell you another stack, Doctor?
> Jones: Get me some bicarbonate of soda and don't call me Doctor.
> Doctor: He was talking to me, I think. No, thank you.
> Chef: You say you don't want no bicarbonate of soda, Doctor?
> Jones: Don't call me Doctor!
> Doctor: No, I don't want any bicarbonate of soda.
> Chef: I thought you say you did.
> Jones: Well, he don't.

The humor here lies as much in Jones's foul nature and the doctor's obliviousness as it does in the chef's stupidity.

Later, Moore's chef takes several pratfalls as the land yacht careens across the countryside chasing Sullivan in the hot-rod with the boy motorist. Sturges turns the scene into slapstick, as when the legs of the secretary (Margaret Hayes) become more and more elevated and her bloomers more and more exposed each time the camera cuts to her bouncing around in the front seat with the driver and the photographer. The chef, however, suffers much more. First, he has water squirted in his face when he falls into the sink and knocks the faucet off its stem. The next time we see him he is on the floor where an oven door falls open and hits him on the head. Then his face lands in a bowl of some kind of batter, and he comes up in whiteface. Moore remains in whiteface throughout the next scene, when the crew from inside the land yacht wonders why the driver was bouncing all over the countryside. Jones asks, "What are you chasin'? A jack rabbit?" The chef says, "Felt more like a kangaroo." No one remarks on the white batter all over his face.

But Sturges is not finished with Moore just yet. Much later in *Sullivan's Travels* the chef stands with the rest of the staff, who had been assigned to protect John L. Sullivan and to promote his journey. Although he is in the back of the group, Moore is wearing a suit and thus assumes a certain degree of equivalence with the white people. Convinced that Sullivan is now dead, LeBrand tells the group, "I suppose I should fire the whole lot of you. Somehow I don't feel like firing anybody today. [Suddenly angry] Well, there's no use hanging around here. Get your things together and go. I'll fly back." When the chef hears that he will *not* be fired, he is the only one in the group who smiles. At the end of LeBrand's speech, Moore enthusiastically says, "Yes, sir," provoking the rest of the group to turn around and look at him indignantly. The chef is much easier to please than the others. Sturges may even have some sympathy for a man who has effectively been programmed to say "Yes, sir," when such servility is hardly necessary.

Even if we consider them to be offensive today, the parts Sturges gave blacks in *The Palm Beach Story* and *Sullivan's Travels* were based on the real-life situation of African American workers in the late 1930s and early 1940s. Numerous black characters appear in *The Palm Beach Story* because so much of the action takes place on a train with Pullman cars. George M. Pullman designed and manufactured the Pullman sleeping car and founded Pullman, Illinois, the ultimate company town.[9] Although he died in 1897, Pullman cars continued to be built and staffed well into the twentieth century. Pullman built his empire after the Civil War, mostly hiring white workers to build the railroad cars. But he took advantage of a vast population of ex-slaves looking for jobs and hired only African Americans to serve as porters. He knew that he could hire the most competent and hard-working ones because he would pay them more than they might earn elsewhere. But he would still be paying them low wages. In staffing his sleeper cars with blacks, Pullman was able to give an upper-class experience to less affluent Americans who traveled by rail. The wealthy were accustomed to liveried retainers at their beck and call, always saying "Yes, sir" and "Yes, ma'am." On a Pullman car with servile workers in crisp uniforms, middle-class Americans received a similar taste of luxury, one they were not likely to experience elsewhere. As for African Americans, being a Pullman porter was an important step up in social class. After other rail lines began hiring porters, waiters, chefs, and "red cap" baggage handlers who were exclusively African American, a new black middle class began to take shape. Some of the workers even had Ph.D.s.[10]

Of course, the Pullman porter was expected to sustain racial hierarchies and put up with a great deal of abuse. In *The Palm Beach Story*, the Ale and Quail shootist played by William Demarest calls the bartender "George," but that is almost certainly not his name. Passengers on Pullman cars would call every porter "George," as if he were George Pullman's "boy," part of the southern tradition of naming slaves after their masters. Pullman porters were also trained to behave exactly as we see in *The Palm Beach Story* when Gerry (Claudette Colbert) says "Shut up" to the waiter passing by her bunk announcing that breakfast is being served. The waiter smiles slightly and simply replies, "Yes, ma'am."

SHARED HUMANITY?

In *Christmas in July*, Sturges makes one of his few appearances on film. Early in the narrative, we see a montage of working people all intently listening to the same radio program hoping to learn the name of the winner of the contest

Figure 7.1 Preston Sturges appears with two anonymous actors in an early scene in *Christmas in July*.

for Maxford House Coffee's new advertising slogan. Without interrupting the flow of the audio, the camera cuts quickly to a butler polishing furniture, nurses listening in a hospital, various men in a barbershop, workers in a Chinese laundry, a group of cab drivers, and several others. The only black faces in the montage belong to a shoeshine man and a man who may be a messenger. Right next to them in the brief shot is Sturges himself sitting in the shoeshine chair and sporting a straw boater.

Could Sturges be reminding us of the inequality in American society with impoverished black Americans indulging affluent whites? After all, when a white man gets a shine from a black man, is he not maintaining racial hierarchies as much as he is improving the appearance of his footwear? Or by inserting himself into this one particular scene is Sturges establishing that he is content with the racial imbalances it connotes? Or is it just one of many unproblematized vignettes in which Sturges, for whatever his reason, has chosen to appear?

I would like to think that by placing himself next to two black actors, Sturges was expressing a certain degree of comfort with and perhaps even respect for African Americans in spite of his willingness to make the occasional black actor play the fool. Jeff Jaeckle's archival research turned up a letter from Jester Hairston, the actor who played the man who lowers the screen during the church scene in *Sullivan's Travels*. The actor wrote, "Because of the gentlemanly manner in which you treated me and all my people during the shooting of that church scene I realized that you had a deeper interest in them than most directors who treat us as just another group of 'darkies.'"[11]

If we look for positive or at least neutral representations in Sturges's films, we should consider the moments when black characters function as foils for white characters or provide information about them that might not otherwise be available. When his black characters seem to be getting rough treatment, Sturges may in fact be asking us to pass judgment on white characters that are contemptuous or simply dismissive of a black person. For example, Dan (Brian Donlevy) in *The Great McGinty* pays absolutely no attention to his valet (Charles Moore), even though he seems to be in the middle of an interesting story. As he brushes down McGinty's clothes, Moore's character asks, "Playing pool tonight, your honor?" When McGinty ignores him, the valet then says, "You know, a funny thing happened to me the other day. I was playin' the twelve ball for the side pocket and the blue ball was right in the way. I look over behind the eight rock, and do you know what happened to the eight rock?" Without even acknowledging that his valet is in the middle of a story, McGinty walks out of the room and closes the door behind him. Because Sturges does not give a reaction shot to Moore's character, the scene seems designed to emphasize the extent to which McGinty is preoccupied with more urgent matters. But the scene may also suggest that McGinty's ultimate downfall may be related to his contemptuous treatment of the people around him.[12] At the risk of putting too fine a point on this scene, I would add that the screenplay for *The Great McGinty* gives a shorter speech to the valet. He only says, "Funny thing happened to me the other day . . . I'm playin' the twelve for the side pocket and the eight is right over."[13] McGinty is a bit more unsympathetic as he rudely walks out of the room while his valet is in the middle rather than at the beginning of an anecdote.

The scene with McGinty and the valet should be distinguished from the scene in *The Palm Beach Story* with Gerry and a black maid (Lillian Randolph). They are on the train in the ladies room trying on clothes while John D. (Rudy Vallee) and the Porter (Charles Moore again) wait outside with still more clothes they have collected from female passengers. The porter seems to be genuinely pleased, and like John D., he smiles broadly. Wearing a bricolage of women's clothes, Gerry is not so pleased. Trying to be of some help, the maid offers Gerry her earrings. As in the scene in *The Great McGinty*, Gerry does not acknowledge what the black person has just said. Although we do not know if the two women conversed further in the ladies room, Gerry emerges wearing the maid's plain white earrings a few moments later. We are probably not supposed to pass judgment on Gerry for not immediately responding to the maid's kind offer. In Sturges's world, Gerry does not have to be sociable when she is upset and in no mood for chitchat with a social inferior. Sturges seizes upon the grotesque power imbalance between whites and blacks to reveal something very specific about his white as well as his black characters.

FLEXING THE LANGUAGE MUSCLES

I was delighted to learn that Sturges loved jazz.[14] Like many white jazz devotees, Sturges was likely to think of African American artists as smart and imaginative, unlike those who had no idea that black people had created a complex, compelling music. It may not be a great stretch to suggest that, therefore, Sturges regularly gave witty, jazzy dialogue to his black characters.

For instance, when Jimmy (Dick Powell) and Betty (Ellen Drew) arrive at his office late in *Christmas in July*, they encounter Sam, the night janitor played by Fred Toones. When asked where the boss is, Sam looks toward the office of Dr. Maxford (Raymond Walburn) and replies, "He's in there connivin' on something or other." Moments later a black cat appears in the frame and Betty asks if it means good or bad luck. Sam says, "That all depends on what happens afterward." This response disappoints Betty, but it definitely reveals a sensibility rooted in reality.

In another scene, Charles Moore appears as a black valet attending to Maxford's clothes after he has been pelted with fish and vegetables on the street by Jimmy's angry neighbors. Handling his jacket, the valet says, "Was you at a fish fry, Dr. Maxford?" When Maxford assures him that this is not the case, the valet quips, "Smells like a seven-course banquet." Of course, Sam the janitor in *Christmas in July* also has multiple lines of "Yassuh, yassuh" like many other black characters in Sturges's films, but Sam and the unnamed valet in *Christmas in July* evince a Sturgean talent with language.

The Palm Beach Story includes some of the wittiest dialogue Sturges ever wrote for black actors. One scene includes a performance by Mantan Moreland, a very funny actor who would be more celebrated today had he not played the fool on so many occasions, especially as the easily terrified chauffeur in the Charlie Chan films. Never having worked with Sturges before or after, Moreland has a cameo as the waiter on the Pullman dining car when John D. and Gerry arrive for breakfast. Thrifty to a fault and then some, John D. insists on the seventy-five-cent breakfast even though Moreland as the waiter attempts to sell him something more expensive. When Gerry orders a prairie oyster, John D. orders one too, adding that he would like it on the half shell. John D. does not know that he has just ordered the testicle of a cow. Rather than addressing his ignorance of Pullman cuisine, the waiter addresses John D.'s parsimony, explaining that "Prairie oysters is à la carte." As the waiter walks away, John D. says to Gerry, "They always get the best of you somehow." Sturges's dialogue is not entirely readable at this moment. Who is the "they" in John D.'s statement? Is he referring to blacks in particular, to waiters in general, or to anyone at all who intends to extract additional money from him?

If he is actually referring to certain African Americans who know what to do because they can see right through him—who "get the best of him"—then he has touched upon one of the principal themes of *The Palm Beach Story*. The staff of the train definitely get the best of the Ale and Quail long before the crew abandon them in the middle of nowhere. Both Gerry and Tom (Joel McCrea) get the best of the John D. and the Princess, even as the Princess gets the best of Toto. Although the black porters, chefs, waiters, and maids may not get more than a dime for their troubles, they understand all too well what the white characters are up to. And in Sturges's world, where speech is often more important than action, the white characters often get hit with zingers from the black characters. Even the film's many millionaires are not exempt.

Charles Moore, for instance, gives an especially distinguished performance as a Pullman porter in *The Palm Beach Story*. Brian Henderson even refers to Moore's character as "Faulknerian":

> one character, uneducated and socially inferior, doggedly clings to a single truth, reasserting it calmly whatever pressures are applied. This infuriates, and finally drives to apoplexy, the more sophisticated and articulate character, who is conducting the interrogation. Such scenes are Faulkner's version of the irresistible force confronting the immovable, and implacable, object, except that in his fiction, the immovable object is never budged and the irresistible force sputters itself to exhaustion.[15]

This may not be exactly what happens when Moore as the porter encounters first Gerry and then Tom. To Gerry, he explains why she cannot get her clothes back after she insists that he has not even bothered to look for them:

Gerry: You just didn't look.
Porter: Oh yes, ma'am, I looked, but I didn't see it 'cause it weren't there. That's why I didn't see it.

He then explains that the conductor set the car off on "a siding in Rockingham Hamlet."

Porter: A very pretty little city.
Gerry: Never mind the geography.

In the more famous encounter, Moore's porter tells Tom that Gerry was alone when she got off the train in Jacksonville:

Porter: You might practically say she was alone. The gentleman that got off with her gave me ten cents from New York to Jacksonville. She's alone, but she don't know it.
Tom: Well, never mind the philosophy. Then she's in Jacksonville?
Porter: Yes, sir. No, sir. She said that he said he was gonna take her down there on his boat. I suppose she means yachet, but I don't see how no gentleman can give me a dime from New York to Jacksonville can have a yachet. Maybe a canoe or a bicycle. Yes, sir.

The porter has delivered a devastating judgment of John D. and registered his disappointment over the miniscule tip while still maintaining the "professional" demeanor in which he was trained.

John Pym praises Moore for his "pistol-shot pronunciation" of "YAT-CHET," but also for the slight changes he seems to have made to the lines that Sturges wrote for him. The screenplay has the porter saying, "I don't see where no gentleman who come up wid ten cents from New York to Jacksonville get off to have a yachet." But in Moore's mouth the line comes out more elegantly, with "dime" replacing "ten cents" among other changes. While acknowledging that Sturges could have rewritten the line himself, Pym is almost certain that Moore "exercised his art, flexed his muscles and added his own touch to a corner of the canvas."[16]

If Pym is right, Moore has pulled off a miniature version of the "uplift" that Paul Robeson accomplished as Joe in the 1936 production of *Show Boat*. Richard Dyer points out that Robeson wrote his own lyrics to "Old Man River," transforming "suffering and resignation to oppression and resistance." The lyrics that Oscar Hammerstein II wrote for Jerome Kern's music originally read:

> Git a little drunk an' you'll land in jail.
> Ah gets weary an' sick of tryin'
> Ah'm tired of livin' and scared of dyin'.

When Robeson sings "Old Man River," however, we hear instead:

> Show a little grit and you land in jail.
> But I keep laughin' instead of cryin'
> I must keep fightin' until I'm dyin'.[17]

Charles Moore has not undertaken the wholesale transformation of the script that we hear in Robeson's new lyrics. Substituting "dime" for "ten cents" is small change, pardon the expression. But like many black actors in Sturges's films, he has also cleaned up some of the dialect, allowing his character to sound a bit more literate. Moore's rewriting of the line, for example, allows him to dispense with the "wid" in the original phrase "no gentleman who come up wid ten cents . . ." by recasting it as "no gentleman can give me a dime . . ." Elsewhere, Sturges's black actors regularly replace "de" in the script with "the," "sumpin'" with "somethin'," and "warn't" with "weren't," as well as "wid" with "with."[18]

Sturges wrote all of these lines in dialect because he thought audiences would find them funny. He must have been satisfied that the scenes turned out just as funny when the black actors found the music in his dialogue even as they rejected some of the substandard pronunciations. The talented actors he used did not exactly "get the best of him," but they did flex their artistic muscles, as Pym suggests.

"LET MY PEOPLE GO"

African Americans get more screen time in *Sullivan's Travels* than in any of the other films written or directed by Sturges. In the church scene, Jess Lee Brooks plays a benevolent, charismatic preacher at the head of the congregation. This was the only time that Brooks, a busy actor who moved back and

Figure 7.2 Jess Lee Brooks sings "Go Down, Moses" to his congregation and the visiting members of a chain gang in *Sullivan's Travels*.

forth between Hollywood and race movies, acted in a Sturges film. As the preacher, Brooks tells his congregation:

> Well, brothers and sisters, once again we are going to have a little enter-
> tainment . . . And once again, brothers and sisters, we're gonna share our
> pleasure with some neighbors less fortunate than ourselves. Would you
> please clear the first three pews so they may have seats? And when they
> get here, I'm going to ask you once more, neither by word nor action nor
> look to make our guests feel unwelcome, nor draw away from them or act
> high-tone. For we is all equal in the sight of God.

As the prisoners walk up the aisle wearing their chains, their steps are carefully synchronized so that they resemble the workers marching in formation
toward their dehumanizing labor in Fritz Lang's *Metropolis* (1927). While the
prisoners enter, the preacher leads his congregation in singing "Go Down,
Moses." Once they are seated, Sturges gives the preacher an extra level of cen-
trality, if not dignity, by placing him precisely in the middle of the aisle with
his arms outstretched.

He has become a living cross, the embodiment of Christian sacrifice.
Having finished his rendition of "Go Down, Moses," the preacher asks that
the lights be turned down so that everyone can watch the cartoon. A well-
dressed black woman looks at the convicts and smiles as she dims the lights.
"How do?" she says.

No less than Walter White wrote to Sturges to praise the "decent treatment of Negroes" in the church scene in *Sullivan's Travels*. White directed
the National Association for the Advancement of Colored People for many
years and was instrumental in numerous civil rights victories, including
the Supreme Court's 1954 ruling that the segregation of public schools was
unconstitutional. In his letter to Sturges, White says nothing about Charles
Moore in whiteface earlier in the same film, but he does write:

> I was in Hollywood recently and am to return there soon for confer-
> ences with production head writers, directors, and actors and actresses
> in an effort to induce broader and more decent picturization of the
> Negro instead of limiting him to menial or comic roles. The sequence in
> *Sullivan's Travels* is a step in that direction and I want you to know how
> grateful we are.[19]

At the time of *Sullivan's Travels*, White and his organization were joined by
many outside the black community in lobbying for better roles for blacks. In

particular, Elmer Davis of the Office of War Information was urging filmmakers to give better treatment to blacks in films, if only so that they would be more likely to get behind the war effort. Hollywood, however, ended up creating fewer roles for blacks, since "if the portrayal of blacks was offensive, it was easier to eliminate them than to change them."[20]

According to Thomas Cripps, at the time when many groups were insisting that Hollywood treat black people with more respect, Sturges was using the church sequence in *Sullivan's Travels* to "haze" "conscience liberalism" by placing a "defeated white chain gang" in a black church.[21] For one thing, the chain gang is not exclusively white—several of the prisoners are most assuredly black. Throughout *Sullivan's Travels*, in fact, blacks are mixed in with whites. Both races are present in a hobo camp and later in a soup kitchen as well as in the chain gang. I also do not agree that Sturges is ridiculing Hollywood's attempts at the beginning of World War II to put more black faces into films and to treat them according to the strictures of "conscience liberalism." The case could be made that Sturges was hazing the liberals earlier in the film when he sustained the demeaning image of the chef in whiteface. But in the church scene, Sturges is not presenting an upside down world in which blacks are on a higher ground than whites in order to thumb his nose at Hollywood liberals. The demeanor of the preacher and his congregation suggests a much more sincere attempt to depict the hopeless situation of the prisoners and perhaps even a touching moment when people are practicing Christian charity at its most authentic. The predicament of the prisoners is so desperate that Sullivan has an epiphany when he realizes the importance of laughter to people who have very little to laugh about. I also think that Sturges is sincere when he shows a group of black people making a heartfelt attempt to give the convicts a moment or two when they *do* have something to laugh about.

The singing of "Go Down, Moses" in the church scene recalls Charles Musser's argument about Al Jolson and his black audiences.[22] Musser is especially interested in a sequence in *Big Boy* (1930) in which Jolson plays an African American jockey who, at one moment, leads a group of black workers on a plantation in song. Jolson and the choir sing "Go Down, Moses," a song that perfectly combines the history of the Jewish people with the situation of African Americans: "When Israel was in Egypt's Land. Let my people go! Oppressed so hard they could not stand. Let my people go!" In the 1920s and 1930s, Musser argues, a Jewish man playing a black man and singing the sacred and profane music of African Americans was well-received by many in the black audience. Except when they are singing, no one in the church mentions Jews. But the prisoners are as much in bondage as the Israelites of the hymn and the slaves of the previous century. And the kind of solidarity that Jolson dramatizes in *Big Boy* is just as powerful in the black preacher's appeal for tolerance and in the unity of blacks and whites laughing together. Walter White was surely not the only African American viewer who would have been moved by Sturges's church scene.

Ella Shohat and Robert Stam, however, take an anti-auteurist approach to Sturges's handling of black people in *Sullivan's Travels*. For them, the film exemplifies what they call "the generic coefficient of racism."[23] They argue persuasively that blacks in the 1930s and 1940s were given specific roles in each of the era's cinematic genres. In *Sullivan's Travels'* early slapstick moments on the land yacht, Charles Moore "conforms to the prototype of the happy-go-lucky servant/buffoon," while in the documentary-style scenes with groups of desperate unemployed people, blacks "are present but voiceless, very much in the left/communist tradition of class reductionism."[24] Shohat and Stam point out that the church scene strongly recalls all-black musicals like *Hallelujah* (1929)—I would add *Green Pastures* (1936)—in which blacks are a scrupulously religious people united in prayer and song. By closely adhering to well-established conventions in each of the scenes with black actors, the Sturges of one generic scene bears little resemblance to the Sturges of another, revealing the extent to which "racial attitudes are generically mediated."[25]

We must also confront the debate about the "message" that ends *Sullivan's Travels*. As many have argued, the lesson that Sullivan learns at the church perfectly fits Hollywood ideology and gives audiences one more reason to like the films they already like.[26] And as any good Marxist will tell you, the entertainment industry is devoted to maintaining the status quo. Even the prisoners who are so unjustly victimized can tolerate their lot if they are occasionally amused by images of animated dogs. The good Marxist would also point out that religion is "the opiate of the people" and that the African Americans in Sturges's church are less likely to rise up against daily indignities—not to mention a culture that embraces lynching—if they imagine a divine reward for welcoming "neighbors less fortunate." And finally, in terms of how blacks are represented, the scene in the church is consistent with what James Naremore has called the 1930s "folkloric" view of African Americans as a simple people torn between a righteous path and the pleasures of the flesh. Naremore singles out the all-black-cast film *Cabin in the Sky* (1943) as a good example of the folkloric view, especially in the early scenes when Little Joe (Eddie "Rochester" Anderson) must choose between attending church with his pious wife Petunia (Ethel Waters) and rolling dice at the dance hall.[27] Although Sturges shows us only one half of this folkloric dichotomy, he buys into the tradition with the devout, homespun parishioners in *Sullivan's Travels* as well as with the folk wisdom the janitor dispenses in *Christmas in July* when he tells Ellen what to make of the black cat rubbing against her leg.

STURGES AND COMPANY

Except for a few scenes in which he has written piquant dialogue for porters and janitors, Sturges was very much a creature of his historical moment and consistently embraced the old racial stereotypes. Sturges nevertheless deserves praise simply for giving work to black actors. The handful of African Americans working regularly in Hollywood surely earned more than they could have with almost any other employer. As Hattie McDaniel famously observed, "I'd rather play a maid than be a maid." And at Paramount, according to Tom Sturges, bit players who spoke lines were not paid by the week, as was usually the case in Hollywood, but for the duration of the shoot. Since Sturges gave lines to almost all of his African American characters, they were making a better living than the average actor with a small part in an American film.[28]

At least two black men were part of the Sturges repertory company even if they were not as ubiquitous as William Demarest, Jimmy Conlin, Robert Grieg, and Franklin Pangborn. Fred Toones (1906–62), the bartender in *The Palm Beach Story*, has the astounding distinction of having appeared in more than two hundred films, many of them race films but even more being from the Hollywood mainstream. He also performs memorably as the janitor in *Christmas in July* as well as in *Remember the Night*, which Sturges wrote.[29] Charles R. Moore (1893–1947), who appeared in more than one hundred films throughout his career, was even more active in the Sturges circle. He plays the exceptionally observant Pullman porter in *The Palm Beach Story* who doubts that John D. really owns a "yachet." He is also in *The Great McGinty*, *Christmas in July*, *Sullivan's Travels*, *Hail the Conquering Hero*, and *The Sin of Harold Diddlebock*. In addition, Moore appeared in two films in which Sturges had a hand, *Diamond Jim* and *I Married a Witch*. Diane Jacobs reports that Sturges would pick on William Demarest, especially after the actor began disagreeing with Sturges's claims that he was responsible for Demarest's career.[30] But by all accounts, Sturges was friendly with almost all of the many actors who repeatedly show up in his films. With his black actors, he may have been as consistently "gentlemanly" as he was with the actor in *Sullivan's Travels* who took the time to thank him in a personal letter.

Rather than anachronistically condemn Sturges for not treating African Americans with the respect we now believe everyone deserves, we should think of him as a successful and talented artisan working in a popular medium more than ten years before a vigorous civil rights movement would put black schoolchildren in previously all-white schools and Martin Luther King, Jr. on the cover of *Time* magazine. Treating black people as equal participants in America's experiment with democracy was surely not a priority with Sturges, just as it was of little concern to those in his overwhelmingly white audience.

Sturges was probably much more interested in pleasing the Breen Office than in pleasing his black audience. Nevertheless, he must have had real respect for African American actors such as Jess Lee Brooks, to whom he gave so much face time in *Sullivan's Travels*. He was even more devoted to the black members of his repertory company, bringing them back in film after film and making sure that they made the most of the time they were on the screen. They may never have got the best of Sturges, but Sturges definitely got the best that they could give as members of the acting profession.

NOTES

1 John Pym, *The Palm Beach Story*. BFI Film Classics (London: British Film Institute Publishing, 1998), 38.
2 Born Siegfried Aron in 1895, Sig Arno was a German Jew who began his film career playing mostly comic roles. He has small but significant parts in *The Love of Jeanne Ney* (1927), *Pandora's Box* (1929), and *Diary of a Lost Girl* (1929), all directed by G. W. Pabst. After fleeing Germany in 1933 he eventually landed in Hollywood, where he regularly played eccentric European waiters, musicians, professors, and socialites, but none as over-the-top as Toto in *The Palm Beach Story*.
3 Ruth Vasey, "Diplomatic Representations: Accommodating the Foreign Market," *The World According to Hollywood, 1918–1939* (Madison, WI: University of Wisconsin Press, 1997), 158–93.
4 Eric Lott, *Love and Theft: Blackface Minstrelsy and the American Working Class* (New York, NY: Oxford University Press, 1993). Also see W. T. Lhamon, *Raising Cain: Blackface Performance from Jim Crow to Hip Hop* (Cambridge, MA: Harvard University Press, 1998), William J. Mahar, *Behind the Burnt Cork Mask: Early Blackface Minstrelsy and Antebellum American Popular Culture* (Urbana, IL: University of Illinois Press, 1999), and Robert C. Toll, *Blacking Up: The Minstrel Show in Nineteenth-Century America* (New York, NY: Oxford University Press, 1977).
5 Michael Rogin, *Blackface, White Noise: Jewish Immigrants in the Hollywood Melting Pot* (Berkeley, CA: University of California Press, 1996).
6 Donald Bogle, *Toms, Coon, Mulattoes, Mammies, and Bucks: An Interpretive History of Blacks in American Films*, new ed. (New York, NY: Continuum, 1992), 54.
7 Louis Armstrong made "When It's Sleepy Time Down South" something of an anthem. He sang it at virtually every one of his performances throughout most of his career.
8 Thomas Cripps, *Slow Fade to Black: The Negro in American Film, 1900–1942* (New York, NY: Oxford University Press, 1977), 275.
9 When the economy turned sour in 1894, Pullman lowered wages for his workers but not the amount they had to pay for rent or the prices they were charged in the company stores. When the workers went on strike, Pullman persuaded President Grover Cleveland to suppress them with federal troops. The troops eventually fired on the strikers, killing several. After the report of a national commission and a Supreme Court ruling, the town of Pullman was divested and made part of the city of Chicago. See Dominic A. Pacyga, *Chicago: A Biography* (Chicago, IL: University of Chicago Press, 2009).
10 Larry Tye, *Rising From the Rails: Pullman Porters and the Making of the Black Middle Class* (New York, NY: Henry Holt, 2004).

11 Preston Sturges Papers (Collection 1114). Department of Special Collections, University Research Library, University of California, Los Angeles, Box 71, Folder 1.

12 But as Jeff Jaeckle pointed out in a comment on the first draft of this paper, McGinty was initially successful *because* he was contemptuous and self-centered. His downfall only comes *after* he has begun to care. When he kisses his sham wife, for example, he says, "I musta been blind."

13 Brian Henderson, *Five Screenplays* (Berkeley, CA: University of California Press, 1985), 137.

14 Diane Jacobs, *Christmas in July: The Life and Art of Preston Sturges* (Berkeley, CA: University of California Press, 1992), 64.

15 Brian Henderson, *Four More Screenplays of Preston Sturges* (Berkeley, CA: University of California Press, 1995), 61.

16 Pym, 48.

17 Richard Dyer, *Heavenly Bodies: Film Stars and Society* (New York, NY: St. Martin's, 1986), 103.

18 In this context, see Sarah Kozloff's arguments in this volume about Sturges and his collaborators, including actors, as well as Diane Carson's chapter on acting.

19 Jacobs, 262.

20 Clayton R. Koppes and Gregory D. Black, "Blacks, Loyalty, and Motion Picture Propaganda in World War II," *Controlling Hollywood: Censorship and Regulation in the Studio Era*, ed. Matthew Bernstein (New Brunswick, NJ: Rutgers University Press, 1999), 142.

21 Thomas Cripps, *Making Movies Black: The Hollywood Message Movie from World War II to the Civil Rights Era* (New York, NY: Oxford University Press, 1993), 94.

22 Charles Musser, "Why Did Negroes Love Al Jolson and *The Jazz Singer*? Melodrama, Blackface and Cosmopolitan Theatrical Culture," *Film History* 23.2 (2011): 196–222.

23 Ella Shohat and Robert Stam, *Unthinking Eurocentrism: Multiculturalism and the Media* (New York, NY: Routledge, 1994), 210.

24 Shohat, 210.

25 Shohat, 210.

26 See Virginia Wexman's chapter in this volume for an extended discussion of the various "messages" in *Sullivan's Travels*.

27 James Naremore, *The Films of Vincente Minnelli* (New York, NY: Cambridge University Press, 1993), 54.

28 See the interview with Tom Sturges available at <http://www.youtube.com/watch?v=c7DIuzWsdBA> (last accessed 17 April 2015).

29 Of all the black characters in Sturges's work, none is as stupid or as hapless as the valet played by Toones in *Remember the Night*.

30 Jacobs, 266.

CHAPTER 8

Falling Hard:
The Sin of Harold Diddlebock

Joe McElhaney

A STRANGE EPIPHANY

The Sin of Harold Diddlebock (1947) occupies an uncertain position in the filmography of Preston Sturges. It was the first and, as it turned out, last film he made as an independent producer after leaving Paramount, the studio where, between 1940 and 1944, his reputation as a writer-director was established. In 1944, Sturges and Howard Hughes formed California Pictures, an early example of the move toward independent production then being made by directors who had previously worked within the Hollywood studio system. But 1944 would also be the year Paramount released two of Sturges's biggest commercial successes, *The Miracle of Morgan's Creek* (which opened in January but was filmed two years earlier) and *Hail the Conquering Hero* (which opened early in August). Late in August 1944, however, Paramount finally released *The Great Moment*, an important project for Sturges and, like *Miracle*, shot two years earlier. *The Miracle of Morgan's Creek* was, in spite of the enormous challenges it presented in terms of the dictates of the Hays Code (which were largely responsible for delaying the film's release), eventually shown in a version close to Sturges's intentions. *The Great Moment*, on the other hand, was significantly recut by the studio's head of production, B. G. De Sylva, a decision on De Sylva's part that was central in Sturges leaving Paramount.[1] *The Great Moment*, a departure for Sturges, was a major critical and commercial disappointment. *Diddlebock*, which began shooting in September 1945, promised far greater control for Sturges and, consequently, the possibility of a return to critical and popular favor. But it, too, faced post-production problems, as well as an enormously protracted shooting schedule brought on by the comparative freedom Sturges was now luxuriating in as his own producer. Tentatively released two years later in Miami, Portland, and San Francisco to good reviews, the film was soon withdrawn by a dissatisfied Hughes and held up for three years, recut by him, and released in 1950 as *Mad Wednesday*. It, too, was a financial failure. In the years between *Diddlebock* and *Mad Wednesday*, Sturges signed a contract with Twentieth Century-Fox, where he made *Unfaithfully Yours* (1948) and *The Beautiful Blonde from Bashful Bend* (1949). The former of these is now regarded as one of Sturges's major achievements. But on its release, it confirmed the general sense of a decline, as did *Beautiful Blonde*, a film featuring the studio's biggest star, Betty Grable, but one that nonetheless did not find either financial or critical favor.

Unlike *The Great Moment*, *The Sin of Harold Diddlebock* survives in a (non-*Mad Wednesday*) form that allows one to arrive at a sense of Sturges's intentions. Moreover, scholars have not entirely neglected the film. For example, two recent book-length studies of the director, Alessandro Pirolini's *The Cinema of Preston Sturges: A Critical Study* and Jay Rozgonyi's *Preston Sturges's Vision of America: Critical Analyses of Fourteen Films*, devote sustained attention to *Diddlebock*. On the other hand, a Sturges biographer, James Curtis, has argued that the film "lacked the polish and drive of Sturges's Paramount pictures," while also complaining of how the film's "pacing faltered" and that the "overall look" of the film gave the appearance of something shot on a low budget (when the opposite was the case).[2] I would not necessarily dispute this general observation of Curtis's. But I prefer to follow the lead of another biographer, Diane Jacobs, when she writes that the film amounts to a strange type of "epiphany" for Sturges, in which we find "the one time in his working life when he did exactly as he pleased."[3]

Since the mid-1970s, *The Sin of Harold Diddlebock* has been in the public domain and largely circulates in low-grade 16mm prints. As of this writing, the only DVD/home video versions of the film have been derived from this second-rate source material (also the source for most television showings). Such an orphaned status is entirely fitting for this *film maudit*. For most screenings today, *Diddlebock* looks like a ruin of its former self. But even in its original state, it is unlikely that it had anywhere near the professional sheen of the films that Sturges made for Paramount—presupposing that such professionalism is, in itself, inherently a virtue.[4]

That the film's substantial budget and long shooting schedule did not translate into a lavishly detailed visual spectacle could be regarded as a type of failure. As we shall see, though, such a cavalier attitude toward money, and to those who are in control of it, is one of the essential projects of the film. *Diddlebock* is, in fact, a work in which many of the fundamental implications of Sturges's cinema are being articulated in a manner that is often unlike his previous work at Paramount. The film is sometimes exploratory in form and tone, as though Sturges is attempting to stake out entirely new territory for himself, even as he also falls back on strategies and effects from earlier films. In particular in terms of the latter, the film reworks elements of *Christmas in*

July (1940), Sturges's second film as writer-director. But *Diddlebock* revisits
that earlier film in order to pursue its implications in different ways. *The Sin of
Harold Diddlebock* is a major achievement for Sturges, even as it also requires
the spectator to adjust certain expectations. In its story situation, and in the
conflicts facing its protagonist, the film is overtly *about* failure and decline:
physical, mental, social, and economic. But it is also willing to implicate itself
in the very process it is dramatizing, to become (in a very deliberate sense) an
allegory of failure.

COLD HANDS OF TIME

In *The Palm Beach Story* (1942), the elderly businessman, the Wienie King
(Robert Dudley), propels the dramatic action forward. Early in the film,
he lectures on the importance of taking action in life because "cold are the
hands of time that creep along, relentlessly, destroying slowly but without
pity that which yesterday was young." Dudley was part of a group of character actors who formed Sturges's "stock company" at Paramount and he,
along with most of the group, appears in *Diddlebock*. The actors forming this
company were middle-aged or older, and in many of the Paramount films this
allowed for them to contrast with the dynamism or movie-star glamour of
the romantic leads and to become part of a vital community of mutually supportive chaos. With *Diddlebock*, however, this has given way to an oppressive
atmosphere of thick dust, of hostile work and family environments, and with
a movie star at its center who is not only aging but tied to another era of the
cinema: its silent period.

When *Diddlebock* opened in France in 1951, in its *Mad Wednesday* form,
it was the subject of an André Bazin review. Central to Bazin's review was
the presence of the lead actor playing Diddlebock, the great silent comic star
Harold Lloyd, returning to the screen for the first time since 1938. For Bazin,
Sturges bringing Lloyd back to cinematic life becomes the comic star's "final
reason to exist." Yet by "revealing the physical imprint of time on Lloyd's
face—with a distressing and almost lewd cruelty—Sturges ultimately reduces
to ashes the idol whom he had just restored to glory."[5] Such a concern with
aging and death, and with the "imprint of time" on an actor's face, is not
unusual for Bazin. It is central to his writings on Humphrey Bogart, Jean
Gabin and, especially, another great silent comic star, Charles Chaplin, as
these actors are appearing in projects in which the ravages of aging are increasingly visible.[6] Nonetheless, we are dealing with a passage of time that is not
simply personal and biological. We are also dealing with this passage in terms
of the cinema as an aesthetic, cultural, and technological form, in which the
actor's physical and symbolic body becomes implicated. The cinema changes,

continually testifying to the historical moment in which it is being made even as it leaves in its wake a sense of things left behind. Of Chaplin's *Monsieur Verdoux* (1947), released the same year as *Diddlebock*, Bazin writes: "The transition from orthochromatic stock to panchromatic should itself alone have brought on a veritable morphological disorder, more serious perhaps than even the introduction of the spoken word: acknowledging and revealing that the actor was aging, it ate away at the character."[7]

Bazin's melancholy, informed by a dialectical awareness of history, is the product of postwar attitudes toward the cinema. Access to older films, via film clubs, repertory houses, museums, and (somewhat later) television, gives birth to a variety of discourses on cinema and leads to an increased awareness of the breadth of film history. This is particularly the case in France, where Sturges would soon settle and where he would make his final film, *Les Carnets du Major Thompson* (1955). Within such a climate, an "old" Chaplin film can culturally coexist on the same level as *Monsieur Verdoux*. And a Harold Lloyd silent film, such as *The Freshman* (1925), can be placed side by side with *The Sin of Harold Diddlebock*. And yet such coexistence is not without historical ironies, especially the degree to which one may be continually reminded of past glories that are not being fully achieved in the present day—or, at least, not in the same manner. In particular, we are aware of historical passage; since the aging star is also a myth, the mythology is bound up with the cultural moment from which that stardom emerged.

In the case of Lloyd, the myth is that of "Harold," a naive young man (defined iconographically by his circular-rimmed glasses and straw hat), often middle- or working-class but optimistically striving for something more spectacular. By the time of *Diddlebock* Lloyd was middle-aged, and even though he is again "Harold," wearing the iconic glasses and, at first, the straw hat, his aging is quite apparent, with the film's cinematography doing virtually nothing to disguise this. Sturges performs an ironic linkage by opening *Diddlebock* with an extended excerpt from the final sequence of *The Freshman*. He explicitly identifies the earlier Lloyd film through an intertitle even as he simultaneously absorbs *The Freshman* into the universe of *Diddlebock*, inserting some of his own footage into the original Lloyd material, with one of his own actors, Raymond Walburn, seen cheering from the bleachers (This cheering individual will soon become a major character in the film, E. J. Waggleberry.)

Customarily, critics see such a gesture by Sturges as a tribute to the slapstick tradition of silent comedy. The dedication of *Sullivan's Travels* (1941) "to the memory of those who made us laugh: the motley mountebanks, the clowns, the buffoons, in all times and in all nations, whose efforts have lightened our burden a little" could supply further evidence of this nostalgia. When Manny Farber and W. S. Poster wrote their 1954 essay on Sturges, they argued that the director "was the only legitimate heir of the early American film, combining its various methods, adding new perspectives and developing the whole in a form suitable to a talking picture."[8] Sturges deceptively implies a continuity between Lloyd's cinema and his own near the end of the opening sequence by cutting from footage of Harold winning the football game in *The Freshman* (his teammates hoisting him up on their shoulders) to a shot of Waggleberry cheering, followed by a dissolve of Harold, again on his teammates' shoulders as they carry him into the dressing room. However, the second image of Harold being carried by his teammates was filmed more than twenty years after the first, a sleight of hand that briefly manages to create the possibility that not only the myth but also the face and body of Harold Lloyd are ageless. But such a fondness for the simple and timeless pleasures of physical comedy, and its attendant creative figures, is also for Sturges the site of ambivalence.

Diddlebock was, after *Sullivan's Travels*, *The Miracle of Morgan's Creek* and *Hail the Conquering Hero*, the last of the Sturges films that Bazin reviewed when these works were eventually shown in Paris after the war. In all of his reviews, Bazin is unable to get away from the notion that Sturges is at once reviving older comic traditions and obliterating them, self-consciously marking their end. *Sullivan's Travels*, for example, "constitutes a kind of self-destruction of the genre with which it appears to be connected."[9] If we are to take *The Sin of Harold Diddlebock* as a sequel to *The Freshman*, offering us a new Harold Lloyd for the postwar era, something about the world of that earlier film has gone horribly wrong. Harold Lamb of *The Freshman*, a film that ends on a note of personal and romantic triumph, has become Harold Diddlebock, stuck in a low-paying, dead-end bookkeeping job at an advertising agency run by Waggleberry and about to be fired after twenty-two years of service to the company.

"His body looks like that of a desiccated 200-year-old locust weighed down by an enormous copper hat," write Farber and Poster of Walburn in *Diddlebock*[10] (whose Waggleberry has clear links with his equally nefarious Dr. Maxford in *Christmas in July* and Major Noble in *Hail the Conquering Hero*). But he does not seem markedly older than Lloyd. In reality, Walburn was only six years Lloyd's senior. Diddlebock is supposed to be 44 but Lloyd was 50 when the film was being shot. In the sequence in which Waggleberry fires Diddlebock, he gives Harold a watch (with its own "cold hands of time") as a severance gift, a brutal gesture in light of the reason he is firing Diddlebock: as time and history have moved forward, Diddlebock does not. This forward movement of history is overtly signaled prior to this through a montage sequence built around a presidential calendar hanging on the office wall, that takes us from June 1923 (photo of Warren G. Harding) up through June 1945 (photo of Harry Truman), set to an orchestral version of "America the Beautiful." Waggleberry's speech in relation to this firing, though, suggests that Harold's problem is more complex than a question of either time standing still as the world moves forward or of Harold simply decaying: "You have not only ceased to go forward, you have gone backward. You have not only stopped regressing, you have stopped thinking. You not only make the same mistakes, year after year, you don't even change your apologies. You have become a bottleneck."

Diddlebock's stasis, which is both physical and mental, creates an awareness of time that is not so much linear as negatively dialectical. Stasis turns in on itself while moving both backward and forward, all of this creating the pervasive sense of waste and decay. Within such an environment, even the young become implicated, placing particular pressure on the function of romance. The male/female couple had been central to the structure of virtually all of Sturges's previous films, albeit often characterized by comically uneven pairings rather than romantic ideals of equality between the sexes. But in *Diddlebock*, Harold's romance with Miss Otis (Frances Ramsden) is secondary, at best, and caught up in the film's obsession with stalled temporality and repetition. Miss Otis is the seventh and youngest of a family of sisters with whom Harold had fallen in love over many years, all previous Miss Otises having finally deserted Harold for more decisive men. "I was even in love with the same girl all my life," Harold later says, "except in different bodies." Ramsden (a fashion model and Sturges discovery) was twenty-two years younger than Lloyd and the credit sequence of the film makes a great show of presenting her as an exciting new talent ("And for the first time a young girl called Frances Ramsden playing the youngest Miss Otis"). But like Lloyd, Ramsden would make no more films after *Diddlebock* and her youthful presence, almost as much as Lloyd's aging one, is absorbed into the film's atmosphere of failure.

BALANCING ACTS

"Most Sturges heroes," Penelope Houston has written, "have some difficulty in keeping their balance."[11] Time and again throughout his films, Sturges draws upon the image of falling. This may be a simple pratfall, such as the recurring gag of Officer Kockenlocker (William Demarest) in *The Miracle of Morgan's Creek* attempting to administer a swift kick to his daughter, Emmy (Diana Lynn), but instead missing the mark and falling on his own rear end. But Sturges is obsessed with the question of "the fall" in all of its implications, including the Fall of Man, which *The Lady Eve* (1941), with its witty Garden of Eden citations, makes overt. Beyond this, however, the metaphor of "the fall" has become part of Sturges's own mythology: the star director whose brilliance quickly exhausted itself and whose final years were spent on the fringes of the industry of which he once was such a central figure. Only seven years after *Diddlebock*, Farber and Poster would write that Sturges was "leaping into relative obscurity."[12] Given the degree to which some of Lloyd's most indelible screen moments during the silent era involve him precariously attempting to balance himself in relation to spaces of great height a collaboration with Sturges might initially promise to be a seamless one. But critics have widely remarked/noted that Sturges and Lloyd did not get along during the shoot of *Diddlebock*.[13] This would only be of anecdotal interest if it did not also affect the form of the film itself.

Lloyd's presence in *Diddlebock*, while part of the film's original conception, creates an unresolved tension in the work. Central to their collaborative disharmony were their opposed approaches to the material: for Lloyd, the comedy needed fundamentally to arise from sight gags and visual set-pieces; for Sturges, it had to arise from dialogue. It would be simplistic, however, to establish a strong opposition between Lloyd's comic world of the visual and Sturges's of the verbal. *The Freshman*, for example, exhibits frequent playful attention to language (via intertitles), through Harold's rehearsals as a potential college cheerleader ("Brack! Kack!! Brack Kack!!" or "Hi Ta Ticky Bing! Bang! Blooey! Chop!"); and the coach in the film engages in alliteration that would find a happy home in a Sturges film ("You dubs are dead from your dandruff down"). Moreover, a Sturges film is likely to contain a good deal of slapstick comedy. "I happen to love pratfalls," Sturges writes.[14] However, it is one thing for *The Freshman*, with its extended comic set pieces, to periodically engage in playful intertitles and quite another for Lloyd to be given (as *Diddlebock* does) extended amounts of spoken dialogue, which must frequently be recited while standing up, gesture and physical movement kept to a minimum, as though Sturges wanted to work *against* some of Lloyd's strengths as an actor.[15] And it is one thing for Sturges to ask sound-era actors to submit to occasional slapstick bits and quite another for Sturges to be confronted, for the first and last time in his career, with an actor whose stardom was founded on his relationship to physical comedy rather than dialogue. But we might trace the tensions between the two men to other matters.

Lloyd's silent films, for all of their skillfulness, essentially accept the world in its present state in a way that Sturges's films never do. Thanks to Harold's ingenuity, all suffering, pain, and injustice are a temporary inconvenience. *The Sin of Harold Diddlebock* is far more skeptical about such energies. As I have argued elsewhere, the ferocious drives of Sturges's characters are often tied to exhaustion, even death.[16] To take possession of the world in Sturges, to enact one's goals is at once a conscious mental activity *and* a physical one, a literal putting into action. At the same time, due to the enormous resistance of the surrounding world, such drives (even if temporarily successful) often expire or implode. By opening *Diddlebock* with the final sequence of *The Freshman*, Sturges moves what would otherwise be a traditional climax for a film to its beginning so that the remainder of the film involves an attempt to return to that sense of triumph with which the narrative began. But *Diddlebock* also effectively begins as a silent film, the historical setting of the story in the time of silent cinema, before moving ahead in the life of not only Diddlebock but also the cinema itself. For both Harolds, this passage constitutes a fall: for Diddlebock, from his brief stardom in winning the football game to being quickly hired to serve at the bottom of the economic ladder at an advertising agency; and for Lloyd, from being one of the top stars of the silent era to being a comparatively minor figure in sound cinema, now trapped in the midst of a film made by a major comedy director whose style is nevertheless rather different from his own.

Either through predetermined design or through the tensions in their collaboration, the humor of much of *Diddlebock* resides in the dialogue, but with the film bracketed by extended visual comic set pieces: the prologue (comprising primarily footage from *The Freshman*) and the final third of the film, in which some of Lloyd's other silent films are evoked, in particular *High and Dizzy* (1920) and *Safety Last* (1923), with their sequences of Lloyd precariously attempting to balance himself on the ledges or facades of tall office buildings. In contrast to these earlier Lloyd silent classics, however, Sturges shoots these echoing moments in the studio. In the Lloyd originals, because of the location shooting, viewers feel a sense of immediacy, even of danger, when Lloyd climbs the buildings or teeters on a ledge. Lloyd's silent films acknowledge and incorporate a realistic surrounding environment into their stylized physical action. *Diddlebock* removes this realism and, along with it, the element of physical risk, so that the slapstick becomes more remote, almost theoretical. In *High and Dizzy*, Lloyd follows a sleepwalking Mildred Davis out of the window of a tall building as both of them walk about on a small ledge, Lloyd dangerously teetering about and initially oblivious to the real danger. When Lloyd teeters on the ledge of an office building in *Diddlebock*, he does so not only on an obvious studio set but with rear projection used to suggest the surrounding environment of Lower Manhattan. Moreover, Lloyd does not ascend the building through the ingenious and miraculous methods of his silent films (as in *Safety Last*, when he literally crawls up the side of an office building) but instead more prosaically ascends through a fire escape.

Revealingly, Sturges's dedication in *Sullivan's Travels* is to the "memory" of the tradition of the clown, not to its potential ongoing vitality. Lloyd reportedly did not wish to perform the stunts in the film himself at all ("I've gotten a little past that point," he told Sturges) and had to be persuaded to do so, after the initial footage with a stunt double proved unsatisfactory.[17] The Harold Lloyd of *The Sin of Harold Diddlebock* is not the naively dynamic young figure of *The Freshman*, a target of practical jokes and cruel laughter who ultimately triumphs. Diddlebock cannot transform his environment but is weighed down and oppressed by it. "I'm just an old has-been," he states, a line that has a clear resonance in relation to Lloyd himself, here for the first and last time being asked to directly enact his own aging and faltering command of the world around him. Such a faltering is especially apparent in the film when Harold is called upon to speak.

LANGUAGE, MONEY, POWER

In virtually all of Sturges, command of spoken language is crucial to a command of the world. In *Christmas in July*, for example, a contest for a new advertising slogan for Maxford's coffee is, for Jimmy (Dick Powell), not *simply* a contest: its $25,000 prize amounts to his escape from the world of the working class, a miraculous and overnight form of upward economic mobility. The world of advertising returns in *Diddlebock*, but in a more savage vein, in which a fall is partly enacted *through* language. Even though the historical time period for the first meeting with Waggleberry is that of silent cinema, spoken language quickly engulfs Diddlebock. Waggleberry (who, in spite of his excitement at witnessing Diddlebock win the game, does not even remember him when he is standing in his office several months later) does most of the talking:

> We don't start people at the top, you understand. That would be too easy. We do it the American way: we give them an opportunity to work up from the bottom. What satisfaction! What a feeling of accomplishment you will have when you are able to look back from whatever rung of the ladder your, uh, go-gettiveness would have placed you for and say, "I, I did that!"

A little bomb ticks inside of this motivational speech. The speech taps into the American myth that individual initiative and hard work are all one needs in order to succeed, even as the same words (delivered by Waggleberry in a tone of blatantly exaggerated gusto, with emphatic gestures, foregrounding the hypocrisy of what is being spoken) imply the overwhelming odds against anything of the kind happening. The speech given by Betty (Ellen Drew) to her boss, J. B. Baxter (Ernest Truex) at the end of *Christmas in July* provides another perspective on the same issue, but recited with a breathless sincerity by a less cynical individual. Betty defends her boyfriend Jimmy's right to receive a promotion at his company, even though they have just discovered that Jimmy's winning of the contest was a hoax. Betty's speech unwittingly makes clear that such success is available to a distinct minority even as the economic system itself engenders a non-stop supply of fantasy for just such success:

> He belongs in here because he thinks he has ideas. He belongs in here until he proves himself or fails. Then somebody else belongs in here until

he proves himself or fails, and somebody else after that, and somebody else after him, and so on and for always. Well, I don't know how to put it into words like Jimmy could. But all he wants, all any of them wants is a chance to show, to find out what they've got while they're still young and burning like a shortcut or a stepping stone. Oh, I know they're not going to succeed. At least most of them aren't. They'll all be like Mr. Waterbury soon enough, most of them, anyway, but they won't mind it. They'll find something else and they'll be happy because they had their chance. Because it's one thing to muff a chance when you get it, but it's another thing never to have had a chance.

The Mr. Waterbury to whom she is referring is her own and Jimmy's immediate (and deeply punctilious) supervisor who, early in the film, delivers his own justification to Jimmy for his own mediocre standing:

I'm not a failure. I'm a success. You see, ambition is all right if it works. But no system could be right where only half of one per cent were successes and all the rest were failures. That wouldn't be right. I'm not a failure. I'm a success. And so are you, if you earn your own living and pay your bills and look the world in the eye. I hope you win your $25,000, Mr. MacDonald.

This last sentence of Waterbury's that I have quoted above suggests that, like Waggleberry (although from a different position of power, their last names at once linked and contrasted with one another), he does not quite believe in the ideology to which he is giving voice. But Jimmy is, as Betty makes clear, young and filled with a desire to succeed.

Harold, on the other hand, is oblivious to the rapid passage of time that occurs around him and, as a result, language becomes primarily a collection of mummified clichés. Jimmy's slogan ("If you can't sleep at night, it isn't the coffee, it's the bunk."), while certainly avoiding mastery, at least demonstrates an attempt to transform language to a particular economic and social purpose. By contrast, Harold can only repeat the most careworn aphorisms and proverbs. Even at his initial meeting with the voluble Waggleberry, Harold mainly responds to him with statements such as: "He who loseth honor, loseth everything." Or: "Every man is the architect of his own fortune." (Both of these will assume an ironic function in relation to the narrative that develops.) In the space the company gives Harold to work in as a bookkeeper (alternately referred to by Waggleberry as a "nook," a "niche," and a "cranny"), he nails over a dozen of these proverbs and aphorisms, printed on signs, to a billboard. Harold accepts language's function and meaning in its present state while being simultaneously surrounded by advertising, a world in which the primary rhetorical function of language is to sell a product. Harold tells Waggleberry at their first meeting that he is "bursting with ideas." Waggleberry, however, tells him to "contain them, save them, don't squirt them all out at once. The Idea Department is a little congested at the moment. It always is, for that matter." In the environment at Waggleberry's, thought is solely tied to the flow and logic of capital, and in which the worker must also be young, "full of zing, full of zest, full of zowy," as Waggleberry phrases it. Even though Waggleberry insists that a "man is as young as his ideas" clearly biology plays no less important a part for him in determining success or failure. "A firm is only as young as its employees," Waggleberry explains to Diddlebock, as he begins the process of dismissing him. "My father fired anyone who got over fifty. Man, woman or child, it didn't matter to him. That was the cornerstone of his success." Diddlebock's atrophied use of language becomes the verbal equivalent of his aging face and body, and of the dust that literally and metaphorically gathers around him.

Even Diddlebock's being fired does not immediately shock him out of his tendency to speak in cliché. His meeting of the itinerant Wormy (Jimmy Conlin) on the street outside of the firm involves an exchange between the two men in which Wormy initially undercuts each of Diddlebock's aphorisms with a line that suggests an alternate logic in relation to questions of money and ethics:

Harold: A fool and his money are soon parted.
Wormy: Yeah, but think what beautiful memories he lays up.
Harold: He who lendeth money, endeth friendship.
Wormy: Oh, that's all right. We ain't friends. I never even seen you before.

This exchange, with its evocation of vaudeville comedy, is still not quite enough to shake Diddlebock out of his stasis, and instead Wormy challenges Harold by responding to each aphorism or proverb with another equally well-known one that contradicts the message of the previous one:

Wormy: You're never too old to learn.
Harold: You can't teach an old dog new tricks.
Wormy: Every dog is entitled to one bite.
Harold: Let sleeping dogs lie.
Wormy: A barking dog never bites.
Harold: He who sleepeth with dogs, riseth with fleas.
Wormy: A little wine for thy stomach's sake—that's from the Good Book. . . He who hesitates is lost.
Harold: Lips that touch liquor shall never touch mine.

Wormy: Eat, drink and be merry.

Harold: The priest and the prophet have erred through strong drink. They are swallowed up of wine; they are out of the way of strong drink; they err in vision; they have stumbled in judgment. *Isaiah*: 28

But then, along with Wormy, the teetotaling Harold enters a bar. Diddlebock must literally descend, down a flight of stairs to the basement that houses the huge space of this bar (contrasting with the nook/niche/cranny of his former work space). It is another type of fall, but, in this case, connected to the possibilities of rising again. The bar becomes a new space of language into which Harold is initiated, a space presided over by the brilliantly verbose bartender, Jake (Edgar Kennedy), whose control over spoken language is of an entirely different nature from Waggleberry's. For Waggleberry, all matter and manner of the world is tied to the accumulation of capital. Even his excitement at Harold winning the football game is immediately coopted: "We need your spirit in my business." Jake, on the other hand, turns his profession into a space of performance and creation. "You arouse the artist in me," he tells Harold when he discovers that Harold has never had a drink before in his life, while also adding, "Opportunities like this come along all too rarely for a man with his heart in his work." But Wormy also refers to Jake in this sequence as a scientist and a professor. Jake's approach to both language and the phenomenal world is intuitive and associational while also steeped in concrete knowledge and experience, and he turns the limitations of Harold's world on their head. Work, for Jake, is not tied to drudgery and the absence of thought but to a full-bodied engagement with the world.

"Diddlebock" the cocktail transforms Diddlebock the man into a non-stop monologist, at last setting him free from the world of clichéd utterances and into the world of irony, in which the myth of the American pioneer spirit is initially mythologized before finally given comic contempt:

Look at our forefathers. Look at Washington. Look at Valley Forge. Look at the pioneers ... Men were men in those days ... They mined the earth and doused the rivers and tamed the wilderness and brought forth peaceful homesteads in the shadow of evil and the echo of thundering herds. And in the final analysis, where are they I ask you? Dead, my friends, deader than a boiled mackerel.[18]

There's more. The Diddlebock also causes Harold to go on a bender that lasts for a day and a half. He gambles on a horse and visits a tailor, Formfit Franklin (Franklin Pangborn), who outfits him in an outrageous plaid suit and Stetson hat. All of this functions within traditional comic logic: a repressed character loses inhibition and comes to embrace a spontaneous conception of the world.

But the additional implications of these gestures become clearer when placed in relation to what follows.

BEYOND THE LION'S DEN

As early as Sturges's first important screenplay, for William K. Howard's *The Power and the Glory* (1933), the famous non-chronological structure there complicates the sense of character agency. *The Power and the Glory* deals with the rise of a powerful industrialist while simultaneously muting this figure's capacity to transform himself and his environment, making Sturges's experiment even more remarkable. Through its structure, the film undercuts the American myth of individual initiative and hard work, something that *Diddlebock* articulates in a comic vein. "Diddlebock's real sin was his refusal to think," said Lloyd, "to rise from his inertia."[19] The final third of the film is a laborious attempt by Diddlebock not simply to take action but to regard action and thought as intertwined and to enact this on a scale that he has never before experienced.

The final third of *Diddlebock* is largely set in the world of corporate finance, Wall Street, in which the primary motivating force, the intertwining of thought and action, is that of profit. In Martin Scorsese's *The Wolf of Wall Street* (2013), itself a type of farce in which command of language is central in attaining access to economic and social power, the opening sequence shows a TV commercial in which a lion prowls the offices of an investment bank, the lion becoming a symbol of the "jungle" of capitalist power. A lion is no less central to *The Sin of Harold Diddlebock* and its own journey into Wall Street, but the beast is used in a markedly different manner. When Harold awakens from a blackout brought on by his Diddlebock-infused rampage, he discovers that he has bought a circus, a package deal that includes thirty-seven lions. Of these lions, one emerges as a character in his own right: Jackie.

In contrast to the studio-controlled artifice that surrounds the slapstick elements of the final thirty minutes of the film, Jackie emerges as all too real: a beast of the jungle placed within the stylized world of *Diddlebock*. (Lloyd's understandable fear of this animal, a fear confirmed after the lion snapped at him, became a major source of tension on the set.[20]) Jackie serves as the primary impetus for the physical comedy in the film's final section, sending Diddlebock (wearing his plaid suit and Stetson hat) and Wormy out onto the ledge. In itself the use of a lion (or any animal) in slapstick comedy is unremarkable. But in *Diddlebock*, Jackie becomes the catalyst for the combination of thought and action for which Harold is so desperately searching. Without Jackie, Harold effectively has no power. In the film's final third, Harold brings Jackie into a series of banks, creating terror and essentially blackmailing the bankers into donating to a free circus for impoverished children, a bit of moral do-goodism that marginally links the film with the work of Frank Capra. But the film fundamentally has other (non-Capra) things on its mind.

In praising Chaplin's *The Circus* (1928), Bazin would write that it, like other films from the great silent tradition, bases its sight gags on a "comedy of space" that addresses "the relation of man to things and to the surrounding world."[21] In one notable sequence, Chaplin's Tramp gets into a cage with a lion. "Chaplin is truly in the lion's cage," Bazin writes, "and both are enclosed within the framework of the screen."[22] Nonetheless, when the lion turns and roars at the Tramp, Chaplin quickly runs out of the cage, and our laughter arises through Chaplin's speed and dexterity in extricating himself from the harsh reality of this "enclosed framework." Lloyd's Diddlebock is not permitted such an easy escape and must remain in the enclosed framework of the film's final section. Even though it is clear that some shots involve doubles for Lloyd or the lion, the overwhelming experience of these later sequences is of an actual lion placed within the cardboard sets of a movie and extensively coexisting with human beings. One may also be reminded here of the use of the leopard Baby in Howard Hawks's *Bringing Up Baby* (1938), an animal likewise set loose within an ostensibly civilized community. But in the Hawks film, we are closer to the realm of Shakespearian romance, in which human relations with the natural world become tied to a magical, transformative and reciprocal energy and in which the formation of the couple becomes central. *Diddlebock*, by contrast, remains firmly urban and avoids any placement of its characters in natural settings. Instead, its journey takes us into the heart of the concrete jungle, as Jackie becomes the most extravagant example of the drive toward chaos and destruction that underpins so much of Sturges.

When Harold first consumes the Diddlebock, he makes a noise that sounds like an animal letting out a howl. Before he finds a new gift for speech he must first perform an animal-like cleansing ritual, leaving behind the more repressive aspects of a humanity-based civilization of semantics in order to coexist with the world of animals. The animal motif runs through the film. "What is it—a horse blanket?" Harold's puritanical sister (Margaret Hamilton) asks Harold in relation to a vulgar plaid jacket he is wearing the morning after his alcohol-induced rampage. That jacket, part of the suit that Formfit sells Harold, was originally made for a dog act, at once implying a connection to vaudeville comedy that Wormy has already introduced into the film, and to animals as entertainers for human amusement. Harold throwing his money away on a horse race not only takes a philosophical step back from the literal and metaphoric investment in capital that dominates his environment (money, he drunkenly declares in the horse race sequence, "is nothing but a symbol that costs practically nothing to print"), but also further links humans with animals in that the horse he invests in is named Emilene, the name of his aunt. In

Sturges's screenplay for Mitchell Leisen's *Easy Living* (1937), where Edward Arnold's banker character is nicknamed the Bull of Broad Street, black cats are an uncertain symbol for bad luck, a symbol that returns in an equivocal fashion in *Christmas in July*.

Although Jackie is part of this world of trained animals, the film also positions him as a sheer force of nature, terrorizing the banking system and the humans working for it who perpetuate its financial dealings.[23] All of the men Harold and Jackie confront on Wall Street are themselves aging, the most extreme of these being the nearly-blind Robert McDuffy (played by the Wienie King himself, Robert Dudley), who initially mistakes Jackie for a dog. The aging here, however, is tied less to questions of physical decline than to the ossification, the deep entrenchment of this economic environment. The film implies that the only possible form of resistance to the immutability of capitalist economics is through a threatened violence outside the realm of conventional human confrontations. In his sheer size and scale, Jackie is almost too much for Sturges's world; its structured artifice can barely accommodate the messiness of animals striding (or, in the case of the snake in *The Lady Eve*, slithering) into its studio-controlled universe.

ENDLESS

The resolutions to most Sturges films depend upon sudden ironic changes in the narrative structure or unexpected twists of fate. In *Christmas in July*, for example, Jimmy is first the victim of a hoax in claiming that he was the winner of the Maxford contest but then miraculously wins the contest prize after all. But the ending to a Sturges film will often not so much engage in narrative closure as push the basic issues and conflicts of the film into a seemingly endless spiral of repetition and duplication: the sextuplets in the final sequence of *The Miracle of Morgan's Creek* becoming tiny embodiments of this resistance to things coming to an end. *Diddlebock* does not aim for such bold formalist strategies in its resolution and, by contrast, offers a rather abrupt final sequence in which the burden of exposition is placed on the shoulders of the frail Miss Otis: during a second consumption of the Diddlebock, we are told, Harold blacked out again and his circus was sold to Barnum & Bailey for $175,000; Waggleberry has not only restored Harold's job but elevated him to an executive position; and Harold has married Miss Otis. Harold howls one final time here, not due to the drink but to the happy news of his marriage, as the horse-drawn carriage that he purchased during his first blackout takes off, this one-time sound of rebellion and transformation now giving itself over to romance and marriage.

That Diddlebock has not only gotten his job back but has been promoted to a high position within the firm can be taken, like Jimmy's promotion, as a miraculous form of upward mobility, albeit in this instance occurring very late in life. But the film has so systematically criticized the entire system on which the Waggleberrys of this world achieve their power that Diddlebock's inclusion back into that system can be interpreted less as a happy ending than as a cruel, ironic joke. Far from escaping that world, Diddlebock falls back into it. And as Miss Otis herself notes, Barnum & Bailey purchase Harold's circus not in order to follow through on Harold's desire for free admission but rather to circumvent the possibility that such an altruistic gesture could ever occur. A temporarily revitalized (but nevertheless still aging) Harold returns to an environment of short-term memories and relentless forward progress, marrying a woman who is, in her youth, a symbol of new beginnings while also being the sixth copy of the same woman he has been in love with for many years, the attraction in Sturges for duplication and repetition manifesting itself once again. For Farber and Poster, *The Sin of Harold Diddlebock* marks "a kind of ultimate in grisly, dilapidated humor."[24] For Sturges, though, the film was little more than "amusing nonsense with a small grain of sense under it all."[25] What is this "small grain of sense"? Sturges doesn't say. As with so much that surrounds *The Sin of Harold Diddlebock*, we mainly face ambivalence, equivocation, and unresolved questions.

NOTES

1   See *Preston Sturges by Preston Sturges*, ed. Sandy Sturges (New York, NY: Simon & Schuster, 1990), 297–9.

2   James Curtis, *Between Flops: A Biography of Preston Sturges* (New York, NY: Harcourt Brace Jovanovich, Publishers, 1982), 219.

3   Diane Jacobs, *Christmas in July: The Life and Art of Preston Sturges* (Berkeley, CA: University of California Press, 1992), 346.

4   The film's cinematographer is the German refugee Curt Courant (here billed as Curtis Courant), whose important credits include Fritz Lang's *Woman in the Moon* (1929), Alfred Hitchcock's *The Man Who Knew Too Much* (1934), Jean Renoir's *La Bête humaine* (1938), and Marcel Carné's *Le Jour se lève* (1939), all visually striking films, suggesting that *Diddlebock*'s visual spareness has a degree of premeditation. He is credited as technical director, due to union restrictions. See Curtis, 204.

5   André Bazin, *The Cinema of Cruelty*, ed. François Truffaut, trans. Sabine d'Estrée (New York, NY: Seaver Books [1975] 1982), 46–7.

6   For an extended treatment of this issue in relation to Bazin and Chaplin, see Ivone Margulies, "Bazin's Exquisite Corpses," in *Opening Bazin: Postwar Film Theory and Its Afterlife*, Dudley Andrew and Hervé Joubert-Laurencin (London: Oxford University Press, 2011), 186–99.

7   André Bazin, *What Is Cinema?* Volume II, trans. Hugh Gray (Berkeley, CA: University of California Press, 1971), 20.

8   Manny Farber, written with W. S. Poster, "Preston Sturges: Success in the Movies," from *Negative Space: Manny Farber at the Movies* (New York, NY: Da Capo Press, 1998), 94.

9 Bazin, *The Cinema of Cruelty*, 37.

10 Bazin, *The Cinema of Cruelty*, 37.

11 Penelope Houston, "Preston Sturges," from *Cinema: A Critical Dictionary*, ed. Richard Roud (London: Secker & Warburg, 1980), 993.

12 Farber, 89.

13 See e.g. Jacobs, 342–3.

14 Sturges, 294.

15 Lloyd's collaboration with another great comedy director, Leo McCarey, on *The Milky Way* (1936) is useful as a point of comparison. While another example of Lloyd attempting to adapt his comic style to sound cinema, McCarey almost continually integrates physical movement and gesture with spoken language and sound in the film so that they form a fluid whole, in contrast to the more strictly demarcated worlds of spoken language and the visual in *Diddlebock*.

16 See Joe McElhaney, "Fast Talk: Preston Sturges and the Speed of Sound," in *Cinema and Modernity*, ed. Murray Pomerance (New Brunswick, NJ: Rutgers University Press, 2006), 273–94.

17 Jacobs, 342. It should be noted, however, that Lloyd did recreate these kinds of comic stunts, minus optical effects, in his second sound film, *Feet First* (1930), in which he again precariously balances himself on the outside of a tall building.

18 See also my brief discussion of this speech in "Fast Talk," 290.

19 Curtis, 204.

20 See Jacobs, 342.

21 André Bazin, *What Is Cinema?* Volume I, trans. Hugh Gray (Berkeley, CA: University of California Press, 1967), 52.

22 Bazin, *What Is Cinema?*, 52.

23 Jackie was eighteen when the film was shot, making him also part of the film's supporting cast of aging players, although the film itself makes no obvious point of Jackie's age.

24 Farber, 104.

25 Sturges, 305.

PART 3

Technique:
Scripting, Performance, Music

CHAPTER 9

The Unheard *Song of Joy*

Jeff Jaeckle

In the foreword to his posthumously published autobiography, Preston Sturges penned one of the most enduring quips about his filmmaking career: "Between flops, it is true, I have come up with an occasional hit."[1] James Curtis used this remark as the linchpin for his book *Between Flops: A Biography of Preston Sturges*, while numerous scholars have replicated this binary of failure and success, in part because it maps so well onto Sturges's filmography. Hits such as *The Great McGinty*, *The Lady Eve*, and *The Miracle of Morgan's Creek* are offset by flops such as *The Great Moment*, *The Sin of Harold Diddlebock*, and *The Beautiful Blonde from Bashful Bend*. Those eager to uphold Sturges as a genius can focus on the string of hits, mostly between 1940 and 1944, while those hoping to account for his misjudgments or loss of talent can concentrate on the flops, which appear regularly after 1944.

In between these much-discussed extremes of hits and flops lie other, unheard projects—some merely incomplete, others painfully aborted. These projects tell different stories, adding nuance and complexity to the familiar arc of Sturges's career. Because they occurred between films, we know less about them, thereby making their study all the more necessary and potentially rewarding. For these reasons, I've chosen to concentrate on a film that never was: *Song of Joy*, a backstage musical about Hollywood that mixes satire and romance and calls to mind not only *Sullivan's Travels* but also *Going Hollywood* (Walsh, 1933), *Singin' in the Rain* (Donen and Kelly, 1952), and *A Star is Born* (Cukor, 1954). Written early in his screenwriting career, in 1935, revised in the midst of his glory days in 1941, and then largely abandoned until his death, *Song of Joy* is one of the most outlandish and charming screenplays Sturges ever created yet never realized on film (Table 9.1).

Up until recently, no one other than a few executives at Universal, MGM, Paramount, and Fox had seen the script for *Song of Joy* (which they all

Table 9.1   *Song of Joy* among Sturges's other projects of the period.

1933	1934	1935
The Power and the Glory	*The Good Fairy*	**Song of Joy drafted** **Song of Joy rejected—** **Universal and MGM** *Diamond Jim*
1936	**1937**	**1938**
Love Before Breakfast (uncredited) *Next Time We Love* (uncredited)	*Easy Living*	*If I Were King* *Port of Seven Seas*
1939	**1940**	**1941**
Song of Joy rejected— **Paramount** *Remember the Night*	*The Great McGinty* *Christmas in July*	**Song of Joy rejected—Fox** *The Lady Eve* *Sullivan's Travels*

rejected); likewise, few film scholars have read it, since it remains unpublished and available in only a handful of libraries, most notably UCLA's Charles E. Young Research Library, which has since 1975 housed the Preston Sturges Papers. It was here that biographer Diane Jacobs rediscovered the script, which she considers a forgotten masterwork. Referring to it as "a real hysterical spoof . . . far more biting, more farcical" than *Sullivan's Travels*, Jacobs contends that the story remains "as appropriate today as it was then. Writers are still treated badly in Hollywood and everyone is still an egomaniac."[2]

Song of Joy is indeed an hysterical story that goes further than *Sullivan's Travels* in its satire of Hollywood, but its significance as a precursor doesn't end there. When compared with Sturges's other written-and-directed films, *Song of Joy* often shows less restraint and more exuberance in testing the boundaries of the Hollywood studio system, especially in terms of plotting, meta-cinema, and dialogue; in this respect, his films can be read as *toned-down* versions of his creative experiments in *Song of Joy*. Tracing these extremes can clarify why the script was so disliked and why so many studios rejected it. These analyses can also illustrate the intensity of Sturges's creative ambitions at this point in his career—that period between his roles as playwright and writer-director when he took an even more over-the-top approach to screenwriting. In this way, *Song of Joy* is both an unrealistic dream project and a touchstone for the real breakthroughs to come.

THE BASICS: PLOT, CORRESPONDENCE, AND CASTING

Song of Joy centers on a famous opera singer, Lilli Pogany, who arrives in Hollywood to make her first film, a musical for the Apex Film Company. Little does she realize that studio head, Adolph Apex, has entirely no memory of hiring her, nor of signing her to an exorbitant $19,000-per-week contract.[3] With only four weeks until Lilli leaves for Milan to sing at La Scala, Apex immediately commands his best writer and director, Jasper Balcom and Vladimir Von Stark, to cobble together a script and start shooting the next morning. Their warring personalities, coupled with Apex's insistence on producing a commercial hit, result in a goofy and often nonsensical story about Trudel Edelweiss, a Pennsylvania Dutch girl with an angelic voice who comes to Hollywood to film the musical "Song of Joy."

Meanwhile, Lilli flirts with a young copyist in the music department, known as "The Boy," who immediately assumes she is just an extra—a pretense she perpetuates in part by calling herself Lilli Bushmiller.[4] Their romance quickly blossoms and The Boy pens Lilli the love song "For You Alone."[5] Soon after, however, he makes a number of boneheaded and sexist comments, including the insult that opera singers make terrible wives, which infuriates Lilli, who storms off. The Boy's troubles multiply after Apex catches him writing noncommercial songs on company time and immediately fires him.

Nevertheless, love and happiness prevail, as The Boy and Lilli (still pretending to be an extra) soon reconcile and, out of the blue, decide to elope to Yuma, Arizona. As luck would have it, the screenwriter Jasper eavesdrops on their reunion and is inspired to make their relationship the crux of the musical. In the final scene, on the steps of a preacher's home in Yuma, reporters and marching bands crowd around the newlyweds as The Boy learns that Lilli is the famous opera singer and the couple discovers that "Song of Joy" will now be about *them*, a quite literal instance of art imitating life.[6]

This meta-cinematic ending echoes Sturges's initial inspiration for the script. He was to write a star vehicle for Marta Eggerth, the Hungarian-born opera singer and actress who, like the character of Lilli Pogany, was offered a lucrative contract to showcase her operatic talents by playing a singer in a Hollywood musical. Known as the "Maria Callas of operetta," Eggerth was a coloratura soprano who had already established her acting career in Europe, with over a dozen films produced in Germany, Austria, Italy, and the U.K. *Song of Joy* was to mark her breakthrough in Hollywood, with Universal hoping that her career would mirror the successes of other recent crossover opera stars such as Jeanette MacDonald (MGM), Grace Moore (Paramount/ Columbia), and Lily Pons (RKO), who had risen to fame with the introduction of synchronized sound.[7] However, the ensuing controversies over *Song of Joy* ultimately ruined these prospects, as Eggerth soon left Universal to sign with

MGM, where she would play supporting roles in two Judy Garland musicals, *For Me and My Gal* (Berkeley, 1942) and *Presenting Lily Mars* (Taurog, 1943). Since no more star vehicles came her way, Eggerth never reached the same heights in Hollywood as her character Lilli Pogany or her real-life counterparts.

Song of Joy was also a potential springboard for Sturges, since it marked his first assignment for an original screenplay at Universal. After his high-profile sale of *The Power and the Glory* in 1933, Sturges had adapted several stories and scripts, but nothing with the degree of complexity and originality seen in *Song of Joy*. He had also tried, and failed, to complete and produce several musicals, starting with a stage musical based on Irvin Cobb's comic essay *Speaking of Operations* (1916), which he wrote (and immediately abandoned) in 1929 while recovering from appendicitis. He would try again that same year with *After the Rain*, another stage musical that went unsold, and again the next year when writing the libretto for his 1930 play *The Well of Romance*, which flopped. With so much riding on this script, we need not wonder why Sturges would come to devote so many years to its production.[8] (See Karnick's chapter on the revealing aspects of another long-stewing yet unproduced Sturges script, *Matrix*.)

Jacobs speculates that the stakes for *Song of Joy* were especially high because producer Paul Kohner, who had hired Eggerth and worked with Sturges earlier that year on *Next Time We Love* (1936), had personally assigned him to write the script. (Kohner likely also had a hand in choosing the film's director, Eddie Sutherland, who had recently worked with Sturges on *Diamond Jim* [1935]). She suggests that Sturges "must have felt particularly inclined to write precisely what he liked, knowing this sophisticated man was his producer."[9] Sturges did exactly that, creating a ludicrous behind-the-scenes story of greedy producers, pretentious directors, clueless choreographers and wig designers, and—unsurprisingly—sympathetic and downtrodden screenwriters and copyists.[10] The resulting 126-page script, which divides into eight sections (A–H), includes an additional 27 pages of music continuities for the final trio of Gounod's *Faust* (in sequence A), Strauss's "Blue Danube Waltz" (between E and F), and Liszt's "Hungarian Rhapsodies" (H).[11]

Sturges was on a tight deadline to produce a draft because Eggerth, like Lilli, had to return soon to Europe. Yet Jacobs notes that he procrastinated, as he was wont to do, perhaps because he was hesitant to share a script that so blatantly bit the hand that fed him. He judged correctly. Upon receiving the initial draft of *Song of Joy*, Sutherland complained to Universal studio head Carl Laemmle, Sr. and general manager Fred S. Meyer (as well as Kohner and Sturges) that the script was "dangerous" and would destroy everyone involved. In a letter dated November 7, 1935, Sutherland insisted that "making fun of producers, writers, etc. is not entertainment," and he warned that, if released, the film "would make enemies of all the other motion picture companies and producers."[12]

Sturges pleaded his case the next day to Laemmle himself, pointing out the script's originality and freshness, not to mention Eggerth's approval. He also rejected Sutherland's claims about the boundaries of film entertainment, arguing that Universal had already released a satirical behind-the-scenes film in 1932, *Once in a Lifetime*, and that the studio could do so again, with greater success.[13] Sturges must also have been thinking here of the long tradition of Hollywood spoofing and self-referentiality in silent cinema, to which he owed much of his style as a writer and director. Films such as *Behind the Screen* (Chaplin, 1916), *Movie Star* (Hibbard, 1916), *The Extra Girl* (Jones, 1923), and *The Cameraman* (Keaton, 1928) are tongue-in-cheek stories that satirize many of the same topics Sturges spoofs in *Song of Joy*.[14] Understandably, then, Sturges saw plenty of opportunities to continue these traditions. "It is my belief," he insists to Laemmle, "that the Motion Picture Industry is sufficiently well established and sufficiently dignified to be able to withstand some 'spoofing.'"[15] The UCLA archives do not contain any responses from Laemmle or any follow-up letters from Sturges, Kohner, or Sutherland; and since Sturges chose not to discuss *Song of Joy* in his autobiography, we do not know how he coped with this rejection.

However, we can follow the controversy through the archive's news clippings, which reveal both the high-profile nature of the project and the speed with which Universal abandoned it. On November 12, 1935, five days after Sutherland sent Laemmle his list of concerns, *Variety* ran the headline "Sutherland, U Scowl on Eggerth Satire," indicating that the script's revision would include "elimination of some satiric targeting of Hollywood tin hats."[16] Yet within two days, *Variety* announced that Laemmle had dropped the script and reassigned Eggerth's contract to producer Edmund Grainger. Then, on November 20, *Variety* revealed that Sturges and Kohner had pitched the script to Louis B. Mayer at MGM. Although Mayer reportedly loved the story, Jacobs says he scoffed at paying Eggerth's weekly salary and turned it down.

Even after two high-profile rejections by two major studios, Sturges kept faith with the script, pitching it at least two more times over the next six years. First, after leaving Universal for Paramount, he tried unsuccessfully to convince William LeBaron to purchase the rights. In a letter dated April 26, 1939, Sturges declares:

> I believe it is a very good picture. I believe it can be bought for beans from Universal including its full shooting script and full musical score. I believe Eggerth is a very good bet. I believe Mitch [Leisen] could direct it with great charm. Or could that new fellow Sturges or whatever the Hell his name is.[17]

The script then seems to have lain dormant until 1941, when Sturges attempted to sell it to Darryl Zanuck at Fox, which was owed a film in exchange for loaning Henry Fonda to Paramount for *The Lady Eve*. In a January 20 letter to Frank Orsatti, Sturges's agent, Zanuck dismissively refers to the script as "something out of Preston's trunk," and suggests that revisions would prove too costly, as "the handicaps of this story, *Song of Joy*, are too heavy."[18] Little did Zanuck realize that two of Sturges's previous and most successful films—*The Great McGinty* and *Christmas in July*—were also trunk projects, which he revised extensively both before and during their productions.

Since Sturges doesn't outline his possible revisions to *Song of Joy* in any of his letters to the studio heads, we are left to wonder how he might have reconceived the script during the intervening years between 1935 and 1941, or why he held it so close to his heart all those years. Perhaps he wanted to prove that he could finally produce a successful musical (a feat that had escaped him since 1929), or perhaps he wanted to court the controversy (and celebrity) that a controversial musical might inspire. After his precedent-breaking sale of *The Power and the Glory* and ascension to writer-director status with *The Great McGinty*, it could be that he considered *Song of Joy* the next summit. As Henderson rightly notes, "What Sturges would have done with *Song of Joy* is a tantalizing possibility."[19] Although we can never fully answer many of the questions swirling around this project, we can examine other existing documents, including the script itself, to make these tantalizing possibilities slightly more tangible.

We do know, for instance, that Sturges would continue to flesh out the production details for *Song of Joy*. Included with the script at UCLA is a single-page cast sheet dated February 27, 1941, five weeks after Zanuck's rejection. Among the nine names listed are:

> Don Ameche—The Copyist (a.k.a. The Boy/Bill)
> Marta Eggerth—The Operatic Star (a.k.a. Lilli)
> Akim Tamiroff—Vladimir, The Director
> Ned Sparks—Jasper, The Writer
> Alan Hale—Mr. Adolph Apex, Pres.
> Edgar Kennedy—Dave, the Talent Scout[20]

This list reveals a good deal about Sturges's conception of the characters while confirming what we already know about his relationships with actors. For instance, fans of Sturges's films will immediately recognize names that would form part of his familiar troupe, including Tamiroff (*The Great McGinty* and *The Miracle of Morgan's Creek*) and Kennedy (*The Sin of Harold Diddlebock* and *Unfaithfully Yours*). The proposed casting of Tamiroff suggests that Vladimir's character would likely have been shady yet sympathetic, as Tamiroff is in his repeated roles as "The Boss"; likewise, Kennedy's casting as a talent scout suggests that this character may have been awkward and verbose yet not devious, as Kennedy is as a bartender in *Diddlebock* and as a detective in *Unfaithfully*. This cast list also points to Sturges's investments in working with actors from his previous screenwriting projects, including Alan Hale (*Imitation of Life* and *The Good Fairy*), Ned Sparks (*Imitation of Life*), and Don Ameche (*Broadway Melody of 1939*), which is in line with his career-long interest in deploying familiar faces and voices in his films; this includes Ameche's well-known crooning style, which would have made a notable contrast to Eggerth's coloratura singing. Finally, and perhaps most importantly, the casting of Eggerth as Lilli reveals that Sturges continued to consider *Song of Joy*, despite its six-year hiatus, a big-budget, A-quality picture, given Eggerth's top-tier salary. Jacobs reports it as $3,500 per week as part of Eggerth's contract with Universal, while *Variety* listed the total contract at $35,000—an amount comparable to those for other crossover opera singers of the period, including Jeanette MacDonald's $4,000-per-week salary for MGM's *The Cat and a Fiddle* (1934) and Grace Moore's $50,000 fee for Columbia's *One Night of Love* (1934).[21]

Other possibilities and patterns emerge when setting *Song of Joy* against Sturges's written-and-directed films. These comparisons underscore the script's boldness and audacity in terms of plotting, meta-cinema, and dialogue—a notable feat, given the groundbreaking nature of those movies.

PLOTTING: A CRUEL GAME OF FALSE PRETENSES

Some aspects of *Song of Joy* are quite similar to those of Sturges's later works, including the pairing of characters from radically different backgrounds: the wealthy Lilli Pogany opposite the working-class The Boy; the rural Trudel Edelweiss opposite the cosmopolitan The Fur Collar. Typical of the screwball genre, these characters engage in some type of deception; or, as Sarah Kozloff has observed, "calculated masquerades" that are "endemic to screwball comedy."[22] These masquerades are equally endemic to the plots of Sturges's films, many of which are foundational examples of the screwball genre. As Penelope Houston notes, "If there is one consistent element running through Sturges' films, it is a view of life as some gigantic game of false pretense."[23] Yet this is exactly where the plot of *Song of Joy* strays from the familiar Sturges model. Although he experiments here with two of his favorite forms of pretense—class-based masquerade and widespread deception—the degree of cynicism in *Song of Joy* is arguably unmatched, as the characters' lies go unexposed, unexplained, or unpunished.

The games begin with the false pretense that Apex Film Co. is prepared to launch the acting career of opera star Lilli Pogany. Studio head Adolph Apex has no knowledge of signing Lilli's contract, while screenwriter Jasper and director Vladimir have no script, sets, or vision for the musical. Dance numbers are made up on the spot and song choices are random and unconnected. Lilli, however, has no knowledge of these backstage shenanigans, as Apex and his associates do their best to deceive her. This includes misleading her about which songs will appear in the film, presumably her most important contribution to the project. When Lilli insists that Vladimir include her rendition of The Boy's noncommercial "For You Alone," the director feigns acquiescence to her demands, speaking to her "as to a child or a lunatic," while behind her back "he simulates scissors, cutting and with both hands does a throw-away gesture."[24] Ultimately, Vladimir, Jasper, and Apex refuse to come clean to Lilli about their tomfooleries, so she remains essentially a pawn of the studio system, a fact made more pronounced by her supposed "star" status. The script's happy ending is therefore sullied: Apex will make "Song of Joy" and likely score a commercial hit, while Lilli—as well as her entourage of singers and agents, and even The Boy—will remain largely ignorant of the studio's machinations.

Compared with those in Sturges's written-and-directed films, the unacknowledged and unresolved nature of these deceptions is darker in tone. For instance, even though Dan McGinty lies to his constituents for the majority of *The Great McGinty*, he tries to do right by them after becoming governor, just as Woodrow Truesmith attempts to make amends in *Hail the Conquering Hero* by confessing to his family and friends that he misled them about being a combat veteran. Even the three despicable pranksters in *Christmas in July*, who concoct a fake telegram notifying Jimmy that he has won the Maxford House slogan contest, apologize for their lies and purchase a convertible sofa for Jimmy's mother to assuage their guilt. And while Sully never publicly admits to his masquerades as a hobo in *Sullivan's Travels*, he does hand out five-dollar bills indiscriminately to the poor in gratitude for the life lessons they've unwittingly taught him.

Even when characters do admit to their masquerades in *Song of Joy*, they do so without sincere or satisfying explanations. While the studio misleads Lilli about the making of "Song of Joy," she is mired in her own false pretenses after lying about her identity to her love interest, The Boy. In this way, she is both a victim and a perpetrator of lies. Calling herself "Lilli Bushmiller," she pretends to be a working-class extra struggling to succeed in the industry. This includes wearing plain clothes, and lying about where she lives, how much money she has, and even how well she can sing. After only a brief moment of honesty, in which she records herself singing beautifully for The Boy, Lilli quickly resumes the ruse when the Apex talent scout Dave Horner appears. After pretending to fumble the record, which shatters, Lilli purposely mangles her voice the next time she sings. Sturges describes her visual and vocal masquerade in detail:

> She arranges her features into the high-class sneer of an amateur parlor performer and places her hands under the heart. She begins with a very

throaty note, then slips into a headtone like a steam whistle. Passing now through a very inaccurate run, she arrives at an extremely unpleasant trill. She makes this doubly unattractive by cocking her head on one side, smiling archly and shooting it directly into Mr. Horner's ear.

Lilli maintains this subterfuge until the final seconds of the film, when the unavoidable presence of the studio heads and reporters at her wedding to The Boy make lying any longer impossible. Yet even her confession is an evasion. After Apex hands Lilli a bunch of roses and says her last name, The Boy turns to her, perplexed:

The Boy: The opera singer?
Lilli: Yes (seductively). But darling, I don't sing all the time.

In these closing lines of the film, audiences see Lilli's charming manipulations still at work, as she immediately shifts the focus from her false identity to her sexual allure. At no point, however, does Lilli *explain* her reasons for lying to The Boy. She is not jilted, on the run, or particularly spiteful; instead, it seems, she lies to him for a lark. This fact is all the more disturbing when we consider that Lilli has (off-screen) just married The Boy under an assumed name and identity, all for no particular reason.

Fans of *The Lady Eve* might be tempted to hear in Lilli's closing response to The Boy an echo of the penultimate lines to that film, when the confused and hesitant Charles reunites with the all-knowing Jean:

Charles: I have no right to be in your cabin.
Jean: Why?
Charles: Because I'm married.
Jean: But so am I, darling, so am I.

Jean's suggestive reply comes as she closes the door to the cabin, presumably leading Charles to the bedroom. As with Lilli, she quickly swaps honesty for sex, an effective bait and switch that concludes the film. However, in Jean's case, audiences know her to be a jilted lover with cause to mislead Charles because of his snobbish and cruel behavior to her earlier in the film. Jean might be crafty, but we at least can understand *why* she behaves as she does. The same holds for Gerry in *The Palm Beach Story*, who lies to a host of potential suitors, and comes quite close to becoming engaged to John D. Hackensacker, all for the prospect of financial security. Gerry is an unabashed gold digger, a disreputable yet honest admission; however, even these calculating motivations are softened by her desire to share the wealth—$99,000 to be exact—with her estranged husband Tom. A similar desire to provide for and protect loved ones comes across in *Hail the Conquering Hero*, as Woodrow repeatedly expresses his preference to leave town or live a lie rather than disappoint his mother or dishonor his family's military legacy. Finally, much the same is true of Norval Jones in *The Miracle of Morgan's Creek*: he is willing to participate in a sham marriage and endure a lifetime of indignities if it means protecting the reputation of his unrequited love interest, the pregnant Trudy Kockenlocker.

To a greater extent than any of these films, *Song of Joy* treads on the acceptable boundaries of masquerade, since Sturges withholds scenes of sincere confession and reconciliation. No wonder, then, that so many studio heads objected to the script. Perhaps they sensed in this story the possibility that audiences would be hard-pressed to sympathize with the characters or even understand their motivations, which remain somewhat murky. As written, none of the malingering characters in *Song of Joy* is villainous; instead, they are better described as thoughtless or careless. Apex forgets that he signed Lilli's contract, and rather than admit to this fact, he sets in motion a cascade of lies; Lilli pretends to be an extra when first meeting The Boy, and rather than easily undo a white lie, she allows the pretenses to grow unfettered. Sturges's decision not to clear up these confusions ultimately results in a blacker comedy, yet subtly so, since the seemingly happy ending—yet another form of masquerade—effectively masks the characters' ongoing pretenses.

META–CINEMA: RELENTLESSLY REFLEXIVE

Like Sturges's written-and-directed films, *Song of Joy* takes several opportunities to remind audiences that they're watching a movie, whether through dialogue that explicitly references films and filmmaking (as happens in *Sullivan's Travels*) or through the staging of scenes that include film screenings (again, as in *Sullivan's Travels* but also *The Sin of Harold Diddlebock*). For Alessandro Pirolini, these tendencies reveal Sturges's penchant for meta–cinema, whereby he "overcomes Hollywood's invisible self-consciousness, and pushes the practice of cross-reference in the postmodern realm of overt textuality, meta-lingualism, and self-reflexivity."[25]

Sturges delights in these tendencies to an unprecedented extent in *Song of Joy*, likely in part because he was well-aware of the conventions of the Hollywood musical, perhaps the most inveterately self-referential of film genres. Rick Altman contends that "the musical from its very beginnings has been a self-reflective genre,"[26] while Jane Feuer argues that "musicals, in being about Hollywood, are also about themselves."[27] This holds true, she suggests, not only for backstage musicals, but for any film in the genre, since they all operate on at least two levels of signification: "Musicals not only *showed* you singing and dancing; they were *about* singing and dancing."[28] In writing *Song of Joy*, then, Sturges may have sensed an opportunity too good to pass up: the chance to indulge in his love for meta-cinema with a genre thoroughly steeped in it. In this way, *Song of Joy* is his most relentlessly reflexive narrative—one that, like his cynical uses of masquerade, is tinged with comic pessimism.

Since the bulk of the script takes place in a film studio, characters talk a good deal about the movie business, much of it echoing the real-life arguments Sturges found himself embroiled in at Universal. For instance, when screenwriter Jasper Balcom describes "Song of Joy" as a Hollywood story full of shady producers and naive starlets, Adolph Apex flies into a rage:

> Mr. Apex (horrified): A *Hollywood* story! Who asked you for a Hollywood story? What's Hollywood got to do with it?
> Jasper: It's all about Hollywood.
> Apex: Not with *my* money it isn't. I wouldn't put a dime in a Hollywood story. They're sick and tired of Hollywood stories. Who cares about Hollywood stories? I don't . . . What are you trying to do . . . give the industry a black eye? . . . let us not foul our own nests.

Despite Apex's vitriol here, audience sympathies are meant to align with Jasper, who is younger and more clever yet also downtrodden. Sturges telegraphs this quality in one barbed sentence of direction: "His face, with one single expression, reflects all the grievances of the Writers Guild." Adolph Apex and his company, by contrast, represent all the pomposity of the major studios, not only in the name, which recalls Paramount, but also in the logo (a blatant amalgam of those for Paramount, MGM, and RKO), which Sturges describes in detail:

> To the sound of martial music, the base of the mountain descends like an elevator and brings into view its snow-capped peak. On this sits a lion holding on one raised paw the world . . . radio waves flash from the peak of this mountain and on top of the world appear the glowing letters "APEX."

Given the preponderance of these overtly cynical meta-cinematic references, we need not wonder why Eddie Sutherland described this script as "dangerous" or why Carl Laemmle, Sr. so quickly abandoned it. These arguments and references also complicate the easy pleasures of the backstage shenanigans, as the whimsical song-and-dance numbers become mired in damning evidence of the characters' incompetence and egos.

Sturges takes this self-awareness further by mocking the films themselves, including their trite and repetitive titles. When Apex, Jasper, and Vladimir debate the name of Lilli's musical, they toss out "Rhapsody in Red," "One

Day of Love," and "It Happened One Morning," all tongue-in-cheek references to previous films, but with a single word changed. Sturges pushes this gag to the extreme when describing the marquee listing the movies Lilli and The Boy see on their first date:

THREE FEATURES: ONE NIGHT OF LOVE. ONE HEAVENLY NIGHT. IT HAPPENED ONE NIGHT ... NEXT WEEK: THE NIGHT WAS MADE FOR LOVE. NIGHT AFTER NIGHT. WHAT A NIGHT!

As the couple exit the theater, a dazed and confused Lilli puts her head in her hands and says, "Phew! It make you dizzy . . . I don't know who married who—or why. I go home now." Yet again, these references and commentaries complicate an otherwise sweet love story by drawing comparisons between the budding romance on-screen and the cavalcade of hackneyed movie titles.

Lilli's reactions here might call to mind Sully's aggravating experience at the movies in *Sullivan's Travels*, during which Sturges again uses titles to comment on the hackneyed nature of the films:

3 Features Tonight
Beyond These Tears
The Valley of the Shadow
The Buzzard of Berlin
also
SWINGO

Sully's bored expression and fidgety behavior suggest that the images on-screen are dull and uninteresting, while the intrusive noises of crying, hiccupping, and crunching in the cramped and dingy theater only exacerbate the feeling of agitation. Coupled with the film's opening conversation, in which Sully's producers urge him to make a comedy or, if he must, a drama "with a little sex in it," moviegoing and moviemaking appear worthless and bankrupt. Yet Sturges ultimately pulls back from the edge of despair by leaving audiences with at least two hopeful takes on cinema. First, in capturing Sully's experiences as a hobo, Sturges renders scenes of poverty in ways that effectively and non-ironically illustrate the dramatic power of socially conscious cinema. Second, he uses Sully's closing speech to underscore the emotional value of film comedy, which he suggests is important not because of its commercially viability but because people sincerely benefit from it.

In stark contrast, *Song of Joy* offers no solution to the dilemma of Hollywood greed and incompetence, except to mock and laugh at it while glossing over its unfunny realities. *Sullivan's Travels* is therefore not the pinnacle so much as a toned-down version of Sturges's experiments with meta-cinema. First drafted on February 3, 1941—just two weeks after Darryl Zanuck rejected *Song of Joy*—the script and film show greater restraint when it comes to Hollywood studios and movies in general. *Song of Joy* therefore makes explicit the degree to which Sturges's subsequent projects relaxed and reduced the use of meta-cinematic techniques, especially satirical ones, to achieve more subtle balances between engrossing audiences and provoking them.

DIALOGUE: A MOST MALAPPROPRIATE IDIOM

Readers of *Song of Joy* will find in its pages much of the trademark dialogue for which Sturges has been so rightfully celebrated. The rapid-fire debates between Apex, Vladimir, and Jasper recall the heated exchanges between Sully and his producers in *Sullivan's Travels* or the dizzying conversations between Gerry, Maude, and John D. in *The Palm Beach Story*. Readers are also treated to perfectly phrased *bon mots*, such as Jasper's aphoristic quip, "Irritation is the mother of invention." Even minor characters raise the verbal bar with their provocative and poetic language. An unnamed cameraman, for instance, blurts out a bizarre, jargon-laden line about lighting—"Kill that Baby and gimme a Mama Dietz in there"—while a grinning undertaker, J. P. Smiley, appears for only seconds in the script to ask Lilli, "What can I do for you, my child, in this time of trouble and tribulation?"

Common as well in *Song of Joy* are instances of misspeaking—stutters, malapropisms, and outright nonsense—which are so typical of Sturges's screenwriting that Richard Corliss once characterized his dialogue as a "racy, malappropriate idiom."[29] Indeed, misspeaking is central to the design of Sturges's screenplays, as frequent verbal pratfalls work in tandem with slapstick to punch up the humor of a given scene. Having traced these patterns in my previous work, I expected to find them in *Song of Joy*, but was surprised by their sheer density and frequency, which outpace anything in Sturges's written-and-directed films.[30] This excess is due in part to the polyglot backgrounds of the characters, who speak Russian, Hungarian, French, and Italian—a more diverse assortment of languages and accents than Sturges would use in his films. When these characters switch to English, their native tongues are not far behind, often there to trip them up. Sturges accentuates this dialogue by transcribing it in a roughly phonetic form, capturing national languages and dialects as inflected through English while exaggerating accents, thus drawing comedic attention to their mistakes in pronunciation, word choice, and syntax.

These mistakes frequently apply to Lilli, whose Hungarian ancestry (like that of Marta Eggerth) seeps through all of her dialogue. These errors can be brief, such as her mangling of "picture talking" and "up-slip," but they are just as likely to take over the conversation, as happens when Lilli and her European companion Sophie Schnortz read from conversation books and debate pronunciations:

> Mme. Schnortz (reading in very bad English): Does your grandmother possess an ow-tomobile?
> Lilli (reading from her book): No, but my ooncle has a fountain pen.
> Mme. Schnortz: Vot does he do vit dis instrument?
> Lilli: He vrites checks for my ah-oont.
> Mme. Schnortz: Good. Vhre does he vrite de checks?
> Lilli: In his hooss.
> Mme. Schnortz (laughing): No, no, no. In his ho-ooze.
> Lilli (pointing to her book): No, hooss. (in Hungarian she spells; h-o-u-s-e, and adds as if it were obvious) Hooss.

The debate escalates until Lilli seeks the opinion of a nearby stranger—The Boy—who disappoints both women by insisting that the word is pronounced "house." Often, however, The Boy plays along, either repeating Lilli's mispronunciations or choosing not to correct her. In this way, Sturges extends and perpetuates the error, thereby making them more obvious and comedic. For instance, when Lilli attempts to use the word "hippopotamus" to describe opera singers—pronouncing it "hipp-popo-papa"—The Boy nods understandingly, adds "Like an elephant," and the two move on. Sturges reuses this exchange in the script's closing scene, when The Boy discovers Lilli's true identity:

> The Boy: So you're the elephant.
> Lilli: Yes . . . I'm the hippo-popo-papa . . .

In this way, misspeaking becomes a form of communication, a shared vocabulary that highlights the characters' differences while underscoring their chemistry or connection.[31]

Sturges's uses this gag again with conversations between Jasper and Vladimir, the vaguely European director. For instance, when Vladimir comes up with the title for the musical, no one other than Jasper can seem to understand him:

> Vladimir (inspired): Don't move! I've got a great title! The Song . . . of Yoy.
> Jasper (considering): The Song of Yoy.
> Vladimir (furiously): Not *Yoy*. Yoy!

Jasper: Yoy . . . I should say that fitted the story about as well as anything else right now.
Vladimir: Yoy.
Jasper: I get you.[32]

As with Lilli and The Boy, Jasper plays along, making the pronunciation error more explicit and comedic yet also illustrating the writer and director's strangely functional relationship.

Similar exchanges predominate in "Song of Joy," the film-within-a-film, especially when the Hollywood producer ("The Fur Collar") attempts to decipher the Pennsylvania Dutch characters' garbled English. Although Trudel seems interested in the producer's offer, her mother is skeptical:

The Fur Collar (perplexed): What did she say?
Trudel: She said in der whole world she didn't gewusst drei hundred dollars gives.
Mrs. Edelweiss (clucking to herself): Drei hundred dollars for nu rein jahr!
The Fur Collar: What?
Trudel: She says for only one year only so much it gives.
The Fur Collar (laughingly): You tell your mama I wasn't by the year getalking . . . you've got me doing it now . . . I meant you might get that much a week.
Trudel: Oh, you are jokes gemaking?
Mrs. Edelweiss: Vas sagt him?
The Fur Collar: No I am not jokes gemaking. I am seriously gespeaking.

Like The Boy and Jasper, the producer plays along, finding himself caught up in the mispronunciations and using them as a form of communication to convince Trudel's mother to allow her to leave for Hollywood.

While this sophisticated balance of fluid and flummoxed speech pervades all of Sturges's films, *The Palm Beach Story* is perhaps the most cited example. However, when compared with *Song of Joy*, this film is almost relentlessly articulate. One reason is that Sturges condenses most of the misspeaking into the one character of Toto, whose vocabulary appears limited to three decipherable words, "yitz," "nitz," and "gritniks." As Kozloff observes, Toto is "so 'Other' that we are not sure where he's from."[33] The other characters—mainly Tom, Gerry, Maude, and John D.—represent the opposite extreme: so familiar and deft in their speech as to make misspeaking a largely isolated case. Notable exceptions are pointed uses of malapropism, such as Gerry's mistaken use of "millstone" for "milestone" to describe her unfitness as a wife, or John D.'s flub of "mess" for "mass" in his analogy of marriage as a grafting of two trees. However, these characters are immediately and explicitly corrected, since unlike in *Song of Joy*, the other characters do not play along or adopt the speech errors. Finally, *The Palm Beach Story* features no other non-native speakers, whereas in *Song of Joy* Sturges experiments with several languages. The opening scenes, for instance, are presented in untranslated Russian, Hungarian, French, and Italian. When these speakers arrive in Hollywood, they do not let their lack of English impede their desire to be heard, but rather talk over the native speakers and insist on using their own, mangled pronunciations.

In this way, *Song of Joy* is Sturges's most sustained experiment with a multilingual cast of misspeaking characters—a complicated verbal juggling act that also sings!

CONCLUSION

This chapter has aimed to illustrate some of the untapped riches of *Song of Joy*, both in terms of its pivotal timing in Sturges's filmmaking career and its unappreciated achievements in screenwriting. We see that, between flops and hits, Sturges repeatedly returned to this joyful, self-reflexive attack on all the powers that held back his effervescent experimentation. Although we will never know exactly how he might have adapted the story to film, or how audiences and critics might have received it, we can use the existing primary documents to dig deeper into the script's fascinating possibilities, including how they compare with Sturges's creative experiments as a writer-director. This includes analyzing the wealth of accompanying materials that shape the plotting, dialogue, and meta-cinematic features I've outlined here, including musical cues, camera and editing directions, and notes on costuming and lighting. Work on this script has therefore just begun, and much remains before the *Song of Joy* can be fully heard.

NOTES

1 Preston Sturges, *Preston Sturges* (New York, NY: Simon & Schuster, 1990), 12.
2 Steven Rea, "At Temple, An Appreciative Look at Works of Preston Sturges," *Philadelphia Inquirer*, 24 January 1993.
3 Jacobs incorrectly lists this salary as $1,900 per week.
4 Sturges refers to The Boy as "Bill" in the 19-page treatment, but not in the script; Lilli Pogany has the same name in both the treatment and script. This naming may be a reference to *Going Hollywood*, which includes the protagonists Bill (Bing Crosby) and Lili (Fifi D'Orsay). It also echoes that of Lily Pons, the crossover opera star for RKO.
5 Henderson incorrectly refers to it as "Song of Joy."

6 This final, unnumbered script page is missing from the UCLA copy, but it is present in the copies at the Lilly Library (Indiana University) and the Margaret Herrick Library (Academy of Motion Picture Arts and Sciences), Beverly Hills, CA.

7 See the three-volume *Hollywood Songsters: Singers Who Act and Actors Who Sing* for reviews of the careers of these and other crossover opera stars (James Parish and Michael Pitts, Routledge, 2003). See also Edward Baron Turk's *Hollywood Diva: A Biography of Jeannette MacDonald* (Berkeley, CA: University of California Press, 1998). Currently, no biography is available for Marta Eggerth, and her career remains largely a footnote in existing literature on the film musical.

8 Sturges would attempt numerous musicals in the 1950s, all aborted or abandoned, including adaptations of *The Good Fairy* and *The Great McGinty*. Nevertheless, music plays substantial roles in all of Sturges's written-directed films, most explicitly in *The Palm Beach Story* ("Good Night Sweetheart"), *Hail the Conquering Hero* ("Home to the Arms of Mother"), and *Unfaithfully Yours*, which centers on life of orchestra conductor Sir Alfred de Carter, who conducts pieces from Rossini, Wagner, and Tchaikovsky. See Martin Marks's chapter for an extended discussion of scoring in these and other Sturges films.

9 Diane Jacobs, *Christmas in July: The Life and Art of Preston Sturges* (Berkeley, CA: University of California Press, 1995), 165.

10 Universal sent a portion of this controversial script to the PCA on November 5, 1935, and submitted the remainder on November 7. Joseph Breen responded on November 19, making no reference to Sturges's satire on Hollywood. Rather, his concerns are that the director Vladimir not appear to be Jewish, that the wig designer does not come off as homosexual ("pansy"), and that questionable references to religion, sex, and Boris Karloff be altered or removed. See PCA Files *Song of Joy*, Special Collections, Margaret Herrick Library (Academy of Motion Picture Arts and Sciences), Beverly Hills, CA.

11 Henderson's account of *Song of Joy*, published in *Five Screenplays by Preston Sturges* in 1985, is based on a 19-page treatment that stops abruptly near the end of the equivalent of sequence G in the script. Since this treatment leaves out the denouement of sequence H, Henderson unknowingly drew inaccurate conclusions about the story's ending.

12 Brian Henderson, *Five Screenplays by Preston Sturges* (Berkeley, CA: University of California Press, 1985), 513. Henderson quotes most of the letter, which can be found in its entirety at UCLA: Preston Sturges Papers (Collection 1114). Department of Special Collections, University Research Library, University of California, Los Angeles, Box 42, Folder 17.

13 Bernard F. Dick provides a brief account of *Once in a Lifetime* that supports Sturges's take on the film. See *City of Dreams: The Making and Remaking of Universal Pictures* (Lexington, KY: University of Kentucky Press, 1997), 85.

14 See Robert Stam's *Reflexivity in Film and Literature: From Don Quixote to Jean-Luc Godard* (New York, NY: Columbia University Press, 1992).

15 Henderson, 513. Once again, the full letter can be found in the UCLA archives—see previous endnote.

16 All of the *Song of Joy* clippings are available in Box 103: Preston Sturges Papers (Collection 1114). Department of Special Collections, University Research Library, University of California, Los Angeles.

17 Jacobs does not reference this letter, while Henderson only alludes to its existence. It can be found here: Preston Sturges Papers (Collection 1114). Department of Special Collections, University Research Library, University of California, Los Angeles, Box 74, Folder 33.

18 Henderson quotes this letter in full on page 514, but it can also be found here: Preston Sturges Papers (Collection 1114). Department of Special Collections, University Research Library, University of California, Los Angeles, Box 42, Folder 17.

19 Henderson, 514.

20 Preston Sturges Papers (Collection 1114). Department of Special Collections, University Research Library, University of California, Los Angeles, Box 42, Folder 17.

21 See Jacobs, 169 and the Preston Sturges Papers. (Collection 1114). Department of Special Collections, University Research Library, University of California, Los Angeles, Box 103. Eggerth's salary was also much higher than those of other singing actresses: Ginger Rogers's weekly salary for *Top Hat* (1935) was $1,550 per week, while Judy Garland's 1935 contract at MGM was for $100 per week, with a seven-year option topping out at $1,000 per week.

22 Sarah Kozloff, *Overhearing Film Dialogue* (Berkeley, CA: University of California Press, 2000), 180.

23 Penelope Houston, "Preston Sturges," *Cinema: A Critical Dictionary*, ed. Richard Round, Vol. 2 (New York, NY: Viking Press, 1980), 992.

24 All quotations of script directions and dialogue are from my transcriptions of the screenplay.

25 Alessandro Pirolini, *The Cinema of Preston Sturges: A Critical Study* (Jefferson, NC: McFarland, 2010), 52.

26 Rick Altman, *Genre: The Musical*, ed. Rick Altman (London: Routledge, 1981), 159.

27 Jane Feuer, *The Hollywood Musical* (Bloomington, IN: Indiana University Press, 1993), ix.

28 Feuer, x.

29 Richard Corliss, *Talking Pictures: Screenwriters in the American Cinema* (New York, NY: Penguin, 1974), 26.

30 See Jeff Jaeckle, "On Misspeaking in the Films of Preston Sturges," *Film Dialogue*, ed. Jeff Jaeckle (London: Wallflower Press, 2013), 140–56.

31 See Kozloff for a broader discussion of verbal chemistry and friction (86).

32 Lines like these may have been what Breen had in mind when stressing that none of the characters should appear to be "of a Jewish or any other specific racial type." See PCA Files *Song of Joy*, Special Collections, Margaret Herrick Library (Academy of Motion Picture Arts and Sciences), Beverly Hills, CA.

33 Kozloff, 196–7.

CHAPTER 10

The Eye of the Storm:
Preston Sturges and Performance

Diane Carson

Preston Sturges has received numerous accolades for his writing and direct-ing, but much less acknowledgment for the superb acting on display in his films. In fact, an electronic and hard copy search turned up no articles devoted solely to analysis of acting in Sturges's films, though diverse comments on individual actors' performances are peppered throughout books on individual stars and genres. In fairness, Richard Dyer and James Naremore (1979 and 1988, respectively), among others, contributed significantly to scholarship on stardom and on acting; but over the past decade, in film study as a whole, per-formance remains an area still relatively under-examined.[1] As Paul McDonald observes, this is particularly regrettable since "examination of acting has a vital role to play [in] . . . considering how the signification of the actor's voice and body contribute to a film's meaning."[2]

Given Sturges's character-driven stories and the performative role-playing by characters within many of his films, analysis of the acting proves both richly deserved and profoundly intriguing. I will argue that the sustained, exceptional acting is in fact the key element in creating the dynamic appeal of his work, earning his scripts the esteem they merit. To this end, Sturges often cast major stars of the studio system in his films. But while "stardom" is fertile ground for further interrogation of all it entails, for the purposes of this essay use of the term "acting" will follow James Naremore's definition that designates "a special type of theatrical performance in which the persons held up for show have become agents in a narrative."[3] Also assumed is that acting involves a "mastery, skill, or inventiveness that is implied in the normative use of the word performance."[4] In addition, in agreement with Andrew Klevan, I will treat performance as one element in the totality of film style and explore "the achievement of expressive rapport."[5]

This more inclusive analysis of acting includes "the relationship of the per-former to the camera"[6] and the composition of the shot, as well as all aspects of art direction. As Cynthia Baron and Sharon Marie Carnicke explain, "[W]here actors' work is treated as a primary cinematic element, human movements and interactions often provide the basis for a film's visual and aural design . . . Such films use lighting, setting, costuming, camera movement, framing, editing, music, and sound to give audiences privileged views of characters' inner experiences."[7] Even so, "the research in mirror neurons suggests that audiences do not respond directly to framing and editing choices but instead to gestures and expressions that serve as the locus of meaning," or, put another way, "the connotatively rich features of actors' performances."[8] Experienced in stage work,[9] Sturges respected the importance of the actor while attending to the technical elements that would foreground performance and direct attention to critical details.

Sturges keeps the pace so brisk, writes dialogue so dazzling, and fashions a *mise-en-scène* so precise that the audience gets swept along, buoyed by the acting. Attuned to verbal rhythms that reveal characters' personalities and nonverbal attributes that reinforce their individuality, Sturges consistently coaxed clear, compelling choices from his actors. His cinematic elements complemented his emphasis on what the characters say and how they say it.

Sturges integrated the cinematic aspects of his work to highlight his dialogue and the actors' performances as *the* vital ingredients. Sturges knew the rhythm and inflection he needed, and so he often modeled the behavior he wanted. "What Sturges looked and listened for," according to biographer James Curtis, "was a close facsimile of what he had seen in his mind. The same cadence to the words, the same pitch to the voices."[10] He'd cajole, he'd encourage, he'd push and suggest. One of his stock players, Bill Demarest, observed that Sturges "always rehearsed people too much."[11]

With his uniquely deft touch in staging the complexity of a performer's relationships within a film, Sturges foregrounds actors' strengths, even when they must adopt uncharacteristic (and multiple) personas. While deceptive disguise figures prominently in screwball comedies,[12] Sturges pushes his characters' dissembling to extremes. As Richard Dyer writes, the best performances "collapse this distinction between the actor's authenticity and the authentication of the character s/he is playing."[13] This is particularly striking when actors adopt distinctly different roles and convincingly and smoothly transition from one persona to another.

In *The Lady Eve, Sullivan's Travels, The Great McGinty, The Palm Beach Story* and *Hail the Conquering Hero*, among others, actors present diverse facades as they navigate an elaborate plot. Eve Harrington, John Lloyd Sullivan, Dan McGinty, Gerry Jeffers, and Woodrow Truesmith, respectively, dramatically alter personality traits within the narrative. Throughout the kaleidoscopic shifts, Sturges reveals his actors as unfailingly compelling characters, however contrived the story. Henry Fonda swoons, loses perspective, plays the fool and becomes a slapstick comic. Joel McCrea fumes and fusses, protests in vain, and follows dutifully after his wife. Brian Donlevy swaggers, barks orders, acts the tough guy and falls tenderly in love. To be sure, throughout their varied roles and shifting guises within a film, actors verbally and nonverbally honor the acting conventions of the time, that is, of the 1940s studio system.[14] Sturges achieved results that enliven whip-smart dialogue and showcase the acting.

PERFORMANCE IN *THE LADY EVE*

The Lady Eve stars Barbara Stanwyck as Jean Harrington and Henry Fonda as Charles "Hopsie" Pike, a repressed intellectual who specializes in snakes (an ophiologist). Along with her cardsharp father Colonel "Handsome Harry" Harrington (Charles Coburn), Jean cons wealthy marks out of considerable sums on transatlantic ocean liners. There Jean and Charles/Hopsie fall in love, until, learning Jean's true identity, Charles spitefully ends their relationship, prompting Jean's revenge in the assumed persona of British Lady Eve Sidwich. Enticed into marriage, Charles wants a divorce after Eve, on their wedding night, confesses multiple previous relationships. Thanks to Jean's machinations, they reunite on another steamship and Charles's education in forgiveness is completed.[15]

After the critical and commercial successes of *The Great McGinty* and *Christmas in July*, Sturges had the clout to demand the two stars he wanted: Barbara Stanwyck, under contract to Paramount, and Henry Fonda, borrowed from Twentieth Century-Fox.[16] His choices proved wise. As he wrote in his autobiography, *Preston Sturges by Preston Sturges*, "Barbara Stanwyck had an instinct so sure that she needed almost no direction; she was a devastating Lady Eve."[17] Among the most prominent reviewers, *The New York Times*' influential Bosley Crowther singled out the actors for praise: "No one could possibly have suspected the dry and somewhat ponderous comic talent which is exhibited by Henry Fonda as the rich young man. And Barbara Stanwyck as the lady in the case is a composite of beauty, grace, romantic charm and a thoroughly feminine touch of viciousness."[18] Crowther's appreciation of the acting extended to Sturges's stock players as well. "Other beautiful performances are contributed by Charles Coburn as a wry and lovable cardsharper, William Demarest as hard-boiled bodyguard and gentleman's man, Eugene Pallette as a much-abused tycoon and Eric Blore as a confidence worker."[19] Praise for the acting has not abated over the years. David Thomson calls it "virtually the only good comedy that Fonda ever made, tribute to Stanwyck's wit, to Sturges's grace, and to Fonda's own solemnity" and praises Stanwyck as "giving one of the best American comedy performances."[20]

Studying the nonverbal acting choices in *The Lady Eve*, Laban Movement Analysis offers "a conceptual framework that facilitates observation and analysis of human movement."[21] This useful framework offers a rubric for identifying critical performative details because Laban pinpoints direction and speed of movement, as well as the performers' degree of control. It is worth considering that "through study, Laban and his collaborators located eight basic efforts: pressing, thrusting, wringing, slashing, gliding, dabbing, floating, and flicking."[22] Analysis accounts for a range of variations, for example, a movement's weight or weakness and whether the movement is sustained.

Using this methodology, we see that Sturges's actors seldom use what are labeled the "Strong and Sudden" movements—Thrust, Crush, Cut, or even the "Strong and Indirect" ones—Slash, Beat, Throw. Sturges's actors lean toward the "Light and Direct" such as Glide, Dab, Tap, or the "Light and Indirect" such as Float, Stroke, Flick.[23] Stanwyck, for example, works in the light, indirect range in most of her interaction with Hopsie. She doesn't need force, because she has the advantage through sheer, crafty manipulation.

We might note that despite the woman propelling the plot while the man struggles to keep up, adding a modest feminist undertone, the film's success still derives from surprisingly familiar messages embedded within unique role reversals: a woman needs an irresistible man to take charge of her, to teach her true love; the wealthy are imperious, disdainful bores; outwitting them provides amusing diversion; and the course of true love never runs smoothly. We see, though, that despite the uncritical endorsement of marriage as love's goal, Sturges resists the sentimental indulgence and playful escapades of Hollywood's romantic comedies. As James Harvey sees it, "The special tone of *The Lady Eve* is a kind of energetic cruelty, a malicious exuberance, reflected chiefly in Stanwyck's treatment of Fonda: a kind of relentless and systematic humiliation, extending over the whole film with all its changes of direction and transformations of character."[24] Moreover, all seven films[25] Sturges made between 1940 and 1944 stand

> as an insouciant rebuke to the mythic America of John Ford, the inspirational America of Frank Capra, and the cozy America of MGM's Andy Hardy series. If those movies were a warm hug to their audience, the Sturges pictures were a jab in the ribs, a sexy joke whispered in church— a wink, a kiss, and a hiccup.[26]

Or, as the esteemed French theorist André Bazin wrote in *L'Écran français*, Sturges was the anti-Capra.[27]

In order to sell this potentially dissonant content to a 1940s audience, Sturges insisted Stanwyck star in *The Lady Eve*. Given Sturges's emphasis on clever dialogue and its credible delivery, "the Sturges gift for a kind of offhand profundity has its ideal exponent in her, with her directness, and the feeling she gives of so many levels of comment *behind* the directness: the smile behind the eyes."[28] Sturges

> knew the speed at which the lines had to be delivered and the volume as well. And he allowed Stanwyck to dictate the piece. As she moved, so moved the rest of the story. And since she was fast and clever and resourceful, the film acquired the same attributes.[29]

In other words, Stanwyck's performance infuses her vindictive retaliation with a joyful, naughty mischievousness. By the emotional complexity she "acts," accenting manipulative dialogue with transparent pleasure in the charade, Stanwyck conveys multiple layers of pleasure and tenderness, pain and vulnerability.

Stanwyck embodies Jean Harrington *and* Lady Eve Sidwich, with both personas convincingly segueing through this wide range of emotions and moods. Roger Ebert appreciated this, finding there "one of Stanwyck's greatest performances, a flight of romance and comedy so graceful and effortless that she is somehow able to play different notes at the same time," adding, "there has rarely been a woman in a movie who more convincingly desired a man."[30] Stanwyck's engaging performance is an even more remarkable achievement given that a significant difference exists between the character of the central woman in *The Lady Eve* and the earlier, more good-natured screwball comedy women. For Jean/Eve "is a predator," writes Kendall, and so successful as to "forecast the forties, that decade in which any clever female in the movies was assumed to be duplicitous."[31] Sturges's inclination to push cynicism and romanticism to an extreme resulted in a virtual reversal of the screwball formula within the confines of the familiar "battle of the sexes." Sturges's protagonists contrast markedly, for example, with Capra's or Cukor's heroines.

Heretofore the women in the famous screwball comedies of the 1930s and 40s played their stereotypical roles without double-dealing guile, even when they were riotously unfettered. Claudette Colbert in *It Happened One Night* (1934), Irene Dunne in *The Awful Truth* (1937), Katharine Hepburn in *Bringing Up Baby* (1938) and *Holiday* (1938), and Rosalind Russell in *His Girl Friday* (1940)—to name notable screwball comedy women—epitomize formidable partners but foreswore the devious vindictiveness practiced by Lady Eve Sidwich. And this difference in the female character comes through in Stanwyck's acting choices, for she smiles and defers less to men, most notably her father and Charles/Hopsie. In the other screwball classics, women may temporarily have the upper hand, but in *The Lady Eve* Jean dominates her relationship with Charles/Hopsie both verbally and physically until the concluding scene, when she allows him to assert himself. But throughout the rest of the film, rather than epitomizing the aggressive male, Hopsie, through the softness of his face and body, embodies and expresses stereotypically female characteristics: emotional innocence, naiveté about human nature, and inflexible ethical standards.

Several iconic scenes highlight Stanwyck's and Fonda's acting choices. As Hopsie, Henry Fonda expresses a "softer," more malleable male persona through a myriad of performance details while Stanwyck presents an assured, assertive, manipulative presence throughout her dual personas. Without ascribing authorial agency to the director, the actor, or others, let's acknowledge the collaborative enterprise of film production. What matters, as McDonald suggests, is analysis of "the signification of the body and voice in those fragmentary moments when the actions and gestures of the performer impart significant meanings about the relationship of the character to the narrative circumstances."[32] And given the playful, mischievous interaction between Jean and Hopsie, and later Lady Eve and Hopsie, the filmic context matters considerably.

In an early, roughly four-minute scene, verbal and nonverbal elements produce what McDonald calls micromeanings[33] that resonate through the rest of the film; that is, Stanwyck's and Fonda's acting choices reveal rich macro and micro levels of connotation. In their first, prolonged interaction, Jean lures Hopsie to her cozy cabin to change her shoes, having tricked Hopsie into accompanying her. Jean broke the heel off one shoe when she purposely tripped Hopsie who, naive gentleman he is, believes he caused the accident. Appropriately, she's in black, he's in white; she's in control, he's flummoxed. Stanwyck communicates her emotions and ideas through a skillfully honeyed inflection of her voice and half-suppressed chuckles. As Maria DiBattista describes it, "There is Barbara Stanwyck's voice, modulated and enriched by all the under- as well as overtones of a young woman already burdened with a full, often checkered past."[34] Using minute details such as the shifts in her stance and her eye contact, a light and direct approach, Jean establishes her control and her growing interest in Hopsie, along with her increasing disbelief in his naiveté. Stanwyck portrays myriad emotions as she visually scrutinizes her prey and registers Jean's tangled conflict over Hopsie's increasing appeal.

Jean and Hopsie enter the cabin, she throws an errant piece of satin clothing to the side, and looks up at Hopsie smiling, nervously tapping the broken heel on her hand, accompanied by a half-hearted, small laugh. Jean follows a slowly moving Fonda into the room where they mirror each other's position perfectly, both turned with their profiles to the camera. They're already a mismatched couple, not facing each other at the moment, his white and her black clothes in opposition: Hopsie wobbly, Jean poised.

Hopsie/Fonda communicates his awkwardness by, first, standing completely still, arms handing at his side. He's struck by the perfume and turns to face the camera, expressing his unease. Jean verbally acknowledges it, then takes Hopsie's arm, points to the shoe trunk, and leads Hopsie to it as the camera pans with them. She delivers her lines with a subtext of sexual innuendo when she turns toward the camera, leans back, puts her right hand defiantly on her hip, meets Hopsie's gaze and asks, "See anything you like?"

Jean physically controls the space within the scene through her decisive movement. Using primarily her eyes, she conveys her astute assessment of Hopsie as an easy mark. His minimal energy expressed through the slowness of his movements and of his speech telegraphs his lack of power. In addition, as he kneels to unfasten Jean's shoe, Hopsie's facial expression telegraphs anxiety bordering on illness. He displays his pain, looking as though he might throw up. Fonda pulls his facial muscles back, opens his eyes, and haltingly speaks as he exhales, "I hope I didn't hurt you." He nearly swoons and faints, all with minimal movement, just before Sturges cuts to his out-of-focus subjective gaze at Jean.

Jean infuses energy into the dialogue with quick questions, though she remains seated on the stool, her leg dominant in the frame, Hopsie focused on it. He becomes more animated as he differentiates ale from beer and finishes buckling Jean's shoes, but even as they stand, Hopsie on the dominant right-hand side of the frame, he remains the physically and emotionally subordinate character. As Jean exits frame right, still half smiling and enjoying her charade, Hopsie staggers slightly, tugs at his collar, and weakly follows Jean off screen.

Through Jean and Hopsie's first protracted interaction, they establish a meticulously nuanced relationship expressed through Stanwyck's and Fonda's infinitesimal inflections and poses. Jean is sizing Hopsie up, evaluating the target of her and her father's con, and evaluating their difficulty or ease of success. Through his posture and delivery, Fonda communicates Hopsie's lack of control, as the camera literally reproduces his faulty lack of vision with a blurry, point-of-view shot of Jean. His physical dizziness and imbalance are complemented by his halting verbal delivery. To emphasize Hopsie's lack of power, Sturges keeps Hopsie's back to the camera as he surveys Jean's shoes.

By contrast, Jean moves forcefully on a diagonal toward the camera, stands with her right hand cocked on her hip in a strong, direct, commanding pose, and speaks with decisiveness. Eschewing Hopsie's halting vocalization, Stanwyck pauses in her line delivery only to signal Jean's sizing up a hapless, flustered Hopsie. Twice Jean cannot suppress a slight laugh as Hopsie swoons in response to her seductive enticements: her exposed leg and her teasing *double entendre*. Her amusement, obvious in her facial expressions and her whimsical line readings, lightens the mood and sustains the comic atmosphere that, in a less able actor's performance, would risk losing its entertaining quality. Indeed, Stanwyck shows that Jean is clearly toying with Hopsie: the timbre of her voice, her lilting delivery, and her open posture. But her amusement and the weightlessness of her delivery keep the scene adroitly humorous.

To borrow from Cavell, Stanwyck "carries the holiday in [her] eye."[35] As Roger Ebert observes, "Watch her eyes as she regards Fonda, in all of their quiet scenes together, and you will see a woman who is amused by a man's boyish shyness and yet aroused by his physical presence."[36]

Given Jean's manipulative dominance in the first encounter, Hopsie must regain some stature in order to establish a volatile, interesting contest. To accomplish this, in the subsequent scene, Hopsie and Eve go to his cabin where Hopsie's snake Emma has escaped. Upon confronting Emma, Jean screams in abject terror and races, in speeded-up, cartoonish shots, down to her cabin, a hysterical, neurotic wreck, the only time this controlled and controlling woman is so thoroughly unnerved, losing her verbal and physical control. Sturges releases the sexual pressure cooker, inserting this farcical scene with its obvious, symbolically Freudian suggestion. Cavell prefers to read it as testimony to the fact that "sexuality is for this sophisticated and forceful woman still a problem."[37] More accurately, as Harvey notes, "The Stanwyck temperament and style are at the heart of that tension between experience and innocence which so much preoccupies Sturges."[38] Pulling herself together, reverting to her enjoyable control over Hopsie, Jean quickly directs this passive boy-child once her panic has subsided.

Figure 10.1 A dominant Jean (Barbara Stanwyck) teasing a physically uncomfortable Hopsie (Henry Fonda) in *The Lady Eve*.

Jean lowers her voice and coos, "You don't know what you've done to me." Hopsie's smile has disappeared and his delivery slows as he yields power. He slips off the chaise longue and she trails her fingers through his hair, mussing it slightly, as he barely moves.

Fonda is stiff, Stanwyck relaxed and back in control, the eye of the storm. Stanwyck places Stanwyck just slightly above Fonda, right side of the screen. His clothes are disheveled, reflecting his emotional discomfort. She ends the scene with a broad smile and half laugh.

In the dialogue exchange as Jean musses Hopsie's hair, typical of Sturges, the dominant character/actor, here Jean/Stanwyck, underplays a role that could so easily have tipped over into uncomfortable mockery. Her calm control, ease of movement, and minimal fussiness signal an equal confidence by writer-director Sturges: a trust in his material and his players, who need only to invite the viewer to embrace and enjoy the entertainment as much as they. To maintain momentum and energy, Sturges supplements with bursts of slapstick from which he quickly retreats, reestablishing his focus on the characters' interaction. His nimble actors segue through these moods and styles with slight, subtle shifts of verbal and nonverbal details. This relative stillness by the more commanding character and the constrained bewilderment by the secondary participant define Sturges's approach. His lead actor consistently resists exaggerated strong and sudden expressions, gestures, or movements.[39]

After a naive Hopsie loses $32,000 to Harry, after Hopsie learns the real identity of Jean and her father, and after Hopsie refuses to listen to Jean's explanation, Hopsie breaks off his relationship with her, exposing a self-righteous, unforgiving side to his character. The softness disappears from Fonda's facial expressions and his body becomes rigid, less yielding than he had been earlier in response to Jean's literal and figurative maneuvers.

Stanwyck's and Fonda's acting choices shift in response to the tone and intent of the scene, their verbal and nonverbal force, or lack thereof, telegraphing the dominant character. This is equally evident in the critical confrontation between Lady Eve and Hopsie when Hopsie first sees Lady Eve at the Pikes' dinner party. In that critical scene, as Lady Eve, Stanwyck adds a level of animation beyond Jean's earlier, more restrained enactment. At the Pikes' home, Eve gestures often with her hands, moves her head from side to side and up and down, and turns her upper torso right to left while her appreciative, fawning audience remains, for the most part, inactive, merely smiling and laughing as if on cue. In effect, Eve channels her emotional and ethical anxiety as she speaks with her body. Typical of Sturges's films, stronger gestures increase and activity accelerates in later scenes, evidence of actors calibrating their performances to express rising tension with increasing plot complications, finally culminating in a satisfactory resolution.

Figure 10.2 Preston Sturges regularly used slapstick humor to relieve verbal tension, as he does with Charles (Henry Fonda) in *The Lady Eve*.

During this recognition scene, as activity peaks at the Pikes' estate, Hopsie remains physically calm, the stunned look on his face similar to his "soft" facial appearance in Jean's cabin. To intensify this impression, Sturges lingers on the close-up of Hopsie's face, emphasizing stillness, vulnerability and disbelief. The close-up of Eve, the shot answering Hopsie's close-up, is from a slightly higher camera position, angled down, further reinforcing Hopsie's perspective. Sturges reestablishes Eve's dominance by a series of slapstick falls that mock Hopsie: he falls over a couch that, as his father says, has "been there for fifteen years," trips and tears down a drape, has a platter of roast beef and gravy dumped on his chest, and, after freeing Eve's train, comes up under a tray filled with coffee and cups whose contents fall on him.

Sturges's second detour into heavy-handed slapstick functions as his first foray did, that is, to defuse the mildly uncomfortable mistreatment of Hopsie. He's clueless when his family and their friends are having such a good time, and the audience is invited by their joyful camaraderie to join in the laughter. Though he forged ahead with this series of pratfalls, Sturges admits, "I was scared to death about *The Lady Eve*. I happen to love pratfalls . . . [but] my dearest friends and severest critics constantly urged me to cut the pratfalls down from five to three."[40] By his own admission, he held his breath watching the film with an audience. "But it paid off. Audiences, including the critics, surrendered to the fun."[41] Sturges also used physical humor to sell Hopsie's most thorough humiliation, which occurs after he leaves the honeymoon berth, steps off the train, and falls on his backside, in semi-slow motion, into rain-soaked, sloppy mud. Sturges pushes Hopsie's bungling beyond that visited upon conventional leading men, finding refuge in a closing pratfall to prompt audience laughter. Fonda registers shock at Eve's revelations with a breathy, high voice (noticeably different from his masculine quality in other dialogue scenes) and his unrestrained physical flop into the mud. His adept acting sells the comedic connotations.

The reliance on physical humor also makes palatable several jabs at class affectation. This extends to secondary characters as well. For example, the introduction to the Pike household establishes Mr. Pike (Eugene Pallette, called the human bullfrog because of his raspy voice) as a childlike patriarch. He enters his first scene from his upstairs bedroom singing "Roll Out the Barrel." Through a phone call he accidentally learns about a party at his own home, and, because he cannot get breakfast quickly, insistently rings a bell, pounds on the table, and bangs two silver dish covers together. Pallette plays Pike for farce, becoming increasingly childish, just one way in which the film mocks the rich through their unsophisticated behavior. His acting reinforces his infantile persona with his unselfconscious, energetic, forceful banging. He plays the child.

Sturges concludes his satire on the pompous, vacuous attitude of the rich, as well as their fawning over British royalty, in the exchanges during dinner between Eve, the Pikes and their friends. Eve says nothing really humorous, but the Pikes and their guests laugh merrily, gush and defer to the Lady Eve. Stanwyck exaggerates her delivery and her reactions, prompting our laughter at the Pikes' and their guests' unwarranted, inane reverence for her phony status. As one of Jean and Harry's previous acquaintances tells them when they encounter him at the track (Gerald/Sir Alfred McGlennan-Keith, another con man), "The chumps? My dear boy, when your name is Sir Alfred McGlennan-Keith, R.F.D., you don't have to meet them; you fight them off with sticks."

Because costumes constitute the actor's "skin" and props, *The Lady Eve's* costumes contribute to the cumulative effect of the performances. To accentuate Jean's guises and her physical allure, Edith Head (who won more Academy Awards than any other costume designer in Hollywood's history) created twenty-five gowns for her and, to signal Charles's elegance and character, fourteen outfits for him. Aware of the contribution intelligently designed clothes made in communicating Jean/Eve's personality, Head ensured that the elegant Lady Eve in the second half of the film "was a complete metamorphosis; in the first half of the film she was one person and in the other half, another."[42]

Emphasizing the tropical environment in the early scenes, Head "gave her bare-midriff evening gowns and other glamorous outfits with a decidedly South American flavor at a time when Latin American music was sweeping the radio stations and the American government was promoting good Pan-American relations."[43] When Jean becomes Eve, Head explains, "Naturally I chose much richer, more luxurious fabrics when she was supposed to be of noble birth" and "used different colorations that would show up more subtly in black and white." In effect, Head reinforced Stanwyck's qualities as Jean and Lady Eve: her sexiness, her class status, and her physical movements which Stanwyck's acting emphasized.

Costumes enhance performance in other scenes as well. Once Hopsie learns that Jean is a cardsharp exploiting the cruise ship clientele, he breaks up with her despite her protestations and honesty. Head enhanced Stanwyck's performance in this sequence by putting a distressed Jean "in a suit with a box jacket and a full, pleated skirt. When Stanwyck falls onto the bed crying, the outfit gives her a little girl vulnerability that is surprising and effective."[44] As Harvey sees it, this romantic, more innocent reaction is exactly "the sort of thing that Hopsie means to her—recovering that little girl again in some way."[45]

In the dinner scene discussed above, the dress and the tiara Eve wears to the Pikes' home sparkle to highlight Eve as the center of attention. But Stanwyck added much more, and Head realized this, writing, "It wasn't merely a change of costume. The way she stood and walked was different. Her makeup and hair became much more elegant to suit her character."[46] Stanwyck also changed her verbal and nonverbal details, increased the pace, and kept the humorous ambience with verbal and nonverbal buoyancy. Using her luxuriously feathered fan as a prop, Lady Eve punctuates her story about her trip to America with hand gestures, controlled eye contact, periodic bursts of laughter, and dramatic pauses. For his part, Charles's gorgeous tuxedos reinforce his physical appeal as an object of desire as they also heighten the humor of his pratfalls.

Without Stanwyck's pervasive cheerfulness, conveyed by her lilting verbal and a flowing nonverbal delivery, the revenge motif would collapse into pathos, and Sturges edges dangerously close to cruelty. James Harvey considers it odd, ambiguous and troubling, this "exuberant, coldly brilliant comedy about the humiliation of a man by a woman"[47] and stresses Charles's deep snobbery when he won't listen to Jean. Part of what makes the film engaging is watching Stanwyck wrestle with the problem of Jean/Eve's tough persona as Sturges's script compromises her in ways that have not found their parallel in representations of typical male protagonists. The tension between tough and vulnerable, patriarch and matriarch, boy and girl, savvy and naive gives *The Lady Eve* its edge, delicately delivered by Stanwyck and Fonda.

This is nowhere more apparent than when Charles proposes. In addition to infusion of his beloved slapstick to alleviate the tension, Sturges rescues the sunset scene in which Charles sentimentally announces his love for Eve by using an intrusive horse to distract from and add silliness to Charles's awkward marriage proposal. Nibbling, nuzzling, pushing, rolling one wild eye, and whinnying, the horse steals the scene. But Stanwyck's and Fonda's acting choices add levels of enjoyable silliness to this three-ring circus: Charles reaching for strained profundity, Eve amusedly taking his comments literally and misinterpreting them, and the horse making a mockery of it all.

In a busy (and ugly) jacket, Charles futilely tries to ignore the intrusive horse, continuing to deliver his proposal and his philosophy to a receptive Eve. Stanwyck maintains an uncharacteristic stillness using her eyebrows, her half-closed eyes, her open-mouth half smile, and her soft voice to anchor the scene. She lets Fonda dictate the scene's pace and mood as he asserts his love. Coyly and kindly, Stanwyck cedes the scene to Fonda, whose attempted gravitas is, characteristically, undermined with tomfoolery. But as Charles's offer solidifies Eve's victory, we feel it is a thoroughly hollow one. She looks terribly heartless for the first time. Wisely for the comedic climate, Sturges provides little time to dwell on Eve's distasteful success as the horse upstages Charles's proposal.

Throughout *The Lady Eve*, through physical movement, costuming, line delivery, and pacing, Sturges foregrounds and entrusts his actors with the success of his story. Their acting expertise in both broad strokes and minute details delivers the accomplished film Sturges designed.

PERFORMANCE IN *THE PALM BEACH STORY*

A year after *The Lady Eve* Sturges wrote and directed *The Palm Beach Story*, an enormously successful film though its plot design showed none of the potentially revolutionary gender reversals of *The Lady Eve*. Claudette Colbert and Joel McCrea,[48] both of them photogenic and appealing actors, present engaging performances true to the Sturges style: that is, underplaying in a manner that suited their characters. Colbert and McCrea, in ways reminiscent of Stanwyck and Fonda, argue and entertain as Gerry and Tom Jeffers.

The simple premise revolves around a woman who leaves her inventor husband in an attempt to secure the $99,000 he needs to build a prototype of a suspended airport. After an opening wedding montage sandwiched in between the credits (all silent film slapstick with a payoff only at the film's conclusion), the Wienie King (Robert Dudley) gives Gerry money for past rent due, leading to a confrontation between Gerry and Tom. On the run, Gerry throws herself on the mercy of John D. Hackensacker III (Rudy Vallee), one of the wealthiest men in the world. Immediately enamored, John D. offers to help her "brother" (Tom) who has flown to meet them in Palm Beach. John D.'s crooning sends Gerry and Tom back into each other's arms. They remarry, each has a twin: hers weds John D.; his weds John's sister, Maude, also known as Princess Centimilla (Mary Astor).

The weight of the film rests firmly on Colbert's and McCrea's shoulders, their performances the heart of the film, with little subtlety in supporting roles. This diminishes the satirizing of the wealthy, especially given that Sturges depicts only one wealthy man as humane, the Wienie King, and he is old, silly, extremely hard of hearing, and symbolically impotent. The millionaires in the Ale and Quail Club are boorish, stupid, drunken louts. They intrude into the narrative so awkwardly that, after their riotous scenes, Sturges leaves them behind, never to be heard from again. John D. is "more cut off from life than Hopsie . . . [he's] been so cloistered and puritanized that Hackensacker resembles a parsimonious old maid more than a man."[49]

John D.'s sister Maude is more eccentric than Susan in *Bringing Up Baby*. Mary Astor wrote, "I couldn't talk in a high, fluty voice and run my words together as he [Sturges] thought high-society women did, or at least *mad* high-society women who've had six husbands and six million dollars."[50] And, as expected with Sturges, slapstick periodically took over the already exaggerated, ludicrous depiction of the rich in the person of Toto (Sig Arno), Maude's houseguest, who singlehandedly destroys the comic rhythm of every scene. A parody of a parody (Carlo/Mischa Auer, the gigolo in *My Man Godfrey* 1936), he suggests that Sturges was serious about his eleventh rule for box-office appeal, "A pratfall is better than anything."[51]

Hackensacker doesn't comprehend his humiliation, mild as it is, and Gerry is the recipient of the largesse of everyone from taxi drivers to millionaires. Colbert and McCrea in their verbal and nonverbal, active/passive *pas de deux* emerge, then, as the central reason for the film's appeal. They amply demonstrate their unique compatibility and on-screen chemistry in two pivotal scenes: first, Gerry's attempt to explain the $700 given her and, second, Gerry and Tom's reuniting once in Florida.

Numerous similarities exist between Jean's seduction of Hopsie and Gerry's interaction with Tom. Though *The Palm Beach Story* scene dramatizes a very different conflict, it is noteworthy that in both films the man is verbally and nonverbally awkward and inflexible, looking stunned as the women, Gerry and Jean, are relaxed and in control, upbeat and animated, obviously enjoying the exchange. Colbert's performance delivers this through Gerry's bubbly, direct address and bemused attitude, expressed through her barely suppressed smile.

In their first encounter in their apartment, Tom enters the living room and Gerry cheerfully greets him, their vocal intonations in conflicting registers. Tom is angry and alarmed, having just learned from Mike the doorman (Monte Blue) that Gerry has paid their rent from money given her by an older man. In his exchange with Mike, Tom keeps his hands in his pockets, makes no nonverbal gestures, and makes only minimal use of his eyes and shifts of his head to communicate both his desire to avoid the Park Avenue apartment manager and his irritation upon learning of the gifted money.

Using the Laban Movement Analysis to explore acting choices, we find that McCrea consistently opts for light and indirect gestures. For example, even though Tom is annoyed about the money, when he confronts Gerry, McCrea chooses to glide across the room, unhurried, arms held immobile at his side. In her performance, Colbert commands the energy of the scene with strong, indirect gestures.

She casually flicks the ash from her cigarette into the ashtray, moves her arms upward to emphasize the rent receipt, leans her body forward and back to underscore her comments, shakes her head, holds up the receipt a second time to point at the "Paid" stamp, takes a step back, points at her new dress and hairdo, and holds up at face height and counts $14 she's saved for Tom. Gerry dominates the scene with her movements, her placement on the right side of the composition, and the shiny satin beauty of her dress versus Tom's dark suit, position on the left side of the composition, and verbal and nonverbal immobility.

Colbert insisted on wearing gowns designed by Irene, her personal designer at Bullock's Wilshire store.[52] Elegant without being ostentatious, Gerry's

Figure 10.3 An animated Gerry (Claudette Colbert) in her new, satin dress and a stiff, immobile Tom (Joel McCrea) in *The Palm Beach Story*.

gowns accentuate Colbert's lithe movements. In addition, Irene "was equally renowned for her suits which were tailored, full of choice detail, yet softly feminine,"[53] another enhancement of Colbert's actions. For example, the horizontal and vertical striped suit Gerry wears upon the yacht's arrival in Palm Beach adds a zany touch that doesn't distract from or interfere physically with Gerry's racing up a ramp to confront Tom, walking with Hackensacker, and later circling the room in dialogue with Tom at Hackensacker's estate. Tom's suits are less arresting, nicely tailored, but as staid as he is.

The sartorial contrast between the two actors extends further. Colbert's musicality and her multifaceted, inflected delivery differ from McCrea's speaking his lines in a near monotone with a flat cadence. Gerry smiles, the camera pans right and back left to follow her as the conversation turns to the issue of sex appeal and how it mattered in her exchange with the Wienie King. As the dialogue concludes with Gerry's gleeful description of being discovered hiding in the bathtub, Colbert amplifies her delight with a strong, sustained smile. McCrea sounds increasingly like Hopsie in *The Lady Eve's* honeymoon scene. Tom's voice is deep and angry, his delivery clipped, his body posture stiff. Implicitly addressing Tom's metaphorical and literal stance, Gerry even says, "You don't have to get rigid about it." Of course, stillness and a quiet presence can convey immense power, but in this instance, McCrea conveys Tom's inflexibility and unyielding certainly that he is right. Tom and Gerry explicitly articulate oppositional attitudes to accommodating their monetary windfall. Similarly, McCrea and Colbert demonstrate their characters' mindset through their vocal and postural choices.

In both *The Lady Eve* and *The Palm Beach Story*, the dynamic performances of Colbert and Stanwyck drive the plot forward and animate the film's appeal. The conspicuous and arresting similarities behind Colbert's and McCrea's choices and Stanwyck's and Fonda's verbal and nonverbal qualities in *The Lady Eve* indicate that Sturges had a guiding directorial role in Colbert's and Fonda's as well as Colbert's and McCrea's performances.[54] Moreover, for a scene to have texture, the actors must project different levels of intensity, both emotionally and physically. In ensuring this occurs, Sturges opposes the vivaciousness of his female character, in this latter case Colbert, against the formality of McCrea. In our earlier case, Stanwyck, craftier given her hidden agenda, is also the catalyst with Fonda, the character out of his element. In *The Palm Beach Story*, as the wayward wife, Gerry also activates the plot and commands center stage in the early confrontation with Tom, as she will throughout the film.

After she flees with no money, Gerry throws herself upon the mercy of man after man, all of whom quite happily rescue her by rewarding her helpless little-girl act with shelter (an apartment, a train berth and a mansion), travel (by taxi, train, yacht, car and, for Tom, airplane), money, food, clothes, and other gifts, in particular, the agreement by John D. to build Tom's prototype. She trades her lowered eyelashes, sweet smile, breathy thank yous, and leggy appeal for what she and her husband need. As in *The Lady Eve*, Sturges inserts slapstick physical action to break the verbal tension. As Gerry leaves Tom, he falls down the flight of stairs in their apartment and runs to the elevator with a comforter wrapped around his waist. In another scene, Gerry twice steps on and breaks John D.'s pince-nez as she clumsily attempts to climb into an upper berth on the train after fleeing the Ale and Quail Club.

In a climactic scene late in *The Palm Beach Story* Tom greets Gerry upon her arrival by boat in Palm Beach. She is surprised and unnerved by his presence, and her movements now become strong and indirect, in Laban's terms. She wrings her hands, speaks and gestures quickly, and grasps her purse nervously. The subsequent confrontation at the Hackensacker's estate between Tom and Gerry echoes the earlier one between husband and wife. While McCrea chooses to incorporate a few stronger, indirect arm movements and a bit more alarm in his voice, Gerry again controls the action. She strides toward the camera as it retreats, panning left to right with her. As Gerry walks 360 degrees around a table looking for a cigarette in the four empty boxes there, Tom walks slightly toward and then away from the camera, his arms hanging motionless (again) at his side. Gerry continues to smile, enjoying the charade that has Tom perennially out of sorts. With minor variations, this pattern characterizes their subsequent encounters up to the *deus ex machina* ending.

The Lady Eve and *The Palm Beach Story* reflect Sturges's preference for active/passive pairings of his central male and female characters as well as in his supporting roles. Extending this model of relatively active characters paired with comparatively inactive ones, Sturges repeatedly stages scenes featuring supporting characters delivering sudden or sustained gestures, moving and gesturing much more than the principal actors. Sturges tends to position his stars near the center of the composition, anchoring the action but contributing primarily a strong presence in many scenes. For example, Gerry with the Ale and Quail Club and Jean describing Hopsie's exchanges with women flirting with him during the first dinner scene on the ship and in the card game with the Colonel illustrate this approach. The supporting characters make strong, sudden and sustained, even alarming (in the case of the Ale and Quail Club) movements. The principal character remains calmer, central to the action, as anchor and as catalyst.

This calm vs. excitable performance pattern extends to other Sturges films as well. In *The Great McGinty* McGinty (Brian Donlevy) argues in numerous scenes with excitable criminals and staff; in *Christmas in July* Jimmy MacDonald (Dick Powell) interacts with more demonstrative colleagues, clerks, and neighbors; in *Hail the Conquering Hero* Woodrow Truesmith (Eddie Bracken) debates his "hero" status with the six excitable marines; and in *Sullivan's Travels* John Lloyd Sullivan (Joel McCrea) encounters more demonstrative individuals in multiple locations.

Sturges's films' visual and tactile interactions provoke pleasure as showcases displaying skilled actors listening to each other, speaking witty dialogue, and delivering amusing, and incisive, social satire via strong character exchanges. Joel McCrea, who needed, by his own admission, strong directing from Sturges, has said that he told Sturges he couldn't learn a long speech. And yet, McCrea adds, he could rattle off Sturges's dialogue, so well-crafted and natural that it just flowed.[55]

In the two Sturges films under consideration here, the actors sustain the carnivalesque spirit of the narrative through their deceptively effortless performances. Only a director and actors at the top of their game could achieve such a high-wire act with such apparent ease in a truly difficult endeavor. Sturges and his actors deserve acknowledgment for the masterful, nuanced performances Sturges guided as he, the eye of the storm, delivered enchantingly entertaining films.

NOTES

1   My extensive June 2014 literature search included hard copies of film journals (*Cineaction, Cineaste, Cinema Journal, Film Comment, Journal of Film and Video, Sight and Sound, Wide Angle, et al.*) and of cinema studies books, as well as electronic resources such as MUSE and EBSCO. I found no articles focused exclusively on analysis of acting in any Preston Sturges film. The diverse comments on individual actors were included in scattered commentary on various individual films and in articles and books on genre studies, e.g. screwball comedy. However, I found no in-depth analysis of acting in Sturges's films.

2   Paul McDonald, "Why Study Film Acting?" *More than a Method: Trends and Traditions in Contemporary Film Performance*, ed. Cynthia Baron, Diane Carson, and Frank P. Tomasulo (Detroit, MI: Wayne State University Press, 2004), 25.

3   James Naremore, *Acting in the Cinema* (Berkeley, CA: University of California Press, 1988), 23.

4   Naremore, 26.

5   Andrew Klevan, *Film Performance: From Achievement to Appreciation* (New York, NY: Wallflower Press, 2005), Preface.

6   Klevan, Preface.

7   Cynthia Baron and Sharon Marie Carnicke, *Reframing Screen Performance* (Ann Arbor, MI: University of Michigan Press, 2011), 38–9.

8   Baron and Carnicke, 59.

9   Sturges, Preston, *Preston Sturges by Preston Sturges*, ed. Sandy Sturges (New York, NY: Simon & Schuster, 1990), 274–5. Sturges writes about watching theater audiences night after night through a peephole to see where they looked and when. He also experimented with his own focus on an object, to understand what his eyes were doing.

10 James Curtis, *Between Flops: A Biography of Preston Sturges.* (New York, NY: Harcourt Brace Jovanovich, 1982), 132.

11 Curtis, 132.

12 I think in particular of Lucy Warriner (Irene Dunne) masquerading as ex-husband Jerry's (Cary Grant's) sister in *The Awful Truth*; Godfrey (William Powell) posing as the butler in *My Man Godfrey*; Susan (Katharine Hepburn) briefly pretending to be Swingin' Door Susie of the Leopard Gang in *Bringing Up Baby*; and Peter Warne (Clark Gable) pretending he's a gangster kidnapping Ellie in *It Happened One Night*; among others.

13 Richard Dyer, *Stars*, new ed. (London: BFI Publishing, 1998 [1979]), 21.

14 For more on acting conventions of the studio system, see Cynthia Baron and Sharon Marie Carnicke, especially Ch. 1, "Crafting, Not Capturing 'Natural' Behavior on Film," 11–32. See also the Introduction to Cynthia Baron, Diane Carson, and Frank P. Tomasulo, eds, and subsequent chapters which discuss acting ideas and styles of naturalistic acting.

15 As was his custom when he penned a screenplay, Sturges thoroughly rewrote Monckton Hoffe's 19-page story "Two Bad Hats," written in 1937 or 1938, and Jeanne Bartlett's 1938 adaptation of it. His first completed version, dated November 30, 1938, went through several more revisions before the October 18, 1940 shooting script became the official blueprint for the film released in February 1941.

16 Curtis reports that Sturges insisted on Fonda even after being encouraged to cast Brian Aherne. Paramount Executive Y. Frank Freeman (the first person awarded the Jean Hersholt Humanitarian Award) had to negotiate a costly deal with Twentieth Century-Fox's Darryl Zanuck.

17 Sturges, 294.

18 Bosley Crowther, "*The Lady Eve*, a Sparkling Romantic Comedy," *The New York Times*, 26 February 1941, accessed 19 June 2014 at http://query.nytimes.com/mem/archive-free/pdf?res=9D07E2DD133DE33BBC4E51DFB466838A659EDE

19 Bosley Crowther, "The New York Film Reviewers Choose the Year's 'Bests' With Gracious Harmony." Eighteen New York film critics voted *The Lady Eve* the second-best film of the year "because it was one of the most delicious screen comedies we've ever seen." *Major Barbara* received first place. They considered *Citizen Kane* "a superior picture." Joan Fontaine won the best actress award but the critics "admired tremendously" Barbara Stanwyck's performance. *The New York Times*, 4 January 1942. Accessed 19 June 2014 at http://query.nytimes.com/mem/archive-free/pdf?res=9806E0 DC163CE33BBC4C53DFB7668389659EDE

20 David Thomson, *The New Biographical Dictionary of Film* (New York, NY: Knopf, 2002), 298 and 832.

21 Baron and Carnicke, 190.

22 Baron and Carnicke, 199.

23 See Baron and Carnicke for more on Laban analysis.

24 James Harvey, *Romantic Comedy in Hollywood, from Lubitsch to Sturges* (New York, NY: Knopf, 1987), 570.

25 *The Great McGinty* and *Christmas in July* in 1940, *The Lady Eve* and *Sullivan's Travels* in 1941, *The Palm Beach Story* and *The Great Moment* in 1942 (release of *The Great Moment* in 1944), and *Hail the Conquering Hero* in 1944.

26 Doug McGrath, 9 June 2014.

27 Quoted in David Spoto, *Madcap: The Life of Preston Sturges* (Boston, MA: Little, Brown), 219.

28 Harvey, 561.

29 Curtis, 146–7.

30 Roger Ebert, "*The Lady Eve*." Written 23 November 1997. Available at <http://www.rogerebert.com/reviews/great-movie-the-lady-eve-1941> (last accessed 9 June 2014).

31 Elizabeth Kendall, *The Runaway Bride: Hollywood Romantic Comedy of the 1930s* (New York, NY: Knopf, 1990), 248.

32 McDonald, 32.

33 McDonald, 32.

34 Maria DiBattista, *Fast-Talking Dames* (New Haven, CT: Yale University Press, 2001), 12.

35 Stanley Cavell, *Pursuits of Happiness: The Hollywood Comedy of Remarriage* (Cambridge, MA: Harvard University Press, 1981), frontispiece.

36 Roger Ebert, "*The Lady Eve.*" Written 23 November 1997. Available at <http://www.rogerebert.com/reviews/great-movie-the-lady-eve-1941> (last accessed 9 June 2014).

37 Cavell, 54.

38 Harvey, 561.

39 On stillness as power: one of the best anecdotes in this regard involved Spencer Tracy. Often acknowledged as the best actor of this generation and this time period, Tracy knew quite well the power of composure and calm whatever the circumstances, and he earned a reputation as restrained *and* forceful. As Tracy said to Robert Wagner when shooting *Broken Lance* (1954), "Did you really think you could underplay me? Do you *really* think you could? Because you could *never* underplay me." In James Curtis, *Spencer Tracy: A Biography* (New York, NY: Knopf, 2011), 658.

40 Sturges, 294.

41 Sturges, 294.

42 Quoted on the Criterion DVD, excerpted from Edith Head and Paddy Calistro, *Edith Head's Hollywood* (New York, NY: Dutton Books, 1983).

43 David Chierichetti, *Edith Head: The Life and Times of Hollywood's Celebrated Costume Designer* (New York, NY: HarperCollins, 2003), 67. In his earlier *Hollywood Costume Design* (New York, NY: Harmony Books, 1976), 60, Chierichetti adds, "The results were sensational. Latin-American clothes swept the country. Head had launched a major trend, and for the first time, Stanwyck was regarded as a clothes-horse and she loved it."

44 David Chierichetti, 67–8.

45 Harvey, 574.

46 *The Lady Eve.* Paramount Pictures, 1941. DVD. The Criterion Collection. 2001.

47 Harvey, 570.

48 Curtis, 160. Sturges admired Colbert's acting and, in fact, originally wrote *The Lady Eve* with her in mind in 1938 while working with producer Al Lewin. He told Stanwyck that he would write a comedy for her. Sturges wrote *Sullivan's Travels* with McCrea in mind and, according to McCrea, liked him because of his "blank, no-nonsense quality" (Curtis, 152). Similarly, Rudy Vallee impressed Sturges when he saw him in a Three Stooges comedy, *Time Out for Rhythm.* He spied Vallee's comic talent as he was preparing *The Palm Beach Story* and immediately invited him to lunch and cast him.

49 Kendall, 257.

50 Curtis, 161.

51 Curtis, 163.

52 Chierichetti, 52. Beginning with *Midnight* (1939) she, as with other stars, "wanted to start wearing Irene clothes onscreen as well." She being under contract with Paramount for two films a year, they acceded to her request as long as she had her fittings at Bullock's, which she did. Head resented the arrangement.

53 David Chierichetti, *Hollywood Costume Design*, 32.

54 While the energy Stanwyck shows here as Jean is similar to that shown in her performance as Sugarpuss in Howard Hawks's *Ball of Fire* (1941) and Colbert's performance reminiscent of her approach in Mitchell Leisen's *Midnight* (1939), there are subtleties in

both their Sturges roles to suggest some measure of decisive direction teasing out a richness not always present in their other films.

55 *Sullivan's Travels*, Paramount Pictures, 1941. DVD. The Criterion Collection, 2001. Interview with McCrea.

CHAPTER 11

Presto(n) con Spirito: Comedies with Music, Sturges-style

Martin Marks

INTRODUCTION: UP WITH MUSIC

Well that sounds very deep dish and high falutin'.
> —Coffee magnate J. B. Baxter in *Christmas in July*

When we recall the great Hollywood comedies from the first two decades of the sound era, chances are we don't remember much about the music—unless it happens to play a role in the diegesis. In *Bringing Up Baby* (Hawks, 1938), for example, a memorable musical moment comes within a lengthy sequence set in the Connecticut woods at night, when the two leads, Susan and David (Hepburn and Grant), begin to sing the popular song "I Can't Give You Anything but Love (Baby)." They are trying to entice Susan's new pet, a leopard named "Baby," down from a stranger's rooftop. Susan launches into the melody, and David joins her by harmonizing. But their duet turns into a cacophonous quartet when Baby starts to caterwaul and George, the story's pesky terrier, chimes in with strident barking.

I show this scene to my students to demonstrate how pointed such musical nonsense can be. It confirms our sense that Susan and David are destined to go through life, as the cliché has it, "making beautiful music together" (though "beautiful" is hardly an accurate descriptor of their performance). Notwithstanding all the trouble Susan has caused poor David, the scene shows how much *fun* their relationship has become. Most importantly, in an amusing way the performance of "I Can't Give You Anything But Love" reinforces its function as the film's "theme song."

Written a decade before *Bringing Up Baby* was made, the song offered a comforting message to Depression-era audiences: one doesn't have to be rich to be happily in love.[1] It's intriguing to note that the lyrics make light of the importance of money, and to surmise that the filmmakers might have chosen to feature it for this very reason, as a counterweight to the film's money-dependent plot. But even if for no more zany reason than to make a punning connection between the film's title and Susan's "baby," the filmmakers frame the story with this song. Besides its performance as a hideous serenade, we hear it in two jazzy orchestral arrangements during the opening and closing credits. Apart from these segments, the soundtrack contains only a few instances of diegetic background music, none of it of any thematic importance—and no other non-diegetic scoring at all. If we do not feel the lack, there is a good reason: the film's dialogue affords us an abundance of "music" all its own, with several actors' voices functioning like different orchestral instruments.

As the contributors to other chapters of this volume note, Preston Sturges's characters also capitalize on the musicality of their voices and dialogue. Yet unlike *Bringing Up Baby* and most romantic comedies of the period, the Paramount comedies Sturges wrote and directed also contain considerable music *per se*, much of it non-diegetic. This departure from the generic norm did not come about all at once, nor did each successive Sturges film offer some sort of musical "advance" over the previous one. All the same, as can be seen in Table 11.1, these comedies collectively display an increase in the sheer *amounts* of music, well beyond the scope of the music in most other comedies made between 1930 and 1945.[2] From *The Lady Eve* forward, the amount of music adds up to an average of around forty minutes per film, compared to twenty minutes in *The Great McGinty* and fifteen in *Christmas in July*. The greatest amount by a sizable margin—fifty-five minutes in a 101-minute film—belongs to *Hail the Conquering Hero*; but even in the films that contain relatively little music, it still plays important supporting roles.

In parts two and three of this chapter, the reader will find detailed examples of musical designs and patterns within four of Sturges's Paramount films made between 1939 and 1942: *The Great McGinty* (in part two), *Christmas in July*, *Sullivan's Travels*, and *The Palm Beach Story* (in part three). The concluding part of the essay leaps forward to *Unfaithfully Yours*, which Sturges made at Fox in 1947–8. Since music is of supreme importance in the latter film, we might be tempted to see it as the director's "final cause" (and a lost one at that, in terms of audience response when it was initially released). But let us be wary of treating the Paramount films as way-stations on a journey: such a teleological narrative not only distorts the significance of music in the earlier films, it also begs the question of authorship. The presence and power of music in the Paramount films is impressive, but just how much credit should we give *Sturges* for that? Was the writer-director a musical "auteur" behind the scenes? Or do we more properly credit the scores to individuals on staff at the studios—or to what Thomas Schatz calls the "genius of the system"?

To proclaim Sturges as the dominant musical auteur is problematic. On the one hand, his upbringing—saturated as he was, while a child, in European opera and other types of high musical culture—must have helped him at least to appreciate what composers could do. On the other, we know precious little about the depth of his musical understanding. In his unfinished autobiography, Sturges tosses off humorous anecdotes about the operas he encountered many years earlier.[3] He writes vaguely about early, less-than-effective piano lessons, and about having co-composed a four-hand ragtime duet called "Winky"—though here, too, he adopts a self-deprecating manner.[4] We learn, too, from both Sturges and his biographers that in adulthood his musical experiences expanded. We know, for instance, that he sought out a more serious dose of piano lessons; that he supplied a set of lyrics for the operetta *The Well of Romance*; that he took pointers about lyric-writing from composer Ted Snyder, with whom he also collaborated on a published song, a foxtrot; and that he subsequently wrote some songs on his own, including funny ones performed on-screen in *The Miracle of Morgan's Creek* and *Hail the Conquering Hero*.[5] But none of this information suffices to convince us that he had a well-informed, insider's knowledge of the art of music. Furthermore, any attempt to estimate what part Sturges played in scoring the Paramount comedies requires us to keep in mind several points about how the studio worked at the time he took to the director's chair.

First, by the late 1930s the studio had become musically conservative. During the early years of the decade, Paramount produced several innovative musicals (e.g. *Monte Carlo* and *Love Me Tonight*). In the middle years it gave a few relatively "modern" composers opportunities to work on A-list films (notably, *The General Died at Dawn*, scored by Werner Janssen). In 1936 the studio even hired Borris Morros, its new "Director-in-Chief of Musical Production," who cavalierly asserted that "only modern composers should write the scores of the modern motion pictures of today"; but despite getting good PR, his supposed efforts to bring icons like Stravinsky and Schoenberg to Paramount went nowhere—and he was gone from the studio within a year.[6] After that, compared to the other major studios, Paramount produced little music to shout about, which partly explains why historians of music for early sound films have mostly ignored the studio. Instead they have focused on scores by Max Steiner (who worked first at RKO, then Warner Bros.), Erich Korngold (Warner), Franz Waxman (Universal, then MGM), Alfred Newman (principal composer for Goldwyn, then at Fox), and Bernard Herrmann (RKO). Of all the composers active at Paramount at that time, only one, Victor Young, has received more than passing notice, although as yet no scholar has written about his scores for Sturges's *The Palm Beach Story* and *The Great Moment*.[7]

Secondly, Paramount was so conservative at this time because the studio continued to favor intensive divisions of labor in the scoring process. Film by film, the studio parceled out tasks among multiple composers and arrangers—a workshop system that discouraged the creation of unified film scores. (Many scores included "stock" cues and song arrangements taken from the Music Department's ever-growing library.) As McCarty notes, such "collaborative scores . . . were gradually phased out in the 1940s," but not much change is evident until after Sturges had left the studio.[8] His films thus date within a period when scoring practices at Paramount were in transition, but at a fairly glacial pace, and innovators could easily get themselves into trouble. For example, as Marmorstein notes, composer Miklós Rózsa, who joined the Paramount staff in 1943, quickly rose to Academy-Award-level prominence with his imaginative scores for two Billy Wilder films in succession, *Double Indemnity* (1944) and *The Lost Weekend* (1945). Yet Paramount executives Louis Lipstone and Buddy DeSylva gave Rózsa such a hard time for these that he soon abandoned the studio to seek out more supportive environments at Universal and MGM.[9]

Thirdly, due to this divide-and-recycle method of scoring, we have difficulty pinning down the workings of the process from one film to the next. Concerning personnel, McCarty's *Filmography* is a reliable guide, because he labored meticulously to verify as many music credits as possible. Yet as he notes, terminological troubles mount due to inconsistent usage of basic terms: "Music Score," "Music Director," "Arranger," "Orchestrator"—all these credits were slippery. Compounding the confusion was the peculiar logic of copyright law, according to which each studio was deemed the "author in fact" of the music for its own films—meaning that in contractual terms, musicians were simply producing "work for hire," and thus need not be credited on screen.[10] Composers might be listed, but orchestrators almost never were at that time.

Thus, on-screen music credits can be confusing or downright misleading. (For the following details presented in schematic form, see Table 11.1.) At the opening of *The Great McGinty*, Frederick Hollander gets sole credit for the score; but according to McCarty and to Paramount's recording session log sheets, three others contributed: Leo Shuken, Charles Bradshaw, and John Leipold. After that, Shuken and Bradshaw supplied most of the original music for *Christmas in July* and *The Lady Eve*, yet the only on-screen credit was to Sigmund Krumgold, for "Musical Direction." This means that he conducted the studio orchestra at the recording sessions (where the composers may or may not have been present).[11] Then, for reasons unknown, the studio's crediting methods changed, such that Krumgold was listed on three more films as Music Director, while other men got credit for the scores: Shuken and Bradshaw jointly for *Sullivan's Travels* and *The Miracle of Morgan's Creek*, Werner Heymann for *Hail the Conquering Hero*. The only Sturges comedy for which the music credit is by and large unambiguous is *The Palm Beach Story*: Victor Young both composed and conducted the music, and he received sole

Table 11.1 Overview of music in seven Paramount comedies directed by Preston Sturges.

	Film length in minutes	Length of music in minutes	Number of music cues	Music credits on screen	Composer and orchestration credits per McCarty	Additional credits from various sources
The Great McGinty, 1940	82	21	24	Score: Hollander Direction: Krumgold	Score: Hollander (with Leipold)	Arr./orch.: Bradshaw, Shuken Songs: Rainger, Carmichael.
Christmas in July, 1940	67	15	17		Score: Shuken (with Leipold)	
The Lady Eve, 1941	94	46	27	Direction: Krumgold	Score: Shuken (with Boutelje, Krumgold, Grau, Bradshaw, Leipold)	Paramount songs include "Isn't It Romantic" and "Lover" by Rodgers & Hart; "Cocktails for Two" by Arthurs Johnston. Public domain song: "Landlord Fill the Flowing Bowl." Also included: arrangement of "Thunderstorm" movement from Beethoven's "Pastoral" Symphony; "Pilgrim's Chorus" from Wagner's *Tannhäuser* Overture.
Sullivan's Travels, 1942	90	47	32	Score: Shuken, Bradshaw Direction: Krumgold	Score: Shuken (with Bradshaw)	Comic cues feature arrs of Beethoven, Mendelssohn, Rossini, Wagner, Suppé, Chopin. One segment based on a cue by Shuken from *The Lady Eve*. Two public domain songs. Additional borrowings from Paramount catalogue likely.

The Palm Beach Story, 1942	87	38	28	Score: Young	Score: Young Orch.: Parrish, Scharf, Shuken	Comic cues feature arrs of Rossini, Wagner, Mendelssohn.
The Miracle of Morgan's Creek, 1944	99	42	43	Score: Shuken, Bradshaw Direction: Krumgold	Score: Shuken (with Bradshaw) Orch.: Parrish	Song: Sturges.
Hail the Conquering Hero, 1944	101	55	49	Score: Heymann Direction: Krumgold	Score: Heymann Orch.: Parrish, Shuken, Marquardt	Song: Sturges. Reuse of march fragments by Bagley *et al.*, from *The Great McGinty*.

credit for the score on-screen (though according to McCarty he was assisted behind the scenes by three staff orchestrators).

To sum up: on the Paramount mountain, it could be a long climb from a composer's sketch to a conductor's full score—as arduous a climb as from a writer-director's vision of a finished film to the actual final cut. It would be nice to think that Sturges, sherpa-like, led the way up the mountain as the musician's guide. However, we have no proof. The best answer to the question of authorship is to jointly credit the results to all three: Sturges, individual composers, and the studio system itself.

What, then, we do know for certain? Just this: within Sturges's funny and "deep dish" Paramount films, we hear music that matters.

THE FIRST COMEDY: THEME AND TONE IN *THE GREAT MCGINTY*

> *Down went McGinty . . . Dressed in his best suit of clothes.*
> —Line from an old popular song

Typically enough for an early sound comedy, *McGinty* doesn't have much music. The film contains twenty-four distinct segments ("cues"), ranging in length from a few seconds to a few minutes; these add up to around twenty-one minutes of the eighty-two-minute running time. In accordance with the studio's usual methods the score was a composite product, with different men responsible for different types of cues. Hollander composed six of the eight non-diegetic cues, and they are the most important ones, both for setting a comic tone and also for tying the film together musically with a single theme. Shuken, Bradshaw, and Leipold worked on the non-diegetic cues, in each case by drawing upon pre-existing music that had to be adapted and/or edited to fit individual scenes.[12]

As the man who had written the songs for *The Blue Angel* ten years earlier, Hollander might seem an odd choice for *McGinty*; but after emigrating from Germany and joining the Paramount staff in the mid-1930s, he demonstrated stylistic flexibility and took whatever films he was assigned.[13] As with many busy composers in the studios, Hollander's craft was *adaptable*; and adaptation is the key to his work on *McGinty*, in the sense that in the score he reworked material from an old English music hall song, "Down Went McGinty"—which became the working title of the film in the final (1939) version of Sturges's script.[14] We do well to pause to consider what the song is about—to understand what it must have signified to Sturges, when he settled on that name for his film's central character, originally known as "the vagrant."

The song's Dan McGinty is a hapless fellow whose behavior conforms to contemporaneous anti-Irish prejudice: he is so cheap he lets himself be dropped off a wall, breaking many bones, rather than being carried all the way to the top, which would require him to pay off a $5 bet (verse 1); next, celebrating after his wife bears him a child, he drinks so heavily that he trips at night and falls into a coal chute (verse 2); arrested for being drunk and disorderly, he sulks in a jail cell (verse 3); after he is released, he discovers that his family has deserted him, so he jumps into the sea and drowns, because "water he had never took before" (verse 4). In the chorus that comes after each of these verses, the opening and closing words are always the same: "*Down went McGinty* [the accent falling on the first word] *to the bottom of the Wall* [then *Chute*, then *Jail*, then *Sea*]/*Dressed in his best suit of clothes.*"

In literal terms, the film's Dan McGinty suffers only one of these misfortunes: he too winds up in jail, dressed in an impeccable suit. But contrary to the song, his fall from power is due not to stereotypical Irish faults, but rather to his intrinsically "American" character traits: whether as bum, mayor, or governor, McGinty is determinedly independent and resourceful. But he is also self-centered and ignorant of what others think and feel. "I musta been blind," he admits, when he finally realizes his feelings for Catherine and takes her in his arms, for the film's sole romantic love scene. Willful blindness—to rampant corruption and graft—trips McGinty up, and though his wife's love and encouragement lead him to try to "reform" himself and the system, it is too late. He sinks into a metaphorical sea of exile and anonymity: lost to his wife and stepchildren, he tells his story to other hapless souls as a moral lesson.

For this serio-comic tale, Hollander's musical cues eschew sentiment and take inspiration from the comic muse. In the music that accompanies the opening credits (Cue 1, the "Prelude"), we hear a boisterously free "adaptation" of the old song. Never presenting the tune straight, Hollander focuses our ears on repetitions of one buoyant phrase that appears in both the song's verse and the chorus.[15] He ignores the tune's square-cut and somewhat pedestrian phrases, instead opening up the melody into an expanded form. The middle phrase unit has a good-humored, country-bumpkin quality (especially due to its static drone bass, long a musical sign of rustic or "simple" folk). But at the end, after the opening phrase has returned, comes a grander closing section of a polished "classical" nature: the cadence phrase sounds like a pointed reference to Wagner's *Meistersinger* overture.[16]

We can be more certain of Hollander's general interest in merging classical with less "highbrow" musical styles. A prime example is Cue 6 (labeled "Voting Montage" on the film's recording sheet), which accompanies McGinty's visits to multiple polling places; it constitutes the first non-diegetic music in the body of the film. Lasting less than fifty seconds, this dense and atypical cue begins with a comic fugue, while the second half departs from strict fugal procedure to emphasize colorful orchestral effects, leading in turn to a surprising blues-harmony cadence at the close. As witty as it is unexpected, this music provides a definitive illustration of the score's mixture of musical styles.

So, too, does the concluding "Finale" (Cue 23). After Demarest's character utters the last line ("Time out, Gents, here we go again"), and while McGinty and the Boss begin to scuffle one more time, Hollander rounds off the film musically by recalling the main title in a fresh-sounding key (A-flat Major). The film races to its end, and the music quickly arrives at another grand "Wagnerian" cadence.[17] But this is not quite the end: a cast list follows, accompanied by a still fresher version of the Main Title: it has been transformed into a nifty swing-band piece arranged by Bradshaw (Cue 24). While such up-tempo exit music was hardly unusual at a comedy's end,[18] this conclusion sounds definitive, as if the tune has finally found its true nature. Putting the finishing touches on the film's picture of the main character, the final cue seems to tell us that by escaping and surviving the indomitable McGinty has triumphed after all.

Important as they are to the film, Hollander's cues last only eight minutes. What do the other thirteen minutes of music add? Most of these cues are diegetic, emanating from McGinty's world. Written in a variety of styles, they reinforce the narrative's many shifts of time, place, and tone.

All of the film's "present-day" scenes are set in an unidentified banana republic (as Sturges terms it in his script) within one locale: the unnamed "café" where McGinty works as a bartender and narrates his tale. Throughout these frame scenes runs a continuous stream of instrumental songs and dances (Cues 2–5, 9, 16, and 22), and these, to borrow ideas from Claudia Gorbman, provide both "narrative cueing" of the geographical setting, and also "connotative cueing" of particular moods.[19] The first of these is in a "Latin" style: a rumba by Ralph Rainger called "The Magic of You," which appeared in a 1935 film (itself titled *Rumba*).[20] The music establishes the "exotic" setting while reflecting the vogue for such dance-band music within the U.S. and abroad at the time *McGinty* was being made. Additionally it connotes the devil-may-care attitude shared by the denizens of this American-dominated, rather sleazy hangout. Cue 5, another Latin tune by Rainger, plays a more dramatic role, intensifying a sordid twist of Tommy's attempted suicide in the café's men's room. This music's pacing is frenetic, and it grates on the ear due to the prominence of an abrasive solo trumpet—its longest and shrillest flutter-tongued notes timed to sound precisely when Tommy fires his gun. Moreover, this music is *needed*, because (to appease the censors) Sturges showed Tommy's suicide attempt within a blurred mirror shot; the soundtrack therefore brings this dramatic moment into sharper "focus."

All the other café numbers sit in the sonic background to contribute to melancholy moods. Of these, the first and last (Cues 3 and 22) provide the most poignant moments. Cue 3, played while Tommy sits with "The Girl" and mourns the life he has left behind, consists of a sentimental version of "Louise" (another song from Paramount's catalogue).[21] While most vocalists sang this number in a carefree manner, the piano solo here sounds like a nostalgic reverie.[22] Cue 22, heard when McGinty's story ends and the last café scene begins, resurrects "La Golondrina," a famous Spanish ballad connoting exile and lost love.[23] While a conventional choice, the music's sentimentality subtly belies The Girl's jaded reaction to McGinty's story. She calls him "a big liar," but the music tells us that his story has moved *her* as much as Tommy.

In their own ways, these two cues illustrate how music can bring to a narrative what Michel Chion calls "added value."[24] Within the film's main story a majority of diegetic cues add much more: they function ironically by seeming to give wholehearted endorsements to the film's political action. Cue 7, for example, serves up a *very* quick and jazzy solo piano for the first of the film's crowd scenes—a noisy party celebrating Tillinghast's reelection. While hungry McGinty grabs food from the table, a tracking shot keeps the focus on his hands, which creates an intriguing parallelism, since his hands seem to move as busily as the unseen pianist's. More important, the music is exuberantly brash; we understand that these grafting politicians feel like they're sitting on top of the world.

Even more exuberant medleys of marching band music—a longstanding tradition in American politics—run through montages of McGinty's campaigns for mayor and governor. For their comedic value, Sturges had personnel in the studio Music Department to thank. The script called for the scenes of the mayoral campaign to be accompanied by "Hot Time in the Old Town Tonight," "The Battle Hymn of the Republic," and "The Stars and Stripes Forever," but none of these was used.[25] "Hot Time" *might* have worked: it had become familiar as Teddy Roosevelt's campaign song, and later was associated with other Democratic campaigns, including FDR's; thus it could have underscored the irony of McGinty's claim to be a "reform" candidate. But by 1940 the song was stale. As for Sturges's other two suggestions, one Paramount executive who read the script feared an audience backlash against bringing familiar patriotic anthems into so rowdy a satire.[26] By keeping them out of the film, the studio toned down Sturges's political cynicism. Even so, the music selected for these scenes becomes ironic by virtue of its very aptness. The cues reverberate with all-American optimism—especially the "National Emblem March" by Bagley—and the way its strains and those of different marches are bluntly jammed together increases the sense of crowds and hubbub. Their effectiveness must have echoed in Sturges's head when he worked on *Hail the Conquering Hero*: in the latter film we hear a similar jumbling of marches, even some of the very same tunes in the latter film's lengthy scene of Woodrow's return.[27]

This music conveys the feeling of a political bandwagon rolling at break-neck speed, especially in the last campaign montage, which builds to a "verbal-music" climax. Through carefully scripted crosscutting, the film juxtaposes campaign speeches being delivered by "The Politician" (Demarest) who speaks on McGinty's behalf, and an orator who lambasts McGinty and sup-ports his opponent. Sturges thus mocks the interchangeable hollowness and hypocrisy of their rhetoric; and the editing—first via swish-pans, then by cuts at an accelerating rate—adds rhythmic zest. Toward the climax, the volume level of the band music recedes, until we hear a brief, suspenseful pause, after which the Politician concludes by proclaiming McGinty's greatness. The crowd erupts in cheers, and the march music swells into the foreground one last time, ushering the montage into shots of McGinty's victory parade.

For all the political satire, this optimistic music is double-edged. Yes, it can imply ironic mockery, but it can also stir pride in America's no-holds-barred, democratic culture. But if the music pulls the viewer in opposite directions, it honors something essential. Henderson puts the matter this way: McGinty "like most Sturges films, confounds audience expectations by belonging to no single genre and by outmaneuvering, with remarkably sustained invention, modes of response inherited from other films."[28] We can expand his idea by noting how much our "modes of response" throughout the film are influenced by music. If, for all their wrongdoing, we end up by liking both McGinty and The Boss, one reason is that Hollander's deft and light-hearted music inclines us to do so.

SIX MORE COMEDIES: CONNECTEDNESS, DISJUNCTION, "MUSICAL MONTAGE," TRANSFORMATION

The Great McGinty hasn't much music; Christmas in July, a shorter and simpler film, has even less (Table 11.1). But despite its brevity, the second film score connects more strongly to the longer ones that enliven Sturges's Paramount comedies to come. One affinity between them is that, unlike McGinty, they all contain more non-diegetic than diegetic music.[29] In three of the longer comedies—The Lady Eve, The Miracle of Morgan's Creek, Hail the Conquering Hero—the score moves from predominantly diegetic cues during the opening reels to non-diegetic ones as the story intensifies. A second affinity is that in all of these films—again, unlike McGinty—a love theme warms up many key scenes. Love themes became necessary, it seems, because Sturges made a romance between two leads central to his plots in the post-McGinty comedies, although in characteristic fashion he maneuvered them in peculiar directions.

In Christmas in July Sturges makes Jimmy and Betty's scenes a counter-weight to a series of escalating mishaps caused by the coffee slogan contest.

Their partnership (as well as Jimmy's expansive love of family and friends) occupies one position, in opposition to the film's other spheres of business and salesmanship. The story thus pulls in two opposed directions, toward domestic contentment versus public humiliation, while the score favors one side of the struggle. The Main Title introduces the love theme simply (the arrangement resembles a conventional popular song). It does not play under the initial rooftop scene, because at that point Jimmy and Betty have a minor spat; but it enters quietly when they make up some thirteen minutes later, and subsequently the theme recurs five more times in various transformations, some of surprising intensity for so slight a tale.[30]

Otherwise, music in *Christmas in July* provides comedic enhancement, and some of the humorous cues prefigure stylistic elements in scores to come.[31] For example, a threefold connection originates with a key short cue played when Jimmy finds the bogus telegram on his desk telling him he has won the slogan contest. By means of an inserted close-up we see the telegram through Jimmy's eyes, and while he takes the words in, the music climbs upward dissonantly; then it breaks off without resolution when he lets out an explosive "Wow!" Though amusing to us (since we know that the telegram is a fake), this is a moment of high tension for Jimmy. In subjective fashion the music "cues" us into sharing his mounting excitement.

A parallel cue (titled "The Photograph") expresses the hero's tense mental state in *The Lady Eve*, though in a more serious manner, when Hopsie looks at a picture of Jean and learns her true identity. Once again the music climbs step by dissonant step, with stronger accents than before ("stingers," to use Hollywood parlance). The resemblance might have been accidental, although this seems unlikely, since both cues were the work of the same composer, Leo Shuken; but certainly it was no accident that led Shuken to recycle the very same *Eve* cue at the denouement of *Sullivan's Travels*, when the hero confesses to (his own) murder. By his confession Sullivan succeeds in getting his picture in the paper—and that visual parallel probably gave Shuken the idea of reusing this bit of music at such a different narrative juncture.

As noted above, to recycle a cue, or by extension, to write one that sounds very much like something already written, was par for the course at Paramount, and at other studios too: film music was expected to be conventional, and it was only common sense for composers to repeat themselves (literally or figuratively) as they moved from one hastily written score to the next.[32] But the connections in the scores for Sturges's films tend to be more significant than that: they are not just due to a system rooted in expediency; they reflect deeper recurring narrative patterns and unresolved contradictions.

Consider, for example, another humorous cue in *Christmas in July*. Early on, Baxter finds out that his company's slogan contest jury hasn't yet actually picked a winner, and he runs madly down a hallway to the jury room.

While he does, the orchestra both expresses and mocks his fury by launching into an old-fashioned, stormy *agitato*—the music being loosely based on the "Thunderstorm" (Movement 4) that Beethoven evoked in his "Pastoral" Symphony. This kind of musical parody, whereby the orchestra races forward on hackneyed warhorses dating from the nineteenth century, recurs in all of Sturges's Paramount comedies to come.[33]

In the penultimate scene of *Christmas in July*, we hear the sixth iteration of the love theme, played by the oboe. This cue underscores the lovers while they slowly exit their office, contentedly resigned to their latest turn of fortune. But when Betty stops to look wistfully out the window at the Maxford House building, the distant glimmering source of all their trouble, there erupts out of nowhere an anarchic *glissando* played by a slide whistle. This sound effect is matched to a joltingly quick dolly shot in which the camera races toward the building, ending with a cut into Maxford's office for a "codetta" to the story. Sturges here acts like a vaudevillian stage manager who, becoming bored by some sentimental number, gives a performer the hook. The following year, for the pantomimic resurrection scene of *Sullivan's Travels*, a virtually identical slide whistle effect celebrates the moment when Veronica sees Sullivan's picture in the newspaper and joyfully tosses it in the air. The two sequences occupy nearly identical positions in the narrative—the moment when all the serious matters are quickly resolved by comically satisfying but patently unreal machinations. And in both cases, the soundtrack makes them more so.

Many other instances of Sturges's fondness for auditory hijinks, often with gender-bending implications, occur in these comedies. Early in *The Lady Eve*, Hopsie comes out of the jungle on a tiny steamboat that announces itself with feeble high-pitched gasps and gurgles. He is about to board an ocean liner on which he will meet Jean, and *her* ship replies to his with massive bass-register blasts. The joke, based on sonic inversion, prefigures the way Jean will overwhelm and manipulate Hopsie through most of the story. Of course, not all sonic twists were so thematically significant—or at least not obviously so. In *The Miracle of Morgan's Creek*, when the audience gets its first glimpse of Trudy, she entertains a group of soldiers in the record store where she works by comically lip-synching to a deep bass-voice rendition of "The Bell in the Bay," an absurd mock-somber ballad written by Sturges.[34] What this goofy sight-and-sound gag has to do with the central story is not clear—though it does tell us that Trudy has a great sense of humor (and an excellent gift for clowning), putting us on her side before she gets "in trouble."

To extend Henderson's remark about *The Great McGinty*, Sturges's risky, unyielding interest in bending genres and "confounding expectations" must have challenged, and stimulated, Paramount's sound and music departments greatly. Careening from one musical "idiom" to another—classical to popular, serious to silly, genteel to jazzy, rollicking to romantic—the scores keep us as off-balance as the narratives they serve. Of all these comedies, the two with the richest bundles of contradictory effects are *Sullivan's Travels* and *The Palm Beach Story*; yet they are also the films whose scores make the richest sense, because in their musical designs they replicate the crazy-quilt odysseys of the main characters.

In the first half of *Sullivan's Travels*, after the Main Title, comedic cues abound. Beginning with a cue by Bradshaw called "The Tramp," they mock Sullivan's initial attempts to put on the costume and carefree air of a hobo, and thus to set out on the open road in search of "suffering" and adventure.[35] These musical cues sound cartoonish and corny, especially two short ones that quote Mendelssohn's all-too-familiar *Spring Song*.[36] Moreover, they are by no means the only instances of musical clichés placed in the score for parodic purposes. At the start of the film's first scene—a film within a film, showing (as Sullivan grandiosely puts it) a fight to the death "between capital and labor"—the orchestra plays a furious arrangement of the third movement of Beethoven's *"Moonlight" Sonata*, one of the staples of the repertoire during the silent period. Still more frantic is the music that accompanies the film's runaway go-cart chase: this cue jumbles bits of Rossini's *William Tell Overture*, Suppé's *Light Cavalry Overture*, and Wagner's *Ride of the Valkyries* into a chaotic mash-up of clichés. Later, when Sullivan goes to the movies with Miz Zeffie and her spinster sister, we don't get to see the picture, but we can tell it's a tragedy from the musical accompaniment: the orchestra is playing another silent-era chestnut, Chopin's *Prelude in E Minor*, for an invisible scene of intense misery, melancholy, and/or death.[37] Sturges treats the film's soundtrack here as dissonant counterpoint to what we actually do see and hear: on the one hand the coy attempts by Zeffie to seduce Sullivan; on the other, his increasing irritation with audience noises (a baby's cries, a brat with a toy whistle, a man munching crackerjacks).

While the score's two principal themes differ in style and purpose, both are original, and both subjected to multiple transformations. The film's love theme is the less prominent of the two. First heard in the background of the scene by the swimming pool, the cue has an easy charm. In later cues the tune becomes more passionate but never attains the intensity of the love themes for *Christmas in July* or *The Lady Eve*.[38] Indeed, one of the triumphs of the score is that in his love-theme cues Shuken followed Sturges's lead: underplaying the attraction that builds steadily between Sullivan and "The Girl." While "there's always a girl in the picture," as Sullivan says, in this film that's the only name she gets—a telling sign that the love story is secondary in importance to his quest to learn what it means to suffer.

The more important plot thread, of course, is Sullivan's odyssey, which is supported by the score's more important theme. Its essential character is that of a lament,[39] but it takes on additional meanings almost from the start. After being introduced in the Main Title, the theme is repeated more forcefully during a short prologue, while a title card states that the film is "Dedicated to the memory of those who made us laugh." The use of the past tense, combined with the musical style of this dedication, makes the film seem truly elegiac, as if comedy *were* a thing of the past—and for large portions of the film that becomes true. I am referring to two exceptionally long "musical montages" (Sturges's term)—a remarkable pair of extended wordless segments at the film's heart. Shuken wrote the music for the first of these, a well-crafted tone poem that runs nearly seven minutes. He cast the segment, called "Adventure in Poverty," into free rondo form: the music keeps returning to versions of the main theme, separated by contrasting episodes that follow the changing content of the sequence closely.[40] For a Hollywood film composer in the studio era, because dialogue was normally the dominant soundtrack element in narrative films, such a lengthy music-only cue was a rare opportunity.

The second musical montage (labeled "Charity and Tragedy") was divided into separate parts, composed successively by Shuken and Bradshaw. Shuken's portion begins with a reprise of his previous cue; this is an appropriate strategy because the sequence begins with shots of Sullivan's return to the same world as before, now to hand out money to the dispossessed. But when a sinister figure begins to follow him, Bradshaw's action music takes over; no longer elegiac, his music uses a much tenser style. What this montage sequence lacks in musical coherence, however, it makes up for by the striking visuals and the increasingly suspenseful, dissonant music. As the segment continues, unlike the previous montage, the noises of train engines, bells, and whistles become increasingly compelling. At the climax of the opening film-within-a-film sequence we heard a strident three-note musical figure blasted by a trumpet. That same trumpet motif appears at the climax of the later montage sequence, just before the train obliterates the robber.

Why the musical link? Consciously or not, Bradshaw must have sensed that one key to the meaning of *Sullivan's Travels* derives from the story's associations of mayhem with vehicles in rapid motion: trains, motorcars, and at the very end, an airplane. These machines, we come to learn, can easily backfire or spin out of control, just as do the hero's attempts to learn about suffering. As a result, when order and good sense are restored at the film's end, the resolution seems to owe more to chance than purposeful action. This is the implication of the film's last "musical montage," the sequence when Sullivan comes back to life. In this segment, adults behave childishly—recall The Girl's jubilant "Whoopee!"—and run amok. In keeping with the craziness, Bradshaw's fast and funny montage cue is filled with musical imitations of a train running *prestissimo*, musicalized whistles and all. Speaking the film's last lines, Sullivan describes life as a "cockeyed caravan." This is true enough for him, whose motorized caravan has traveled in a series of crazy circles. After this line comes the closing shot, a swirl of laughing faces, accompanied by music that confirms the nobility of his quest and celebrates the value of comedy and laughter.

The film's final shot also reminds us of one more film within the film: the fragment of a cartoon that Sullivan and others watch at the Baptist church. This too presents an example of musical "montage" (if we stretch the term a little), but it stands apart from all the others in both style and musical accompaniment. To begin, the scene possesses an intrinsically American social irony: a congregation of poor blacks and their Moses-like preacher behave kindly and accommodatingly to the white convicts. Paramount also includes musical irony, because even though the Disney cartoon was made with sound, here it is run on a silent projector. While one can rationalize the anomaly as a function of the church's not having money to buy an expensive new projector, a deeper meaning lies submerged in the music. The accompaniment is *not* a musical parody of silent film styles, like the Mendelssohn cues or the obtrusively noisy Beethoven music played at the film's start; nor is the cue a thematically-based interpretation or enhancement of the visuals, like the music for the montages at the film's center. Rather, the accompaniment is completely diegetic, played on a little pedal organ inside the church.[41] What we hear may have been written out but sounds as if improvised by the on-screen organist, and skill-fully so. The "score" has many so-called "mickey-mousing" effects (musical imitations of the action and imaginary sounds on-screen), but no themes. With self-effacing modesty, the organist's music supports the idea that the sound of audience laughter is what matters. Thus, this radically a-thematic segment stands apart from the rest of the score; and for that matter, so does the earlier deeply moving *a capella* performance of "Go Down, Moses" by the congregation and the preacher. This scene, we may say, is too important for its points to be undercut by any hint of musical mockery or insincerity. When this audience of the underprivileged and outcast begins to laugh, Sullivan finally realizes the value of his profession. Thus, in narrative terms the segment is the story's turning point. It is also the one with the film's least "composed" and most "authentic" music.[42]

The Palm Beach Story has a similar climactic scene of transformative signif-icance and musical authenticity. Here is a film in which comedy cues abound, and Young's farcical music bedazzles. But the most telling segment operates outside Young's score, when Rudy Vallee, as John D. Hackensacker, gives a fine characteristic performance of the song "Good Night Sweetheart." It was one of the many songs Vallee had become known for singing on radio and gramophone recordings, as well as in films, a decade or so earlier.[43] His goal is to win Gerry (Claudette Colbert) by serenading her; yet with an irony Sturges was so fond of, Hackensacker/Vallee does so both in and out of character. At first he is the hapless Hackensacker, who begins to sing at the wrong point, only to realize that he has been holding the sheet music upside down. Once the song gets underway he becomes Vallee the vocal artist and sings three full choruses, the musicians playing right next to him on the set. For each successive chorus the key rises a half step, a technique that makes both the sound of the voice and the emotional temperature warmer.

"Sweetheart" is not all that distinguished a song in its own right; nevertheless, it triggers the film's emotional climax through its effect on the two leads, Gerry and Tom (Joel McCrea). Sturges therefore focuses the camera on what happens to them psychologically while they listen, and what happens is wonderful to see. Arrested by the music, posed in gorgeous costumes and half-lit interiors, they become so moved as to cast aside their problems and reunite as a couple. When Sturges cuts back to Vallee singing one more "Good night," his closing words are set to an affecting falling major third as in a lullaby—an unknowing benediction of the couple's "remarriage."

The sonic richness of this song, and of music more broadly in this and Sturges's other comedies, surely implies the director's unusually effective awareness of music's transformative power. In each film he made at Paramount we can find simple themes and songs alongside intricate and densely wrought cues. Yet they seem to work in tandem and in opposition; they fit together and they don't; they enhance and they confuse. They are, in sum, mere and marvelous examples of the patchwork art called "film music"—perhaps the most problematic of dramatic genres, especially when it aspires to "classical" heights. With characteristic daring, Sturges made those aspirations a key subject of *Unfaithfully Yours*.

SCREWBALL FANTASIA; OR, OF FOOLISH MEN AND SERIOUS MUSIC[44]

Music does strange things—very strange things.

—Sir Alfred

With its odd mix of screwball comedy and satirical treatment of "serious" music, we can understand why the publicity department at Fox was unsure how to promote *Unfaithfully Yours*, and why it fared poorly with many critics and the general public.[45] We can also honor Sturges for his persistence. He based the film script, completed in October 1947, on a sketch written fourteen years before. (The script and sketch had the same title, *Unfinished Symphony*.) Readers at both Fox and Paramount had deemed the proposed film unlikely to please a general audience. Yet Sturges came back to it anyway, "gambling—at high stakes," as Henderson writes, "that there was a successful feature picture in his 1933 story."[46]

Had the film retained the script's title, *Unfinished Symphony*, the film-going public might have grasped the point more readily, and even understood that it was based on subverted meanings. The title, by association with the composer's best-known orchestral work, would have implied a film about Franz Schubert. Audiences would have expected a romanticized story of the composer as a struggling, lovestruck, and probably underappreciated genius, because in the years just prior to the film's release such biographies of composers enjoyed a minor vogue.[47] But Sturges turned those ideas upside down, since his film was about a successful, rich, happily married musician, whose extravagant creative energies are meant to make us laugh rather than weep. Equally important, he made his "hero" a conductor, not a composer. In that respect Alfred becomes kinsman to Sturges's earlier artist-hero, Sullivan. But while Sullivan looks outward to his audience, seeking to make films that matter, Alfred literally turns his back on them (and on his wife) and retreats into egotistical fantasy. Daphne's point of view becomes that of a stand-in for the whole adoring audience. She is the one who calls him "a really great man" just before the end. After all that has come before, we understand that he is also something of a fraud and a fool.

Sturges uses this contradictory character to show how an artist can be as prone to folly as anyone else, in part by illustrating that Sir Alfred's fantasies while conducting are at odds with the music that inspires them. They become trite miniature plays inspired simultaneously by creaky theater and by popular movies. The first scenario, which depicts a gruesome revenge-murder by razor, harks back to the Victorian penny-dreadful melodrama *A String of Pearls*, and indirectly calls to mind films about criminal masterminds and murderous husbands (as in *Gaslight*). The second is a solemnly ridiculous tearjerker and as such recalls scenes from so-called "women's pictures." The third skit, with its suicidal game of Russian Roulette, brings to mind stories of dueling Russians going back to *Eugene Onegin*.

As with earlier Sturges films, the score in *Unfaithfully Yours* also nods to shopworn fragments dating back to the silent period, but these nods go much further, because now Sturges satirizes film music in multilayered ways. In each of the fantasies, the music begins as diegetic concert music but then slips into pseudo-underscore. As it does, Alfred becomes a stand-in for ourselves as listeners, showing how prone we are to create mental images or narrative "programs" based on what we hear—and how the movies had turned that idea around, making the music seem to belong to such narratives, even when it clearly does not. In his fantasies, Alfred distorts the stories behind the music to self-serving ends; at the same time, Sturges uses those distortions to mock the whole idea of program music—and beyond that, to make us beware of sanctimonious attitudes toward classical music as a whole, along with its illegitimate offspring: movie music.

Consider the example of *Tannhäuser*. Here is an excerpt from a translation of the text note Wagner supplied for the overture when it was to be played in concert in Zurich in the early 1850s:

> As [the Pilgrim's] *Chant* draws closer, yet closer, as the day drives farther back the night, that whir and soughing of the air—which had erewhile sounded like the eerie cries of souls condemned—now rises, too, to ever gladder waves . . . So wells and leaps each pulse of Life in chorus of Redemption, and both dissevered elements, both soul and senses, God and Nature, unite in the atoning kiss of hallowed Love.[48]

This is not Wagner's prose; rather, it is a late Victorian's way of describing music's meanings in rarefied terms. As such it was ripe for mockery, and Sturges obliges. In the film, while the overture plays, Alfred fantasizes about earthly things more than the spiritual. When he says to Daphne by way of pardon, "Youth belongs to youth, beauty to beauty," he is thinking of bodies, not souls. He is also thinking about money as he writes her a check for $100,000, with this explanation:

> I want you to be rich, comfortable, and free. I don't want you to have to worry about rent or clothing or food, or any of the *unromantic* things [my emphasis], which should always be provided for you. That little head was never made to worry . . . or these little hands to work. Only to love . . . to love, so dearly.

Alfred patronizingly turns the whole *Tannhäuser* story around: *he* forgives *her*, because she is the adulterous one, and he "redeems" her both from sin and from material needs. He has the noble soul; she is nothing more than a prop.

Consistent with this scenario, when he conducts the overture during the concert, the Venusberg music, which connotes the eponymous hero's indulgence in sensual love, is absent. This elision occurs despite dialogue that Alfred will be conducting "the Paris version with the Venusberg music." On recordings, the overture usually lasts somewhere between thirteen and fifteen minutes, but in the film it takes less than five. What we hear is the "Pilgrim's Chorus" as it appears at the beginning of the piece, with a rewrite of the overture's final few bars tacked on at the end.

The bookend effect and distortions of meaning are still more extreme when it comes to Tchaikovsky's *Francesca da Rimini* as the basis for the third fantasy—compression again being the soul of Sturges's wit. Tchaikovsky's interpretation of Dante's vignette (from Canto V of the *Inferno*) takes a good twenty-three minutes to play, but in the film this concert performance spans but five. As they had with Wagner's overture, the film's musical arrangers condensed this elaborate tone poem to its ominous opening and hysterically tempestuous close, entirely omitting the central, lyrical love epi-sodes. Notwithstanding the original tale, the heartfelt bond between the adul-terers is entirely absent. Within the skit Daphne and Tony become sniveling cowards, foils to Alfred's vision of himself as melodramatic hero entitled to self-vindication. However, when at the end of the fantasy he shoots himself, Alfred falls "swooning" like Dante himself after he has heard the story.[49] His head is framed in a swirling eddy, suggestive of the whirlwind that torments the sinners in Hell's second circle. With his muddle-headed fakery, Alfred falls into a hell of his own making—until the end, when Daphne unwittingly becomes his Virgil and Beatrice in one.

Rossini's overture from *Semiramide* is the film's centerpiece: the longest and most ingeniously scripted of the three fantasies. It begins with nearly ten minutes of the overture played straight. As it unfolds, Sturges challenges his audience by making the scenario unusually complicated and shockingly violent. Few in the audience could have foreseen its sudden vivid depiction of Alfred in close-up, gleefully laughing while he slashes Daphne's throat with a razor.

Sturges deserves credit here for his musical intuition. He grasped that Rossini's crescendos release enormous pent-up energies and that often the composer's music, with its sudden stormy eruptions and prolonged climaxes, can be thrillingly brutal and passionate enough to fire the murderous heart. In its original context, the overture to *Semiramide* served to prepare the story of a Babylonian queen who conspires with her lover to murder her husband yet is killed by her own son. Sturges translates the opera plot into a story of a betrayed husband who enjoys a double revenge on his unfaithful "queen" and her lover, with no son or anyone else to stand in his way.

To set up this elaborate skit, Sturges gives us an opportunity to hear a sizable part of the overture in a six-minute rehearsal sequence. Filmed on the stage of an empty auditorium, much of the footage focuses on the orchestral players, with almost a documentary feel. We might go so far as to assert that it replicates a scoring session folded into the diegesis, providing a first hearing of concert music that will later be turned into invisibly rendered "background" score. But *Unfaithfully Yours* is not a concert documentary, and the sequence is also made to serve important narrative and comedic purposes. For one, it shows Alfred's skill and easy mastery of the ensemble: not only does he make clear by his gestures, facial expressions, and dialogue that he knows what he wants, he also makes jokes and treats the whole rehearsal as a lark.

Besides Alfred, Sturges himself adds a series of deflationary jokes in line with the rest of the film's attitude toward "highbrow" music. In the opening shot, while the music plays off-screen, we see a custodian sweeping up back-stage who suddenly reacts to one of Rossini's accented chords with a jerk that sends his broom flying.[50] But the broadest and most important bit of comedy hinges on a pair of cymbals.

Queried by the conductor while the orchestra continues rehearsing, a hesitant cymbalist, Dr. Schultz, expresses his fear of playing too loudly and being thought vulgar, to which Alfred responds, "Be vulgar by all means, but let me hear that brazen laugh!" Now the music becomes a background for comedy, as Schultz rushes offstage to get a much larger pair of cymbals. The sound of his next cymbal crash provokes a double take from Alfred, who then bursts into "brazen" laughter of his own. Significantly, the laughter is dubbed and makes a false match to Harrison's voice; the effect must have been intentional, because it anticipates the way Alfred laughs far *more* brazenly, at the conclusion of the first fantasy, like the pitiless Mephistophelian mastermind he imagines himself to be, when he conducts Rossini's overture that night.

Apart from Alfred's fantasies, the film takes broader aim at classical music's pretensions. Examples abound in the early bedroom scene, when Alfred responds with offhand humor to the questions his secretary Tony has brought him from various journalists. The most telling of these exchanges comes when Tony mentions a "citizen" who wants Alfred to endow "The De Carter Foundation for Serious Music." The conductor says, "Throw him out . . . [There's] nothing serious about music. It should be enjoyed flat on the back, with a sandwich in one hand and a bucket of beer in the other, and as many pretty girls around as possible." Twenty minutes later, after his faith in Daphne has been shattered, Alfred takes a very different tone when he meets with the detective Sweeney. The latter becomes fanatically excited, pouring out some funny lines of idolatry, such as "There's nobody handles Handel like you handle Handel!" To which Alfred replies: "I'm bitterly sorry to hear that you're a music lover! [. . .] I've always hoped that music has a certain moral and antiseptic power, quite apart from its obvious engorgement of the senses, which elevates and purifies its disciples."

Much of what goes on inside the first fantasy sequence seems designed to contradict those noble sentiments, including the way Rossini's music is toyed with as the scenario continues. The overture is too short to cover the whole skit, and other music by Rossini has been skillfully blended in. While the added music comes from other numbers in the opera's score, at two points it is arranged in pop styles. The first is a boogie-woogie harmonica solo (played by virtuoso "Toots" Thielman), the second a swing dance featuring a loud soprano saxophone. This, we are meant to conclude, is the kind of "vulgar" music Daphne would enjoy. Alfred has craftily placed her 78-rpm albums of these pieces into the pile of classical discs on his record player—all part of the master plan. But they are also some of the fantasy's strangest moments: so "real" has the segment become, we now hear cues as diegetic musical "realities" within a musical dream.

From another perspective, these segments imply that we are no longer inside Alfred's head so much as in that of Sturges, who is himself conducting this skit and inviting us to laugh at the way movies can play with our minds and ears. His love of allusions and stylistic manipulation leads to a brilliant transitional stroke at the fantasy's end. Something must be done to return us to the Rossini and to the concert, so when Alfred turns off the "awful" diegetic music (at the hotel detective's request), he points to the razor on the floor while pocketing the incriminating record. As if sharing Alfred's delight in his own cleverness, the overture's piccolo happily sneaks back in under the dialogue, getting louder, racing to its end, as the fantasy likewise races to a close.

Only at the very end of this fantasy, matched with Alfred's "brazen laughter" and the return to the ongoing concert performance, do the movie's audiences generally begin to grasp what Sturges is up to—and to realize how thoroughly their legs have been pulled. Since the film did not succeed, perhaps for many an audience member it was already too late. For some of us, however, the subsequent fantasies become all the more enjoyable due to their varied dramatic content and unexpected succinctness.

After the concert comes the long sequence of slapstick gags impeding Alfred's obsessive attempts to bring the first fantasy to life. For this portion of the film the Fox composers and arrangers supplied a series of merciless slapstick cues, mocking Alfred's calamities with the most vulgar musical burlesque. We hear mindlessly repetitive fragments that pervert Rossini's music with bizarre phrase twists, crude harmonies, and preposterous orchestrations; adding insult to injury, they are frequently combined with or cut off by zany sound effects.

This section of the film culminates in two gags signifying Alfred's total humiliation. In the first, the conductor's futile attempts to record himself using the so-called "Simplicitas" machine come to a dismal end. Consigned to the lowest possible range, Alfred's recorded voice moans like a dying colossus. Still, he cannot give up his plan of a "perfect" murder, so he retreats into his bathroom to hone his razor, while a portion of Rossini's real overture returns one more time. Futilely he tries to test the blade by depilating himself. When Daphne approaches, he is too wrapped up in his delusion—and too consumed by the music playing in his head—to notice. Mystified, Daphne gently calls to him, and audiences hear a crashing stinger chord (derived from one of Rossini's) just as Alfred cuts his thumb. The chord blows the overture away—its exit a wincing suggestion that music can cut very deep.

As other arguments between husband and wife follow, we hear brief recollections of the other two program pieces. Clearly Sturges wanted the whole concert and all three fantasies to be demolished, to make the shattering of Alfred's dream world and ego complete. Then, when the story has no place left to go, Sturges pulls out one final rabbit. Daphne unwittingly reveals information explaining her nocturnal visit to the secretary's hotel room, and all at once Alfred realizes that his wife has remained faithful. Too ashamed to divulge his lack of faith, he begs forgiveness, which she readily grants. In shots parallel to those from the beginning, Alfred and Daphne once again embrace and kiss in close-up—observed, as at the start, by the other four principal characters of the story. But unlike the opening scene, which has no underscore, a "straight" reprise of the "Pilgrim's Chorus" from *Tannhäuser* accompanies the final one. As the music swells to its noble finish, Sir Alfred utters his memorably poetic yet fatuous last words: "A thousand poets dreamed a thousand years, and you were born, my love."

Wagner, it would seem, has put his seal of approval on the marital reconciliation. Yet after all that has come before, the ending music surely mocks the speed with which Alfred has reverted to "normal" behavior and reaffirmed his undying love. So in fact this reprise of music that celebrates redemption implies its own opposite: that Alfred really *cannot* be redeemed from his elaborate high-flown fantasies. They will continue to swirl in the conductor's brain every time he leads a concert. He will always be two Alfreds, both greatly talented and exceptionally prone to melodramatic thoughts. Quite possibly the closing music we hear is music Alfred himself hears, inside his head, as if he were already conducting another scenario to music. But whether he hears the music or not, we certainly do—and by it we are cued to smile more broadly at his folly.

Yet a higher irony is at work here: Wagner's "high falutin'" music may undermine Alfred's last words, but it also announces "The End" with the conventional big finish that was expected in films of the period. Such a mingling of mockery, exaggeration, and irony has been felt throughout *Unfaithfully Yours*, so why should the ending be any different?

As was so often the case, the director seems to want to make light of his films' troublesome implications in order to keep us from taking them too seriously. Even so, such nineteenth-century orchestral music can be very heavy baggage for a film to carry, because it brings up the whole irresolvable argument about concert music's "pure" and "programmatic" import. If Sturges seems to want to duck these issues, he cannot, because his film is too richly *about* them. The music and the narrative permeate one another, and the music-driven fantasies bend our sense of time, space, character, and narrative this way and that. They enable us simultaneously to dream and laugh (Rossini), to dream and cry (Wagner), to dream and die (Tchaikovsky). Unlike Daphne, we do know what visions Sturges had in his head—and we can see and hear how carefully he worked to bring them to the screen.

NOTES

1　Music by Jimmy McHugh, lyrics by Dorothy Fields. The song was first performed in a small show in January 1928 and reintroduced in the Broadway revue *Blackbirds of 1928*. After that it entered the standard repertoire of both jazz bands and popular vocalists.

2 I am leaving out of this discussion the genre of the film musical, which requires separate consideration.

3 *Preston Sturges by Preston Sturges*, ed. Sandy Sturges (New York, NY: Simon & Schuster, 1990), 39–40.

4 *Preston Sturges by Preston Sturges*, 102–3.

5 These points are all covered briefly in Donald Spoto, *Madcap: The Life of Preston Sturges* (Boston, MA: Little Brown, 1990): see the pages referenced in the index under "musical education, experience, and influences." See also Dan Pinck, "Preston Sturges: The Wizard of Hollywood," *The American Scholar*, 61:3 (Summer 1992), 406.

6 For reportage on Morros, George Antheil's columns in *Modern Music* and also Roy M. Prendergast, *Film Music: A Neglected Art*, 2nd ed. (New York, NY: Norton, 1992), 46–7.

7 On Paramount musicians during this period, the most useful historical surveys are Tony Thomas, *Music for the Movies* (Cranbury, NJ: A. S. Barnes, 1973), 43–8, devoted to Victor Young; and Gary Marmorstein, *Hollywood Rhapsody: Movie Music and Its Makers, 1900 to 1975* (New York, NY: Schirmer Books, 1997), 40–4 and 160–89. In general, other surveys take no notice of any Paramount scores prior to Rózsa's work on *Double Indemnity* and *The Lost Weekend*, in 1944–5.

8 Clifford McCarty, *Film Composers in America: A Filmography 1911–1970*, 2nd ed. (New York, NY: Oxford, 2000), 12.

9 See Marmorstein, 185–9, Thomas, 94–6, and Christopher Palmer, *The Composer in Hollywood* (London and New York: Marion Boyars, 1990), 196–200.

10 See on this point Caryl Flinn, *Strains of Utopia: Gender, Nostalgia, and Hollywood Film Music* (Princeton, NJ: Princeton University Press, 1992), 32. See also Leonard Zissu, "The Copyright Dilemma of the Screen Composer," *Hollywood Quarterly* 1:3 (April 1946); and Ken Sutak, *The Great Motion Picture Soundtrack Robbery: An Analysis of Copyright Protection* (Hamden, CT: Archon Books, 1976).

11 Krumgold remains an obscure figure, with no biographies or studies of his career published to date.

12 Breakdown of cues, with those composed by Hollander in bold. Cue titles in quotes and credits in parentheses taken from cue sheet and score materials in the Preston Sturges Papers at UCLA (box 5, folder 13). Cue timings based on the DVD version in *Preston Sturges: The Filmmaker Collection* (Universal, 2006).

    1. 0:24–1:08 "Prelude" (based on "Down Went McGinty")

    2. 1:09–2:22 "Café #1" (Rainger, "The Magic of You," arr. Shuken)

    3. 2:24–3:22 Café song, piano (Whiting, "Louise")

    4. 3:26–5:06 Café song, piano

    5. 5:08–6:53 "Café #2" (Rainger, arr. Bradshaw)

    6. 10:56–11:42 "Voting Montage" (based on "McGinty")

    7. 12:51–13:41 Election party music, piano

    8. 14:17–14:26 Continuation of Cue 7

    9. 24:25–24:55 Café song, piano

    10. 32:23–32:48 Mendelssohn's Wedding March, organ

    11. 39:27–40:53 "Newspaper Montage" (arr. Leipold; includes "National Emblem March" by Bagley)

    12. 40:53–41:04 "After Election" (Rainger, unident., arr. Leipold)

    13. 41:11–41:40 "For He's a Jolly Good Fellow"

    14. 41:41–42:20 "Home scene" ("Jolly Good Fellow," arr. Leipold)

    15. 45:33–46:06 "Building Montage"

    16. 58:33–59:13 "Café #3" (Young, arr. Bradshaw)

17. 59:14–1:00:19 Campaign music, part 1
18. 1:00:22–1:00:58 Campaign music, part 2 (same as Cue 11)
19. 1:01:05–1:02:48 Victory parade (also repeats from Cue 11)
20. 1:12:20–1:12:28 "Newspaper insert" (stock?)
21. 1:15:15–1:16:00 "The Empty Apartment"
22. 1:19:40–1:20:51 "Café #4" ("La Golondrina," arr. Bradshaw)
23. 1:20:07–1:20:21 "Finale" (based on "McGinty")
24. 1:20:22–1:21:58 "Cast" (based on "McGinty," arr. Bradshaw)

13 According to McCarty's listings, from 1935 to 1940 he worked on 48 films, including two scripted by Sturges, *Easy Living* and *Remember the Night*.

14 Written by Joseph Flynn, who often performed it with his partner, Frank B. Sheridan. One sheet music version (Brooklyn, NY: Spaulding & Kornder, 1889) can be seen online at https://jscholarship.library.jhu.edu/handle/1774.2/17214 (last accessed 14 July 2014). Other versions have different sets of lyrics but have the same opening and closing lines to each of the choruses.

15 In technical terms: the motive Hollander derived from the song is a pentatonic fragment (a trope of traditional folk music styles), the pitches being d–d–c–a–d. In the verse melody the motive appears in mm. 3–4; it recurs in a somewhat different rhythmic shape in mm. 7–8, for the song's concluding phrase, "Dressed in his best suit of clothes."

16 In technical terms: like the *Meistersinger* overture, the key of the Main Title is an unambiguous C Major (in the A sections), and at the end we hear a prolonged dominant pedal point plus trills in the violins, culminating in a full cadence. In Wagner's score, see mm. 25–7, 86–8, and, above all, 207–11 for comparable passages.

17 One difference between the opening and closing music: as was conventional, the Main Title actually does not to come to a stop, but instead bridges into the film's first scene; the Finale concludes with a full stop and brief pause before the End Credit music begins.

18 For excellent overviews of various scoring conventions operative in main titles and end credit sequences, see James Buhler *et al.*, *Hearing the Movies: Music and Sound in Film History* (New York, NY: Oxford University Press), 165–80.

19 See Claudia Gorbman, *Unheard Melodies: Narrative Film Music* (Bloomington, IN: Indiana University Press, 1987), 83–5.

20 In *Rumba*, Rainger's dance number was supplied with lyrics by Leo Robin, his usual songwriting partner at Paramount, but in *The Great McGinty* they are not sung.

21 "Louise," written in 1929 by Richard Whiting (lyrics by Robin), was performed by Chevalier in the Paramount musical *Innocents of Paris*. Sturges's script actually specified the use of a different song at this point, "[My] Blue Heaven". See Brian Henderson, *Five Screenplays by Preston Sturges* (Berkeley, CA: University of California Press, 1985), 52. That song, written by Walter Donaldson (music) and George A. Whiting (lyrics), celebrates marital happiness, and as such would have given ironic underpinning to this scene, in which Tommy mourns the life he left behind. But MGM owned it, and it had been so commercially profitable since its publication in 1927 that a license to use it in Sturges's film would probably not have come cheap.

22 The arranger of "Louise" is unknown; the recording may have been made originally for another film, since this cue is not listed on the recording log sheets for *McGinty*.

23 "La Golondrina" (The Swallow) was by Narciso Serradell Sevilla (1843–1910); it was written, while he was exiled in France, to express in metaphorical terms his sorrow about a swallow that can no longer fly home. It became emblematic for exiled countrymen during the French "intervention" in Mexico.

24 See Michel Chion, *Audio-Vision: Sound on Screen*, trans. Claudia Gorbman (New York, NY: Columbia University Press, 1994), 5.

25 Brian Henderson, *Five Screenplays* 119–20.

26 Preston Sturges Papers (Collection 1114). Department of Special Collections, University Research Library, University of California, Los Angeles, Box 37, Folder 29: "In view of the respect with which we always wish the National Anthem to be treated, we question whether this is a good spot to play the "Star Spangled Banner" . . . the use of the National Anthem is in bad taste" (memo to Sturges from Paramount executive Luigi Luraschi dated 12 August 1939).

27 Bagley's march also makes a brief appearance in *The Miracle of Morgan's Creek*, at 1:34:18–1:34:46, when Norville enters the hospital after the sextuplets have been born. He has (unknowingly) become a national hero, and the music turns his entrance into a one-man parade.

28 Henderson, *Five Screenplays*, 45.

29 Of the 17 music cues in *July*, only four are clearly diegetic; these last around five minutes altogether, about a third of the score's overall length.

30 Using timings from the DVD in *Preston Sturges: The Filmmaker Collection* (Universal 61031126), the six cues that use the love theme after the Main Title are distributed as follows: 13:44–15:17, 42:51–44:07, 55:19–56:28 (for solo player piano!), 56:29–58:38 (the score's lyric climax), 65:05–65:40, and, to close the film, 66:31–66:53.

31 Two particularly inventive *original* comic cues in the score for *Christmas in July* that are unlike anything heard in Sturges's later films accompany the "going-to-work-in-the-morning" scenes at Baxter & Sons: these are machine-like bits, driven by dehumanized percussion and rhythmic effects. See 16:36–16:58 and 17:53–18:33.

32 For further reading on the conventionality of film music during the studio era, an excellent place to start is the anthology of readings collected and edited by Julie Hubbert, *Celluloid Symphonies: Texts and Contexts in Film Music History* (Berkeley, CA: University of California Press, 2011), esp. Part III, "Carpet, Wallpaper, and Earmuffs (1935–1959)."

33 For this comic *agitato*, see 48:49–49:41.

34 Sturges's song alludes mockingly to a famous ballad from the mid-nineteenth century, "Rocked in the Cradle of the Deep" (music by J. P. Knight, set to a poem by "Mrs. Willard").

35 "The Tramp" begins at 7:08. In the score the music is credited as Bradshaw's arrangement of "We Are Four Bums," a song in the public domain. Two subsequent cues by Bradshaw, similar in style but original, are "The Escape," Parts I and II, at 20:10 and 20:35. These consecutive cues accompany the slapstick comedy scenes of Sullivan's flight from the clutches of Miss Zeffie.

36 See 11:24 and 16:52. These cues do not appear in the conductor's score for the film contained in the Sturges collection at UCLA. However, a very similar arrangement of Mendelssohn's piece, by Bradshaw, appears in *The Lady Eve* score as Cue 18. (In the film this cue begins at 1:12:15.)

37 In *Motion Picture Moods*, the Nocturne is indexed under "sadness." The film affords us a glimpse of this rural theater's marquee, indicating that the film segment came from one of "three features tonight—*Beyond These Tears*—*The Valley of the Shadow*—*The Buzzard of Berlin*."

38 The love theme for *The Lady Eve* actually began life as a light popular song, "With the Wind and the Rain in Your Hair," music by Clara Lawrence (and lyrics by Jack Lawrence: not sung in *The Lady Eve*). Originally published in 1930, it became a major hit about a decade later—just before work on *The Lady Eve* began—in recordings by dance band

orchestras and their vocalists. An instrumental version of this song (which was owned by Paramount) makes a cameo appearance in *Sullivan's Travels* as diegetic background music that emanates from a radio in the roadside café where Sullivan and The Girl first meet.

39 In technical terms: the theme is based on a descending tetrachord, a common element of tragic songs and instrumental pieces (often in the form of an ostinato bass-pattern) since the early Baroque period.

40 See 50:52–57:26. The piece is placed at the end of the UCLA piano score (instead of being inserted in cue order); apparently the music was reworked in certain details from what Shuken originally composed when it was incorporated into the film.

41 Actually, the music sounds like it is coming not from an organ but from either an accordion or a harmonium, which is the instrument called for in the script (to be played "off key"): see Henderson, *Five Screenplays*, 668. Once the film cuts to the church exterior, signaling the end of the sequence, a pedal organ resumes playing.

42 For this crucial scene, Sturges's script called for "a silent comedy, possibly Chaplin in *The Gold Rush*, possibly a Laurel and Hardy two-reeler" (Henderson, *Five Screenplays*, 671).

43 "Good Night Sweetheart" was written by Ray Noble, Jimmy Campbell, and Reg Connelly; one ed. (published in 1931 by Robbins Music Corporation in New York) carries an additional credit, "Introduced in America by Rudy Vallee," with the singer's picture on the cover.

44 In this section I have reworked extensive portions of my essay "Screwball Fantasia: Classical Music in *Unfaithfully Yours*," *19th-Century Music*, 34:3 (Spring 2011), 237–70. Readers with backgrounds in music theory are encouraged to consult the earlier essay, which has many additional technical details.

45 For a balanced appraisal of the film's strengths and weakness, and its problem-filled promotion and critical reception, see Diane Jacobs, *Christmas in July: The Life and Art of Preston Sturges* (Berkeley, CA: University of California Press, 1992), 370–8.

46 Brian Henderson, *Four More Screenplays of Preston Sturges* (Berkeley, CA: University of California Press, 1995), 762.

47 Two prime examples were *A Song to Remember*, about Chopin (Columbia, directed by Charles Vidor, 1945); and *Song of Love*, about Clara Schumann, Robert Schumann, and Brahms (MGM, Clarence Brown, 1947). For a concise view of these and other films, see Mervyn Cooke, *A History of Film Music* (Cambridge: Cambridge University Press, 2008), 422–36.

48 William Ashton Ellis, trans., *Richard Wagner's Prose Works*, III: *The Theatre* (1894; repr. New York, NY: Broude Brothers, 1966), pp. 229–31. For Wagner's original essay see "Ouvertüre zu *Tannhäuser*," in *Sämtliche Schriften und Dichtungen*, V, 177–9.

49 See Robert Pinsky, *The Inferno of Dante: A New Verse Translation*, Bilingual ed. (New York, NY: Farrar, Straus & Giroux, 1994), Canto V, line 127 in the English version.

50 In his initial draft of *Unfinished Symphony* Sturges had placed a similar joke at the film's start. Two so-called English charwomen are listening to a rehearsal (of an unnamed piece) while cleaning up an auditorium balcony. At a sudden explosive musical passage, one of them reacts like the sweeper in *Unfaithfully Yours*, and then the two launch into a fretful discussion (in cockney slang), wondering why anyone would want to listen to such stuff.

PART 4

Impact: Reception/Reputation

CHAPTER 12

Thrust with a Rapier and Run: The Critics and Preston Sturges

G. Tom Poe

The 1982 biography of Preston Sturges by James Curtis, *Between Flops*, reflects Sturges's own evaluation of his Hollywood career. Curtis quotes Sturges as saying: "Between flops, it is true, I have come up with an occasional hit, but compared to a good boxer's record, my percentage has been lamentable."[1] Indeed, the current master narrative regarding Sturges's place in film history is that of a publicly flamboyant, self-promoting Hollywood writer-director who experienced a dramatic critical and box-office rise and fall. This personal story is made even more compelling in that it parallels a key theme in his most canonical films, the collision of luck, fate, and human fragility played out in both personal and public spheres. As Jared Rapfogel noted with regard to Sturges's films:

> None of Preston Sturges's characters are allowed to have purely private lives . . . In almost every film, the private becomes (if it isn't already) public—the characters' individual stories are seized upon and inflated into (more often than not a political) spectacle, sometimes according to their wishes, usually not. Sturges's protagonists therefore tend to become a kind of gateway into a broader portrait of a community and its political and social functioning (or more accurately, malfunctioning).[2]

Indeed, Sturges has become something like a character in one of his own movies, and his very public career in Hollywood has often overtaken a nuanced critical study of his body of work. As Dan Pinck complained in a 1992 essay in *The American Scholar*, in the five decades following the end of Sturges's Hollywood career the smattering of books on the writer-director had largely been limited to popular biographies. Pinck's review of three influential Sturges biographies—Curtis's *Between Flops* (1982), the adapted semi-autobiography by Sandy Sturges, *Preston Sturges by Preston Sturges* (1990), and Donald

Spoto's *Madcap: The Life of Preston Sturges* (1990)—found all three wanting in providing critical insight into the value of Sturges's body of work. As Pinck says of Spoto's biography, "Moviemaking becomes a sideline, almost a framework of irrelevance; what is lacking is a sharp understanding of his movies and how Sturges made them . . . Analysis of Sturges's movies or what might have influenced his perceptions of comedy is thin."[3] Granted, since the publication of Pinck's essay, a short list of books has offered critical studies of Sturges's work, such as Jay Rozgonyi's *Preston Sturges's Vision of America* (1995) and *The Cinema of Preston Sturges: A Critical Study* by Alessandro Pirolini (2010). Still, Pinck's complaint continues to beg two interrelated questions with regard to the critical reception of Sturges's films, questions this essay will attempt to address.

First, how did Sturges's public persona as a "madcap" character in the history of the Hollywood studio system create a master narrative that both informed and influenced the critical reception of his films, and by extension, serve as an early precursor to what would, some decades later, be deemed "auteur criticism"? Second, how did the theme of public (often directly political) spectacle in *both* the life and films of Sturges incite theoretical/critical debates with regard not only to his place in American film history as an "auteur," but also to the final purpose of film comedy, particularly the role of satire and irony versus cynicism and nihilism?

Because the word "auteur" is a loaded term in film theory and criticism, I need to clarify that this essay is not intended to be a study of Sturges as an auteur, much less an argument for the use of auteur approaches to a textual analysis of his films. Rather, I find instructive the degree to which the critical reception of Sturges's work reveals the early development of a set of critical assumptions/logics that help to establish the concept of the "auteur" director as an individualist working in a communal/collaborative art form, including how the concept of the sole genius filmmaker reflects cultural logics constructed around "difference" defined by such interlocking categories as cultural geography, socioeconomic class, ideological loyalties and aesthetic sensibilities. Decades before the term "auteur" entered the lexicon of film studies, these logics were clearly visible in the *promotion* of Sturges by his studios, the industry press and film critics alike, as representing something *new* and different for Hollywood: a writer-director with a personal, biographically determined sensibility.

Indeed, Sturges is important in American film history as an early sound-era writer-director; we can refer to Sturges using "auteur" as a descriptive term rather than as a broad, often vague and problematic concept in critical theory. Thus, this chapter seeks to reveal something of the history of the concept of an auteur in Hollywood, wherein Sturges plays an important role, particularly in setting up the conditions for a conflation of what film theorist Paul Sellors identifies as a film's textual "meaning" ("authorial intention") and its "significance" ("understandings and judgments") as *read* (interpreted) by film critics (and audiences).[4] As a vocabulary guide to what follows, the term "meaning" will refer to Sturges's "authorial intention," and the term "significance" to his critics' *reading* and *writing* about his films.

Clearly, Sturges was one of Hollywood's most iconoclastic film writer-directors who constantly trespassed the boundaries between madcap comedy and social realism, satire and farce, humanism and nihilism. Indeed, film historian James Shokoff noted that

> the history of criticism of Sturges's films shows more reserve than one might expect from the responses of . . . recent admirers. Many critics have expressed strong ambivalence about the films. On the one hand, they delight in their expansive, witty iconoclasm, yet on the other they have found the works in some ways incomplete and lacking, as if Sturges were unwilling or unable to do more than thrust with a rapier and run.[5]

Richard Corliss wrote, "Though he deserves praise for his courage in throwing stones through the stain-glassed windows of chauvinism and self-righteousness, Sturges's aim was not always precise . . . [being] admirable in its audacity but chaotic in character resolution."[6]

The ambivalence that marks the history of critical writing on Sturges makes a study of the critical reception of the Sturges canon a particularly useful site, not only for contributing to Sturges scholarship, but also for offering a greater understanding of the cultural practice of film criticism itself. To that end, I will give particular attention to the critical debate provoked by three films, *The Great McGinty* (1940), *Sullivan's Travels* (1941), and *Hail the Conquering Hero* (1944).

AN "AUTEUR" ARRIVES IN HOLLYWOOD

Unlike most Hollywood directors who came up through the ranks of the studio system, before Sturges arrived in Hollywood he was already a New York Broadway theater celebrity. Following the critical success of his first major Broadway play, *Strictly Dishonorable* (1929), the New York press presented him as an artistic child prodigy who had developed into a quintessential New York sophisticate. A September 1929 profile published in *The New York Times* was titled "Mr. Sturges Takes a Bow." The paper assures its readers that Sturges had "not lingered long enough" in the city of his birth, Chicago, to "become stamped with its characteristics," adding, "He has for many years been a New Yorker, so it is more natural that he should have chosen for his play's setting the jovial atmosphere of one of those thugless West Forty-ninth Street speakeasies whose name is legion."[7] This introduction of Sturges established his public persona as a worldly-wise, artistic child of privilege destined for fame. According to Sturges historian Ray Cywinski, Sturges had "gone from a hard-luck dreamer to the biggest new celebrity on Broadway."[8]

Having achieved Broadway critical and box-office success, along with New York celebrity status, Sturges set his sights on conquering the new cultural capital of American popular culture, Hollywood. At the time, he was not the first or only major Broadway (or literary) lion to make his way to Hollywood. While celebrated New York writers like Ben Hecht began working in Hollywood at the beginning of the sound era (Hecht arrived in 1927) primarily because it proved financially rewarding, Sturges appears to have made the move with one goal: to make himself Hollywood "royalty." In 1932, Sturges moved to Hollywood to begin his climb to the top.

Sturges's rise to prominence in Hollywood began with the critical success of his 1933 screenplay for *The Power and the Glory*, directed by William K. Howard. The screenplay was largely inspired by the rise and tragic end of C. W. Post, the grandfather of Sturges's wife, Eleanor Hutton. That fact invited critics and the press alike to draw a connection between the screenplay and Sturges's personal life. Additionally, the narrative structure of the script was heavily promoted by the film's producer Jesse Lasky and Fox studio as being outside Hollywood norms and highly individualistic. The screenplay presents the rise and fall of a wealthy industrialist, beginning with his suicide as recounted by a friend who narrates the story by flashing back and forth through the man's dark and tragic life. The studio launched a massive publicity campaign about this new technique for storytelling, one the studio called "narratage." Lasky proclaimed to the press, "I believe Mr. Preston Sturges is the first author to avail himself of the full resources of the new medium."[9] *The New York Times* ran a lengthy article on the film's "novelty" and found the narrative structure "eminently well suited for this particular story."[10] *The New York Times* also commends Sturges's sense of irony in the cynical use of the Lord's Prayer in the film's title. *Variety* predicted that the film's radical storytelling would hurt its box-office appeal outside of the largest cities, noting that "it's no smash and its b.o. reactions may be spotty." Still, "reviewers in keys and hinterlands will gobble it up, and that's not going to hurt."[11]

No doubt, the critical praise for the film helped, but not much. Outside New York City the film did poorly at the box office. In seven years it grossed less than $700,000. While the positive critical reception for the film greatly benefited Sturges's profile in Hollywood, the film's poor box-office performance didn't pay out for Sturges, who had made a groundbreaking and highly controversial financial deal with Jesse Lasky. In exchange for a completed script by one screenwriter (rather than the normal practice of using a script prepared by a team of studio-salaried, contract writers), as widely reported, Sturges received $17,500 upon signing and a percentage of the profits, Sturges's percentage share exceeded his $17,500 advance by a little under $2,000.[12] Still, the Sturges–Lasky deal played out in the Hollywood press and initiated the first major debate around the concept of film "authorship."

Paramount producer B. P. Schulberg wrote an article for *The Hollywood Reporter* warning both studios and screenwriters against such deals. In Schulberg's opinion, good films are a result of collaboration between as many as eight writers, because films attempt to appeal to a wide audience, unlike Broadway theater audiences; thus, film scripts must include low comedy, high comedy, heart appeal, and "many other elements of intellectual or emotional stimulation."[13] In a response to Schulberg's article, Sturges drafted a reply to *The Hollywood Reporter*: "I for one can think of no surer way of stamping out originality, initiative, pride of achievement, and quality."[14] Today, *The Power and the Glory* is mostly remembered as the film that influenced Sturges's drinking buddy, Frank Mankiewicz, in his telling the story of Charles Foster Kane. For Sturges, the critical praise set him at the threshold of becoming Hollywood royalty. That goal would be reached in 1940 with Sturges's chance to both write and direct *The Great McGinty*.

THE GREAT MCGINTY: "SOMETHING UNUSUAL"

As widely reported in the film industry press, Sturges made a landmark deal with Paramount to both write and direct a film. Sturges would later say, "When a picture gets good notices, everyone but the writer is a prince. So I decided, by God, I was going to be one of the princes."[15] He went to Paramount with a much-publicized offer, to sell the studio his screenplay for $10 if he could direct his own film. Paramount agreed, as long as he could bring its production costs in on a low-risk $325,000 budget. As Cywinski notes, "Sturges, at 42, was hailed by the press as the new young 'genius' of Hollywood–the creator of the 'one-man' pictures. Not since the silent days had there been anything like a 'writer-director' . . . More importantly, he opened the door for a whole generation of writer-directors to follow."[16] Like Orson Welles, albeit seven years later, Sturges's public performance as a New York sophisticate in the land of Hollywood fantasy and celebrity would engender both notoriety and, in time, professional animosity. A survey of both the press coverage and film reviews of *The Great McGinty* demonstrates how two themes dominate and blend together: Sturges as a highbrow outlier in Hollywood, whose films represent something *different*.

Reviews of *The Great McGinty*, positive and negative, are largely a response to how the film challenges audience expectations for Hollywood films. This critical reaction is framed, again, by extensive press coverage of Sturges as a "different" kind of Hollywood *player*. Indeed, days before the premiere of Sturges's directorial debut, with *The Great McGinty*, *The New York Times* ran a glowing article on Sturges, highlighting his exotic upbringing in Europe surrounded by leaders of the avant-garde and noting that he stood out in the Hollywood studio system, whose directors are "usually dedicated early to the pragmatic, or red-necked, pattern of life."[17] Indeed, the *Times* presented Sturges as a child prodigy destined for artistic greatness, writing: "When two years old, he was conveyed to Paris by his mother . . . a friend and biographer of Isadora Duncan . . . The infant Preston, a brand plucked from the burning, was exposed straightway to the Eurhythmic, or neo-Delarosa school of esthetics . . . and at the age of eleven Sturges could knock out one large painting a day. The discipline was, in the Athenian phrase, terrific."[18]

Sturges's gamble to trade his script for the chance to direct the film would pay off. *The Great McGinty* was a great critical and a respectable box-office success. Following the film's opening night, Paramount's New York office wrote to the studio in Los Angeles: "Reviews are unanimously excellent with most of them raves," adding that in New York, the Paramount Theater would be "changing entire theatre front to play up reviews and expects on basis these reviews and word of mouth picture will build rapidly."[19] Bosley Crowther in *The New York Times* declared, "*The Great McGinty* which blew into the Paramount yesterday with all the spontaneous combustion and pyrotechnic display of an old-time Tammany parade through the streets of the lower East Side."[20]

The trade paper, *The Hollywood Reporter*, was ecstatic in its praise of the movie, starting with the headline: "'McGinty' A Socko: Sturges's Writing, Direction Tops."[21] The review goes on to say, "Well, boys and girls, here's your answer to great screen entertainment; better written, better directed and better acted;" adding, "Here's the answer to any exhibitor's prayer for a picture that will send an audience out talking, and here's the reason why the motion picture is the greatest institution for entertainment on this earth."[22] The review goes on to note that it was a "very reasonable cost picture. If Paramount had a Clark Gable to tie into the picture and maybe the name of a big feminine star to work in his support, the picture would grab about all the coin that's waiting to be spent at any box office."[23]

The New Yorker's review of *The Great McGinty*, titled "The Great Sturges," is particularly instructive in that it hardly reviews the film itself, focusing on its critical reception. Indeed, two decades before what we today would deem "auteur criticism," *The New Yorker* critic Russell Maloney announces the importance of the arrival of the individualistic writer-director (albeit somewhat tongue-in-cheek, foreshadowing current debates around the overvaluing of auteur criticism), declaring that the film is "refreshing *merely* because it is so different" (italics mine). He writes:

> I liked it, and so, apparently, did everybody else—the professional critics, the finicky upper-bracket moviegoers, and the pimply members of the intellectual underworld who patronize the Broadway cinema palaces . . . The film is refreshing merely because it is so different from those that have been coming along for the past few years . . . The payoff is one of the credit lines: "Written and directed by Preston Sturges" . . . He travels the fastest who travels alone, eh, Sturges?[24]

Despite *The New Yorker* critic's faint praise for *The Great McGinty* as "merely" different (noting, "It's just a good little comedy that keeps you happy for an hour and some odd minutes"), most critics found it powerful because it was so "different." The film's eccentric narrative structure, employing both flashbacks and flash-forwards, would, like *The Power and the Glory*, famously predate and influence that of *Citizen Kane*. Moreover, for a film deemed a comedy, it tells a depressingly dark political fable where doing the right thing is its "own reward" and its *only* reward. Being true to oneself leads to the "Great" McGinty's fall from political grace into exile and obscurity. (Some might say it's a parable that foretells the "Great Sturges's" own fall from Hollywood's grace.)

The New Yorker's admission that Sturges's first film had generally charmed film critics is borne out in the film's generally enthusiastic reviews. *Time* magazine hailed it as "shrewd, salty, adroit."[25] In *The New Republic*, Otis Ferguson found it "a little different and quite a lot of fun," even if it has "its rather soggy moments and occasionally, a heavy touch right in the middle of the deftest humor."[26] Still, Ferguson was quick to point out what other critics would come to recognize as Sturges's particular gift, his "sense of the incongruous."[27] The trade paper *Variety* published one of the more perceptive reviews in regard to Sturges "sense of the incongruous," and how that unique characteristic of Sturges's work might win him the affection of many professional film critics, while perplexing many in the moviegoing public. Noting the film's lack of "marquee strength," *Variety* predicts that the picture "may not catch unanimous top-of-bill bookings through the regular runs, but will enjoy much favorable comment as something unusual and off the beaten track, without being arty . . . It looks like he will establish himself as a writer-director *individualist*" (italics mine).[28]

The movie also proved a respectable financial success. Despite the film's critical praise, it did not make it into the year's top twenty moneymakers, perhaps, as *Variety* opined, because it lacked "marquee strength" or it was just too "different" in its lack of a likable hero to win over the average moviegoer.

Still, given its low budget, the film made Paramount a respectable profit. James Curtis reports the film was "modestly profitable,"[29] while, according to Hal Erickson, it made back its low budget "several times over"[30] and was so embraced by critics and the Hollywood establishment that Sturges would win the first Academy Award for Best Original Screenplay, beating out Ben Hecht, John Huston, and Charlie Chaplin.

The film's critical success thrust Sturges into the status of one of Hollywood's most celebrated directors. He was, for a time, Hollywood's new *wunderkind*. Two weeks after his Academy Award win, *The Saturday Evening Post* published a two-part biography with pictures of him working on the set of *The Lady Eve*.[31] That new status would guarantee that his next films would have ample budgets and stars with major "marquee strength." By the night of the Academy Award ceremony, Sturges had completed directing his next film, *Christmas in July* (1940), and was well into directing one of his most critically acclaimed films, *The Lady Eve* (1941), with Henry Fonda and Barbara Stanwyck. These critically and commercially successful films would spur him to complete his most personal project, *Sullivan's Travels* (1941).

SULLIVAN'S TRAVELS: PRESTON STURGES VS. JOHN SULLIVAN—A DIRECTOR'S DILEMMA

Sullivan's Travels is Sturges's movie about the political, social, and personal uses of moviemaking and moviegoing. Indeed, one can read the film's fictional film director, John L. Sullivan (Joel McCrea), as Sturges's stunt-double, a trapeze artist, swinging between comedy and drama, social commentary and cynicism, between humanism and nihilism. It is one of his most "experimental" films, at least in the screenplay's transgressing the usual boundaries of genre in the "Classic Hollywood" tradition. A majority of critics either decried *Sullivan's Travels* as a dismissal of serious moviemaking in favor of mindless entertainment or found its brutal scenes a betrayal of his gift for comedy. It also proved to be a box-office disappointment. Sturges brought the film in, over budget, for just under $677,000. Granted, the film received some positive reviews in the New York press, and *The New York Times* named it Best Film of the Year. Likewise, it had an excellent opening in New York, setting an all-time house record of $75,650 in its first week at New York's Paramount Theater. But given the film's juxtaposition of wacky comedy and dark drama, the studio had a hard time marketing it to the rest of the country, settling on a national ad campaign dominated by a picture of Veronica Lake's peek-a-boo hairdo with the tag line "Veronica Lake's on the take," a line that grossly misrepresents the film's storyline.

Figure 12.1 Publicity poster for *Sullivan's Travels*.

Sturges blamed much of the film's failure on its critical reception, saying, "One local reviewer wanted to know what the hell the tragic passages were doing in this comedy and another wanted to know what the hell the comic passages were doing in this drama."[32] Still, Sturges later acknowledged the film's faults, admitting that the ending wasn't right, but I didn't know how to solve the problem, which was not only to show what Sullivan learned but also to tie up the love story . . . There was probably a way of doing it, but I didn't happen to come across it. It might be profitable for a young director to look at *Sullivan's Travels* and try not to make the same mistakes I did.[33]

After a month, the film disappeared from theater screens. Indeed, a survey of reviews for *Sullivan's Travels* reveals the discomfort critics (and paying audiences) had in "reading" and making judgments with regard to the film's "significance," that is, the difficulty critics had in employing their usual understandings and critical facility for making a judgment, particularly with regard to mood and genre. This would incite a significant debate between influential film critics and theorists in their attempts to make a judgment with regard to both Sturges's significance as a writer-director and the *final purpose* of the Hollywood comedy with regard to its moral value and political agency, a debate that continues to inform film theory and criticism to this day.

Unlike the unheroic male propagandists in *The Great McGinty*, the fictional film director John Sullivan may be naive about the ways of the "real" world outside of Hollywood, but he is anything but a "drudge with a dream." Like Sturges himself in his public image, Sullivan is a highly successful Hollywood director of madcap comedies such as *Ants in Your Plants of 1939* who longs to be taken "seriously" as a director of social/politically relevant films. He sets out to move beyond his apolitical nihilism to make his hoped-for social-realism masterpiece, "O Brother, Where Art Thou?" After facing the reality of poverty he will abandon his desire to "visit" reality and return to Hollywood and its role, to offer an alternative to "reality" by providing a miserable America with an antidote: an escape into pure entertainment. Still, to describe *Sullivan's Travels* as Sturges's most personal film is not to say it should be considered autobiographical. Sturges acknowledged that his script was a response to his feeling that his fellow comedy directors had "abandoned the fun in favor of the message," adding that he wrote the script "to tell them that they were getting a little too deep-dish; to leave the preaching to the preachers."[34] That said, Sturges was clear in separating his own view from Sullivan's final declaration that comedy is superior to social-realist message movies. Responding to criticism of his fictional director Sullivan's conclusion that making people laugh through rough times was the highest role of art, Sturges, himself, was quick to add that "now," in a time of war, people need "comedies or tragedies . . . musicals or pictures without music . . . I believe that now is the time for all forms of art, and that now is always with us."[35]

Clearly, the film's internal debate about the social-political role of Hollywood movies left its initial critics perplexed in their own reaction and even more in their ability to predict how the general moviegoer would react to the film's shifting moods. *Variety*'s reviewer, who admitted that the film was a "curious but effective mixture of grim tragedy, slapstick of the Keystone brand and smart, trigger-fast comedy," acknowledged this. The critic asserts that the movie "goes against many of the rules" as Sturges "flits from slapstick to stark drama, from high comedy to a sequence of the Devil's Island prison type of stuff, into romantic spells, some philosophy and, in effect, all over the place without warning."[36]

Indeed, a key tension in many a review of *Sullivan's Travels* is a sense of outrage that their former, highly praised comic genius had personally betrayed Hollywood's critical establishment. In one of the most telling reviews, *The Hollywood Reporter* found the movie a betrayal of the newspaper's past celebration of Sturges as Hollywood's best director of comedy. Its review is not only a pan; the critic seems downright *offended* by the film, arguing that *Sullivan's Travels* is something like a willful betrayal of Sturges's gift for comedy, claiming that the film "lacks the down to earth quality and sincerity which made his other three pictures a joy to behold, and box-office naturals."[37] The reviewer objects to the grim scenes of the film's chain gang section, arguing that the episode "is unnecessarily lengthy," adding that it was "sufficiently emphasized in *I Am a Fugitive from a Chain Gang* that convict life is just plain gruesome, and the public's adequately educated to that fact by now."[38] *The Hollywood Reporter*'s chief complaint is that the film starts off as comedy, "but then it digressed into Saroyanish subtleties and slipped into sobby-faced dramatics."[39] Thus, Sturges failed to "heed the message that writer Sturges proves in his script. Laughter is the thing people want—not social studies. This is something for which director Sturges must answer to writer Sturges."[40]

Beyond the trade papers, the major magazine reviews were generally equally dismissive. *Time* magazine's critic considered it "a confusing mixture of slapstick, drama, melodrama, comedy."[41] The *Nation*'s critic, Anthony Brower, considered it a "blot" on the writer-director's career, adding that if Sturges meant to send a "social message to the effect that everyone wants to laugh and not bother his head over silly old poverty or anything un-pleasant like that," the message "would carry more weight if Mr. Sturges had succeeded in being funny."[42]

One of the most damning reviews came from *The New Republic*'s influential critic Otis Ferguson. He described it as "going from witty banter to the present crude renascence of the Mack Sennett pratfall, from high talk about humanity to the bazzoom of Veronica Lake, from brutality to a *Green Pastures* production number."[43] At the end of the review, he directs a rather personal attack, not only on the film, but also on Sturges as an artist. Ferguson accused Sturges of displaying only a "partial intelligence," whose films are "mixture of snobbism and self-consciousness" with "a professed and knowing scorn for just the kind of thing the dumb sods want."[44]

Indeed, *Sullivan's Travels* became a lightning rod in an important debate that would erupt between esteemed film theorist Siegfried Kracauer and the so-called "Dean" of film criticism, Manny Farber. In 1946, Kracauer prepared an essay on Sturges for the journal *Measure*, titled "Preston Sturges or Laughter Betrayed," in which he contended that while Sturges had created three great American comedies in *The Great McGinty*, *Christmas in July* and *The Lady Eve*, his fourth film, *Sullivan's Travels*, was a selling-out of his artistic birthright for a bowl of Hollywood porridge. For Kracauer, *Sullivan's Travels* marked a failure in Sturges's "gift for inventing funny incidents," giving way to "farcical business."[45] Kracauer argues that with *Sullivan's Travels*, Sturges becomes John Sullivan's counterpart, contenting himself with turning out "conformist" comedies. According to Kracauer:

> And what particular brand of conformism does Sturges–Sullivan administer to the public? It is a streamlined variant of the naïve and uncritical conformism current among us. Sturges first draws on the questionable aspects of our society; and then he gives the audience to understand that this world of ours is in effect a paradise where wrongs right themselves automatically. He conceals nothing and gilds all. He uses the tools of social criticism—only to destroy its constructive power.[46]

To Kracauer, Sturges's use of farce as social satire fails because, finally, the two are incompatible. While Kracauer acknowledges that laughter does not need to have social significance, "the farce in the disguise of satire is dangerous," because "it dulls the edges of a first-rate weapon of human liberation. And it is dangerous at a time when, along with the means of mass communication, methods of psychological manipulation have been developed to an extent unknown before."[47] If nothing else, this critical debate over the political efficacy of Sturges's comedy foreshadows Kathleen Rowe's observation in her 1995 book *The Unruly Woman* that film critics, particularly "on the left[,] have been wary of granting comedy any critical edge, seeing it primarily as a means of reinforcing social norms."[48] Rowe goes on to note that "the lessons about comedy, politics, and pleasure the idealistic but naive John L. Sullivan learned in Preston Sturges's *Sullivan's Travels* (1941) seem to have remained unappreciated, or at least inadequately studied."[49]

Meanwhile, the humanist filmmaker René Clair objected to what he perceived as Sturges's lack of discipline, writing, "Preston is like a man from the Italian Renaissance: he wants to do everything at once. If he could slow down, he would be great . . . I wish he would be a little more selfish and worry about his reputation."[50] In response to Clair's remark, Manny Farber replied, "What Clair is suggesting is that Sturges would be considerably improved if he annihilated himself."[51] Farber goes on to say, "The more popular critics have condemned Sturges for not liking America enough; the advanced critics for liking it too much." Likewise, "He has also been accused of espousing a snob point of view and sentimentally favoring the common man."[52]

Farber's main argument is that the value of Sturges's work in Hollywood was his gift for displaying the dissonance of American society itself in the first half of the twentieth century. Indeed, circling back to the biographical interpretations that have so influenced critics, Farber attributes this to Sturges's life as the child of a capitalist American businessman and his mother's longing to raise him as the European aesthete. Farber writes: "The discrepancies in Sturges's films are due largely to the peculiar discontinuities that afflict his sensibility," going on to note, "such affliction is also a general phenomenon in a country where whole eras and cultures in different states of development exist side by side . . . his years spent abroad prevented his finding a bridge between the two worlds or even a slim principle of relating them in any other way than through dissonance."[53]

Farber argues that it is this dissonance, disparaged by many critics, that makes Sturges "the most original movie talent produced in recent years; the most complex and puzzling," giving his work "a special relevance to the contemporary American psyche—of precisely the kind that is found in some modern American poetry and painting, and almost nowhere else."[54]

Farber's defense of Sturges echoed the stirring endorsement of *Sullivan's Travels* in *The New York Times* by Bosley Crowther, who not only showered the film with high praise, but also followed his initial review, two days later, with a longer essay in defense of the movie. Crowther declares that *Sullivan's Travels* "is a beautifully trenchant satire upon 'social significance' in pictures, a stinging slap at those fellows who howl for realism on the screen and a deftly sardonic apologia for Hollywood make-believe." He adds:

> As a writer and director, Mr. Sturges believes in pictures which will make the customers laugh, but he obviously has his own opinions about the shams of showmanship. And thus this truly brilliant serio-comedy which makes fun of films with "messages" carries its own paradoxical moral and its note of tragedy . . . *Sullivan's Travels* is one of the screen's more "significant" films. It is the best social comment made upon Hollywood since *A Star Is Born*. And that, we quietly suspect, is exactly what Mr. Sturges meant it to be.[55]

If *Sullivan's Travels* was often damned for either being too mindless or too serious, Crowther makes the counterclaim that, coming out just weeks after the U.S. had entered World War II, it actually addresses "a burning question" facing Hollywood in the midst of national crisis and trauma:

Folks in the picture business are talking nervously about "escapist" films . . . Audiences are not interested in anything which stimulates the intellect with too sharp or poignant a trust. Yet Mr. Sturges's picture, which apparently says exactly those same things, is a perfectly splendid example of a thoughtful, sensitive film which entertains. In a manner remarkably facile, Mr. Sturges flings his own teeth into his own words.[56]

So Crowther concludes that "while Mr. Sturges is ably arguing that pictures which stink with messages are so much tommy-rot," and while he is "brilliantly satirizing the pretentious realists of films . . . one cannot say that his picture is purely escapist fare." Indeed, Crowther argues, the film "comes closer to being significant than many another picture which earnestly tries to be." Crowther claims "*Sullivan's Travels* is full of meaning—a 'message' if you choose to call it that. And yet it is quite as beguiling as anything going today."[57]

Crowther's take on *Sullivan's Travels* raises an intriguing question about the relationship between Sturges's authorial "intention" and Crowther's reading of the film's "significance." Crowther's reading of *Sullivan's Travels* may say less about Sturges's authorial intent as a filmmaker than about Crowther's authorial intentions as a critic. There is little reason to think of Sturges as a writer-director of films intent on making socially progressive "messages." Crowther, however, more than Sturges, had long championed the political/social "message" movie: thus his great admiration for a film such as Wyler's *The Best Years of Our Lives* (1946). Indeed, it could be argued that Crowther's reading of Sturges's sense of irony and satire is suggestive of a populist Theater of the Absurd. As I read Crowther, he is suggesting a difference between laughter as an escape from the brutality of history and laughter in its midst. What makes Sturges's films generate such contradictory critical reaction may come down to the paradoxical relationship of satire to cynicism. In *Sullivan's Travels*, how one deals with that question may depend on how closely one relates the motives of the film's fictional director, John Sullivan, to Sturges's own motives. Sullivan may well give voice to the value of comedy as "escapism," while Sturges gives the viewer a film that hardly allows the audience the comfort of escaping the brutality of history. In the midst of the brutality of history, we might need (like Camus's Sisyphus) to *imagine* Sturges—laughing.

HAIL THE CONQUERING HERO: STURGES AND HIS CRITICS GO TO WAR

The critical debates incited by *Sullivan's Travels* would continue unabated around Sturges's next two films, both released in 1944, *The Miracle of Morgan's Creek* and *Hail the Conquering Hero*. If anything, the debate about Sturges's uses of satire was exacerbated by both films being more deeply imbedded in the historical moment of America's deepest involvement in World War II and Hollywood's role in the nation's war effort. In general, the critical and (modest) financial success of both films returned Sturges back into the favor of a majority of critics, including the garnering of Best Original Screenplay nominations for *The Miracle of Morgan's Creek* and *Hail the Conquering Hero*. Even so, both films proved controversial. Here, I will turn to a short overview of critical responses to the more political of the two films, *Hail the Conquering Hero*.

The film's plot is reminiscent of Sturges's first two films as a writer-director, *The Great McGinty* and *Christmas in July*, in that it tells the story of a simpleton, who through fate (with the help of deception) is proclaimed a hero. Unlike the end of *The Great McGinty*, the film had the requisite wartime happy (a.k.a. patriotic) ending that won it praise from the Hollywood branch of the Office of War Information. Much of the middlebrow press agreed. *Time* magazine's critic found the hero's "ultimate ascent from his excruciating little comic hell" an "uncommonly heart warming experience."[58] However, the heated debates incited by *Sullivan's Travels* only increased among the critics of the country's more intellectual/elitist press.

Kracauer discussed the reassuring ending of the film, in which its hapless hero confesses to having deceived his fellow citizens by pretending to be a combat hero, only to be declared a *true* hero for telling the truth. Kracauer complained that Sturges's lame and reassuring, if false, message is that "the world yields to candor."[59] That argument elicited a strong rebuke from Manny Farber of *The New Republic*, who replied, "it should be obvious to anyone who has seen two Sturges pictures that he does not give a tinker's dam whether the world does or does not yield to candor." However, Farber is far from defending Sturges or the film; instead, his point was that Kracauer was giving Sturges too much credit for suggesting that his films have any message at all, even a lame one, Farber concluding, "his pictures at no time evince the slightest interest . . . to the truth or falsity of his direct representation of society."[60] Farber goes further to assert, "There have been few movies, even from Hollywood, which so confusingly and insistently say one thing and immediately its opposite, so as not to be caught to seem to stand solidly for anything."[61] Farber concludes that *Hail the Conquering Hero* is "as rotten and confused inside as it seems pleasant and successful outside."[62]

The National Board of Review's critic James Shelly Hamilton agreed, damning Sturges for "mingling all kinds of hodge-podge things together with a Gothic exuberance and an amorality mixed with disillusionment."[63] Meanwhile, Bosley Crowther took Hamilton to task, by name, praising the film's "deep sincerity" and declaring *Hail the Conquering Hero* as Sturges's most powerful film; indeed, at the end of his *New York Times* review, he declared, "A Hollywood Voltaire is budding. Or shall we just say that Mr. Sturges has arrived?"[64] Crowther's review was too much for James Agee, who replied in *The Nation*, "now that Sturges is being compared, I am told, with people like Voltaire . . . I think there is some point in putting on the brakes."

Agee went on to write an admirably nuanced critique of *Hail the Conquering Hero* that serves as a fitting place to "put on the brakes" on this chapter about Sturges and his critics. Agee acknowledges the difficulty in making a final judgment on the value of the film, admitting, "Any adequate review of this remarkable movie would devote at least as much space to its unqualified praise as I have to qualifying the praise." Then Agee's review takes a surprising turn. Rather than offering a judgment on the film itself, he uses the film to offer "a tentative explanation of why Sturges functions as he does." He continues, "Hollywood is no explanation, surely. Hollywood was made for Sturges and in turn is its apotheosis; but why?" To answer his own question, Agee will turn to Sturges's much publicized and promoted personal narrative.

Thus the methodology Agee employed in his review circles back to the starting point of this chapter and the suggestion that the critical debates provoked by Sturges's use of satire and sense of irony were often influenced by critics reading his films as the work of an "individualist" writer-director representing something "different" from work produced by the usual studio director. For example, Agee devoted the greater share of his review to psychoanalyzing how and why Sturges's films offer conflicting and paradoxical messages. Agee turns to the uniqueness of his personal narrative, claiming on the one hand that "Sturges had reason, through his mother, to develop, as they caromed around high-Bohemian Europe during his childhood, from opera to opera and gallery to gallery, not only his singular mercurialism and resourcefulness, which come especially natural to some miserably unhappy children, but also a retching, permanently incurable loathing for everything that stank of 'culture,' of 'art.'"[65] Agee then turns to Sturges's relationship with his successful businessman father, through whom he "developed an all but desperate respect and hunger for success . . . and this again assumed the dimensions of a complex."

Then, tellingly, Agee seems to step back, admitting his discomfort in relying so heavily on Sturges's publicly constructed personal narrative in making a final critical judgment on the significance of his films. He admits:

> I hesitate to write this sort of thing, drawn only from such superficialities as have appeared in print and from some remarkable photographs of Sturges as a child and young man which appeared in the *Saturday Evening Post*, but I risk the worse than questionable taste because I see no other way to understand what Sturges's films are "about."[66]

Admitting his discomfort with his own critical methodology, Agee concluded that Sturges's movies generate contradictory readings because "in their twisting," they display an "elaborately counterpointed image of a neurosis." Indeed, for Agee, Sturges is such a significant figure in Hollywood *because* his personal neuroses produce films that become "the definitive expression of this country at present—the stranglehold wedlock of the American female tradition of 'culture,' the male tradition of "success.""[67]

CONCLUSION

So, what can we take away from re-viewing how three Sturges films were originally reviewed? First, critics often relied on Sturges's celebrity persona as a sophisticated New York outlier in Hollywood to conflate (returning to Sellors's categories of "meaning" and "significance") Sturges's "authorial intentions" and critics' judgments in regard to his films' "significance." Here we may see certain cultural logics at work wherein Sturges's worldly upbringing and original Broadway success equated to sophistication, which in turn supposedly *explained* his satirical, ironic and/or cynical view of American society. To the film critics of the 1940s, that made Sturges *distinct* from typical Hollywood studio writers and directors, whose work was deemed optimistic and populist.

A second takeaway, related to the first, is that a study of the critical reception of Sturges's work reveals the intersection of a film's "meaning" via "authorial intent," and the "authorial intent" of critics as, themselves, authors. Thus, Sturges's films, deemed more "individualistic" than traditional studio product, became particularly fertile sites for debates (the purpose of comedy, the difference between irony and cynicism, etc.) that reveal the authorial intent of the film critic as an ideological, cultural critic. More than with most directors working in the studio system, Sturges's films generated particularly intense debates over their "meaning."

I'll end with a telling anecdote. However much critics praised or damned *Hail the Conquering Hero*'s happy ending, it earned kudos from the Office of War Information as "a good picture of working democracy in America today," but the OWI went on to declare the film "unsuitable for distribution in liberated areas" because it feared the film might be "misinterpreted."[68]

NOTES

1 Sandy Sturges, *Preston Sturges on Preston Sturges* (New York, NY: Simon & Schuster, 1959), 18, quoted in James Curtis, *Between Flops* (reprinted by Authors Guild, 2000), x.
2 Jared Rapfogel, "The Screwball Social Studies of Preston Sturges," *Cineaste* (Summer 2006): 9.

3 Dan Pinck, "Preston Sturges: the Wizard of Hollywood," *The American Scholar*, 1 June 1992, 406.
4 Paul Sellors, *Film Authorship: Auteurs and Other Myths* (London: Wallflower Press, 2010), 5.
5 James Shokoff, "A Knockenlocker by Any Other Word," *PostScript* 8:1, 1981, 16.
6 Shokoff, 16.
7 "Mr. Sturges Takes a Bow," *The New York Times*, 22 September 1929, 82.
8 Ray Cywinski, *Preston Sturges: A Guide to References and Resources* (Boston, MA: G. K. Hall, 1984), 5.
9 *Newsweek*, 26 August 1933, 31. (quoted in Cywinski, 6).
10 *The New York Times*, 17 August 1933, 13.
11 *Variety*, 22 August 1933, 22.
12 *TMC Notes*. Available at <http://www.tcm.com/tcmdb/title/87010/The-Power-and-the-Glory/notes.html> (last accessed 17 April 2015).
13 *TMC Notes*.
14 *TMC Notes*.
15 Cywinski, 6.
16 Cywinski, 8.
17 *The New York Times*, 4 August 1940, 106.
18 *The New York Times*.
19 Curtis, 135.
20 *The New York Times*, 15 August 1940, 27.
21 Curtis, 135.
22 Curtis, 135.
23 *The Hollywood Reporter*, 26 July 1940, 14.
24 *The New Yorker*, 24 July 1940, 60.
25 *Time*, 21 October 1940, Vol. 44, 93.
26 *The New Republic*, 30 September 1940, 448.
27 *The New Republic*.
28 *Variety*, 24 July 1940, 14.
29 Curtis, 135.
30 Hal Erickson, *Allmovie.com* Available at <http://www.allmovie.com/movie/the-great-mcginty-v20705> (last accessed 17 April 2015).
31 Curtis, 135.
32 Rob Nixon and James Steffen, "Why *Sullivan's Travels* is Essential," *TMC.com* Available at <http//www.tcmdb/title/91851/Sullivan-s-Travels/articles.html> (last accessed 15 April 2015).
33 Sturges, 295.
34 Sturges, 295.
35 Rob Nixon, "*Sullivan's Travels*," *TMC.com* Available at <http://www.tcm.com/tcmdb/title/91851/Sullivan-s-Travels/articles.html> (last accessed 15 April 2015).
36 *Variety*, 10 December 1941, 8.
37 *The Hollywood Reporter*, 5 December 1941, 3.
38 *The Hollywood Reporter*.
39 *The Hollywood Reporter*.
40 *The Hollywood Reporter*.
41 *Time*, 9 February 1942, 39.6, 38.
42 Anthony Brower, *The Nation*, 24 January 1942, 101.
43 Otis Ferguson, *The New Republic*, 26 January 1942, 117.

44 Ferguson, 117.
45 Siegfried Kracauer, *Siegfried Kracauer's American Writings: Essays on Film and Popular Culture* (Berkeley, CA: University of California Press, 2012), 115.
46 Kracauer, 115.
47 Kracauer, 115.
48 Kathleen Rowe, *The Unruly Woman: Gender and the Genres of Laughter* (Austin, TX: University of Texas Press, 1995), 101.
49 Rowe, 101.
50 Rowe, 101.
51 Rowe, 101.
52 Rowe, 101.
53 Rowe, 470.
54 Rowe, 473.
55 Bosley Crowther, *The New York Times*, 29 January 1942, 25.
56 Bosley Crowther, *The New York Times*, 1 February, X5. (ProQuest Historical Newspapers).
57 Crowther, X5.
58 *Time*, 21 August 1944, 19.
59 Farber, 462.
60 Farber, 463.
61 Farber, 463.
62 Farber, *The New Republic*, 21 August 1944, 3, 220.
63 Crowther, *The New York Times*, 13 August 1944, sec. 2,1.
64 Crowther.
65 Agee, *The Nation*, 23 September 1944, 159, 362.
66 Agee, 362.
67 Agee, 362.
68 Clayton R. Koppes and Gregory D. Black, *Hollywood Goes to War: How Politics, Profits and Propaganda Shaped World War II Movies* (London: Collier Macmillan, 1987), 175.

CHAPTER 13

Hail the Conquering Auteur: Preston Sturges in *La Revue du cinéma* (1946–1949)

Christian Viviani (translated by Leah Anderst)

We might expect that, as the first screenwriter-director of the Classical Hollywood era, Preston Sturges would have been the darling of postwar French critics. However, due to a variety of factors, he faced relative neglect. I will trace the coverage he did receive, and try to account for the reasons he was overlooked. These reasons tell us a great deal about the reception of American films in France, and because the esteem of French critics had an outsize influence on British and American tastemakers, they also reveal why Sturges, as an auteur, has received less than his due in the U.S.

Preston Sturges's comedies were discovered in France after World War II; seven films, produced by Paramount between 1940 and 1944 arrived in quick succession, one after the other, but out of order. The first, in September 1945, was *Christmas in July* (1940) and the last, in January 1950, was *The Great McGinty* (1940). In spite of their disrupted chronology, elite French film critics greeted these films enthusiastically. In this regard, Preston Sturges benefited from the patronage of René Clair, whose radiance during the prewar years had never faded. Everyone knew that Sturges and Clair, who were close friends, shared certain actors (leading stars like Veronica Lake or Dick Powell and character actors like Franklin Pangborn or Melville Cooper), and of course that Sturges had been an uncredited producer on Clair's *I Married a Witch* (*Ma femme est une sorcière*, 1942).[1]

Still, the discrepancy between the release of his films in France and the splendor and evolution of Sturges's career had consequences for his subsequent critical fortunes. This former wonder boy, ruined by his extra-cinematic business ventures—especially his notoriously catastrophic management of the restaurant The Players—would soon leave the U.S. After several aborted theatrical projects (notably *Make a Wish*, a musical adaptation of his screenplay for William Wyler, *The Good Fairy* [1935], and *Carnival in Flanders*, based on *La Kermesse Héroïque* [1935] written by Jacques Feyder), the francophile

Sturges returned to France, a country he considered his second home and where he had previously lived with his mother during the early parts of his adventurous life when he served as director of his mother's luxury cosmetics company in Deauville, Maison Desti.

Yet his complicated familial and domestic situation, the ease and sweetness of Parisian life, work conditions that were rather different from those he had known in Hollywood, and his failure to produce a play, *J'appartiens à Zozo* (*I Belong to Zozo*), that he had written in French all worked to anesthetize his creativity. Sturges made only one film, the box-office hit *Les Carnets du Major Thompson* (*The French, They Are a Funny Race*, 1955). An adaptation of the humorous and popular chronicles of the same name by Pierre Daninos, this film gently criticizes the quirks of the French through the eyes of an English major married to a French woman.[2]

If *Cahiers du cinéma*, the official seat of the "auteur theory," spoke little of Preston Sturges's films, the reason was more practical than ideological. In 1951, the year of the celebrated journal's creation, this American filmmaker had already closed the richest and most significant portion of his career: his years in Hollywood between 1940 and 1944. After an announcement, of a purely marketing nature, of the release of *Oh! Quel mercredi!* (*Mad Wednesday*) in the first issues of *Cahiers*, Sturges was included in neither articles nor interviews, and he would only be mentioned in the journal via a few allusions here and there, most notably in echoes included under the category "The Little Film Journal" (*Le Petit journal du Cinéma*), often thanks to Pierre Kast, a *Cahiers* editor and fervent admirer of Sturges. It was Kast who wrote the notice on Sturges in the famous issue 150–1 (December 1963) dedicated to American cinema. This same issue ends with a section titled "The Best American Talking Films": Pierre Kast was the only one to list Sturges, for *The Great McGinty*. However, Kast held a rather particular position because he also contributed from time to time to a review that rivaled *Cahiers*, *Positif*, created in Lyon in 1952. In fact, it was in the columns of *Positif*—not *Cahiers*—that Kast alluded to his deep admiration for, his friendship with, and his enthusiasm for Sturges in an issue published as a tribute.[3] (Kast had also been the assistant director on Sturges's *Carnets du Major Thompson*.)

Thus, Sturges was a filmmaker "forgotten" by auteur theory. He was in good company with Ernst Lubitsch and Frank Borzage, who had created their key works before 1950, and others, like John Ford, who had simply been neglected. If articles, overviews, and dossiers on Preston Sturges indeed found their places in the pages of *Positif*, a journal that dedicates a good deal of space to film history, the editors of *Cahiers*, who had, for their part, tried to retrospectively correct their blindness to Ernst Lubitsch and to John Ford, eventually did the same for Sturges, even if it was very late, in 1989, and on the occasion of a retrospective at the Locarno Festival, which we will return to below.[4]

JEAN GEORGE AURIOL'S *LA REVUE DU CINÉMA*

While *Cahiers du cinéma* is well-known to American scholars, it owed a large debt to *La Revue du cinéma*. *Cahiers* was born in 1951, at the instigation of André Bazin and Jacques Doniol-Valcroze, after the accidental death of Jean George Auriol, founder of the *Revue du cinéma*. The new journal would place itself within the same family of the latest version of Auriol's journal, a publication that Auriol had created and that he later recreated. The editors of *Cahiers* reinforced this sentimental connection to the earlier journal by taking the same format and the same recognizable yellow color of its cover.

Born into a family of artists in 1907, Jean George Auriol (whose real name was Jean-Georges Huyot) worked, from the 1920s on, as a film critic. In 1928 he created a monthly review, *Du cinéma*, which, from October 1929, took the name *Revue du cinéma*. Auriol's ambition was to steer influential literary figures into writing about cinema. The review folded in 1932, but in that short time, over thirty-odd issues, it was able to bring together signatures as prestigious and diverse as André Gide, Marcel Aymé, Louis Chavance, and Jacques B. Brunius. Auriol turned himself from that point on to writing screenplays: he would collaborate regularly with Marcel L'Herbier (on five films); he would assist the writer Colette on her two cinematic contributions, *Lac aux dames* (Marc Allégret, 1934), and, especially, *Divine* (Max Ophüls, 1935); he would work as well with Jacques Tourneur during that director's early stages before he departed for the U.S., *Les Filles de la concierge*, 1934.

After World War II, in 1946, the *Revue du cinéma* was reborn with the prestigious publisher Gallimard, a move that attests to Auriol's continuing ambitions. The journal would last through another twenty issues, until 1949. In reality, the journal's final appearance, issues 19–20, a double issue dedicated to "Costumes in Cinema," had left behind current events in the world of cinema. Auriol assembled a group of literary luminaries such as Brunius and Louis Chavance, but also Jean-Paul Sartre, Jean Cocteau, and Indro Montanelli, whose film projects he had published. He called as well on professional film critics who were already well-known, or were very soon to be, such as André Bazin, Roger Leenhardt, Jacques Doniol-Valcroze, Nino Frank, Lo Duca, Guido Aristarco, and Lotte H. Eisner. Auriol also included figures from other artistic disciplines such as the well-known musicologist Jacques Bourgeois, a regular contributor.

This second iteration of the *Revue du cinéma*, self-contained and well suited to its *époque*, which joined together significant representatives from the intellectual life of the time, allows us to evaluate the audience's and critics' reactions to the discovery of Sturges's films, which appeared in the journal in two forms: in about half of the issues up to March 1948, Sturges mostly figured in allusions included within articles about other films or filmmakers. Sturges's presence in the journal was solidified later within longer analytical articles focused on two of his films: *The Lady Eve* (released in France as *Un cœur pris au piège* in 1946) and *Sullivan's Travels* (1941, released in France in 1947 as *Les Voyages de Sullivan*).

PRESTON STURGES, AN UNDERGROUND PRESENCE

Revue du cinéma never claimed to be focused on current events. Most often the editors solicited for the journal very long articles that focused on major theoretical, historical, literary, artistic, and musical debates, sometimes in a fragmented manner over several issues. Accordingly, from the first issue, Jean George Auriol devoted seventeen pages to the first part of a vast essay under the rather general title "Making Films." "The Origins of *mise-en-scène*" linked cinematic *mise-en-scène* to painting, and was illustrated almost exclusively with black-and-white reproductions of works by Brueghel, Giotto, Botticelli, and Michelangelo, with just one image from the history of cinema: *The Passion of Joan of Arc* of Carl Theodor Dreyer. These articles evoked films from the history of cinema, classics from the silent era and from the 1930s.

Thus, in the context of thoughtful discussion about film, rather than reviews, Preston Sturges's name first appeared. *Revue* published a French translation of an essay by American director Irving Pichel, which first appeared in *Hollywood Quarterly*, a journal edited by the University of California Press.[5] This was a fascinating article because it unambiguously showed that attributing authorship of a film to a single auteur nagged many minds, in Hollywood as much as in Europe, and well before the official birth of the auteur theory in the columns of *Cahiers* by the mid-1950s. Sturges's name appeared on the final page of the article, when Pichel describes "a few writers [who] have likewise absorbed the producer function in order to protect the execution of their work."[6] After Pichel mentions Billy Wilder, Delmer Daves, and Joseph L. Mankiewicz (but, curiously, not Orson Welles), he isolates Preston Sturges as an example of someone who "has absorbed all three functions," of producer, screenwriter, and director, but cites no specific title.[7]

In "Making Film," Auriol bemoans the cinema's objection to "assembling images with the same liberty as the novelist."[8] He cites three exceptions: Sacha Guitry's *Confessions of a Cheat* (1936), Marcel Carné's *Daybreak* (1939), and, a film written by Sturges, *The Power and the Glory* (1933).[9] This last is a film that precedes the other two in time and which Auriol sees as a true cinematic model. It is noteworthy that Auriol attributes cinematic paternity to both the film's writer and its director, Preston Sturges and William K. Howard, but to a screenwriter first of all. So, while he had not yet been the sole object of a focused study, Sturges was, in a manner, firmly integrated within some kind of elite.

In an excellent study of the elaboration of cinematic myths, "Contribution to a Legend of the Stars," Jacques Doniol-Valcroze dedicates fifteen or so lines to Veronica Lake in *I Married a Witch* and *Sullivan's Travels* (the film had just been released in France). He pinpoints Sturges who, he explains, was the sole filmmaker who had provided his audience with "a faithful image" of a rising movie star.[10] A few issues later, Doniol-Valcroze evokes Sturges again within the space of a passionate analysis of Jacques Becker's *Antoine and Antoinette* (1947).[11] Without naming Sturges, the writer mentions the continuity between *The Power and the Glory* and Welles's *Citizen Kane*. This film, certainly well-anchored within the memories of early *cinéphiles* and linked to Sturges, was highlighted as a classic and an often-imitated work. Ironically, in America some cinephiles over-covered this link only in 1971, with the appearance of the famous essay "Raising Kane" by Pauline Kael, which gives the lion's share of credit for *Citizen Kane* to its screenwriter, Herman Mankiewicz, rather than its director, Orson Welles.[12]

Though still not yet listed in the columns of the *Revue du cinéma*, *Sullivan's Travels* already cut the figure of a classic film. In a long essay that the publication encouraged, the philosopher Albert Laffay writes, over seventeen pages, on the "Major Themes in Cinema" (*Grands thèmes de l'écran*). Recent films, not mentioned in the body of the article, formed the focus of photographs with captions tied to the essay. This was the case with Welles's *The Lady from Shanghai* (1947), Billy Wilder's *Double Indemnity* (1944), Lewis Milestone's *The Strange Love of Martha Ivers* (1947), and Sturges's *Sullivan's Travels*. *Sullivan's Travels* is even allowed two photographs and a brief comment that praises Sturges for the use "of all of the essential themes in cinema in his film: the journey, the pursuit, convergence, and unexpected simultaneous presence."[13]

Finally, one last notable mention of Sturges appears in the fifteenth issue, in another study by Doniol-Valcroze focused on an actor. In this instance, Henry Fonda is the subject of a portrait called "Friend Fonda" (*L'Ami Fonda*). In the final section of the article, the author points to the two sides of a talent that he calls "the most solid and the most simple of the American screen"[14] across two memorable films shot within a few months of each other: *The Grapes of Wrath* (1940) by John Ford and *The Lady Eve*. Doniol-Valcroze supports his portrait of this actor with examples from films signed by established filmmakers: Fritz Lang (*You Only Live Once*, 1937) and John Ford (*My Darling Clementine*, 1946). The fact that Sturges would be associated with this collection of film-makers and that, in addition, André Bazin, writing for *L'Écran français*, expressed his admiration for a man he described as the "anti-Capra" speaks to the high regard in which his work would thereafter be held.

From these different allusions, we can easily deduce that Preston Sturges's name was common within French film criticism as well as among French intellectuals generally. His name appears equally as often as those of other major filmmakers discovered in France during the postwar period: Orson Welles and Billy Wilder, for example. We can go even further than this, though, because his name springs notably from the pens of Auriol and Doniol-Valcroze, who singled out this filmmaker's 1933 screenplay. Not only did *Revue* establish the link between Sturges's work as a scriptwriter and his more recent work as a director, in order to defend the idea of a cinematic auteur *avant la lettre*, but the journal also underlined the influence *The Power and the Glory* had on Welles's *Citizen Kane*. Preston Sturges may have been historically forgotten by the chief auteurists of *Cahiers*, such as Truffaut, Godard, and Chabrol, but he was also a precursor to whom the concept would apply before the label "*politique des auteurs*" was itself born.

TWO CLASSIC FILMS ANALYZED: *THE LADY EVE* AND *SULLIVAN'S TRAVELS*

La Revue du cinéma brought together the praises of many French critics (notably André Bazin, writing for *L'Écran français* but also for more mainstream publications such as *Cinémonde*, wherein 1947 Sturges was interviewed by Maurice Bessy) by dedicating detailed overviews to two of Sturges's films: *The Lady Eve*[15] and *Sullivan's Travels*.[16] The criticism, focused on *The Lady Eve* (which had already been released in France for more than a year), made up the second half of a large group of pieces called "American Chronicles" (Chroniques américaines), written by Jean George Auriol himself. The first part of the essay focused on Elia Kazan's *Boomerang*. In effect, the introduction ended in this way: "The most brilliant recent example of Hollywood directing that shirks the studio routine and is, without a doubt, highly distinct from the terrific cinematic attempts of Orson Welles, is the personal effort of Preston Sturges. We have wanted to speak of him for a long time now."[17]

After including a quotation from Maurice Bessy's interview with Preston Sturges, mentioned above, Auriol writes of Sturges's "professional experience, of his talent, even of genius"[18] in order to justify the presence of a personality that might appear frivolous in the face of the more serious, realist tendency represented by Rossellini (also mentioned in the article) then in dominance. From the third paragraph, *The Power and the Glory* again allows Auriol to situate the filmmaker: "[it is] an exceptional work that European critics speak of today, but often without having seen it, as a masterpiece realized almost in opposition to the American industry."[19] Auriol also makes mention of slapstick and Mack Sennett in reference to *The Lady Eve*. Auriol narrates certain situations, describes certain gags, before a conclusion which is surprising, to say the least. In effect, he links the revenge of Eve (Barbara Stanwyck) to that of Hélène (Maria Casarès) in Robert Bresson's *Les Dames du Bois de Boulogne* (1945), primarily because of the cruelty of the sleeping car scene that Sturges "knew how to orchestrate with a frenzied ardor."[20] This scene seemed to justify in advance François Truffaut's decision to include Sturges, in a collection of André Bazin's writings, among what he called "the cinema of cruelty"[21] and his decision to link Sturges with Eric von Stroheim, Carl Theodor Dreyer, Luis Bunuel, Alfred Hitchcock, and Akira Kurosawa.

This analysis of *The Lady Eve* remained summary. The latter half of the article moves away from the film itself while Auriol develops an extended tribute to Preston Sturges, as if to excuse the fact that, up until then, the journal had only mentioned his name in brief allusions. He calls *Sullivan's Travels* "a strange odyssey" and a "burlesque voyage," ideas which correspond precisely to the approach taken by Joel and Ethan Coen who titled their homage to Sturges *O Brother, Where Art Thou?* (2000).[22] Auriol then mentions *The Palm Beach Story*[23] and *Christmas in July* (*Le Gros lot*). He concludes his stirring tribute by observing, justly, that Sturges is "a director who never forgets that a scene's rhythm, its flow of images, depends as much on the words spoken as on the activity of the actors."[24] This is an apt description that wonderfully captures the genius of this filmmaker, a magician of words and editing, and a director of actors. The article ends with a stunning photograph of Veronica Lake and Joel McCrea in *Sullivan's Travels* (which had been out in France for already a year), with a caption that called it a "curious and original film" and that announced an article that would be focused on it in the next issue of the journal.[25]

Revue du cinéma's respect for chronology allows us to end this brief inventory with an essay that is at once an overarching tribute and an advancement of several reservations: an article written by Grisha Dabat, the future collaborator of Roger Vadim,[26] focused on *Sullivan's Travels*. The article's title alerts us in advance: "A Failed Masterpiece" (Un chef d'œuvre manqué).[27] Dabat certainly judges Sturges very highly in this piece. The writer speaks of no less than the filmmaker's "Hegelian dialectic,"[28] rightly alluding to a model in philosophical tales, linking his comedy to that of George Bernard Shaw and Aldous Huxley and multiplying the references by adding to familiar ones (like Mack Sennett, Fatty Arbuckle, Chaplin, and René Clair) that of Ernst Lubitsch. But Dabat quickly corrects himself by saying: "the style of his comedies recalls Lubitsch most of all, even though their spirit and their tone belongs only to him."[29] In sum, does Sturges resemble Lubitsch or not? The answer is not clear.

More seriously, but once again rather unclear, is Dabat's impetus behind the disappointment announced in the article's title. Dabat sees the film as a philosophical demonstration, reduced to a thesis (up until the death of the vagrant thief, crushed by the train), an antithesis (the prison episode), and a synthesis (the film's conclusion). Dabat characterizes this "demonstration" as one of "constantly surprising skill."[30] The thesis, according to Dabat, "is marvelously demonstrated."[31] "The dialogue shines, and the satire is brilliant."[32] The antithesis, however, pleases Dabat less. He judges that "the film becomes violent and the lesson hardens."[33] How exactly does Dabat reproach what he calls the antithesis? If we understand what he means, he accuses the film of being overwritten (but could it be otherwise?). According to Dabat, "the antithesis has the whiff of ebonite, of a Parker 51 fountain pen. It was born of *othédrine*[34] in the early morning hours of a sleepless night and recalls a well-endowed gentleman who slips ten dollars to an out-of-work father of four, telling him to take a good long bath and to clean his fingernails well."[35] This argument finally turns to reproach Sturges with the same complaint that the studio folks in the film brought to the character of Sullivan. Dabat's criticism, clumsy and to my mind without merit, underscores the personal side of the film as well as the skill of its author and director.

Dabat names his own text a "vivisection of the script": more modestly, though, it amounts to a criticism devoid of a solid argument. Dabat complains that the time he spent writing about the script "evidently left him little room for a deep analysis of Sturges's writing which [. . .] remains always marvelously flexible."[36] In sum, we can see in this essay that Dabat refuses to offer too much admiration, a well-known thread of a certain style of French criticism that at times faults films for being *too* perfect. Beyond these unconvincing reservations, and most of all with the hindsight of history, the vital place Preston Sturges occupies in postwar French criticism remains untouched. Dabat's critique uses a plethora of laudatory phrases and more than once places Sturges at the heart of a fundamental debate that took shape at that very moment in history: that of the "auteur," the filmmaker as the complete author of a film. However, the reservations Dabat expresses reflect well the reticence toward Sturges held by one branch of French criticism. Such reticence even appears in the writing of André Bazin, one of Sturges's principal admirers.

PRESTON STURGES "AFTER" *LA REVUE DU CINÉMA*

When compiling a fine volume of Bazin's writings, Truffaut would include Sturges within what he called "the cinema of cruelty," an appellation that mixes admiration and reticence, which may account for Sturges's sidelining from what would later become "auteur theory."[37] We find an article on *Sullivan's Travels*,[38] and shorter articles on the paired films *The Miracle of Morgan's Creek* and *Hail the Conquering Hero*,[39] as well as an article on *Mad Wednesday*.[40]

The first of these articles is the longest and the most interesting. From the first paragraph, Bazin links Preston Sturges to Orson Welles, a connection that he often made, as was seen in his admiring references to Sturges in *La Revue du cinéma*. Bazin, in fact, used the opportunity of the release of *Sullivan's Travels* to return to Sturges's films that had previously screened in France and to submit them all to a kind of critical appraisal. From the beginning of his essay and in a very straightforward manner, Bazin reminds readers that *Christmas in July*, *The Palm Beach Story*, and *The Lady Eve* "did not have great success in France."[41] He notes, however, that these films still circulated in France outside of commercial theaters and within the network of ciné-clubs, an audience that "he [Sturges] still didn't always please."[42] The viewers who persisted for the zaniness, sometimes insouciant (McCarey, Hawks) sometimes optimistic (Capra), of prewar screwball comedy resisted or remained indifferent to the biting irony, "the self-destruction of the genre" that Bazin spoke of.[43] Bazin's admiration is clear, but so is his reticence, which is, no doubt, of the same order as that felt by confused audiences. In effect, if Bazin appreciated *Sullivan's Travels*, he wondered why the film "leaves us feeling unsatisfied," and he proposed as an explanation that it was necessary for "tragedy to dialectically annul comedy."[44] In sum, it was the mixture of tones that finally unsettled audiences and that tempered Bazin's enthusiasm. On the other hand, he was seduced by *Mad Wednesday*'s homage to silent-era burlesque.[45] He gave this film the most indisputably favorable assessment, and even though it was often considered a hybrid, even precarious work, he saw in it "the most intelligent homage one can make to Harold Lloyd and to the great school of American comedy."[46]

The discrepancies between the films' releases and the appearances of articles about them in *La Revue du cinéma* are an invaluable indicator: it was late that the journal addressed the films directly, as if to repair an injustice committed by audiences and by certain critics. Critical curiosity about these films was certainly there, but the violence of Sturges's irony and his tendency toward iconoclasm seemed to have unsettled both the popular and the cultivated public, who in this postwar period seemed to prefer certitude. Also, French cinema of the next fifteen years would be dominated by the "tradition of quality," a movement whose conservatism Truffaut and a few others would end up unseating. Admiration for Preston Sturges remained measured and his films would become difficult to find to watch or rewatch. This is what is quietly reflected in the metaphor that Pierre Kast uses in the only article of consequence written on Sturges and published in *Cahiers du cinéma*:

Films, stored in caves kept deep in the mind, age like wine. We must content ourselves with our uncertain memory of his films in order to situate the work of Preston Sturges in its proper frame. Even Langlois cannot get them, such is the persistence of the old curse, so strong is the violated taboo. But Sturges's films improve over time, like the most robust and most favored wines of Bordeaux.[47]

So it turns out to be very simple: if Preston Sturges did not figure in "auteur theory," that is because his films were, at that time, difficult to screen. After all, Ernst Lubitsch also wasn't cited as an example of auteur theory, probably for similar reasons.

Of course, auteur theory would only announce its name and its principles a few years later in *Cahiers du cinéma*. But the way in which the *Revue du cinéma* took Preston Sturges's works into consideration, notably by linking them with Orson Welles, who was discovered at the same time, demonstrates that the debate can be dated to many years earlier. In the 1920s, Louis Delluc had himself singled out certain filmmakers. The advent, on the Hollywood landscape, of filmmaker-writers, even producers, such as Sturges, Welles, and Wilder, and the assertion of recognizably personal film styles that undercut the privileged grammar and format of mainstream cinema, provided new fodder for the debate. It is clear that the announcement of auteur theory a few years later would be only the (provisional) conclusion of the debate. Preston Sturges was certainly one of the *causes célèbres* of the debate. But we can only note the ironies of history when we fail to include his name among those upon whose work this valorization of the sole author of a film is based. Sturges must, then, retake his deserved place in the foreground of this debate.

Since the late 1980s, Sturges's place has become undeniable. A brilliant complete retrospective at the Locarno Festival in Switzerland in 1989 prompted the first monograph written in French on this *cinéaste*.[48] A few years later, Marc Cerisuelo, a passionate young student, published the first single-authored volume on Preston Sturges in France: *Preston Sturges or the Genius of America*.[49] We are also reminded of the remarkable overview by Grégoire Albout, *Hollywood Screwball Comedy, 1934–1945*, in which he considers Sturges the equal of recognized filmmakers like Frank Capra, Ernst Lubitsch and Leo McCarey and of others who are still little-known, like Gregory La Cava.[50]

In July 2007, a complete retrospective of Sturges's work was organized at the *Cinémathèque française*. It was bolstered by a conference organized by Cerisuelo and by the support of the film-going public, many of whom were just then discovering Sturges's films. Cerisuelo remains the most important specialist on Sturges in France.[51] Collectors edition DVDs for *The Lady Eve*, *The Palm Beach Story*, and *Sullivan's Travels*, as well as the rerelease to theaters of *Sullivan's Travels* and, very recently, *The Miracle of Morgan's Creek* (August 2014, a film practically unedited since its release in 1947), have continued to stoke the interest of French *cinéphiles*, among whom Sturges has finally found the place that is his due.

Although, in recent years, Sturges has been recognized as the equal of other great filmmakers, unlike, say, Hitchcock, whose influence we can trace on French directors, he seems to have had little influence on French filmmaking. Despite the director's many years in France, his sensibility is quite foreign to the French. His special blend of sophisticated comedy and often crude slapstick was perhaps "too American" to be copied here. This "Americanness" may also explain why Sturges, in his day, was only admired by a lucky few.

RELEASE DATES OF PRESTON STURGES'S FILMS IN FRANCE BETWEEN 1945 AND 1950

Since screenings of American films in France between 1945 and 1950 were haphazard (to say the least), readers might find it useful know the order in which Preston Sturges's films reached French audiences and critics:

> *Christmas in July*, 1940/ *Le Gros Lot*, September 1945
> *The Palm Beach Story*, 1942/ *Madame et ses flirts*, September 1946
> *The Lady Eve*, 1941/ *Un cœur pris au piège*, December 1946
> *Sullivan's Travels*, 1941/ *Les Voyages de Sullivan*, February 1947
> *Miracle of Morgan's Creek*, 1944/ *Miracle au village*, May 1947
> *Hail the Conquering Hero*, 1944/ *Héro d'occasion*, April 1949
> *The Great McGinty*, 1940/ *Gouverneur malgré lui*, January 1950

NOTES

1 The French poster for *I Married a Witch* reproduced the complimentary caricature of Veronica Lake, her hair covering one eye, an image which was also part of the American publicity materials for Sturges's *Sullivan's Travels* (1941).

2 Sturges's initial concept for the screenplay, a writer who invents a character but then meets him in real life, was refused. Sturges had to return to a more classic adaptation.

3 Pierre Kast, "Positively Yours: Some Remarks, Notes, and Memories of Preston Sturges" [Positivement vôtre: Quelques remarques, notes et souvenirs sur Preston Sturges], *Positif*, 281–2 (July–August 1984), 3–8.

4 *Cahiers du cinéma*, 426, December 1989, 54–61.

5 Irving Pichel, "Creativeness Cannot Be Diffused," *Hollywood Quarterly* 1:1 (October 1945), 20–5, Trans. in *La Revue du cinéma* as "La Création doit être l'ouvrage d'un seul."

6 Irving Pichel, "La Création doit être l'ouvrage d'un seul" [Creation should be the work of one alone], *La Revue du cinéma*, 2 (November 1946), 61.

7 Pichel, 61.

8 Jean George Auriol, "Making a Film" [Faire un film], *La Revue du cinéma*, 4 (January 1947), 10.

9 Titles in French: *Le Roman d'un tricheur* de Sacha Guitry (1936), *Le Jour se lève* de Marcel Carné (1939) and *Thomas Garner* (*The Power and the Glory*, 1933).

10 Jacques Doniol-Valcroze, "Contribution à une légende des étoiles" [Contribution to a legend of the stars], *La Revue du cinéma*, 6 (Spring 1947), 52.

11 Jacques Doniol-Valcroze, "De l'imitation à propos d'un film original: Antoine et Antoinette" [On the imitation of an original film: Antoine and Antoinette], *La Revue du cinéma*, 9 (January 1948), 64–7.

12 Pauline Kael, "Raising Kane," *New Yorker*, 20 February 1971, 43–89 and 27 February 1971, 44–81.

13 Albert Laffay, "Major Themes in Cinema" [Grands thèmes de l'écran], *La Revue du cinéma*, 12 (April 1948), 18.

14 Jacques Doniol-Valcroze, "Friend Fonda" [L'Ami Fonda], *La Revue du cinéma*, 15 (July 1948), 62.

15 Jean George Auriol, "American Chronicles" [Chroniques américaines], *La Revue du cinéma*, 11, March 1948.

16 Jean George Auriol, "American Chronicles" [Chroniques américaines], *La Revue du cinéma*, 16, August 1948.

17 Auriol, March 1948, 75–9. On the other hand, Elia Kazan's name is never mentioned in this introduction.

18 Auriol, March 1948, 76.

19 Auriol, March 1948, 76.

20 Auriol, March 1948, 78.

21 André Bazin, *Le Cinéma de la cruauté* (Flammarion, Paris, 1975). Preface by François Truffaut.

22 Auriol, March 1948, 75–9.

23 The French release was translated as *Madame et ses flirts*, but Auriol mistakenly called it *Madame et son flirt*.

24 Auriol, March 1948, 75–9.

25 Auriol, 79.

26 Dabat and Vadim co-signed the script for . . . *et Satan conduit le bal*, directed by Dabat in 1962.

27 Grisha Dabat, "A Failed Masterpiece" [Un chef d'œuvre manqué], *La Revue du cinéma*, 16, 77.

28 Dabat, 78.

29 Dabat, 80.

30 Dabat, 78.

31 Dabat, 78.

32 Dabat, 78.

33 Dabat, 78.

34 Othédrine is an amphetamine that was at one time freely available in France. It does not appear to have an English translation.

35 Dabat, 79.

36 Dabat, 80.

37 Bazin, 51–65.

38 This article initially appeared in the journal *L'Écran français* in May 1948.

39 These articles initially appeared in *L'Écran français*, February and May 1951, respectively.

40 This article initially appeared in *Radio cinéma*, May 1951.

41 According to the numbers published in *Film Français, hebdomadaire des professionnels du cinéma a et de l'audiovisuel* (*French Film: The Weekly for Cinema and Audiovisual Professionals*) none of Sturges's films was among the forty films with the highest ticket sales between 1945 and 1951.

42 Bazin, 51.

43 Bazin, 50.

44 Bazin, 55.

45 For its release in France, in 1951, the original title given was *Mad Wednesday*.

46 Bazin, 64.

47 Pierre Kast, "Sturges, Preston," *Cahiers du cinéma*, 150–1 (December 1963–January 1964), 170.

48 With the simple title *Preston Sturges*, and edited by Roland Cosandey, historical articles by Thomas Quinn Curtis, Penelope Houston, Manny Farber, and Siegfried Kracauer, untranslated until then, rubbed shoulders with essays by André Bazin as well as with new pieces and perspectives written by François Thomas, Lorenzo Codelli, and the author of this article.

49 Marc Cerisuelo, *Preston Sturges ou le génie de l'Amérique* (Paris: PUF, 2002).

50 Grégoire Albout, *La Comédie Screwball hollywoodienne, 1934–1945: Sexe, Amour et Idéaux démocratiques* (Arras: Artois Presses Université, 2013, collection Lettres et Civilisations Etrangères).

51 I thank him here for his valuable assistance on this chapter.

CHAPTER 14

O Preston, Where Art Thou?

Sarah Kozloff

In many ways, except for the enduring popularity of *The Lady Eve*, Sturges has faded from view in film history. Certainly he has not enjoyed the constant attention and adulation of a Hitchcock, Hawks, or Ford, thus necessitating this *ReFocus* volume. Even many film scholars have seen only a few of his films. Some titles are hard to find, or available only in poor, unrestored versions.

Yet if one is sensitive to Sturges's themes, tone, and style, in actuality, he lurks *everywhere* in contemporary films. The reason we must bring him back into focus is that, in many ways, modern filmmakers should be counted as Sturges's (multiple) offspring.

THE COEN BROTHERS

Positif: Viewing *Raising Arizona* makes you think a bit about Preston Sturges.
Ethan Coen: We are crazy about his films. We love *The Palm Beach Story*.[1]

Playboy: Several of your films incorporate elements of screwball comedies. What's your favorite of that genre?
Joel: *The Miracle of Morgan's Creek*, although I'm not sure that it's technically a screwball comedy . . .
Ethan: I like all of Preston Sturges's comedies.[2]

Though it adds a clever touch, film history aficionados didn't really need the title, *O Brother, Where Art Thou?*, to see Preston Sturges hiding behind the Coen Brothers' 2000 movie, grinning. In that film alone, we have a picaresque narrative (like *Sullivan's Travels*); government corruption (*The Great McGinty*, *Hail the Conquering Hero*); a stock company of strange male figures speaking odd dialects (John Goodman, John Turturro, Charles Durning); and equally capricious character names, such as "Pete Hogwallop," "Vernon T. Waldrip" and "Ulysses Everett McGill." For Everett to turn out to be the father of *seven* daughters just does the sextuplets of *The Miracle of Morgan's Creek* (1944) one better.

For that matter, critics perceive Sturges's influence even earlier in the Coen canon, in *Raising Arizona* (1987), which throws together physical slapstick, verbal ingenuity, larceny, and . . . actual quintuplets.[3] *The Hudsucker Proxy* (1994)—which adds Hawks and Capra to the masala, specifically in the hard-boiled female reporter character—also explicitly refers back to Sturges. This story of a mailroom attendant suddenly elevated to company president echoes Sturges's constant vision of the humble "schnook" rising to sudden prominence, and illustrates his theme about the capriciousness of money and success, which figure so prominently in *Easy Living* (1937), *Christmas in July* (1940), and *The Sin of Harold Diddlebock* (1947).

I find Sturgean echoes most compelling in *Intolerable Cruelty* (2003), the Coen film that comes closest to a screwball comedy because the romance is the central plot. This is a slantwise remake of *The Lady Eve*, a film in which passion gets crisscrossed with money and a desire for revenge. Miles Massey (George Clooney), the ultra-successful Beverly Hills divorce lawyer, is hardly a Charles Pike innocent, but he falls with just as hard a thud, and Marilyn Rexroth (Catherine Zeta-Jones) is as scheming as Jean Harrington in *The Lady Eve* (1941). The show she puts on with the fake oilman Howard D. Doyle, whose make-believe father and grandfather were both named "John D." (likely after a character in *The Palm Beach Story*), is worthy of the Lady Eve Sidwich.

Like *The Palm Beach Story*, *Intolerable Cruelty* stresses the ways a woman can use her sex appeal for financial advancement. Moreover, *Intolerable Cruelty* is full of Sturgean mannerisms, such as Three Stooges/cartoon scenes, including a private detective chased by rottweilers and two lawyers creeping around a house trying to stop a murder with cans of mace. The offbeat, older, male characters here are embodied not by William Demarest, Franklin Pangborn or Eric Blore, but by Geoffrey Rush (fake Australian accent), Edward Hermann (sexual fetishist mesmerized by trains), and Billy Bob Thornton (fake Texas accent). Playing an effete concierge, Heinz, the Baron Krauss von Espry (Jonathan Hadary) is reminiscent of and yet funnier than any of Franklin Pangborn's characters (though just as offensive a portrayal of a homosexual).

Unlike *The Lady Eve*, however, *Intolerable Cruelty* was only a moderate success with audiences and critics. It earned its higher-than-Coen-normal budget back through overseas distribution.[4] The overall tone is colder: Marilyn never shows the "yen" for Miles that Jean feels for Charles, and she never repents of her trickery or evinces real pain. Sexual desire is fore-grounded, but from the beginning archly clever Victorian cupids in the credits mock love. Though the Coen Brothers admit tenderness into some of their narrative worlds, such as the love between Hi and Ed in *Raising Arizona*, or the union of Marge and Norm in *Fargo* (1996), *Intolerable Cruelty* stresses infidel-ity, gold-digging, lying, murder contracts, and "nailing his ass."

A key scene occurs after Miles has married Marilyn Rexroth Doyle. He is committed to addressing the National Organization of Matrimonial Attorneys, Nationwide (N.O.M.A.N.) the next morning. Ostentatiously, he tears up his prepared text and "speaks from his heart":

> Love need cause us no fear. Love need cause us no shame. Love is . . . good. Love is good. Now I am of course aware that these remarks will be received here with cynicism—cynicism, that cloak that advertises our indifference and hides all human feeling. Well, I'm here to tell you that that cynicism, which we think protects us in fact destroys—destroys love, destroys our clients and ultimately destroys ourselves. Colleagues—when our clients come to us confused and angry and hurting because their flame of love is guttering and threatens to die, do we seek to extinguish that flame so that we can sift through the smolder-ing wreckage for our paltry reward? . . . For my part I have made the leap of love and there is no going back. Ladies and gentlemen, this is the last time I will address you as the president of N.O.M.A.N. or as a member. I intend to devote myself to pro-bono work in East Los Angeles or one of those other . . . God bless you all.

Figure 14.1 Miles and the hardened divorce lawyers giddy after Miles's pro-love speech.

The Coens present this purported eschewal of cynicism cynically. Besotted, Miles falls into the dumbest of clichés: "Love is good." Because he has had one night with the woman he has lusted after for a year, he now imagines himself to be a completely reformed man, who could use his legal mind doing pro bono work in "East Los Angeles or some other—." And since when, exactly, did God's blessing ever enter into a Coen milieu?

Meanwhile, the Coens direct the on-screen audience of hardened divorce lawyers to morph into a crowd from a Capra movie; implausibly, these grim-faced legal vultures are stirred to a standing ovation by Miles's change of heart. The viewer who has actually experienced romance and love (or hopes to do so) is put into the position of being as Capra-foolish as Miles or the lawyers.

When the film was released, David Edelstein wrote that the Coens remain emotionally distant from a love story:

> The reason that many of us still treasure *The Lady Eve* (1941) and *Adam's Rib* (1949) after 50-plus years is that the people who wrote them were serious about exploring issues of constancy and trust, and the jokes allowed them to raise the stakes in ways that most non-comic dramatists don't dare. The Coens are too armored by irony to take those kinds of risks. Cupid would need a rocket launcher.[5]

In many ways, Edelstein's observations apply to the Coens' broader engagements with Sturges. For much as they admire and imitate his films, Joel and Ethan Coen don't capture Sturges's spirit. Their films are more nihilistic, almost as if they are rushing headlong into cynicism. Just as they undercut any notions of romantic love in *Intolerable Cruelty*, so too do they deal cynical blows to beliefs in the power of artistic expression (*Barton Fink*, *Inside Llewyn Davis*), religious faith (*A Serious Man*), and the triumph of good over evil (*No Country for Old Men*). However, they overtly tip their hats to the Master. Thus, they've done him a service; young moviegoers, who may never have heard of Sturges before, may be prompted by the Coens' adoration to seek out his cinema.

In other contemporary films we can also sense Sturges's influence, even if such linear evidence of inspiration is lacking. I believe that this influence shows most strongly in the logocentricity of contemporary films, as well as in their reliance on postmodernism, and cruelty.

WORDS! WORDS! WORDS! I GET WORDS ALL DAY THROUGH; FIRST FROM *HIM*, NOW FROM *YOU*!

Verbal dexterity has become the hallmark of a certain cycle of knowing, ironic, lower-budget-than-mainstream contemporary writer-directors. Partly, as I posited in *Overhearing Film Dialogue*, this stems from the fact that witty dialogue is fundamentally cheaper than car chases or special effects. But the pressure toward highly literate screenwriting stems from a larger cultural shift. In today's networked, global culture and economy, when we hate to wait a second, we expect our on-screen stars to be *smart*, not taciturn, slow-thinking cowboys, nor hard-bodied Terminators. And we expect our screen teenagers to speak like Juno (Ellen Page), who adopts a speech pattern full of allusions to pop culture, rather than Laurel (Anne Shirley) in *Stella Dallas* (King Vidor, 1937), who speaks like an upper-class debutante.

As Jeff Daniels remarks, "It can be as thrilling as a car chase to see two actors walking down a hallway going back and forth if they're smart people saying smart things."[6] Comedies have always relied upon "repartee." The word, coined in the 1600s, comes from a French fencing term. Nowadays we do not pick up swords against enemies, nor do we have competitive jousts with friends. But we do practice verbal toppers; each person proves his wit or her position's superiority through the thrust and parry of conversation.

What *Intolerable Cruelty* does demonstrate, in abundance, is clever scriptwriting. As Joe McElhaney notes in "Fast Talk: Preston Sturges and the Speed of Language," "[Sturges's] cinema is not only verbal but dominated by words, by the act of speaking as a powerful bearer of meaning in and of itself. It is a cinema of great wit and enormous verbal play."[7] Manny Farber and William Poster once wrote that in Sturges, "The audience is fairly showered with words."[8]

In *Intolerable Cruelty*, the shower becomes a flood. Let me refresh your memory of a scene between Miles and his assistant lawyer, Wrigley, after Miles has stolen Marilyn's address book:

Wrigley: Who are you looking for?
Miles Massey: Tenzing Norgay.
Wrigley: Tenzing Norgay? That's someone she slept with?
Miles Massey: I doubt it. Tenzing Norgay was the Sherpa that helped Edmund Hillary climb Mt. Everest.
Wrigley: And Marilyn knows him?
Miles Massey: No, you idiot. Not *the* Tenzing Norgay. *Her* Tenzing Norgay.
Wrigley: I'm not sure that I actually follow that.
Miles Massey: Few great accomplishments are achieved single-handedly, Wrigley. Most have their Norgays. Marilyn Rexroth is even now climbing her Everest. I want to find her Norgay.
Wrigley: But how do you determine which of the people on here are . . .
Miles Massey: How do you spot a Norgay?
Wrigley: Yeah.
Miles Massey: You start with the people with the funny names.

The humor of this passage comes from the metaphor comparing Marilyn's attempt to gain her husband's assets to explorers conquering Mount Everest for the first time; from the unwanted image of Marilyn sleeping with this famous and long-deceased figure; and from repetition of "Tenzing Norgay" eight times. As my co-editor Jeff Jaeckle has demonstrated regarding *The Big Lebowski* (1997), these scripts are held together by a vast amount of repeated catchphrases.[9] In *Intolerable Cruelty*, another oft-repeated phrase is "nail[ing] his ass[ets]." Also, particularly intriguing about the Norgay passage above is that at the end it turns "meta" on us, because "Tenzing Norgay"—for Americans at least—is itself a funny name.

We know that Sturges also used: wild metaphors (Jean: "I need him like the axe needs a turkey" in *The Lady Eve*); funny names ("Luisa Ginglebusher" in *The Good Fairy*); repetition ("With a little sex in it," from *Sullivan's Travels*), and language that calls attention to the fact that it is cinematic dialogue (Sullivan: "What's the matter, don't you go to the movies?").

Jeff Jaeckle has traced the similarities between Sturges and another hip auteur in "The Shared Verbal Stylistics of Preston Sturges and Wes Anderson."[10] Jaeckle specifies wordplay, meta-language, lines that point to their scripted nature, and the use of dialects and national languages as characteristic of both Anderson and Sturges. Jaeckle also suggests that for further examples we look at Noah Baumbach, director of *The Squid and the Whale* (2005), Alexander Payne, famous for *Election* (1999) and *Sideways* (2004), and the writer-director team of Diablo Cody and Jason Reitman, who made *Juno* (2007) and *Young Adult* (2011).

I would add screenwriter Aaron Sorkin to Jaeckle's list, both for Sorkin's cinematic accomplishments and for the influence of his television shows *Sports Night* (1998–2000), *The West Wing* (1999–2006), and *The Newsroom* (2012–14). Sorkin, incidentally, does avow his debt to Sturges (as well as to other screenwriters and playwrights).[11] Although Sorkin's temperament differs fundamentally from the Coens (he is much more serious about social problems and less comic, and he admits to being romantic with a capital "R"), the bleak picture of social and financial success in *The Social Network* (2010), and the narrative complexity of that film, hark back to *The Power and the Glory* (1933). Besides, this opening dialogue between a pretty, self-possessed young woman and a pompous, clueless (brilliant) schnook is worthy of Preston himself:

Mark: Did you know there are more people with genius IQ's living in China than there are people of any kind living in the United States?
Erica: That can't possibly be true.
Mark: It is.
Erica: What would account for that?

Mark: Well, first, an awful lot of people live in China. But here's my question: How do you distinguish yourself in a population of people who all got 1600 on their SAT's?

Erica: I didn't know they take SAT's in China.

Mark: They don't. I wasn't talking about China anymore, I was talking about me.

Erica: You got 1600?

Mark: Yes. I could sing in an *A Capella* group, but I can't sing.

Erica: Does that mean you actually got nothing wrong?

Mark: I can row crew or invent a $25 PC.

Erica: Or you can get into a final club.

Mark: Or I can get into a final club.

Erica: You know, from a woman's perspective, sometimes not singing in an *A Capella* group is a good thing?

Mark: This is serious.

Erica: On the other hand, I do like guys who row crew.

Mark (beat): Well I can't do that.

Erica: I was kid—

Mark: Yes, it means I got nothing wrong on the test.

Erica: Have you ever tried?

Mark: I'm trying right now.

Erica: To row crew?

Mark: To get into a final club. To row crew? No. Are you, like—whatever—delusional?

Typically for screwball comedy dialogue, the conversationalists here don't hear one another; they are following separate trains of thought.[12] In this way, this exchange recalls the conversation between Sully Sullivan and his producers in the way the comments hurl past their intended recipients like missiles. And it is also very similar to Sturges in its use of "hooks," with characters taking a word or phrase and building on it, as you see above with "tried/trying," "final club," and "crew."

Sorkin's dialogue is also fundamentally akin to Sturges's in its *speed*. Speaking quickly is a hallmark of contemporary cinema, because we think it mimics speed of thought. Though its screen running time is only 120 minutes, *The Social Network*'s screenplay stretches for 164 pages, quite a bit longer than the benchmark of one minute per page.[13]

We must keep in mind, however, that not all dialogue-heavy scripts refer back to Sturges specifically. Other screenwriters, directors, or hyphenates, such as Ben Hecht, Charles Brackett, Charles Lederer, Dudley Nichols, Ernst Lubitsch, or Billy Wilder, could be the ghosts in the machines of contemporary moviemaking. Overlapping dialogue, two characters jumping on top of one another's lines, as Joe McElhaney points out,[14] is not characteristic of Sturges.

Moreover, not all fast talk is necessarily Sturgean. Quentin Tarantino and David Mamet made fast talk fashionable with young cinephiles through such films as *Reservoir Dogs* (1992) and *Glengarry Glen Ross* (1992). These two figures in particular step out of Sturges's orbit. Although Mamet is on record that *The Lady Eve* ranks as "Best film ever made. Duh,"[15] these two writer-directors offer a radically divergent model. Sturges wrote during the height of the Production Code: his films are full of innuendo and the not-said, rather than the explicit sexual language, racial epithets, and constant curses that detonate throughout in the movies of Mamet and Tarantino, leaving us shell-shocked. In their movies, words are weapons used to bludgeon characters and audiences alike.

POSTMODERNISM: PASTICHE, ALLUSION, AND IRONY

> With Sturges, the humor of American comedy became irony. If he made use of old themes it was by forcing them to reveal themselves and thereby be destroyed.
>
> —André Bazin[16]

Although of course the dating of "postmodernism" is up for dispute—what about *Tristram Shandy*, finished in 1767?—scholars have long recognized Sturges as postmodern *avant la lettre*. Alessandro Pirolini's study demonstrates how Sturges fits into our contemporary concept of this post-World War II cultural zeitgeist. In particular, Pirolini points to Sturges's constant use of pastiche—for instance, his intermixing of melodrama, silent film, cartoons, and farce—his self-referentiality (such as Governor McGinty reappearing as the Governor in *The Miracle of Morgan's Creek*), and his blending of genres. As Pirolini argues, "Sturges shows a recurrent interest in revealing the structures and mechanisms that Hollywood hides behind its texts."[17] In short, Sturges always departs from classical Hollywood cinema's norm of transparency; he wants the viewer to be conscious that he or she is watching a film, a film by "the genius" Preston Sturges.

Examples abound. In *The Good Fairy*, Sturges lampoons an overblown melodrama. *Sullivan's Travels* starts with a parody of a social problem film. Another famous use of a film-within-a-film occurs in *The Sin of Harold Diddlebock*, which actually inserts within its opening minutes clips from Harold Lloyd's *The Freshman* (1925). Pirolini holds up *Unfaithfully Yours* as Sturges's ultimate departure from classical Hollywood narrative, because in running through three hypothetical scenarios of how Sir Alfred might respond to his wife's suspected jealousy, Sturges puts the process of storytelling/ filmmaking *per se* on display. This allows Pirolini to draw comparisons with such paradigms of postmodernism as *Rashomon* (1950), *Run Lola Run* (1998) or *Sliding Doors* (1998), films in which the attention to the constructedness of stories puts reality itself into question.[18]

From a *Sesame Street* riff in which the Count von Count leads us up "The Thirty-Nine Steps" to *The Colbert Report*'s mock conservatism, contemporary culture revolves around pastiche and irony. As Jedediah Purdy notes, "We are all exquisitely self-aware. Around us commercials mock the very idea of commercials, situation comedies make being a situation comedy their running joke . . . If it is difficult to speak earnestly of personal matters, to speak earnestly about public matters seems perverse."[19]

What effects do pastiche and extratextual references have on viewers? That depends on a host of factors, including the audience's range of knowledge. *Sesame Street* and Disney's *Aladdin* (1992) deliberately reach out to two different audiences, children and their knowing parents, providing separate gratifications for each. Although most viewers can get something out of the films (or TV shows) without recognizing references, those who have seen Harold Lloyd's *Safety Last* will feel a self-congratulatory sense of belonging to the "in crowd" when watching *Diddlebock*. Besides, Sturges's incorporation of the Harold Lloyd film becomes thematic in terms of having the viewer refer back to Lloyd's youth and to the youth of American cinema (see Joe McElhaney's chapter).

Postmodern pastiche and allusions inevitably lead to irony, a sense of double-layeredness, and the recognition that the film is offering a distanced viewpoint on its characters' travails, rather than aiming for the deep engagement of melodramatic pathos.[20] Irony is the stance that says, "We are too wise to accept the official national myths. Hard work doesn't automatically lead to success. Virtue is not its own reward. American leaders have feet of clay. You can't pull the wool over *our* eyes!" What Bazin is pointing to in the epigraph above is that Sturges repeatedly demonstrates a certain skepticism toward official American ideology; witness the empty clichés about success on Diddlebock's cubby, or the ironic question after the wedding scene in *The Palm Beach Story*, where the printface says, "And they lived happily ever after—Or did they?"

No one would be surprised to learn that R. Barton Palmer entitles one of his chapters "The Coen Brothers: Postmodern Filmmakers."[21] Timothy Penner, in his dissertation on Wes Anderson, "The Allusive Auteur," writes:

> Littered throughout his oeuvre are endless allusions to films, directors, authors and books which have had significant influence on Anderson as an artist. In fact, Anderson's films can only be fully appreciated when viewed through the lens of his many sources, since his films emerge as

he carefully collects, compiles and crafts his many influences into a sort of collage.[22]

At the end of *Raising Arizona*, H. I. McDunnough (Nicholas Cage) has a dream about the future. Even though doctors have told his Ed that she is infertile, he dreams that they end up having a large family. In gauzy light, more and more well-dressed, happy, attractive children and grandchildren gather at a Thanksgiving table that stretches on endlessly, revealed by a tracking camera using a wide-angle lens. H. I.'s voiceover comments:

But I saw an old couple being visited by their children, and all their grandchildren too. And the old couple wouldn't [*sic*] screwed up. And neither were their kids or their grandkids. And I don't know. You tell me. This whole dream, was it wishful thinking? Was I just—fleeing reality like I know I'm liable to do? But me and Ed, we can be good too. And it seemed real. It seemed like us and it seemed like, well, our home. If not Arizona, then a land not too far away. Where all parents are strong and wise and capable and all children are happy and beloved. I don't know.
  Maybe it was Utah.

On the one hand, this ending stirs the viewer's deep yearning for an idyllic Norman Rockwell family gathering. At the same time, the exaggeration of the scene—so many grandchildren, everyone dressed in formal clothing, the wide-angle lens—points to this image as a fabrication: dreaming of a land "where all parents are strong and wise and capable and all children are happy and beloved" is a cruel hoax. By the time we get to the devastating "Utah," the viewer has been amply set up for the deflation, especially if, like me, you hear in that line an echo of Robert Frost's equally devastating, 3,000-word ode "New Hampshire" (1923):

It's restful to arrive at a decision,
And restful just to think about New Hampshire. At present I am living in Vermont.[23]

In fact, contemporary filmmakers are even ironic about their irony. Tad Friend writes in his *Vogue* interview with the Coen Brothers, "What saves the Coens from social autism is their own engaging ironic distance on their own ironic distance."[24] I find this claim at least debatable, because their irony in interviews erects more barriers to understanding what they really believe, and because the brothers seem to have lost all perspective on when irony is not an appropriate response.[25] Joel and Ethan Coen are downright *cruel* in a way that Sturges never was.

CRUELTY

As many of the contributors to this *ReFocus* volume have mentioned, François Truffaut gave the title *The Cinema of Cruelty* to a 1975 collection of Bazin's reviews, in which Truffaut includes a section on *Sullivan's Travels*, *The Miracle of Morgan's Creek*, *Hail the Conquering Hero*, and *Mad Wednesday/Diddlebock*.[26] Comedy is always "cruel," because it involves making fun of people, but in some of his films, for his time period, Sturges takes this cruelty to new highs (or lows). Not every director treats black servants the way Sturges does in many films (see Krin Gabbard's chapter). Not every director continually delighted in pratfalls, subjects his alter ego to a mugging and a chain gang, or thought it was funny to have the jealous protagonist fantasize in great detail about slashing his wife's throat with a razor (*Unfaithfully Yours*).

Sturges's tone can be astringent not only toward the characters, but also toward American society as a whole. What a gallery of malapropians, schlemiels, knaves, and sucker sapiens he presents! What mugs we moviegoers are for believing that honest government is possible, that all war heroes were really heroic, or that hard work will lead to success!

Yet, misanthropic as Sturges can be, curiously, people never get physically hurt in his films, no matter how many times they fall down; just as, no matter how many times they suffer humiliation, they appear able to recover. Like the cartoon figures he loves to reference, Sturges's characters are made of rubber. Moreover, the endings of his films always rein in his excesses. In *The Miracle of Morgan's Creek*, instead of being shunned as an out-of-wedlock mother, Trudy Knockenlocker becomes the state heroine for her amazing fertility. Sir Alfred learns that Daphne has a good explanation for her nighttime visit to his secretary's bedroom and repents his wild fantasies, embraces her, and pontificates on the wonders of love. As many of the scholars in this volume point out, Sturges's happy endings are not as convincing as those of his contemporaries in Hollywood, and viewers should (deliberately) be left with doubts and ambivalence. Still, Andrew Horton points to a genuine strain of sentiment in Sturges's early screenplays, particularly the gentle treatment of hometown Indiana at Christmas in *Remember the Night*.[27]

In his own discussion of *Sullivan's Travels*, Sturges wrote, "Art, Tolstoy said, is a medium for the transmission of emotions. We live through emotions. Without them we don't exist."[28] Richard Schickel offers a theory about Sturges, to wit, that he

> operated as a sort of Henry James in reverse. James went to Europe and found innocence imperiled; Sturges came back from Europe to discover that quality in blooming health. And his thesis is a variant on James'. Isolated behind our oceans untainted by the major corruptions of the

Old World—high culture, exquisite manners, a rigid class system—we are permitted to dream on undisturbed . . . We are a nation of eccentric and volatile individualists, each absorbed in his own private variant on the American Dream.

Schickel argues that in Sturges's world we laugh at ourselves and one another "ruefully, and not unkindly."[29]

Many things distinguish contemporary filmmaking as a whole from the 1940s, but chief among these is the intensification of cruelty. Whether this cruelty lies in mockery, humiliation, breaking hearts, stealing assets, or outright physical injury and death, hip contemporary filmmaking often relies on the "energetic cruelty" that James Harvey sees in *The Lady Eve*, offered with thoroughgoing and never-repented "malicious exuberance."[30]

The lapsing of the Production Code not only freed American movies to be more frank about sex or to include naturalistically rough language. Removing censorship also allowed dark demons to roam. Joseph Breen would never have allowed a teacher's vendetta against a student or a student sleeping with a teacher (*Election*), a troubled boy smearing his ejaculate on library books (*The Squid and the Whale*), or suicide attempts and lying about cancer (*The Royal Tenenbaums*).

The Coen Brothers' *Fargo* is a deeply cruel film. Cruel to Mike Yanagita (Steve Park), Marge's lonely former boyfriend who appears in the film mostly, I surmise, because the Coens find it amusing to hear a Minnesota accent in a person of Asian background. Cruel also to Wade Gustafson (Harve Presnell), who wants to get his daughter back from her kidnappers, but whom the Coens shoot both with a gun and with a wide-angle lens, to make his senseless murder "funny." Cruel to Carl Showalter, who is whipped with a belt, shot in the face, axed to death, and then ground up in a wood chipper. And intolerably cruel to Jean Lundegaard (Kristin Rudrüd), who is kidnaped by her husband for the ransom (a plot motif repeated in *The Big Lebowski*), held for days, mocked by the kidnappers and the audience, and then murdered off-screen.

And yet the Coen Brothers hardly provide examples of the summit of cruelty in American cinema. For that we would have to hold up Tarantino, who thinks nothing is funnier than drenching the screen with blood, or to Todd Solandz, who satirizes New Jersey suburban life by going after children with his deadpan treatment of harassment, bullying, pedophilia, and kidnapping.

Sturges's battles with the Breen Office (see Matthew Bernstein's chapter) prove that he dearly wanted free rein to write *double entendres*, lead his characters into sexual situations, and make fun of American puritanism. But no one has evidence that without Breen's interference, Sturges would have maimed or murdered people. In *The Palm Beach Story*, he even uses his *deus ex machina* powers to pull identical twins out of his hat, just so that Maude and John D. will not be disappointed or lonely. You can read this as a deeply ironic comment on marriage (which it is), and as a thoroughly kind gesture toward silly characters whom Sturges did not want to leave broken-hearted.

THE FRENCH, THEY ARE A FUNNY RACE

Donald Spoto intriguingly speculates that during his lengthy sojourns in France, Sturges would have seen some of the sixty farces written by Georges Feydeau (1866–1925), that were then the toast of Paris. Spoto believes these were the major influence on the filmmaker's breakneck pace, his comic vision, and his urge to unmask pretention.[31] The key difference between the romantic, if often adulterous, *comédie boulevardière* of Feydeau and his followers and screwball comedy, Mary Harrod helpfully explains, is that in American screwballs the female leads were played by actresses of higher prestige and were given less stereotyped roles.[32] Harrod traces the globalization of two cycles of romantic comedy—screwball and "the new romance"—and their influence on contemporary French films.

Whether because of the internal influence of Feydeau or because of French cineastes' direct knowledge of Sturges (see Christian Viviani's chapter) and of screwball comedy in general, I propose we look across the pond for more evidence of Sturges in contemporary film. I thought that I was the only one who saw Sturges's fingerprints all over the 2010 film *Heartbreaker (L'arnacœur)*. Thus I was heartened to read, in Laura Kern's *Film Comment* review: "*Heartbreaker* harks back to old-fashioned Preston Sturges-style escapism, with equal parts sophistication, screwball, and heart, that is all but extinct."[33]

Pascal Caumeil,[34] a first-time feature director, and a team of three screenwriters crafted the film. One of the three writers, Laurent Zeitoun,[35] came up with the storyline, based on his family's unhappiness with his cousin's loutish boyfriend.[36] *Heartbreaker* tells the story of a handsome young man whose profession involves breaking up matches that interested parties—such as relatives—find unsuitable for their sisters or daughters. By researching the woman's innermost desires, Alex (Romain Duris), abetted by his sister and brother-in-law, manages an "accidental" meeting, in which his superior qualities illustrate to the woman that she shouldn't be settling for a cad, but instead should find someone who will truly make her happy. After a prolonged setup that shows the team at work with numerous young women, Alex takes on the commission of breaking up the imminent marriage of Juliette (Vanessa Paradis) and Jonathan (Andrew Lincoln), in Monte Carlo.

Like Jean Harrington, who initially treats Hopsie as a mark (or, for that matter, like Professor Harold Higgins, who tries to seduce Marion the librarian for his own gain), Alex gets his foot caught in the door. He falls in love with Juliette, but decides that since Jonathan is actually *not* a cad (though he is a tad stuffy and conventional) he should reject their budding romance for Juliette's own good. But in an exact replay of *It Happened One Night*, at her father's urging Juliette runs away from the altar and into Alex's arms. As Jordan Mintzer notes, the film pits predictability against free-spiritedness,[37] the theme of many romantic comedies. In *Heartbreaker*, we also see the contrast between classes: Alex is deeply in debt, while Juliette comes from ill-gotten wealth.

Heartbreaker certainly demonstrates postmodern pastiche. Just as Sturges refers to other films, so too do Caumeil and company almost literally insert earlier movies. The Monte Carlo setting recalls Hitchcock's *To Catch a Thief* (1955). Not only do the writers directly crib *It Happened One Night*, they insert key plot motif revolving around *Dirty Dancing* (1987), for which Juliette has a secret yen. Alex wins her over by dancing to "(I've Had) The Time of My Life." (Since Quad Films, a French company, co-produced the film with Focus Films International, apparently it had the money to buy American music rights.) Moreover, the poster for the film exactly doubles the poster for *Notting Hill* (1999). Duris, one of France's most popular leading men, famed for his versatility, and Paradis, a singer, actress, and Chanel model, don't really hold a candle in pure screen star wattage to Fonda and Stanwyck, but—to repurpose Gaff's line in *Blade Runner*—"Who does?"

As far as my weak French allows me to judge, the dialogue *per se* is not up to the level of Sturges, the Coen Brothers, or Sorkin. Many lines, however, do become catchphrases through repetition. Once Alex has attracted each mark, he uses the same explanation of a past broken heart to put her off and explain that it is too late for him, but not too late for her to find true love. In addition, the screenwriters put linguistic diversity to comic use. Alex and his team work

Figure 14.2 Juliette (Vanessa Paradis) and Alex (Romain Duris) are watching Juliette's favorite movie, *Dirty Dancing*, in Alex's hotel bedroom.

in French, English, Spanish, Japanese, Arabic, and Mandarin! Alex's schnook brother-in-law, Marc, who yearns to be as good a performer as Alex, tries his hand at impersonating a Polish janitor and an Italian racecar driver, with ridiculous, Toto-like results. Physical comedy includes such slapstick scenes as a barefoot Alex chasing Juliette by stealing a bike from young boys and then bravely vaulting himself onto the wrong tour boat, and Marc unexpectedly knocking Juliette's girlfriend, Sophie, out cold when she comes too close to blowing their plan. As the actor playing Marc, François Damiems, told an interviewer, "On the one hand, we are immersed in full romance. Vanessa Paradis and Romain Duris are a very attractive couple. We must identify with them. And on the other hand, Julie Ferrier and I provide comedy. The film will toss spectators around from one genre to another: surprise and sentiment" (translation mine).[38]

The bevy of minor characters, including Mélanie and Marc, are more central to the plot than in Sturges's films. Mélanie shadows Juliette around the hotel, impersonating a maid, a bartender, a lifeguard, etc., and sometimes gets carried away with her role.

Yet as Laura Kern notes, unlike *Intolerable Cruelty*, the film wears a tender heart on its sleeve. Alex lives by a code of honor not to break up lovers who are genuinely good for one another, and never to sleep with the women he targets. If Juliette needs to learn that she would be happiest with someone unconventional (and not a British millionaire with a snobbish mother), Alex needs to learn that—just like the women he woos professionally—he should be brave enough to follow his own heart.

The film was a large hit in France and played at the Tribeca Film Festival. Universal has bought the rights to an American remake. Romantic comedy has hit a patch of doldrums in recent years; one wonders if *Heartbreaker* could be the film to reawaken the genre.

CODA: STURGES'S TRAVELS

Contemporary discourse about film is studded with references to Preston Sturges. *The New Yorker* chooses *Sullivan's Travels* as its movie of the week to recommend to readers.[39] Harold Ramis, the writer-director of *Groundhog Day* (1993) and *Analyze This* (1999) cites Sturges as the biggest influence on his filmmaking.[40] Sturges's name has been evoked in reference to the *Gilmore Girls*.[41] Francis Veber, the French writer-director of *Le Dîner de cons* (1998) and *La Doublure* (2006), has been held up by critics as a worthy successor to Sturges.[42] *The Boston Globe* sees Sturges in David O. Russell's *Silver Linings Playbook*:

It's as if [Russell] checked the emotional weather, saw the forecast called for snow, and chose to wear shorts and a tank top anyway. He's like

Preston Sturges in that sense, fearlessly—and not always successfully—shepherding crises away from tragedy, sensing we can see the stakes more clearly when we're not watching them through tears.[43]

Not all these comparisons are apt. "Preston Sturges" may have just become a (dead) cliché that signifies witty or fast talking. But the plethora of references does suggest that Sturges's influence is widespread both on filmmakers and viewers. Ideally, books like ours will help make these off-the-cuff remarks a little more explicit and nuanced.

Sturges, who succeeded only "between flops," has become a worldwide representative of the height of Hollywood comedy.

Somewhere, he is laughing.

NOTES

1   Michel Ciment and Hubert Niogret, "Interview with Joel and Ethan Coen," *Positif*, July–August 1987, included in R. Barton Palmer, *Joel and Ethan Coen* (Urbana, IL: University of Illinois Press, 2004), 166.

2   Kristine McKenna, "*Playboy* Interview: Joel and Ethan Coen," *Playboy* (November 2001), *The Coen Brothers Interviews*, ed. William Rodney Allen (Jackson, MI: University Press of Mississippi, 2006), 182.

3   Robert C. Sickels, "'We're in a Tight Spot!': The Coen Brothers' Screwy Romantic Comedies," *Journal of Popular Film and Television* 36:3 (2008): 114–22.

4   "*Intolerable Cruelty*." Available at <http://www.boxofficemojo.com/movies/?id=intolerablecruelty.htm> (last accessed 14 July 2014).

5   David Edelstein, "King George vs Catherine the Great," *Slate*, 10 October 2003. Available at <http://www.slate.com/articles/arts/movies/2003/10/king_george_vs_catherine_the_great.html> (last accessed 15 April 2015).

6   "Aaron Sorkin interviewed by Jeff Daniels," *Interview Magazine*. Available at <http://www.interviewmagazine.com/film/aaron-sorkin#page2> (last accessed 15 April 2015).

7   Joe McElhaney, "Fast Talk: Preston Sturges and the Speed of Language," *in Cinema and Modernity*, ed. Murray Pomerance (New Brunswick, NJ: Rutgers University Press, 2006), 278.

8   Manny Farber, written with W. S. Poster, "Preston Surges: Success in the Movies," from *Negative Space: Manny Farber at the Movies* (New York, NY: Da Capo Press, 1998), 96.

9   Jeff Jaeckle, "The Comforts and Pleasures of Repetitive Dialogue in *The Big Lebowski*," *Fan Phenomena: The Big Lebowski*, ed. Zachary Ingle (Chicago, IL: Intellect Books, 2014), 8–17.

10 Jeff Jaeckle, *New Review of Film and Television Studies*, 11:2, 154–70. Available at <http://dx.doi.org/10.1080/17400309.2012.728917> (last accessed 14 July 2014).

11 James L. Longworth, *TV Creators: Conversations with America's Top Producers of Television Drama* (Syracuse, NY: Syracuse University Press, 2000), 12.

12 See Sarah Kozloff, *Overhearing Film Dialogue* (Berkeley, CA: University of California Press, 2000), 170–200.

13 Aaron Sorkin, *The Social Network*, http://flash.sonypictures.com/video/movies/ thesocialnetwork/awards/thesocialnetwork_screenplay.pdf Retrieved July 2014.

14 Joe McElhaney, 280.

15 "David Mamet and Ricky Jay Share Their Love of the Useless," last modified 18 July 2013. Available at <http://www.filmindependent.org/blogs/filmmaker-spotlight/david-mamet-and-ricky-jay-share-their-love-of-the-useless/#.U8Gl4I1dWpo.> (last accessed 14 July 2014).

16 André Bazin, *The Cinema of Cruelty*, ed. François Truffaut, trans. Sabine D'Estrée (New York, NY: Arcade Publishing [1975], 2013), 35–6.

17 Alessandro Pirolini, *The Cinema of Preston Sturges: A Critical Study* (Jefferson, NC: McFarland, 2010), 66–7.

18 I believe that Pirolini overplays the connection here, because Sturges's dollying in on Sir Alfred's eye repeatedly anchors the scenarios as his fantasies. The viewer is never in doubt about the stories' lack of relation to reality.

19 Jedediah Purdy, *For Common Things: Irony, Trust and Commitment in America Today* (New York, NY: Knopf, 1999), xii, xiv.

20 See Sarah Kozloff, "Empathy and Cinema of Engagement: Re-evaluating the Politics of Film," *Projections: The Journal of Movies and Mind* 7:2 (Winter 2013), 1–40.

21 Palmer, 36.

22 Timothy Penner, "The Allusive Auteur: Wes Anderson and His Influences," University of Manitoba (Canada), ProQuest, UMI Dissertations Publishing, 2011. MR84602, p. 1.

23 Robert Frost, "New Hampshire," 1923, famouspoetsandpoems.com/poets/robert_frost/ poems/733 Retrieved July 2014.

24 Tad Friend, "Inside the Coen Heads," *Vogue* 184:4 (April 1994) repr. in *Interviews*, 69.

25 In their interview with *Playboy*, the brothers were asked about violence. Here is their reply:

> JOEL: The issue of violence in movies bores me. The discussion about it is endless. We get asked about it frequently. There's all this political stuff around it. It's a bore. ETHAN: I was just reading one of Philip Roth's novels, and there's a character in it who talks about trees. He says, "Who gives a shit about a tree," and I feel the same way. I find trees boring. (186)

26 Bazin, 31–47.

27 Andrew Horton, ed., *Three More Screenplays by Preston Sturges* (Berkeley, CA: University of California Press, 1998), 326.

28 Preston Sturges, "An Author in Spite of Himself: Preston Sturges Finds that Playwriting is all Pros and Cons," *The New York Times*, 1 February 1942: X5.

29 Richard Schickel, "Preston Sturges: Alien Dreamer," *Film Comment* 21:6 (November/ December 1985), 34.

30 James Harvey, *Romantic Comedy in Hollywood: From Lubitsch to Sturges* (New York, NY: Knopf, 1987), 570.

31 Donald Spoto, *Madcap: The Life of Preston Sturges* (Boston, MA: Little, Brown, 1990), 103.

32 Mary Harrod, "Sweet Nothings? Imagining the Inexpressible in Contemporary French Romantic Comedy," *Studies in French Cinema*, 13:2 (2013): 175.

33 Laura Kern, "Short Takes: *Heartbreaker* Review," *Film Comment* (September/October 2010). Available at <http://www.filmcomment.com/article/short-takes-heartbreaker-review> (last accessed 14 July 2014).

34 Caumeil has not—to my knowledge—specially acknowledged Sturges. But he does cite classical Hollywood cinema, and Billy Wilder, George Cukor and Ernst Lubitsch. Available at <http://collider.com/heartbreaker-interview-vanessa-paradis-romain-duris-pascal-chaumeil/#ZrWJrFAGF8IqlPhM.99> (last accessed 14 July 2014).

35 Zeitoun also worked as one of the film's producers, as well as producing, with his fellow producers from *Heartbreaker*, Nicolas Duval Adassovsky and Yann Zenou, the French hit bromance *The Intouchables* (2011).

36 Available at <http://www.allocine.fr/film/fichefilm-148441/secrets-tournage/> (last accessed 14 July 2014).

37 Jordan Mintzer, *Heartbreaker*, *Daily Variety*, 306:57 (24 March 2010): 8.

38 Available at <http://www.allocine.fr/film/fichefilm-148441/secrets-tournage/> (last accessed 14 July 2014).

39 Richard Brody, "Movie of the Week: *Sullivan's Travels*," 17 June 2014.
    Available at <http://www.newyorker.com/culture/richard-brody/movie-of-the-week-sullivans-travels> (last accessed 14 July 2014).

40 Jerry Roberts, "Preston Sturges: The Big Inspiration," *Daily Variety*, 269:27 (10 October 2000), B2.

41 Roger Catlin, "Actor says *Gilmore Girls* Is Hitting Its Stride," *The [Hartford] Courant*, 4 November 2004, http://articles.courant.com/2004-11-04/entertainment/0411040300_1_gilmore-girls-producer-amy-sherman-palladino-scripts. Retrieved July 2014.

42 Colin Covert, "Director Is Worthy Successor to Wilder, Hawkes [*sic*] and Sturges," *Minneapolis Star Tribune*, 29 June 2007: B4.

43 Wesley Morris, "*Playbook* Works On Instinct: David O. Russell Gets Serious Comedy Right Again," *Boston Globe*, 16 November 2012: G14.

Index

Note: bold denotes figure, *italic* denotes table